NABOTH'S VINEYARD

THE RUINS OF THE PALACE IN SANTO DOMINGO

Constructed for the Columbus Family

Naboth's Vineyard

THE DOMINICAN REPUBLIC

1844-1924

BY

·SUMNER WELLES

Sometime Chief of the Latin-American Division of the
Department of State of the United States and
AMERICAN COMMISSIONER
to the Dominican Republic from
1922 to 1925

With a Foreword by
THE HON. L. S. ROWE
Director General of the Pan-American Union

In Two Volumes
Vol. I

SAVILE BOOKS
1966

To the indomitable love of liberty
of
the Dominican People
this book is dedicated.

"And Naboth said to Ahab, The Lord forbid it me, that I should give the inheritance of my fathers unto thee." I. Kings, 21, v. 3.

CONTENTS

CONTENTS

ILLUSTRATIONS

ILLUSTRATIONS

FOREWORD

L. S. ROWE, PH.D.

FOR a number of years students of Latin American affairs have been awaiting an authoritative history of the Dominican Republic. The excellent work of Judge Schoenrich is out of print. Moreover, this work was written before the recent significant changes in the Dominican Republic which witnessed the reëstablishment of constitutional government. The termination of military occupation by the United States marked a distinct step in the development of American foreign policy, and it is most important therefore that the successive steps leading to final withdrawal should be presented to the public and especially to students of our Latin American policy.

Mr. Welles, both by reason of experience and equipment, is the person indicated to perform this service. The important part which he played as United States Commissioner to supervise and carry into effect the plan of evacuation, combined with his exceptional acquaintance with Latin American affairs, places him in an extraordinarily favorable position to perform this task. Not only does he possess a thorough acquaintance with every detail of the subject, but he combines therewith a sympathetic understanding of the Dominican viewpoint which was of inestimable value to our Government in the solution of a difficult and delicate situation.

If there is anything lacking in this work, it is the fact that the author, with becoming modesty and self-effacement, has failed to set forth the important part which he played in the reëstablishment of constitutional government in the Dominican Republic and the skill with which the Dominican reorganization plan was carried out.

Mr. Welles has placed every student of Latin American affairs under obligations by his admirable and painstaking study of the history and development of the political institutions of the Dominican Republic.

INTRODUCTION
to new edition of
NABOTH'S VINEYARD

by *JOHN BARTLOW MARTIN*

The publisher is to be congratulated for bringing out a new edition of *Naboth's Vineyard,* long out of print and scarce. For this book is, quite simply, the best history in any language of the Dominican Republic from the beginning to the time of Trujillo—and one of the best books dealing with any Latin American subject.

Sumner Welles was only thirty years old when he went to the Dominican Republic in 1922 on a difficult and delicate mission: to bring to an end the United States military occupation, then six years old, and to help the Dominicans reestablish self-government through free elections.

He succeeded. His difficulties were enormous—virtually no democratic traditions, innumerable quarreling self-seeking politicians, even the mechanical problems of setting up polling places. But Welles persevered, and finally, in 1924, a free election was held, and the U.S. Marines came home.

After Welles departed, the dictator Trujillo seized power in 1930. The next free election did not take place until 1962 (when, as our Ambassador, I faced most of the difficulties Welles had faced a generation earlier).

Welles had left the Republic with the sense of a job well done. But the Republic continued to fascinate him. Why was its stubborn soil so unreceptive to democracy? What had helped shape its people and its history as a nation? The result was our good fortune— *Naboth's Vineyard.*

Perhaps I may be forgiven if I suggest that I feel a special kinship to Sumner Welles. I first read *Naboth's Vineyard* many years ago; I reread it in 1962 when I was appointed U.S. Ambassador to the Dominican Republic; and since resigning in 1964, I too have been unable to let go of the Republic but, like Welles, have devoted my time to writing a book about it, *Overtaken By Events,* an effort to continue the story where he stopped. The Republic's problems, and, even more, one's deep affection for its people, are not easy to shake off.

Welles' admiration for the Dominican people shows on virtually every page of this book. Nor does he conceal his view of their shortcomings and our own. This is an honest book.

It is also, oddly, a very "Dominican" book. Welles understood the tragic, sometimes misguided, and nearly always misgoverned Dominican people so well that he not only seems to share their suffering but at times seems to make their view his own. It has been said that his book is flawed by traces of racial prejudice; by our standards today this is probably true; but we must remember when his book was written and understand that, being so "Dominican," it reflects the Dominicans' own prejudices.

This, however, is a minor point. *Naboth's Vineyard*

is so good that one can only wish that so excellent a book existed on each Latin American country. It is a wise and even a prophetic book. It anticipates by many years the underpinnings of both the Good Neighbor Policy and the Alliance for Progress. Although it was written a generation ago, it speaks directly to us today. By relating the discouraging history of the tragic Dominican people, it helps us understand their difficulties today. By pointing out our own past mistakes there, it may help us avoid similar mistakes in the future.

Leaving the Republic, Welles had scarcely turned his back when Trujillo destroyed, it seemed forever, the Dominican democracy that Welles had done so much to build. Just so did other militarists one night in 1963 wipe out the Dominican democracy that we nearly 40 years later had helped build on the ruins of Trujillo's tyranny. And in 1965 Civil War almost destroyed the Republic itself.

The Dominican Republic is a small country but it has had a great influence on our affairs—and we on its. Indeed, once last century, as Welles relates, we signed a treaty to annex it, though the U.S. Senate refused to ratify the treaty. The Roosevelt Corollary to the Monroe Doctrine, "gunboat diplomacy," Marine Occupation, the struggle to build a democracy under the Alliance for Progress nextdoor to Castro's Cuba, OAS supervision of two elections and an unprecedented Inter-American peace-keeping force—all these resulted from the sometimes happy, sometimes unfortunate, but always close linkage of our two countries.

One of my more pleasant duties as our Ambassador in 1963 was to help dedicate a street in Santo Domingo to Sumner Welles. It was not a grand *Avenida*, just a street. A little group of us gathered at the corner, a handful of men and women looked down curiously from balconies, a crowd of children surrounded us; we spoke briefly. One of the city officials said that Sumner Welles had been not only a distinguished author but a good friend of the Dominican people. He was indeed. And all other friends of the Dominican people will be pleased today to know that Welles' real monument, this book, has outlived Trujillo and other enemies of its ideas and ideals.

May, 1966
John Bartlow Martin
(United States Ambassador
to the Dominican Republic, 1962–4)

NABOTH'S VINEYARD

INTRODUCTION

1.

EXISTENCE in the Spanish colony of Santo Domingo in the earlier years of the latter half of the 18th century had a flavour of romance not equaled, nor perhaps approached, in the other colonies of the New World, however little the residents of the colony may have realized it. The material prosperity of the French half of the Island, now forming the Republic of Haiti, had focused upon it the attention of Europe, whereas the long years of the Spanish colony's gradual decline in commercial rank since the days when the Discoverer of America, Don Cristóbal Colón, had been its Governor, and since the period when Spanish Santo Domingo had been the center of Spain's empire, had caused the Old World to forget the oldest settlement of the New World as it slumbered in its peaceful backwater of the blue Caribbean.

Communication between Santo Domingo and the mother country was limited by royal decree to the Spanish sailing vessels which ever less frequently crossed the ocean from Spain, or to the occasional galleons plying between Spain's richer West Indian colonies, Cuba and Puerto Rico, and the port of Santo Domingo. At the beginning of the last decade of the 18th century, the population of the Spanish portion of the Island had dwindled to some 125,000 inhabitants, of whom only approximately 40,000 belonged to the ruling caste, 60,000 being slaves and the remainder an indeterminate group of mulattoes and quadroons. The 19,000 square miles of the Spanish colony were parcelled out in great plantations, belonging in most part to absentee landlords. Much of the country was arid and had not been rendered suitable for cultivation by irrigation as had been done by the

French across the boundary. In the earlier years of the colony, the chief source of its wealth had been its mines of gold and copper, and when the surface workings had been exhausted, the mines had one by one been abandoned, and by the beginning of the 18th century the colonists were engaged solely in agriculture. The production of sugar, which had commenced early in the 16th century in Santo Domingo before sugar was grown in any other part of the New World, had gradually increased in importance. Sugar planters had developed their fields along the southern coast as well as in the north near the French frontier, wherever exportation of their produce was comparatively easy. The remoteness from all roads or waterways rendered the planting of sugar in the immensely fertile valleys of the central plateau, known as the Cibao, impracticable, and the lands about Santiago de los Caballeros were therefore used for grazing or for the planting of the crops needed for the requirements of each plantation.

The roads which had earlier been built were little by little, as the poverty of the colony increased, encroached upon by the fast-growing vegetation of the tropics, and the great distances between the residences of the owners of adjacent plantations made it difficult for the planters to see one another with any frequency, except in the dry seasons when their heavy coaches could travel, with less danger of being mired, along the muddy trails.

The head of each plantation was virtually a dictator, responsible only unto himself. The difficulty in the means of communication alone prevented the colonial government from maintaining any effective supervision over the colonists, and although the promulgation of legislation prescribing the rights and duties of the colonists as regards one another, their relations to the colonial government and their treatment of their slaves, was frequent, the decrees for the most part were practically unobserved. Life passed tranquilly. One day followed another monotonously. The sun was always shining, except for the half-hour-long showers of the rainy season, or except for the two or three days' long cyclone which came every few years. The cooler months of the dry winter season were followed by the moist heat of the spring and summer. A journey to the neighbouring plantation was an excitement; a longer journey to the capital or to Santiago de los Caballeros was epoch-making; a journey to Spain by a planter's family might perhaps be undertaken once in a lifetime, but most of the Spaniards passed their lives on their own plantations, and native indolence and the initiative-destroying tropical climate made these lotus-eaters not only content with their lot but supremely indifferent to what was going on in the rest of the world.

Men and women matured early. The chief event in a girl's life was her marriage at fifteen or sixteen to some neighbouring planter's son. After that, her sole interest and her sole occupation was the care of her children and the supervision of the household slaves. If the yield was favourable, money was plentiful, but there was little to spend it on. The interest of the men of the family was centered upon the plantation, riding across the fields from sunrise to sunset to make sure that the half-breed supervisor was extracting the necessary amount of labour from the slaves during the planting season, or, after the crop had been harvested, journeying to the nearest port to be sure that it was advantageously sold. Newspapers were unknown. Local news took months to travel. From Spain perhaps once a year might come letters bearing news of events in far off Europe.

In the cities and towns life was not far different. In the capital city, Santo Domingo, numbering some 30,000 souls more or less, there was perhaps the only approach to the more varied existence of a continental city of those days. The city planned by the Comendador Ovando had within thirty years of its construction acquired, with the increasing prosperity of the colony, such traits of magnificence, and such imposing edifices had been built, that the Emperor Charles V was told that the palaces of his Governor-General and of the Archbishop in Santo Domingo were far more magnificent than the imperial residences he posssessed in the many cities of his European dominions. The tradition of luxury remained, but the comparative insignificance into which the colony later sank had deprived the city by the end of the 18th century of much of the glamour of the great days of its commercial hegemony. Its location at the center of the southern sugar-producing area retained for it a certain measure of commercial life, but its chief importance lay in the fact that it continued to be the residence of the Governor-General and of the Real Audiencia, the seat of the Archbishop, and the headquarters of the military establishment, which in the latter part of the 18th century comprised twelve companies of Spanish veterans. The old city walls still stood in their entirety. Within, facing the Ozama River, stood the ancient palace of the Governor-General. The cabildo formed one side of the central square. The palace of the Archbishop, a short block away, and the cathedral, modelled by order of the Emperor Charles V upon a Roman basilica, with other ancient and beautiful examples of ecclesiastical architecture, comprise the list of the buildings of major importance.

The streets of the city were narrow and winding, and the houses, as was customary in Spanish colonial architecture, presented, to the street, walls unadorned save by infrequent balconies and the wrought-iron grilles across the ample windows. These latter, unglazed, were barred, as soon as night had fallen, by massive wooden shutters. The houses were adapted, so far as possible, to permit the free circulation of air during the daylight hours. It was only after sunset, due to the universal belief that the night air was unhealthful, that each aperture was hermetically sealed. Within the houses, which were generally of but one and seldom of two floors, the life of the family was passed in the patio, or central court, and in the rooms opening thereon. In the living rooms the walls were whitewashed, ungarnished by hangings or other decoration.

The social life of the capital consisted largely, as it has until recent times, of the stroll in the central plaza when the day's work was done, and the evening breezes blew in from the Caribbean to cool the city of the burning rays of the sun. It was then that friends met to discuss the events of the day, and the ladies of the city had the opportunity to see one another. The evening walk in the plaza and the High Mass on Sundays or on feast days afforded practically the only opportunities for social intercourse.

During the daytime, except to go to mass, no women of position passed through the streets. When they appeared in public, the Spanish women wore but one universal costume—a short black silk skirt, with a mantilla of the same color falling from their heads below their waists. Beneath the mantilla could occasionally be seen the thin chemise of transparent gauze which was the sole covering of their breasts. For the general monotony of the feminine dress, the vivid colors of the picturesque costume of the men, identical with that worn in Spain during the period, compensated to some extent.

In the best houses and among the wealthiest families the contrast of splendour and poverty was startling to the occasional visitor. The furniture, imported from Spain, or modelled in native woods from Spanish designs, bore all the profusion of carving or of gilding and rococo ornament demanded by Spanish taste of the 18th century. The ladies of the richer class and the masculine members of their families, when they received visitors in their homes, were alike garbed with lavish display, while the slaves who served them, even those who waited upon the ladies, were dressed in rags, and are reputed by writers of the time to have been filthy "to the most disgusting degree."

Entertainments were few and far between, although occasionally the Governor-General or the members of the Audiencia might offer a reception to the city's more distinguished families. Social lines were rigorously drawn, and the population was divided by common acceptance into classes beyond the limits of which the individual might rarely pass. The white resident or official of the highest class was always addressed as Señor Don, the poorer white as Don; the freedman of independent position in whose veins some drops of African blood were believed to flow, merely as Señor. All others in the colony were classed together as being unworthy of any distinctive forms of address. Social intercourse between the classes so distinguished was non-existent.

In the northern plain of the Cibao, the city of Santiago de los Caballeros had gained importance as the result

of the destruction of the towns of Concepción de la Vega,
Puerto de Plata and Monte Cristi through earthquake and
fire, and in the latter part of the 18th century was nearly
equal in population to the capital, although it lacked the
reflected glory which Santo Domingo possessed as the seat
of the royal establishment. There were no other towns of
importance and it is probable that neither Azua, Puerto
Plata, Monte Cristi, Cotuy nor La Vega numbered more
than 5,000 inhabitants each.

Life ran along smooth paths. If the colony possessed
none of the stupendous magnificence, none of the commercial prosperity, none of the febrile activity of its
French neighbour, neither did there exist in it that feeling
of suspense, that sinister sensation of the imminence of
some impending catastrophe, which is sometimes noted in
the writings of travelers to French St. Domingue, where
a sparse 40,000 French colonists were holding in the most
abject servitude more than half a million slaves fresh from
the jungles of western Africa.

In the earlier years of the Spanish colony, manual labor
had been undertaken by the native Arawaks whom the
Spaniards had, immediately after Columbus's first settlement, forced into slavery. Unaccustomed labor, pestilence
and revolt were the contributing causes to the extermination within a century of the native Indian tribes, and
African slavery had been introduced on a small scale into
both the French and Spanish colonies before the close of
the 17th century. Its introduction into the Spanish lands
had never, however, been on the extraordinary scale of
that in the French colony, where the conditions of slavery
apparently were not conducive to the rapid propagation
of the Africans, and where, as a result, the great majority
of slaves working on the plantations were negroes brought

from Africa and where slaves of the second generation were considered a rarity. Abuses on the part of the master towards his slaves in the Spanish colony were undoubtedly of no infrequent occurrence, but it is evident that they were not the matter of course which they were in French Santo Domingo. This, and the fact that a greater proportion of the slaves in the Spanish colony had been born and bred upon their owners' plantations, prevented that hatred of master by slave which was so noticeable on the French plantations.

Neither was there in the Spanish colony the extreme discrimination against the mulatto or quadroon which existed in the colony under French control. In Spanish Santo Domingo, while there was no social contact between the freedman of mixed blood and the whites, there was no evidence of the racial antipathy towards them which existed in French territory.

Communication between the two colonies on the Island was infrequent, and in 1790, the Spanish colonists, secure as they believed in their terrestrial paradise, and pleasantly exhilarated by the news of an unexpected rise in the price of sugar, had no suspicion that the storm clouds already high on the horizon at the other end of the Island could darken their own tropical sky, nor that the hurried drive of the King of France and his family from Versailles to Paris was the first warning that, before many years had passed, their own prosperous plantations would be totally destroyed, and that they themselves, when death did not overtake them first, would be exiles in strange lands.

2.

In 1789, the decree forced upon the French nobility and clergy providing for the renewed representation of the

Third Estate in the Estates General gave rise to general satisfaction among the inhabitants of French St. Domingue. Dissatisfaction with the administration of the Home Government had been rife for many years, and apparently only the Governor of the colony, M. DuChilleau, opposed the action of the Provincial Assembly in construing the decree as including the French colonies as well as the territory of France itself. As the result of this interpretation, eighteen deputies were elected and sent immediately to participate in the deliberations of the Estates General, of whom six were admitted in representation of the colony. Thereupon the mulattoes and negro freedmen, urged on by the society recently formed in Paris known as "Les Amis du Nègre," claimed participation in the direction of colonial affairs. The proclamation of August 20th, known as the declaration of the "rights of man," increased the agitation commenced by the men of color to obtain their political emancipation. Then, and then only, did the colonists who had so blithely accepted the earlier decree of the Estates General begin to rue their decision to beg for representation in the French Assembly. The struggle of the races had commenced.

It was only then that the greater portion of the whites put to one side their local jealousies to unite in confronting the dangers with which their class was threatened. The mulattoes were as one in pressing for the political advantages of which they were ambitious. Both groups, whites and mulattoes, were antagonistic, of necessity, to one another, and equally opposed to the advancement of the numerous negro freedmen. The situation became so tense that in a brief time numerous local disorders had occurred. When the news of these disturbances reached France, it caused the General Assembly momentarily to recede from its former position, and to declare that the rights of representation granted by the decree of 1789 applied solely to the inhabitants of the territory of France itself. The terms of this new decree provoked much ill feeling, and the speeches delivered in the Provincial Assembly, meeting in St. Marc, assumed so radical a character that the Governor-General decreed the dissolution of the Assembly, accusing the members of having conceived the project of declaring the independence of the colony from the mother country. The inhabitants of the northern portion of the colony supported the Governor; the inhabitants of the rest of the colony rose in defense of their announced rights. Civil war was imminent when the Provincial Assembly determined to avoid the conflict by sending eighty-five of its members to France to justify the action which they had taken before the National Assembly. The Governor and the inhabitants of the colony were anxiously awaiting the verdict to be rendered by the National Assembly when an incident occurred significant in the light of later events.

A young mulatto named Ogé, who had been educated in Paris, and who, when the revolution broke out, had become the favourite of the Abbé Grégoire and through his influence a prominent member of "Les Amis du Nègre," sailed secretly for the colony, believing that all that his caste required was his leadership to secure the advantages which they were demanding. After reaching the colony he addressed a letter to the Governor, accusing him of having ignored the decree of the National Assembly establishing the "rights of man," and threatening that unless the privileges of the whites were at once granted to all freedmen of the colony the mulattoes would obtain them for themselves by force of arms. The rebellious mulattoes were at once attacked by the Governor's troops and dispersed, while Ogé and a few of his companions who had taken refuge on Spanish territory were handed over by the Spanish authorities to the Governor of the French colony. Ogé and his principal supporter were executed after their bodies had been slowly broken upon the wheel.

While the mulattoes were crushed for the moment, the death of their leaders provoked them to further revolt, and when these outbreaks were again put down, the execution by the Governor of the ringleaders in the second insurrection had a far more disastrous effect, in that it created such revulsion in Paris as to cause the promulgation of a decree by the French National Assembly declaring that all individuals born of free parents in the colony were thenceforth to have the same rights and privileges as French citizens themselves.

The receipt of this decree in St. Domingue caused general despair on the part of the white population. The colonists determined to take into their own hands that protection of their privileges and of their property which the Colonial Government, now headed by a new Governor-General, Blanchelande, was obviously unable to afford them. The white colonists proceeded at once to elect deputies to a new Assembly convoked to meet in Léogane on August 9th, determined to resist at any cost the National Assembly's ultimate decree. The mulattoes again revolted, but the Assembly, believing that it now had matters firmly in hand, paid small heed to the report. Then suddenly, on August 23rd, the storm broke.

On a plantation at Noé, probably as the result of a widespread conspiracy, seven or eight slaves killed the owner of the plantation and his administrators. Before the day was over, they had been joined by the negroes from adjacent plantations who had likewise slaughtered their masters, and had set fire to the houses and to the cane fields. The conflagration, commencing in the north, spread to the east and to the south. The owners of the plantations, who had known the animosity between the mulattoes and the blacks, and who had seen that none of the negroes had taken part in the successive revolts of the mulattoes, had become unduly confident. They were totally unprepared. As soon as night had fallen and the planters and their families had retired to their homes, the revolting slaves encircled the houses, to which they then set fire. The white men were killed first; they were impotent against the overwhelming number of the blacks. The women and children were reserved for a worse fate, and then, often after indescribable torture, were likewise put to death. The frightfulness of those early days of the terror of 1791 is beyond our modern imagining.

Notwithstanding the lack of means of communication, due to the disturbed state of the colony, the reports spread by those few slaves who remained loyal to their masters, or by the handful of whites who had succeeded in escaping from the general slaughter in the north, must soon have reached the planters of the south and west. Isolated in the midst of the black hordes whom they and their fathers had brought to the country, flight was hardly possible. Each night, when the short twilight of those steaming days of tropical midsummer came to its close, they must have feared that the moment had come for their own destruction. Each dawn brought with it the uncertainty whether they would survive until another night. A few, hunted like animals, escaped to Port-au-Prince and to the Cape, where protection by the French troops was still afforded them. Already a panic-stricken flight from

the country had commenced, and families escaped to the
United States or to the neighbouring West Indian islands,
but by far the greater part of the colonists of the north
coast were murdered in their homes. For days and weeks
the horizon, as an eye-witness has described, was a "wall
of fire from which continuously arose thick vortices of
smoke, and huge black columns which could be likened
only to those frightful storm clouds which roll onwards
charged with thunder and with lightnings."

3.

During the years 1791 and 1792, life in the Spanish
colony continued placidly, without the slightest sign that
the colonists feared the spread of the horrors in the French
colony to their own lands. It is true that the Government
of Spain, when word reached it of the servile revolt which
had taken place in French St. Domingue, ordered a regiment from Puerto Rico to reinforce the garrison at Santo
Domingo, and that the Captain-General of the Spanish
colony, Don Joaquín Garcia, took steps to strengthen the
garrisons on the frontier between the two colonies at
Dajabón and at San Rafael; but apart from these measures
there is no evidence that the rebellion in the western half
of the island perturbed to any considerable extent the
minds of the Spanish planters.

It is probable that the feeble attempts of the first Civil
Commissioners sent by the French National Assembly to
its distressed colony to reconcile royalists to a just appreciation of the "rights of man," and to persuade Jacobins
to love their colored brothers, provoked amusement rather
than anxiety among the Spaniards. After the arrival in
September, 1792, at Cap François, of the second set of
Civil Commissioners, headed by the sinister and corrupt

Sonthonax, the Spanish officials, however, began to express a sentiment of lively contempt, and evident alarm, at the French Commissioners' policy of currying favour with the blacks, but it was not until the astonishing news reached Santo Domingo that the National Assembly of France had declared war on Spain because of the Spanish King's refusal to recognize the Government responsible for the murder of his cousin, that general dread arose, and a positive realization was created of the dangers which threatened their own colony.

War was declared on March 7, 1793. The militia of Santiago de los Caballeros and of other of the Cibao towns was organized, and was ordered by the Captain-General to the frontier, but the French Commissioners were far too occupied with their attempt to reconcile the irreconcilable elements in the French colony to project as yet any offensive against the Spaniards. During the revolts of the two preceding years, many of the French royalists had taken refuge in the impenetrable forests of the high mountains along the border. Here they had obtained the support of a considerable following of former slaves, whose leaders, disgruntled by the policy of the French Commissioners, determined, strangely enough, to link their fortunes with those of their former masters. The white royalists were a negligible quantity, but the value of the support of the negro leaders was at once recognized by Garcia. Through the medium of Don Juan Vásquez, the priest of Dajabón, an understanding was soon arrived at whereby the two supreme generals of these negroes, Biassou and Jean François, agreed to coöperate with the Spanish troops, not only in repulsing any attack which the French might direct across the Spanish frontier, but likewise in making constant raids on French territory, intended to harry the

French and render it more difficult for them to undertake any concerted measures. The satisfaction with which the Spanish authorities viewed the adherence to their colours of the negro chieftains may be judged from the fact that at the request of the Captain-General of Santo Domingo, the Spanish Government accorded some of the negroes not only high decorations but likewise high rank in the Military Establishment of Spain. Among these latter, prominent as the chief lieutenant of Jean François, was the notorious Toussaint L'Ouverture.

Hostilities between the Spaniards and the French continued to be desultory. The intervention of England, which resulted in the landing of an invading force of British troops on the southern peninsula of the French colony, made it more than ever impossible for the French to undertake any offensive against the Spaniards and their negro allies. By the spring of 1794, the fortunes of the Jacobin Commissioners seemed desperate. In the north, the French troops, a fragment only of their former number, were entrenched in Port de Paix. The moment seemed opportune for the Spaniards to take the offensive themselves, and the project was conceived by Don Joaquín Garcia of invading the northern region of the French colony and of capturing the city at the Cape, the strongest position then held by the French. In such a plan, the participation of the negro troops was deemed indispensable, but no sooner had the plan been communicated to the negro chieftains than dissension broke out among them. Toussaint L'Ouverture, who had schemed for many months without success to supersede Jean François in the esteem of the Spaniards, selected this opportunity to negotiate with General Laveaux, who commanded the French garrison at Port de Paix, for the rank and emoluments accorded by the Spaniards to Jean François. Toussaint's overtures were accepted with delight by the French general, and in May of that year Toussaint, with 4,000 of his negro troops, went over to the French, murdering the Spanish officers associated with him, as well as every Spanish soldier upon whom he came.

The Marqués de Armona, referring to Toussaint, only a few days before his desertion had written to his colleagues in Santo Domingo that "in this world God has never entered a soul more pure." But this estimate of the aged negro ex-coachman can more excusably be condoned, on the ground of Armona's ignorance of future events, than can that of our own orator, Wendell Phillips, cherished by Abolitionist audiences of the fifties, who declaimed in one of his most applauded discourses:

"Fifty years hence, when truth gets a hearing, the Muse of History will put Phocion for the Greeks and Brutus for the Romans, Hampton for England, Lafayette for France, choose Washington as the bright, consummate flower of our earlier civilization, and John Brown the ripe fruit of our noon-day; then, dipping her pen in the sunlight, will write in the clear blue, above them all, the name of the soldier, the statesman, the martyr, Toussaint L'Ouverture."

The treachery of Toussaint disorganized completely the plans for the Spanish offensive, and abandoning the positions which they had already won, the Spanish troops retired to the boundary line to adopt again defensive tactics.

There had been little enthusiasm among the Spanish colonists for the war, and when word was received that peace negotiations were in progress between the Home

Government and that of France, general content was expressed. But when the terms of the Peace of Bâle, signed July 22, 1795, were announced to the inhabitants of Spanish Santo Domingo, no earthquake could have wrought greater consternation. The Spanish monarch, with complete disregard of the subjects of whose loyalty he had never had reason to complain, had without hesitation authorized the ratification of the treaty which provided that the Spanish colony of Santo Domingo should be ceded to France and should be governed by the authorities of French St. Domingue.

The terrestrial paradise was now thoroughly convulsed. As soon as word reached them of the latest developments, plantation owners who had not moved from their haciendas for years rolled down in their coaches to the capital to implore the Captain-General and the Audiencia to take some steps which might persuade the king to modify the terms of the treaty. Plan after plan was proposed, discussed, rejected. Deputies were sent to Spain without avail. M. Roume, a member of the first Civil Commission sent by the Assembly to the French colony, was already in Madrid negotiating the details of evacuation with the Spanish authorities. Change of nationality and exposure to the new theories of government so disastrously attempted in the French colony seemed intolerable, but to most of the Spanish colonists even more intolerable seemed the abandonment of their homes and the lands on which their families had lived for generations, and the journey to new countries. Some of them, however, preferred exile to French rule, and migrated to Louisiana, to Cuba, Puerto Rico and Maracaibo, but the reports which gradually filtered back to the colony of the hardships which they had encountered and the ill-treatment to which they had been exposed determined the majority to remain on their properties to await what the future might bring forth.

After his preliminary conference in Madrid had reached a successful conclusion, Roume set sail for Santo Domingo, where he arrived in April, 1796, to complete arrangements for the transfer of the Spanish colony to the French authorities. His negotiations with the Spanish colonial officials were prolonged, although Bayajá, the headquarters of the Spanish forces in the north, was turned over formally to General Laveaux on June 16th of that summer. Toussaint L'Ouverture, whose influence was constantly increasing, now persuaded the French Directoire, in which supreme authority in France had by now been vested, to permit his troops to occupy also Bánica and Las Caobas. The consternation of the Spanish inhabitants may be imagined at this turn of events. Deserted by their king, they were to be exposed to the ruthless domination of the negro leader directly responsible for the murder two years before of their own officers and troops.

Good fortune favoured the colonists temporarily, however, in the arrival of a new British expeditionary force at Môle St. Nicolas under the command of General Howe. The attention of Toussaint was necessarily diverted for the time being from his project of occupying Spanish territory. This momentary respite, however, did not greatly benefit the colonists. The uncertainty of their situation had almost entirely destroyed their means of livelihood. What slight commerce still existed had been brought to a standstill by the rapid increase of piracy in the Caribbean, now permitted by England, indignant at the negotiation of the Treaty of Bâle and more indignant at the notorious "family pact" signed by Godoy at Perignon on August 18, 1796. Produce shipped from the shores of

Santo Domingo was almost invariably seized by the pirates, who were becoming bold to the point of even making frequent incursions along the Dominican coast, which the local authorities were powerless to check. The situation was such that during the next two years almost all the Spanish families of fortune, notwithstanding their reluctance, one by one determined to abandon their homes.

Increasing poverty, lack of discipline, and above all the gradual realization by the Spanish slaves of the success achieved by their brothers on French soil, created such unrest among the negroes in Santo Domingo that it culminated in an armed uprising by the blacks on the plantation of the Marqués de Iranda at Boca Nigua, near the capital, which was, however, crushed by the determined measures employed by the owner's nephew, who was acting as administrator of the plantation. This uprising was followed by others which, while they were likewise quickly checked, increased the general despair of the colonists.

4.

It is probable that Toussaint L'Ouverture had early conceived the idea of the construction of a negro state comprising the entire island, for when the British retired definitely in 1798 from the French colony they had reached an agreement with Toussaint providing for the evacuation of the positions held by them, and their recognition of the Island of "Haiti," its Indian name, as a neutral and independent state. Protesting, at the same time, his loyalty to France, Toussaint now called upon Commissioner Roume to terminate his negotiations for the occupation of the Spanish colony under the Treaty of Bâle, and requested authority himself to undertake its occupation on behalf of the French Republic. Roume evidently suspected the negro's intentions, since he delayed as long as he could his reply to Toussaint's demands. Hoping for a compromise which might cause less distress to the Spanish inhabitants, and which would create less opposition to the transfer of authority, Roume finally ordered the French Commander-in-Chief to appoint General Agé, an intelligent quadroon, to proceed to the capital of the Spanish colony, with white troops, to perfect the arrangements for the occupation. Upon the arrival of General Agé in Santo Domingo, the entire population of the city addressed a petition to the cabildo, imploring a postponement of the final transfer of authority until deputies representing the colonists could be sent to Paris and Madrid to explain the local situation, and to make a last appeal for a revocation of the orders issued by the Spanish Crown.

The petition was approved both by the Captain-General and by the Ayuntamiento, and in consequence Don Joaquín Garcia notified the French Commissioner that General Agé's request that the city be immediately turned over to the French authorities could not be granted until an opportunity had been afforded the colonial delegates to make this final plea. The populace of the city, suspicious that a secret understanding was being arrived at, notwithstanding the assurances given them by the Captain-General, thereupon attempted to assault General Agé in the Monastery of Santa Clara where he was residing, and it was only through the personal intervention of General Garcia, who took General Agé in his own coach without the city walls, that the French general was enabled to reach French territory in safety.

The situation had become so tense that Roume, while ratifying the decree issued for the immediate transfer of sovereignty, proceeded to Port-au-Prince, and sent an agent to the Directoire urging that the occupation be postponed, and that Toussaint be prevented in any event from his purpose of undertaking the occupation himself.

The prolonged absence of Roume from the French colony had made it easier for Toussaint to attain the position of supremacy which he had long coveted, and taking the law into his own hands, as soon as he was aware of the representations which Roume had made, he first threw the latter into prison, and then shipped him summarily to the United States. At once he renewed his plans for the military occupation of the Spanish colony, and addressing a letter to Don Joaquín Garcia in which he demanded immediate satisfaction for the insult offered by the Spanish populace to the French Government in assaulting General Agé, he despatched two armies against Santo Domingo, one by the passes of the south under the command of his brother, Paul L'Ouverture, and the other through the north under the command of his nephew, General Moyse.

The cordiality of the relations between the Spanish authorities in Santo Domingo and the French officials who had already been sent there is evidenced by the fact that they were all present, with those few of the Spanish families who still remained, at a ball on Christmas evening, when the horrifying news was brought that the long dreaded invasion of Toussaint L'Ouverture had commenced.

In the north, a few regular troops and the local militia were speedily destroyed by the negro army of General Moyse; in the south, the garrison of the capital and the local militia, numbering altogether barely 1500 men, under the joint command of the Spanish General Nuñez and the French General Chanlatte, put up a brave fight against the invaders near the River Nizao, but were utterly routed, and forced to retire to Haina. The negro armies, prevented only by their orders to march with the utmost rapidity from undertaking the annihilation of the civilians and the destruction of their homes and fields, joined forces at Boca Nigua, where Toussaint established himself in the house of the Marqués de Iranda. Continued resistance against the invading armies it was realized was impossible, and in order to prevent the assault of the capital by the negro troops, with all its attendant horrors, Don Joaquín Garcia was forced to enter into negotiations with Toussaint for surrender.

On the 27th of January, 1801, Toussaint L'Ouverture entered Santo Domingo at the head of his troops. Picture him as he rode through the narrow streets, followed by his numerous aides-de-camp, decked out with as much gold lace as they could muster, bearing themselves, like their leader, with simian self-importance. All of the officers on the staff were powdered and queued like their commanding general, and attempted to ape the expression of pompous determination depicted on the countenance of Toussaint, which in his case his noticeably prognathous jaw rendered easy. Behind them the common soldiers straggled, dressed in rags or in any incongruous garments they had been able to lay their hands on during the march, and brandishing a strangely assorted variety of weapons, ranging from the more usual machete to the rarer matchlock. Toussaint at once proceeded to the Casa Consistorial, where he received from the Captain-General the keys of the city. Thereupon the French tricolor was hoisted upon the fortress of the Homenaje and a salute of twenty-one rounds was fired. From there, after the delivery of a harangue to the assembled Spaniards urging them to be content that they had now become Frenchmen in nationality, the negro general proceeded to the cathedral to attend a solemn Te Deum. Established in a seat of honour in the chancel of the cathedral, his bloodshot eyes rolling with religious ecstasy, Toussaint there relaxed his rigid pose, prostrating himself low before the Sacrament, as he sang in a loud voice the sacred canticles which he had learned by heart.

The interests of the "martyr and statesman" eulogized by Wendell Phillips appear, however, not to have been confined solely to religion nor to statecraft, since on the day following the taking possession of the capital, orders were given for all the inhabitants of the city to assemble in the central square, the men on one side and the women on the other. After the reading of the proclamation announcing the immediate emancipation of the slaves, Toussaint proceeded with a few companions to pass the members of the feminine sex in review, and the General amused himself for some time by passing from one to the other of the women, prodding with his cane those better favoured by nature, and indulging in coarse pleasantries revolting to the Spanish women. On the following day, a consignment of female members of the population was sent to Toussaint's headquarters at Boca Nigua.

The flight of Spanish families from the colony, which had already assumed such large proportions prior to the negro invasion, now became an exodus. From all parts of the colony those families who were able to do so fled the country, abandoning all their possessions, and embarking for the nearest Spanish ports on sailing vessels, schooners, fishing smacks, and even in some cases in rowboats. An edict was consequently promptly issued by Toussaint, prohibiting the emigration of any inhabitants of the Spanish

colony other than the families of the Spanish officials, who
were permitted to sail from Santo Domingo on February
22nd. For some time Toussaint considered the general
slaughter of all the white inhabitants of the colony. It is
reported that the wife of Paul L'Ouverture spent several
nights upon her knees beseeching the Almighty that her
brother-in-law be dissuaded from that intention. Her
prayers appear to have been efficacious, for no general
order for assassination was issued, although, naturally
enough, the savages under Toussaint's command perpetrated innumerable atrocities.

On February 5th, a decree dividing the Spanish colony
into districts, and convoking the election of deputies to
participate in the deliberations of a Central Assembly to
be held in Port-au-Prince, was promulgated; and the following days brought forth a succession of decrees on
divers subjects, ranging from a decree containing the pro-
hibition to the inhabitants to sell their lands without
authorization of the municipal authorities, to a decree
commanding them to cultivate sugar, coffee, cotton, and
cacao, and forbidding them to cultivate yams and plan-
tains. As soon as these tasks had been completed, Toussaint
departed from the Spanish capital, leaving his brother,
Paul, as Governor of Santo Domingo, and General Cler-
veaux in Santiago de los Caballeros, as Governor of the
North. He himself had previously made a tour of the
Spanish colony, proceeding as far as Samaná, during which
his reception appears to have been particularly cordial on
the part of the clergy. From there he returned to Santo
Domingo, apparently solely in order to issue a decree prohibiting the colonists from exporting mahogany; and
pausing subsequently at the Cape to order the execution
of his nephew, General Moyse, and thirty of the latter's

followers for insubordination, he continued to Port-au-Prince to supervise the deliberations of the Central Assembly, which was already in session, and to which had been elected five delegates from the former Spanish colony.

The new constitution adopted by this body, signed on August 29, 1801, which ignored the authority of France, named Toussaint Governor for life and Chief of the Armies, and provided by various articles for the obliteration, as well, of all that had previously remained of the Spanish methods of administration.

The following spring, the report reached Toussaint that peace would soon be concluded between France and her former enemies at Avignon, and that it was the intention of Bonaparte, as soon as peace had been restored, to send a large expeditionary force to the Dominican colony to reëstablish French control within its confines. The newly-created Governor took at once what measures of precaution he could in preparation for the impending struggle for supremacy, and fortifying to the best of his ability the strongholds of the western half of the island, he proceeded once more to the former Spanish capital to assure himself of the loyalty of the subordinates whom he had left in control of the east. Traveling by way of the Cibao, he reached Santo Domingo January 3, 1802.

While satisfied apparently with the personal devotion of his lieutenants, it could not escape him that dissatisfaction with their lot was general among the Spaniards, and that they would prefer any government rather than the dictatorship which he had attempted to impose. On this brief and final visit to the Spanish colony, Toussaint threw aside all pretense of conciliating the Spanish elements, and instructions were given by him to commence a reign of terror, which his officers were by no means reluctant to carry out. During the preceding months, the greater portion of the Spanish troops with the superior officers had left the island, but lack of facilities for embarkation had rendered it impossible for the Spanish garrison in the fortress at the capital to sail as yet for Puerto Rico. Depriving them of their arms, and surrounding them with negro troops, Toussaint forced these unfortunate Spanish soldiers to march towards French territory when he himself left Santo Domingo on January 26th.

The immense French squadron, bearing the First Consul's brother-in-law, General Leclerc, and the expeditionary force sent to reconquer the colony, had arrived at Samaná during the days that Toussaint was in Santo Domingo, and while the latter was hastening back to the west, General Leclerc had already despatched General Ferrand by land, with a large force, to recapture the Cibao, and General Kerverseaux, with three vessels of the fleet, to proceed around the eastern shore to regain Santo Domingo. The news of the despatch of Kerverseaux, and the receipt of the report that General Ferrand had routed the negroes from the Cibao, brought a ray of hope to the distressed Spaniards in the capital, and a successful conspiracy headed by Colonel Juan Barón, concerted with the knowledge of General Kerverseaux, enabled the latter to force the capitulation of Santo Domingo as early as February 20th. The city was only evacuated, however, after three days of intense fighting in which many of the maddened inhabitants lost their lives, some of them as the result of last-hour atrocities perpetrated by the negro officer, Jean-Philippe Daut, who ignored the orders of his commanding officer, Paul L'Ouverture. The negro invaders, after their defeat, attempted on their return march to Port-au-Prince to induce the negroes on Spanish

soil to rise and join with them against the French. Their
efforts were generally unsuccessful, however, and such few
scattered attempts at insurrection as took place were
speedily put down as the result of the effective measures
of repression taken by Kerverseaux.

The tragic march of the Spanish troops of Santo
Domingo taken as hostages by Toussaint L'Ouverture
came at length to an even more tragic conclusion. When
Toussaint received word of the capitulation of Santo
Domingo, which he correctly interpreted as the beginning of the end of his high hopes, in a spirit of cold-
blooded revenge he gave orders at Verrettes that the
defenseless Spaniards be butchered en masse by his troops.
The full extent of this atrocity was later known through
a handful of stragglers from the Spanish lines who, seeing
some of the Haitian soldiers wearing the ragged uniforms
of their companions, guessed what had taken place, and
were fortunate in escaping, after incredible hardships, to
return eventually to their homes in the Spanish colony.

But Toussaint's own time had nearly come. Betrayed by
his principal followers, Dessalines and Christophe, he was
finally seized by General Leclerc and sent to France. A
year later, dreaming, perhaps, in the delirium of the illness
of his last days, of the blazing sun and the blue sky of the
island which he was not to see again, he died in prison
among the cold mists and barren mountains of the Swiss
frontier.

5.

Since the destruction of the Assyrian hosts, there has
been perhaps no more dramatic catastrophe than that
which overwhelmed Leclerc's proud army. An officer of
demonstrated brilliancy, General Leclerc arrived in French

St. Domingue bearing the most detailed and minute instructions from his brother-in-law, the First Consul, for the recapture of the island. While the negroes put up a stout resistance, they were no match at first for the expeditionary force; but the French had not reckoned with an unconquerable foe which was soon to declare itself against them. With the rains of the spring, yellow fever appeared among their ranks. By midsummer the French forces had been decimated. By autumn their defeat became a rout. In November General Leclerc, whose letters to the First Consul written during the six months of the campaign constitute some of the most tragic documents of history, was himself fatally stricken, and a month later the French abandoned for the last time their richest colonial possession.

The withdrawal of the French from the western half of the island, and the immediate proclamation by the negro chieftains of Dessalines as Governor for life of independent Haiti, created a renewed and even more abject panic among the inhabitants of the former Spanish colony. However, for a time at least, a strong man arose in their defense, and stemmed the tide of negro supremacy, which otherwise would at once have swept over the entire island. The saviour was the French General, Ferrand.

Realizing that a renewal of hostilities between France and England would prevent Bonaparte from making, for some time to come at least, any further attempt to reconquer the colony, he determined to save Spanish Santo Domingo at least for his country. Disregarding the orders sent him to withdraw his troops from the island and to return to France, he gathered together the sparse forces originally under his own command, with a few remnants of the troops which had been fighting under General Leclerc, and induced, as well, a few refugees to return from Santiago de Cuba to swell their number. Learning that his colleague, General Kerverseaux, was wavering as the result of the disasters which had befallen Leclerc, he himself evacuated the Cibao, and by forced marches reached Santo Domingo in the last days of 1803. Finding Kerverseaux unwilling to join in the project he had conceived, he declared himself, on January 1, 1804, Governor of the Spanish colony, and forcing Kerverseaux to embark for Puerto Rico, General Ferrand assumed supreme command.

As soon as the French troops had left the Cibao, the northern provinces had been at once overrun by troops sent from the Cape by Dessalines, who appointed a mulatto born near Santiago, named José Tavares, Governor of Santiago. This attempt at negro domination was readily repelled by Ferrand, who, as soon as he had rendered his position in the capital secure, sent troops to Santiago, where the Haitian soldiers and the Governor imposed by Dessalines were easily defeated.

The chaos which existed in Haiti after the evacuation of the French made it impossible for Dessalines at once to turn his attention towards the accomplishment of his plan for consolidating the whole island under his government. General Ferrand was enabled, therefore, for a brief twelve months, to devote a portion of his efforts towards the amelioration of the condition of the colonists, who were faced, after the tragedies of the preceding ten years, by starvation. As the result of the several struggles which had taken place, agriculture had come to a standstill. No means for shipping the colony's produce existed, and in fact there was no produce to ship. Realizing that the prime necessity of the colony was labour, since the decrees of Toussaint emancipating the slaves had deprived the majority of the plantation owners of the means whereby they might restore their fields to a productive condition, the new Governor soon issued a decree permitting the Spanish residents for a period of twelve years to indulge in the traffic in slaves, limiting this period, however, in the case of foreigners to only six years. The same decree provided that all prisoners taken in engagements with the Haitian troops were likewise to be considered slaves. Prompt steps were taken for the construction of an aqueduct to bring water to the capital from the River Higüero. The crippling taxes previously imposed were remitted. Stimulus was given in every possible way to the planter. Plans were devised for the renewal of commerce with the United States in the export of native woods. A great port, to be known as "Napoléon," was projected in Samaná. In every way possible Ferrand attempted to meet the requirements of the Spanish colonists, and went so far in his efforts to better their condition and to gain their support that he succeeded in obtaining from Bonaparte the promulgation of a decree which authorized the continuance in the colony of the Spanish code, and which established a bi-national colonial court, the Spanish section to hear the cases arising between Spanish inhabitants, and the French section to hear solely cases in which French subjects were involved.

The most distinguished of the Spaniards among the native inhabitants were selected to participate in the colonial administration, the Governor determining to rule his Spanish subjects through the medium of their fellows. Economic conditions reacted quickly to the impulse created by General Ferrand's energy, and within the year many colonists returned to their homes and plantations from abroad, and all signs pointed to the realization of Ferrand's dream for a great and prosperous colony. But the optimism of the Governor, and the confidence which he had succeeded in imparting to the colonists, did not take into reckoning the ambitions of the Haitian Governor, Dessalines.

6.

At the outbreak of the negro insurrection, Jean-Jacques Dessalines had been a slave on the plantation of a free negro, whose name he had assumed and whose property he had seized as soon as the insurrection afforded the slave the opportunity of murdering his master. Like the majority of the negroes prominent in the servile rebellion, Dessalines had been born in the forests of West Africa, and had been brought to the French colony when he was already in his first youth. The savage surroundings of his earliest days were doubtless responsible for his impenetrable ignorance, his cruelty, and the sway which superstitions maintained over him, but only a congenital depravity can account for the fiendish blood lust which has made his name notorious for a century and a quarter. There was no perverted horror of which he was not capable, nor devious torture which his brain did not devise, and his career, from the date when he first participated in the negro revolt to the day of his death, when he was struck down outside Port-au-Prince by one of his own colour, was that of a butcher in a human shambles.

In the early days of the insurrection, Dessalines joined the followers of Biassou. He early obtained the benevolent interest of his chief by the welcome surprise which he was enabled to offer him soon after joining his troops. A large number of white prisoners, men, women, and children, had been captured by the negroes on their plantations,

and the captives had been concentrated in one of the fortresses held by Biassou's troops. When the arrival of Biassou
at the fortress was anticipated, Dessalines personally super-
vised the murder of each of the captives, devising for each
a distinct and agonizing death. He then gave order that
the heads should be struck from the bodies and placed
upon the posts of the stockade surrounding the fort. His
taste in decoration seems so to have drawn to him the sympathy of Biassou, that immediately after this accomplishment he was given prominent command in the regiment.

After the betrayal of the Spaniards by Toussaint
L'Ouverture, Dessalines became Toussaint's right-hand
man and carried out many of the latter's more blood-
thirsty projects, needless to say to the entire satisfaction
of his chief. Far less crafty than Toussaint, and with little
of the latter's astuteness and ability in dissembling his real
intentions, he was distinguished by a greater fixity of purpose and by an utter incapacity for any feeling of pity or
any instinct of mercy. His passion for blood showed itself
not only in his slaughter of the whites, but also in the
destruction of members of his own race, as well as in the
joy of killing animals when human victims were lacking.
Descourtilz records that his wife was at times able to dissuade him from some of the murders which he had
ordained, but the successful intervention of the good lady
appears to have been due more to Dessalines' desire to rid
himself of her importunities, which wearied him, than to
her ability to awaken in him any spark of humanity.

After his association with Toussaint, and the opportunities so afforded him for observation of the customs and
the dress of the French officers, Dessalines, like Toussaint
L'Ouverture, undertook to dress himself in the height of
the fashions of the Directoire. His snuffbox, which he

commenced to carry at that time, became notorious in later years. Almost invariably before determining an execution, Dessalines would open the snuffbox and inspect the small mirror with which the inside of the cover was furnished. Should there be any moisture on the mirror, the project of execution would be temporarily at least abandoned; should the mirror, however, be dry, the augury would be interpreted as a demand by nature for the shedding of more blood, and the signal would quickly be given for the victim to be led to his death. Since the loose tobacco in the box necessarily, except in the most humid weather, absorbed all the moisture within the box, the mirror was almost inevitably dry, and the superstition doubtless proved a satisfactory one to the owner of the magic snuffbox.

After the exile of Toussaint, Dessalines naturally enough assumed chief place among the other negro chieftains, and the evacuation of the colony by General Rochambeau after Leclerc's death made his proclamation as Dictator for life a foregone conclusion. In the proclamation of the indivisibility of the whole island, as Haiti, on January 1, 1804, Dessalines was but carrying out the project which Toussaint had long had in mind, and the decree of General Ferrand permitting the enslaving of captives obtained by the Spanish colonists on the Haitian frontier afforded the Haitian Dictator a welcome pretext for making his proclamation effective.

As soon as the rumours of Dessalines' plans were confirmed to General Ferrand by the masters of some British and American vessels, who had learned of them at Cape Haitian, preparations were at once made to repel the threatened invasion. The city of Santo Domingo contained approximately 6,000 non-combatants, in addition to the garrisons quartered there. Supplies of food were, with difficulty, obtained, but arms and ammunition were lacking, and only the regular troops were granted muskets, the militia being armed largely with pikes and machetes. The few pieces of artillery in the possession of the Governor were mounted on the tower of La Merced, and on the heights of the convents of the Jesuits and of San Francisco, on the fortress, and on the roof of the arsenals in San Fernando and San Carlos. Fortifications were rendered stronger around the city walls.

His lack of resources and his inability to muster a sufficient number of men to strengthen the militia of the Cibao, determined the Governor to concentrate his efforts for defense on the fortification of the city of Santo Domingo. It was realized in advance that the regular troops in Azua, and the militia in the Cibao under the command of Colonel Serapio Reinoso de Orbe, would go to an inevitable death in their attempt to stem the torrent soon to pour across the Haitian frontier.

On February 16, 1805, Dessalines left Cape Haitian by way of Port de Paix and Gonaives. Following the plans successfully carried out by Toussaint in his earlier invasion of the Spanish colony, the Haitian army was divided into two parts; one portion was to sweep from the north through the Cibao; the other, proceeding through the southern provinces, was to meet the northern army outside the walls of Santo Domingo, the two armies concentrating there to capture the capital. The southern army, commanded by Dessalines and by the mulatto Pétion, encountered but slight resistance. Las Matas de Farfán was occupied on February 24th. Three days later, a small number of heroic Spaniards who attempted to delay the onward march of the Haitian army were utterly destroyed, their commanding officer, captured after he had been wounded, being hideously tortured before he was permitted to die. Azua and Baní were occupied without the exchange of a shot, and on March 5th, the southern army reached the capital.

The army of the north, under Christophe, encountered a more stubborn resistance. The inhabitants of the smaller towns in the north of the colony fled before the invading hordes to the protection of the fortifications made along the River Yaque by Colonel Reinoso de Orbe. In the struggle which took place near La Emboscada, the immensely superior numbers of the Haitians rendered the resistance of the Spaniards of short duration. The great majority, including their valiant colonel, perished in that spot.

Santiago was occupied by Christophe on Monday of carnival week, February 25th. The Haitians, rendered jubilant by their easy victory, commenced an orgy of celebration by consuming the stores of tafia which they found in that city. They then turned their attention to rape, loot and murder, and when these pastimes palled, to the more refined pleasures afforded by torture. The greater part of the inhabitants had taken refuge in the church. All of these were slaughtered, and the priest officiating at the Mass, Don José Vasquez, was burned alive, the sacred books and vestments furnishing the fuel. The church itself, piled high with the mutilated bodies of the dead, was then consumed by the flames. Search was made from house to house, and the fugitives who had escaped detection in the early hours of the massacre were now dragged out to more prolonged agonies than those they would have encountered had they met their death when the assault first took place. Children, whose bodies had first been mutilated, were literally torn to pieces; men and women were slowly sliced to bits with machetes. The body of one victim was first mutilated by strokes of the machete, and then lighted cartridges were placed in the wounds, until at length the bleeding mass had been torn to shreds by the exploding cartridges. When no more victims could be found, the march continued; and the following day dawned upon a scene of the most ghastly desolation. When they returned, the few inhabitants who had succeeded in escaping found the bodies of the members of the cabildo, who had all been taken captive by Christophe, naked and mutilated, dangling from the balcony of the Casa Consistorial.

Christophe's troops passed on through the Cibao to Santo Domingo, repeating on a smaller scale in each town and village the scenes which had taken place in Santiago, and so arrived to rejoin the forces of Dessalines two days after the southern army had reached the outskirts of the capital.

For three weeks the siege continued. The Haitians occupied the outposts at San Carlos, and with the capture of Pajarito commanded the left bank of the Ozama. It appeared for a time as if the capital was doomed. The food supply ran short, but was eked out with additional supplies which General Ferrand fortunately obtained from a French vessel arriving opportunely from Martinique. A few sorties were made unsuccessfully, and the inhabitants of the city had begun to resign themselves to the inevitable, when upon awakening one morning they found anchored in the roadstead the imposing fleet commanded by Admiral Missiessy, sent by the newly proclaimed Emperor Napoleon to harass British shipping in West Indian waters. The fleet had sailed with all haste to Santo

Domingo when the news was received by the Admiral of
the invasion of the colony.

Admiral Missiessy at once took steps to assist Ferrand.
Troops were landed to swell the forces of the local garrison. Much needed supplies and ammunition were provided, and with the help so afforded, plans were immediately made to defeat the besieging armies. A column of
French and Dominican troops, under the command of
that same Colonel Juan Barón who had so distinguished
himself in the earlier Haitian invasion, made a sally, on the
afternoon of March 28th, and succeeded in overcoming
the Haitians at San Carlos, although Colonel Barón was
killed in the encounter and Captain Moscoso, the second
in command, was forced to retire. However, the proof
thus afforded the Haitians of the indomitable spirit of
the inhabitants of the capital, and the realization that the
supplies and reinforcements received from the French
squadron would render the early capture of the capital
improbable, compelled Dessalines to raise the siege.

On the morning of the 29th of March, the defenders
of Santo Domingo found the Haitians commencing to
evacuate their positions. The evacuation soon became a
rout, and General Ferrand, sending strong columns in
pursuit of the fleeing Haitians, was able to do considerable damage to their rear. Lack of organization, however,
prevented General Ferrand's forces from continuing their
pursuit for any considerable distance, and the inhabitants
of the south and of the Cibao, who had just commenced
to return to their homes from the mountains and forests where they had taken refuge, were abandoned once
more to the mercy of the retiring Haitians. If any comparison is possible, the horrors of the Haitian retreat were
worse than the atrocities of the invasion.

Dessalines, maddened by this defeat to which he had been subjected, gave orders that utter devastation should mark the passage of his retiring armies. The army of the south, on the march back, was now commanded by Pétion, one of the few admirable figures of the servile revolt, who countermanded the orders of his superior, and was responsible for limiting the excesses of his own soldiery.

Dessalines himself undertook to retreat with the army of the north. Spreading the report, through a few traitorous members of the Spanish colony who had attached themselves to him, that Ferrand had capitulated, and that the Haitian troops were now returning as conquerors to their own territory, Dessalines sent word to the leading inhabitants in each town through which he was to pass that the conquering general wished to treat the colonists as friends, and orders were given that festivals be prepared to celebrate the new era of peace and fraternity. In view of the experience which they had undergone so recently at the hands of the Haitians, it appears incredible that the inhabitants could have been so readily deceived. In Concepción de la Vega, 900 of the inhabitants were taken prisoners and forced to accompany the Haitians on their retreat. In Moca, on April 3rd, the townspeople, 500 in number, assembled in the church to attend a solemn Te Deum of thanksgiving for the peaceful intentions of their supposed conquerors, were all mercilessly slaughtered, only a few small children escaping by being concealed under the skirts of their dead mothers. What remained of Santiago was utterly destroyed. Even towns like Monte Cristi, which lay to one side of the route taken by Dessalines on his return to Haiti, were not immune, for detachments were sent from the main body of troops to destroy them and to murder their inhabitants. The fate of the prisoners taken at La Vega, whose numbers had been increased as the retreat continued, was, if possible, more cruel. Numbers from time to time were murdered as the retreat went on. Many of the women were divided among the officers of Dessalines' or Christophe's staffs. When the survivors, more dead than alive after their forced marches through the devastating heat of the almost impenetrable cactus jungles of the desert lands of Monte Cristi Province, reached the Cape, they were set to work by Christophe at the construction of his famous Citadel. At this task they did not long survive, and only a few fugitives ever succeeded in escaping to Dominican territory to relate the horrors which they had undergone.

7.

The determination of Ferrand to build up a colony worthy of the new French Empire seems to have been rendered only stronger by the setback which had resulted from the invasion of Dessalines. Napoleon, informed by Admiral Missiessy of the brave resistance which Ferrand had put up, disregarding his previous disobedience, confirmed him in his post as Governor of the new colony, sent him reënforcements, and procured for him financial credits in the United States. The Governor at once resumed his plans for the development of the economic prosperity of the colony. Refugees were called back. Every possible incentive was given to the increase of agriculture, and to the fostering of commerce with the United States. Garrisons were established in all the principal towns. Projects of irrigation were commenced; construction of roads was undertaken, and for three years the colony underwent a period of peace, during which the French Governor attempted, by every means within his power, not only to increase the prosperity of his Spanish subjects but also to conciliate them to French sovereignty.

The phenomenon to which the three years of Ferrand's enlightened and progressive administration now gave birth is the most significant in the earlier history of the Dominican people; significant in that there were now sown the seeds of the desire for change which were later to come to such tragic fruition in the bloody revolutions and the shifting governments of more modern times; indicative as well of the passion for independence, and the unwillingness to brook foreign intervention, which alone have enabled the Dominican people to maintain their political integrity notwithstanding the manifold dangers which have repeatedly threatened it. No sooner had the colony settled down to enjoy the period of peace which the determination of the French alone had rendered possible; no sooner had time softened a little the memories of the horrors which the country had undergone; no sooner had the colonists been afforded the opportunity to replant their wasted fields and rebuild their ruined houses, than the spirit of revolt against the French domination became rife.

There were two prime factors in this movement—the first, the sentimental sympathy with which the colonists viewed the struggle of the Spaniards in Old Spain to resist the conquering armies of Napoleon; the second, the belief that the enmity of the Haitians was not directed against the Spanish colonists, but against the French who now controlled Santo Domingo, and the conviction that should the French be forced to relinquish their control of the colony, an understanding could be reached with the Haitians whereby the two sections of the island would respect their mutual independence. The first factor is readily comprehensible. Ties with the mother country were still strong, and it was natural that the Spanish colonists should resent the attempt of the Emperor Napoleon to destroy the independence of Spain, and that they should consequently now resent the French administration which they had so recently welcomed. From the viewpoint of later years, the second factor is one more difficult to understand. It appears strange that the Spanish colonists could so soon forget the miseries which they had undergone at the hands of the Haitians, and could so readily believe that the Haitian chieftains, whose yoke they had with such difficulty succeeded in rejecting, would so soon abandon their determination to dominate the entire island. It is true that Dessalines had by now met his death, and that Pétion was ruling as President in Port-au-Prince; but Christophe was still reigning in his Citadel of the Cape as Overlord of Northern Haiti, and it was not to be supposed that the relative humanity of Pétion could forever restrain the ferocity of those who had installed him, and far less that any sudden change of heart had seized the monster of the Cape at whose hands almost every family in the Cibao had suffered personal injury.

The spirit of revolution against France was, however, general. It was chiefly fostered by Don Juan Sánchez Ramírez, a native-born colonist of Cotuy who had emigrated from the country in 1803, returning in 1807 when conditions in the colony made it seem probable that he could resume with success the lumber business in which he was engaged. Ferrand appears to have had a high opinion of the capacity of Sánchez Ramírez, since upon his return to the colony he was offered by the Government the post of Comandante de Armas of Cotuy. The offer was not accepted, and Sánchez Ramírez, finding his desire to rid the colony of French domination supported by his more intimate friends, commenced in the summer of 1808 the definite task of fomenting a revolution.

During the summer months he was joined in the conspiracy by Padre Morilla, Vicar of the Seybo; Don Manuel Carvajal of Higuey; Padre Moreno, Vicar of Bayaguana; Padre Vicente de Luna, Vicar of Santiago; Don Francisco de Frias, Comandante de Armas in San Francisco de Macorís, and by the commanders of the garrisons in Cotuy and La Vega. The only rebuff of importance which Sánchez Ramírez encountered in his conspiracy came from Don Augustín Franco, Colonel of the Governor's troops in the Cibao, who remained loyal to General Ferrand, and in fact communicated to the latter the suspicions engendered by the overtures of Sánchez Ramírez. Ferrand, sure of the strength of his Government, believing apparently that the prosperity which his administration had brought to the colony and that his invariable consideration for his Spanish subjects made any revolt against him impossible, treated the reports which he received from Franco with scepticism, and paid but little heed to the other warnings of like nature which he received.

The overconfidence of the Governor made it possible for the conspiracy to spread with the utmost rapidity. Negotiations were undertaken by Sánchez Ramírez with the Governor-General of Puerto Rico, from whom the promise of support was obtained should a revolution be attempted. General Ciriaco Ramírez and his brother-in-law, Don Manuel Jiménez, agreed to support the revolution in the southern Dominican provinces.

When General Ferrand at last grasped the gravity of the situation the revolution had already commenced. On October 26th, the revolution was officially proclaimed by Don Juan Sánchez Ramírez near Seybo. There the revolu-

tionary leader raised the Spanish flag, and proclaiming
Fernando VII, King of Spain, as the natural sovereign of
the colony, at the head of a small group of horsemen he
took possession of the town of Seybo in the name of the
revolution, and imprisoned Don Manuel Peralta, Ferrand's
representative.

The energetic steps which General Ferrand now took to
quell the revolt were at first successful in the south. But
the revolutionists, who had now succeeded in creating a
general uprising throughout the country, obtained munitions both from Pétion and Christophe, and likewise received reënforcements from Puerto Rico. They were even
more greatly encouraged by the assistance brought them
by the British frigate *Franchise,* commanded by Captain
Dashwood. The success with which his Government had
been able at first to crush the rebels in the south determined General Ferrand to command in person a column
sent out from Santo Domingo against the troops under
Don Juan Sánchez Ramírez, who had established themselves in a spot known as Palo Hincado, not far from
Seybo. Sánchez Ramírez had succeeded in gathering together troops to the number of some 600 men. The troops
headed by General Ferrand were slightly less in number.
The encounter took place near where the lines of the
revolutionaries had established themselves, and the victory
of the latter was overwhelming. Many of the French
officers were killed in the engagement, and General Ferrand, seeing the rout of his troops, fled towards Santo
Domingo with only two companions, closely pursued by a
body of fifty of the revolutionaries under the command of
Don Pedro Santana. Ferrand, realizing that his defeat
implied the destruction of all his own hopes, and the
definite failure of his ambition to maintain the French flag

over Santo Domingo, committed suicide at Guaquía. His body was found there by Santana, who struck off the head and bore it in triumph to Seybo, where the revolutionists were celebrating their victory. The news of Ferrand's defeat and death caused consternation in Santo Domingo, where General Dubarquier, the second in command to Ferrand, now assumed the Governorship of the colony.

Sending emissaries to advise the delegates of the revolution throughout the colony of the initial success of their plans, Sánchez Ramírez called the delegates to assemble at Bondilla. There, on December 13, 1808, the Pact of Bondilla was signed by the chief leaders of the revolution, who proclaimed their allegiance to Fernando VII and selected Don Juan Sánchez Ramírez as Governor of Santo Domingo.

The siege of the capital by the revolutionists was at once undertaken, but notwithstanding the material assistance afforded them by the intervention of British troops commanded by General Carmichael, General Dubarquier was able to hold the city of Santo Domingo until July 9th of the following year. On that date, representatives of the revolutionists and of the British troops signed an agreement of capitulation with an envoy of Dubarquier, and the revolutionaries with their British allies entered the capital two days later. After coming to an agreement with the revolutionaries whereby British subjects and British colonists were to be accorded favoured treatment, Carmichael sailed for Jamaica bearing with him as prisoners the few last remaining French officers and men.

8.

Sending an envoy at once to Spain to bear the news of the successful efforts of the colonists to free themselves from France, to protest their loyalty to the Spanish Crown, and to beg the assistance of the Spanish Government, Sánchez Ramírez settled down to a survey of the situation. The first measure decreed by the new Governor was the exile of all French subjects from the colony; the second was the creation of *ayuntamientos* in all the towns of any importance.

Encouragement was given the new Governor and his associates by the news which they soon received of the enthusiastic reception which their envoy had met in Spain. Owing to the sequestration at the time of Fernando VII by Napoleon, control of the Spanish Government was vested in the members of the Junta Central de Sevilla, and in the Council of Regency, which governed in the name of the King until such time as his release might be effected. In two edicts issued by the Junta Central de Sevilla and the Council of Regency, January 12, 1810, and April 29, 1810, the colony was welcomed back to the sovereignty of Spain. The promise was officially made to the colonists that a garrison of Spanish troops would be maintained in Santo Domingo for the protection of the colony; that trade between the colony and the mother country, as well as with the other Spanish colonies, would be practically free for fifteen years, and that only nominal taxes would be imposed on Dominican commerce for a period of ten years. All restrictions which had previously existed limiting the colonists to the production of particular crops were rescinded, and financial assistance was assured them. The administration of justice in the colony was once more placed under the control of the Real Audiencia of Caracas. Don Juan Sánchez Ramírez was confirmed in the post to which he had been raised by his fellow-citizens, and was given the additional titles of Intendente and Captain-

General, and Don José Nuñez de Cáceres was named Lieutenant-Governor, Auditor de Guerra and Asesor General. A Royal Commissioner was sent to the colony in the person of Don Francisco Javier Caro, a native Dominican who had been a member of the Junta Central de Sevilla.

It is an astonishing fact that at the very moment when freedom from the control of Spain was being sought by many of the other Spanish colonies of the American Continent, when revolutions were breaking out in Buenos Aires, Venezuela, Nueva Granada, and Mexico, when the cry of "liberty and independence" was being eloquently proclaimed by Bolívar, and the death knell of the period of Spain's colonial expansion had already sounded, the colony of Santo Domingo, in freeing itself from France, should have demanded its return to the Government of Spain.

At first the colonists had no reason to regret the decision reached by the signers of the Pact of Bondilla. The more progressive elements in Spain were temporarily in control of her Government, and the Constitution of 1812, later proclaimed in Santo Domingo, gave added assurance that the period of reform and democracy inaugurated in Spain itself would be shared by the colonies. Under the new Constitution, the colony was given representation in the Spanish Cortes, and Don Francisco Javier Caro was elected as the colony's first representative. But these hopes of autonomy proved to be short lived, since the Treaty of Valencey between Napoleon and Fernando VII permitted the latter to return to Madrid. The King's first step was to abrogate all the acts taken in his name by the Council of Regency and by the Junta Central de Sevilla, and the colonists were dismayed to find that all the progressive measures taken by the Spanish Government since the

INTRODUCTION

colony's return to the Spanish flag were now at one blow overthrown, and that a policy of reaction had been undertaken identical to that which existed prior to the French revolution.

There now began the period commonly known by the Dominicans as the reign of "España boba," or "Silly Spain." The struggle of the reconquest had left the colony in a disastrous condition. The brief epoch of prosperity, which the last years of Ferrand's rule had inaugurated, had vanished, and the government of Sánchez Ramírez had no time to improve economic conditions. Upon his death in 1811 Sánchez Ramírez was succeeded as Governor by a Spanish reactionary of the old school named Urutia, whose interests were concentrated in his own personal advantage, and in the securing of salaried positions for his compatriots and for those of the colonists who catered to him. Little, if any, heed was taken of the general well-being of the colony, and the men who had participated in the struggle of Palo Hincado were consequently ignored, Urutia being surrounded with returned exiles or with Spaniards who had undergone none of the hardships of the preceding years.

Morillas, in his "Noticias," says that the commercial life of the ports was dead except in Puerto Plata, where tobacco in small quantities was still shipped to Europe, and whence a small business in cattle, hides, mahogany, molasses and rum was done with the United States. The production of coffee and cacao had ceased. On a few scattered plantations cane was grown in small quantities, the scarcity of labour making the cost of its production almost prohibitive. The sugar planters had not the wherewithal to improve the machinery of the factories, and the growing of cane and the production of rum were consequently constantly decreasing. The general poverty was so extreme that distinction between classes hardly existed. The ability of the planter and the ability of the free mulatto to purchase were on a par; luxury was a thing of the past. In the capital city there were not half a dozen carriages.

From time to time, the dissatisfaction of the more enterprising of the colonists found vent in the elaboration of revolutionary conspiracies, but these were invariably stifled before they had even been hatched. The arrival of General Bolívar and his 'fellow refugees in Haiti, in 1815, gave the Governor of Santo Domingo considerable alarm, particularly in view of the elaborate reception and the more welcome material assistance accorded them by President Pétion. In consequence of the arrival of the revolutionaries from South America in the neighbouring country, the Governor proclaimed the general mobilization of the militia of the colony. The early departure of General Bolívar, however, made continued mobilization of the local troops unnecessary, and although the Governor in a public proclamation pointed with pride to the rapidity with which the colonists had responded to his call, it is doubtful whether the colonists shared his enthusiasm, since the Governor confessed, with regret, his inability to pay them, or even to bear their expenses for maintenance during the time they were under arms.

The substitution of a more liberal-minded governor for General Urutia, and the reëstablishment of the Constitution of 1812 forced upon Fernando VII by the Spanish Insurrection of 1820, improved slightly the condition of the colonists.

At the same time, however, danger from the west became once more imminent. Upon the death of President Pétion in 1818, General Boyer had been elected President of Haiti in his stead. Boyer appears to have adopted the policy as well as a considerable portion of the strategy of Toussaint, for no sooner had he been inaugurated than he sent secret envoys to the border provinces of the Spanish colony to foster propaganda among the negro inhabitants in order to induce them to rise in favour of a union with Haiti. When rumours of these attempts reached General Kendelán, the Governor of Santo Domingo, he somewhat naively addressed a letter to President Boyer, asking whether there was any truth in the reports that the President of Haiti was attempting to foment discord among the subjects of the King of Spain. President Boyer blandly replied that since such a procedure would be undoubtedly contrary to the law of nations, he naturally could not countenance any such efforts on the part of any of his fellow-citizens, and further assured the Governor that the Government of Haiti held no ambitions for the conquest of additional territory. These assurances appear to have been accepted at their face value by General Kendelán, who published the exchange of correspondence for the benefit of the Spanish colonists; but when the reports continued, and more definite information was obtained that the propaganda was being conducted by order of President Boyer himself, General Real, who had succeeded Kendelán as Governor, determined to send his nephew to Port-au-Prince to make a more careful investigation of the truth of the rumours. Before General Real could obtain any satisfactory information from his agent, however, he was involved in a new and, to him, more serious difficulty.

For some time past, Don José Nuñez de Cáceres, appointed Lieutenant-Governor of the colony by the Junta Central de Sevilla in 1801, had in a half-hearted manner been planning with other prominent men in the colony a

conspiracy to free Santo Domingo from the control of
Spain and link its destinies with those of the newly formed
Republic of Colombia. The time now appeared opportune
to Cáceres to bring the movement to a head, and on November 30, 1821, the freedom of the colony from the
sovereignty of Spain was proclaimed in the city of Santo
Domingo. General Real gave in readily enough; he attempted no resistance, and was in short order packed off
to Spain. The provincial deputies constituted themselves a
Junta Provisional de Gobierno, naming Don José Nuñez
de Cáceres as "Political Governor" and President of the
Independent State of "Spanish Haiti." At the same time a
new Constitution was drafted, declaring that the State of
Spanish Haiti had become an integral portion of the Federation of Colombia, and an envoy was sent, in the person
of Dr. Antonio Pineda, to the President of Colombia
demanding the admittance of Spanish Haiti in the Colombian Federation, and urging that assistance be given
the new state in maintaining its freedom. At the same
time an envoy was sent to President Boyer to propose the
conclusion of a treaty of amity, whereby the Haitian
Government would accord formal recognition to the
independence of "Spanish Haiti."

The opportunity was one which Boyer naturally did not
lose. Before Pineda had time to reach Colombia, where the
absence of Bolívar would have rendered his mission fruitless in any event, the Haitian President, on January 12,
1822, issued a proclamation declaring that the Dominican
people had formally submitted to the laws and Constitution of the Haitian Republic, and in order to render
these verbal assurances doubly sure, two days later Boyer
mobilized the Haitian army for the purpose of occupying
the Dominican territory once more.

The march of the Haitian armies in this new invasion was not delayed. As soon as word reached Santo Domingo of the turn of affairs, the ineffable Cáceres addressed a proclamation to his fellow-citizens counselling them to receive the invading hordes with courtesy, and "with pacific sentiments," and exhorting the Dominicans to show the world how skilled they were in adapting themselves to divers forms of government, since, as he stated, every form of government "is good, if it grants the inalienable rights of liberty, equality, personal security and social peace provided by nature, all of which it is promised you will abundantly enjoy under the Constitution and laws of Haiti." On February 6th, President Boyer reached Baní, where plans were drawn up in accord with Nuñez de Cáceres for the entrance of the Haitian President into Santo Domingo, and three days later Cáceres put into practise the advice he had given his fellow Dominicans by handing President Boyer, on a silver platter, the keys of the city of Santo Domingo.

9.

That date marks the beginning of a period of eighteen years during which the Dominican colony slept a sleep which was almost that of death. No sooner had President Boyer returned to Port-au-Prince than he commenced the effort, which he consistently continued throughout those long years, of stifling every form of culture, and every feature of the Dominicans' proud inheritance, which from time to time glimmered feebly in the gloom of the Black Occupation. The administration everywhere was Haitianized. The families who still possessed some slight property emigrated. Agriculture came eventually to a standstill; commerce was non-existent. Public spirit seems to have sunk so low that only rarely were any sporadic efforts made to raise the standard of a new rebellion. All forms of intellectual progress, which had been encouraged in some slight degree during the years of "España boba," perished in the first year of the Haitian Occupation. The University closed its doors; the great majority of the churches were left without priests.

The following extract of a report submitted by the British Consul-General in Haiti, and presented by Canning to the British Parliament in 1826, provides a graphic description of the depths to which Santo Domingo had sunk:

"The whole isle is divided into departments, arrondissements, and communes. These are all under the command of military men subject only to the control of the President, and to them is entrusted exclusively the execution of all laws whether affecting police, agriculture or finance. There is not a single civilian charged with an extensive authority . . . During the past two years trade has gradually fallen off and . . . it is supposed that it has decreased nearly one half . . . The most important code is the Code Rural, the chief character of which is the enforcing of labor. It is a modification of the old French regulations sanctioned by the Code Noire, with additional restrictions. The provisions are as despotic as those of any slave system that can be conceived. The laborer may almost be considered as 'adscriptus glebe,' he is deemed a vagrant and liable to punishment if he ventures to move from his dwelling or farm without license. He is prohibited from keeping a shop. No person can build a house in the country not connected with a farm. . . . The Code affixes the penalty or fine in some cases, and there is indefinite imprisonment at the option of the justice of the peace. Cultivation would not go on beyond that which daily necessi-

THE MOUNTAINS OF SAN CRISTÓBAL

ties might require, except for the Code. The decrease in population in thirty-three years has been very nearly one-third of the whole population in 1793 . . . The Government has appropriated all the church property to its own use. The clergy rely wholly on the fees, two-thirds of which they are obliged to pay into the Treasury. . . . It is not a subject of surprise that morality should be in as low a stage . . . Marriage is scarcely thought of. . . ." [1]

During the years that passed, the island of Santo Domingo became more and more isolated from the civilized world. In a decree dated April 17, 1825, the French King, Charles X, recognized "the entire independence of the Government of the present inhabitants of the French portion of the Island of Santo Domingo," terms which specifically excluded from such recognition the former Spanish colony. In return for this recognition the Haitian Government obligated itself to pay to the French Government an indemnity of 150,000,000 francs, "destined to repay the former colonists who claim indemnification," and to grant French vessels in Haitian ports a preferential rate of 50 per cent in the exaction of duties or port dues. Commercial relations, however, with France or with any other European nation were constantly diminishing. Moreover, relations of any character with the new Republics to the south had been estopped by the refusal of the Colombian Government to receive an Haitian envoy because of Boyer's disregard of the declaration by the Government at Santo Domingo that it had adhered to the Federation of Colombia.

The determined opposition of the representatives of the slave-holding states in the American Congress long pre-

[1] From a report of Charles McKenzie, British Consul-General in Haiti, submitted September 8, 1826, by the Rt. Hon. George Canning to the Parliament.

vented the maintenance of diplomatic relations between the United States and the Haitian Republic. While American Commercial Agents were occasionally appointed to Port-au-Prince, the Haitian Government resolutely refused to permit such agents to establish themselves in the Spanish portions of the island, and when in 1837 the United States Government appointed Daniel William Carney as its first Commercial Agent to Santo Domingo, President Boyer instructed General Carrié, the Governor of that "Arrondissement" to arrest him should he attempt to perform any official act in that capacity.

If the attention of the American people was directed at all towards conditions in Santo Domingo, it was due to the interest shown by several of the recently organized abolitionist societies, which warmly welcomed the invitation of Boyer to assist negroes in leaving the United States to populate the barren lands of the Spanish portion of the Island. But this enthusiasm soon died out, since a considerable number of the emigrants from the United States died shortly after their arrival in the Dominican provinces of an epidemic of typhus, and since some of the negroes who returned to the United States horrified their New England patrons by dilating upon the conditions of gross immorality existing among the Haitians. A few of the former American slaves remained, however, in the Province of Samaná, willing apparently to overlook the immorality of the Haitians, or else agreeably impressed by the climate. There their descendants remain in considerable numbers to the present day.

The systematic oppression of their Haitian overlords, the terror which the methods of repression employed created among the Dominicans, eventually stifled not only all semblance of concerted public spirit, but even crushed the normal instincts of virile pride in the individual. A pitiful instance of this fact is found in the correspondence published on March 4, 1838, in *Le Telegraphe* of Port-au-Prince.

Dr. José Maria Caminero, a distinguished resident of Santo Domingo, who later served his country, after its liberation, as the first Diplomatic Agent of the Dominican Republic in Washington, had brought suit for divorce from his wife, charging that it was notorious that she had been taken under the "protection" of General Carrié, the Haitian Governor of his "Arrondissement." Affecting offense at this aspersion upon his father, Carrié's son, who was also his aide-de-camp, published, in the sheet referred to, a letter calling Dr. Caminero to account for the "satisfaction of feeling in these cases as in all others the sacred obligations of a son and of an aide-de-camp towards his father and towards his general," and published as well the following humiliating retraction of the charges which he had forced Dr. Caminero to address to him:

"Santo Domingo, January 30, 1838,
"Monsieur Carrié, fils,
"Santo Domingo.
"M. le Capitaine:
"In response to your demand that I throw light upon the phrases which I employed in the petition presented to the Court of Cassation for divorce from my wife, Guadeloupe Heredia, which phrases are as follows:
'The notorious protection of the Supreme Authority of this Arrondissement,' and, 'She counted upon the influence of her protector,' I declare to you that I had no intention of referring even remotely to the private character, honor, and administration of General Carrié, your father, since in accordance with the wise precepts of the Chief of State,

each Commanding Officer of an Arrondissement must always protect all of the citizens under his jurisdiction.

"I sincerely hope that these explanations will be agreeable to you.

"I greet you affectionately.

"CAMINERO"

10.

It was not until 1838 that hope dawned in the future Dominican Republic. Juan Pablo Duarte, a young Dominican whose father had taken a prominent part in the public life of the colony in the early years of the century, and whom fortune had favoured in those earlier years, had been sent to Europe to be educated, far removed from the asphyxiating effects of Haitian domination. Duarte returned to his native land fired with the purpose of freeing his fellow-citizens and of restoring his country to a place in the family of nations.

The impressions made upon Duarte on his arrival may be imagined when account is taken of the fact that almost his entire life had been spent in the most civilized countries of the modern world. The streets which he remembered filled with members of his own race going about their business, which even "España boba" had not been able wholly to destroy, were now deserted save for a few negroes lounging on the street corners; the Casa Consistorial and the Governor's Palace, where formerly the resplendent figures of the Spanish officers and the members of the Governor's staff had been seen, were now occupied by a horde of arrogant Haitians; at the entrance to the city gates, where the Spanish troops were once on guard, now a few ragged Haitian soldiers squatted in the shade, or slouched by in bare feet.

But if the material ruin of the country was shocking, how much more disheartening must have seemed the supine indifference with which so many of his countrymen regarded their fate.

Duarte's personality was magnetic, his determination was irresistible, and his creed of "God, Country and Liberty" breathed life into the souls of the younger generation at least, for some of the older men had been too long ground beneath Haitian heel to feel any response.

After months of effort, Duarte at last formed a revolutionary society known as La Trinitaria. The original members of the society, numbering nine, met secretly on July 16, 1838, in the house of one of the members, Don Juan Isidro Pérez, which still stands opposite the Church of the Carmen. There they solemnly took the oath of allegiance to the creed of their leader, and swore to continue the work of obtaining proselytes throughout the country until the flag of red and blue quarterings bearing the white cross, designed by Duarte as the symbol of the new nation, should wave over the independent Dominican Republic.

Once the movement was launched, it met with general response. The plan of procedure was so devised that new members of the conspiracy were kept in ignorance of the names of all the original members of the revolutionary group, except that of the member responsible for their own induction. In that manner the danger of the defeat of their plans was avoided, since betrayal could never involve more than one of the nine leaders at the same time. The task of propaganda was not carried on alone by word of mouth, but the spirit of revolution was fostered as well by the priest in the confessional and by the master in the secret school. Amateur theatricals were even devised in which many of the conspirators took part, in order that patriotic sentiments might be proclaimed to the audiences thus obtained.

For five years Duarte and his fellows worked on unfalteringly, and at length the moment approached for the consummation of their hopes. The despotism of Boyer, absolute as it was in the eastern half of the Island, had at length become intolerable even in Haïti proper. A revolution against him broke out in 1843, commencing in the Haitian town of Jérémie. At the instigation of Duarte, the Dominican revolutionaries secretly lent their moral support to those Haitians involved in the attempt to overthrow Boyer. The revolution consequently gained adherents throughout the Island, and Boyer, at length giving in to the inevitable, fled from Haiti, where he was succeeded as despot by Charles Hérard.

The moment was now believed propitious by the members of the Trinitaria to proceed openly along the path they had set for themselves. On March 24, 1843, Duarte, accompanied by Francisco del Rosario Sánchez, Ramón Mella and numerous leaders among the Dominicans, as well as by several Haitians of the liberal party, marched through the streets of the capital to demand from the Governor, General Carrié, reform of the Constitution and reform in administration. The movement was at first suppressed and its chief leaders were constrained to flee for their lives, but eventually General Carrié was forced to give in, and the desired reforms were officially proclaimed. A step in advance had thus been taken by Duarte, but the Haitian liberals, who had until now supported him, broke away as the result of discord which developed between them and the Dominicans, and the arrival in Santo Domingo of General Hérard, determined to stamp out, at any cost, the

Dominican cry for independence, caused an abrupt check to the plans of the conspirators.

As soon as Hérard arrived in the capital, orders were issued for the arrest of the chief conspirators, whose names by now had become generally known. Duarte, Piña and Juan Isidro Pérez succeeded in escaping from the country. Sánchez, too ill at the time to travel, was hidden by his family, and the Haitian general, advised of his sudden death, was fortunately credulous enough to believe the story, and abandoned further attempts to ascertain his whereabouts. The Santana brothers, Pedro and Ramón, sons of Ferrand's opponent, escaped to the Seybo, where they found concealment. For a time, which proved to be but brief, plans for the revolution were abandoned. Duarte reached Curaçao with the intention of proceeding to Venezuela, in the vain hope of obtaining foreign assistance in carrying out his plans. But before he was afforded the opportunity of returning to his country, the ideal for which he had so long laboured was at last realized.

On February 27, 1844, at ten o'clock at night a band of some hundred members of the conspirators seized the fortress of the Puerta del Conde, whose commanding officer had been suborned by one of the conspirators. Here the cry of "Separation, God, Country and Liberty" was raised. Leaving a number sufficient to guard this outpost, the conspirators, dividing into smaller groups, succeeded by a ruse in obtaining control of the strongholds in the city, and on the following day the Haitian commander, General Desgrotte, was compelled to sign his capitulation. The declaration made by the revolutionary Junta in their negotiations with Desgrotte is significant of the inspiration which Duarte had bestowed upon his countrymen. "The denial," stated the Junta, "of their rights, and the evil administration of the Haitian Government, have created among the Dominicans the firm and imperishable determination to be free and independent, should it cost their lives and their property, and no menace will be capable of weakening this resolution."

Two days later, Desgrotte and his fellow Haitians retired from the soil of the new Republic, and the history of the independent Dominican Republic had commenced.

NABOTH'S VINEYARD

CHAPTER I

1.

ON February 29, 1844, the last of the Haitian officials left the capital. The Provisional Junta, diminished in its membership by the fact that Tomás Bobadilla, Manuel Jiménez and Vicente Celestino Duarte had been sent to different parts of the Republic to encourage the inhabitants of the outlying provinces to rise in support of the revolution, and to concert with all possible speed plans for the formation of a national militia to repel the anticipated attack from Haiti, declared itself a "Junta Central" to direct the destinies of the new nation until the people could determine upon a form of constitutional government. This Junta Central, composed of Francisco del Rosario Sánchez, Ramón Mella, José Joaquín Puello, Remigio del Castillo, Wenceslao de la Concha, Mariano Echavarria, and Pedro de Castro y Castro, despatched Juan Nepomuceno Ravelo to Curaçao to bring Juan Pablo Duarte to the Republic. On March 14th Duarte arrived in Santo Domingo and was received upon his arrival as the nation's idol.

Support of the revolution in the eastern provinces was evidenced at once, due in large part to the popular prestige in the Seybo of Pedro and Ramón Santana. Azua joined later. The early reluctance of its inhabitants was due to the disinclination of their local leader, Buenaventura Baez, to support the Junta Central in its determination to proclaim the independence of the Dominican provinces rather than to follow the course which Baez favoured of seeking a protectorate from France. Divergence in the policies of the leading men in the Republic thus early became marked.

The original failure of some of the most influential men in the country to join the revolution proclaimed by the patriots of the Puerta del Conde was caused by their sincere belief that the independence of the country could not be maintained, and by their conviction that separation from Haiti could only be rendered permanent were some foreign power to afford the Dominicans effective protection. For this reason Pedro Ramón de Mena, sent by the Junta Central to the Cibao to obtain the adherence of the northern provinces, met at first with considerable opposition in his mission, but eventually Cotuy, La Vega and Moca, as well as San Francisco de Macorís, were brought into line, and the enthusiasm among the inhabitants of Santiago was finally roused to such a pitch that the Haitian authorities discreetly capitulated and evacuated the strongholds of that city. Soon after, Puerto Plata and other northern towns announced their participation in the revolution, and before the middle of March the Junta Central had obtained the declared support of the whole Republic with the exception of a few small towns near the Haitian border. To grant representation to all parts of the Republic, the membership of the Junta Central was again changed before the first of April, and Juan Pablo Duarte himself after his return to the capital, was appointed a member of the Junta, although Tomás Bobadilla and General Manuel Jiménez were elected its President and Vice President.

The speed with which the provinces rose at the proclamation of separation from Haiti was fortunate, since as soon as Hérard, the President of Haiti, learned that the Dominican Provinces were in revolt, he mustered as large a force as he could raise, and sending an army from the north under the command of General Pierrot, he himself invaded the Dominican Republic from the south with an equally large force, encountering little resistance until he reached the town of Azua. The army gathered together to oppose the invasion of Azua was composed in large part of farmers from the Seybo under the command of General Pedro Santana, who had been ordered by the Junta Central to proceed to Azua with all possible haste. The untrained and undisciplined Dominicans fought with the utmost valour, and succeeded in completely routing the greatly superior numbers of the Haitian hordes. But Santana, for reasons which were not then explained, and which gave rise in later years to bitter recriminations between himself and Buenaventura Baez, who was at the time one of the officers fighting under him, failed to follow up his victory and retreated to Baní, permitting the Haitians, notwithstanding their defeat, to occupy the town of Azua without further opposition. As soon as news of General Santana's retreat was received by the Junta Central, General Juan Pablo Duarte was ordered to Baní to coöperate with Santana. Duarte arrived in Baní on March 21st, but after two weeks, during which he found it impossible to persuade Santana of the necessity of taking the offensive, and obtained small support in his contentions from the Junta Central, he was ordered to return to the capital on the ground that his presence was necessary in the Government. In the meantime, the Dominicans in the north under the command of General José Maria Imbert were successful in repelling the onslaught of the Haitians under General Pierrot.

After the recall of Duarte to Santo Domingo, Santana notified the Junta Central that he considered it impossible to take the offensive against the Haitians until he received further supplies, and in particular more men and greater quantities of ammunition. Small engagements occurred from time to time in which the Haitians were worsted, but the two armies remained stationary for several weeks until fortune favoured the Republic by the outbreak in Haiti, towards the end of April, of a revolution headed by General Pierrot against the Administration of Hérard. In order to attempt to arrest the revolution within his own boundaries, Hérard abandoned Azua on May 9th, and embarking part of his forces, and retreating at the head of the remainder overland to the Haitian frontier, burned and sacked, in accordance with the best traditions of his predecessors, all towns and villages lying along his path. Now at last Santana was willing to move, and following up the retreating Haitian armies he proceeded at the head of a considerable column to the frontier, where he established garrisons in all of the frontier towns of any importance.

The fundamental differences which had existed even prior to the revolution between the leading men in the Republic became still more strongly accentuated with the retreat of the Haitian armies from Dominican soil.

On the one hand was the small band of patriots, the liberals, led by Duarte and Mella—whose cry of Liberty and Independence, still re-echoing down the years, alone had made the revolution a living, inspired fact, and who had time and again risked their lives, their families, their property, in the support of their faith that the Dominican people were destined to become a sovereign, an independent nation; on the other, the protectionists—a few timorously seeking that protection from abroad which they feared their own strength could not afford against the dreaded Haitian menace; the many, and among these the more prominent, seeking the security for their property, or the more definite advantages to themselves which the French agents, the Spanish authorities in Cuba and Puerto Rico, and the representatives of European commerce had long asserted would be ensured by a foreign protectorate, or by annexation to a European Power.

The prime mover in the protectionist policy from its very inception appears to have been Buenaventura Baez— "all his life," [1] as Charles Sumner afterwards characterized him, "adventurer, conspirator and trickster, uncertain in opinions, without character, without patriotism, without truth, looking out supremely for himself, and on any side according to imagined personal interest . . ." Born about 1810, the grandson of the Spanish priest and author, Don Antonio Sánchez Valverde, and the son of a mulatto slave girl, he was recognized as a legitimate member of a large family long settled in Azua, possessed of considerable property, and of preponderant influence in the local affairs of the Province. Baez had been sent in his early youth to Europe to receive those means of education which it was not possible for a Dominican student to obtain during the Haitian Occupation. Upon his return to his own country he had served in various offices under the Haitian Government, and in 1843 was sent as delegate from the Province of Azua to the Haitian National Assembly in Port-au-Prince. It was at that time that, meeting Adolphe Barrot, then Special Commissioner of France to the Haitian Republic, and obtaining facile assurances from the French envoy that a Dominican revolution concerted for the purpose of placing the Dominican Provinces under a French protectorate would receive the active support of France, Baez conceived the policy which the vigilance of the Trinitarios at first rendered abortive.

[1] Speech of Senator Charles Sumner of Massachusetts, delivered in the U. S. Senate March 27, 1871.

Not until long afterwards was it known that, in a rage at the thwarting of his plans by the uprising of February 27th, Baez had sent a secret emissary to Port-au-Prince to warn the Haitian President of the revolt and to advise him of the movements of the revolutionary troops. Baez, ever a shrewd judge of character, was able to gather about him in support of his schemes many of the leaders in the Republic whose firm belief in the promises of the French agents was worthy of a better cause. But that the Government of France was at least interested in developments could not be doubted.

Immediately after the outbreak of the revolution two French war vessels were despatched to Dominican waters under the command of Rear Admiral de Moges. The French Vice-Consul in Santo Domingo, Juchereau de Saint Denis, coöperating to the limit of his ability with Admiral de Moges, had no small part in the decision of Santana to withstand the urgent pleas advanced by Duarte, when the latter was sent by the Junta Central to Baní, to take up the offensive against the Haitian armies; for the French representatives believed that the further the Haitians were permitted by Santana to advance towards the capital, the more disposed would the liberal members of the Junta Central be to seek French protection.

A confidential letter written at this time from Baní by General Santana, who had come to share the protectionist views of Baez, to Tomás Bobadilla, President of the Junta Central, and likewise one of the leading reactionaries, makes Santana's motives very plain. He wrote:

"I am sure that in the troops which are following the Haitians there is a large number of Spaniards (Dominicans); and holding as they do six Spanish towns, they will fight us with our people and at our expense while we at

the same time are ruining ourselves, our efforts paralyzed
and ourselves exhausted in this difficult task of war, particularly when we are not accustomed to it; and that is the
reason why, in my way of thinking, the longer the struggle
lasts the more uncertain becomes the victory, . . if, as
we have agreed and discussed so many times, we do not
obtain help from across the ocean . . . You are able to
judge the truth of all that which I wish to say to you, and
you have sufficient ability not to delude yourself and to
realize that we should pursue with despatch those negotiations which in the opinion of every sound mind alone
can make our victory sure. I will be grateful if you will
answer me giving me definite information concerning the
state of *those negotiations;* and if by chance they are stationary, take them up again by any means within your
power, since it is our duty in such crucial moments to
make every effort *in behalf of the public welfare and in
order to assure the triumph of our policy."*

As soon as rumours commenced to be current in the
capital regarding the reactionary policy favoured by those
members of the Junta Central who were acting in concert
with Santana and Baez, the liberals demanded the expul-
sion from the Junta of Bobadilla, Dr. José Maria Caminero,
and their adherents. Consequently, on June 9th, a meeting
was called in the fortress of all the leaders prominent in the
rising of the Puerta del Conde. A resolution was there
unanimously adopted demanding the elimination of the
reactionaries from the Junta Central, and, with the support
of the troops in the capital, orders were given for the
arrest of Bobadilla and Dr. Caminero, as well as of
Buenaventura Baez, who was then in Santo Domingo.
Those selected for arrest were successful in escaping, due
probably to the warning given them by General Francisco
del Rosario Sánchez, elected President of the Junta Central

in place of Bobadilla, whose allegiance to Duarte's ideals was already wavering. The Junta Central as now reorganized determined to take all measures possible to maintain itself in power, and despatching General Duarte to the Cibao to prevent the fomenting of any plots against its control in the northern provinces, appointed General Sánchez himself to take command of the army in the south, giving orders at the same time that General Santana should be removed from his command "because of his ill-health."

General Duarte reached Santiago June 30th and was acclaimed the popular hero of the revolution. On July 4th, he was proclaimed President of the Republic by a commission headed by General Ramón Mella. Duarte, however, while expressing his willingness to accept the Presidency, refused to take office unless elected by the majority of the votes of his fellow-citizens. Support of Duarte had become general throughout the Cibao, when, to the consternation of all, information was received that the troops under General Santana had refused to agree to his removal as their commander, and that Santana himself had marched with his army to San Cristóbal, whence he had entered the capital on July 12th. There he had been proclaimed by his own troops "in the name of the Dominican people and of the army" Supreme Chief of the Republic, with the powers of Dictator.

Immediately after his entrance into the capital, Santana threw the leading liberals, including General Sánchez, into prison. Duarte and Mella, who had both withdrawn to Puerto Plata, believing that negotiations begun with Santana would make possible free elections in which the people could for the first time express their choice for the Presidency, were soon after arrested by agents of Santana, and with their leading followers were brought to the capital on the vessel *Separación Dominicana*, from which they were removed in chains to share with the other liberal leaders imprisonment as common criminals in the Torre del Homenaje.

On August 22nd a new Junta Central, appointed from among the reactionaries by Santana, decreed that "for the safety and tranquillity of the country, it was a prime necessity that punishment be imposed upon all the authors and conspirators of sedition at whose head had figured General Juan Pablo Duarte; whose object had been to cause the fall of the supreme government which had been established . . . ; that Generals Juan Pablo Duarte, Ramón Mella, Francisco Sánchez, and their leading supporters had been traitors and faithless to their country and as such were unworthy of the positions which they held; that consequently they were removed from them and condemned to perpetual exile, to suffer the penalty of death should they ever again set foot on their natal soil." Consequently, shortly afterwards, Sánchez and Mella were sent with other leaders of the liberal party to England, and on September 10th Duarte, with a few companions, was embarked upon a vessel bound for Germany.

A policy of reaction thus early triumphed, and the proponents of the absolute independence of the Republic, who alone had been responsible for raising the national spirit of the Dominican people from the lethargy into which the twenty-two years of subjection to Haitian rule had sunk it, were removed from the political stage. It is hardly a matter for conjecture that the history of the Republic would have been far different had it, during the early years of its independent life, been governed by a patriot with the

ideals and the purity of purpose manifested by Duarte
throughout his life.

Utterly disillusioned by gross ingratitude, disheartened
by the rapidity with which the ideals for which he had
spent himself were submerged in the tides of corruption
and lust for power, he fades—an admirable, a proud figure
—from the Dominican scene, to which in life he returned
but for a few brief days. It is by the deathless spirit of the
man, in the last analysis, that his true greatness must be
judged; for Duarte's ideals have not been tarnished, his
spiritual voice has not been stilled; and in the moments
which were sometimes to occur in after years, when his
fellow-citizens, granted respite from the turmoil of in-
ternecine war or foreign danger, were enabled to ask
themselves where the true interests of their land might lie,
it was by the doctrine and by the inspiration of Duarte
that they were to attempt to be guided. In the long line
of patriots of the Americas who lived and, often, died that
the creed of liberty might not perish from the New World,
Duarte will ever hold an eminent place.

The few brief months of his public career made manifest
that his very lack of personal ambition, and his belief in the
innate worth of his fellow-men, would perhaps have incapacitated him from being the ruler that the times demanded. While his ability as an executive he was never
granted the opportunity to demonstrate, he probably
lacked the practical gift for government required during
the years which elapsed before constitutional government was an established fact. But his overwhelming love
of country and his eager desire for the well-being of his
people cannot be questioned.

During his last days in the Cibao there came to him one
evening a group of citizens of Puerto Plata bringing a

proclamation telling him that Puerto Plata as one man supported his candidacy for the Presidency. A group of friends stood about him in the dusty street as the leader of the delegation read laboriously through the long pages. The swift tropical sunset was darkening. Duarte stood quiet in the fading light—erect—the deep-set eyes under the broad forehead glowing with eager emotion—his hand in an habitual nervous gesture going to the heavy mustache which partly concealed his ascetic smiling lips. When the monotonous reading was done, the leader roused himself. In a few phrases he expressed his gratitude for the support tendered, and in these touching sentences, which contain the gist of the man's faith, bade them go their way:

"Be happy, citizens of Puerto Plata," he said, "and my heart will be fully satisfied even without the office which you desire I may obtain; but first of all, be just, if you desire to be happy, for that is man's first duty; be united, and thus you will put out the flame of discord and conquer your enemies, and the fatherland will be free and safe, and your wishes will be gratified; so shall I obtain my greatest recompense, the only one to which I aspire: that of seeing you peaceful, happy, independent and free."

Through the years which followed, years of exile and want, to which in a far country he was at length reduced, the crowning sadness of his life may well have been the fact that he never did see the Dominican people united, happy or peaceful, and not even securely independent and free.

2.

The Junta Central appointed by Santana had issued, on July 24th, a decree calling for elections to the Congress.

The elections took place during the last ten days of August, and the representatives elected assembled in San Cristóbal on September 21st, under the Presidency of Don Manuel Maria Valencia, one of the earliest members of the Francophile group. Five days later, a delegation of members of the Junta Central Gubernativa accorded the newly elected Congress the official recognition of General Santana.

Dissension appears to have broken out between the Dictator and the Congress at the start, since the refusal of the Congress to approve a loan contract entered into by the Junta with a British subject caused the Junta Central to remind it that its faculties were limited to those of drafting the first Constitution of the Republic. The Congress accepted its rebuff meekly enough and limited its discussions from then on to those relative to the drafting of the Constitution, which was finally approved November 6th. In large part, the first Constitution of the Republic was modeled on that of the United States, such amendments being grafted upon that creature of the Anglo-Saxon genius as were rendered necessary by the Spanish system of local government to which the country had been originally accustomed. Consequently, ayuntamientos were created in all the communes which existed prior to the Haitian Occupation, and the college of electors was entrusted with the duty in the future of electing the President, the members of the Tribunado and of the Consejo Conservador (or House of Deputies and Senate), and the members of the Provincial Deputations. As soon as the Constitution had been approved, the Congress elected General Pedro Santana President of the Republic for the first two terms, each term being of four years.

The Congress, however, had omitted to grant Santana,

in the Constitution, the dictatorial powers which he desired. The latter consequently replied that he was unwilling to accept the Presidency under those conditions. Thereupon, at the instance of Tomás Bobadilla, Santana's leading henchman, the Congress reformed the Constitution, incorporating in it the famous Article 210, which permitted the President of the Republic, until such time as peace with Haiti had been proclaimed, to have full and untrammeled control of the military forces of the Republic, and to take such steps "for the security of the country" as he might desire without responsibility to the Legislative Body. As soon as Bobadilla's amendment had been approved, Santana accepted the Presidency, and on November 13th, 1844, appeared before the Congress in San Cristóbal to take the oath of office as the first President of the Republic.

Immediately after his inauguration, Santana appointed to his Cabinet his closest followers: Manuel Cabral Bernal as Secretary of Interior and Police; Ricardo Miura as Secretary of Finance and Commerce; Tomás Bobadilla as Secretary of Justice, Public Instruction and Foreign Relations; and General Manuel Jiménez as Secretary of War and Marine. The members of Santana's Cabinet were noted primarily for their subservience to their chief, and the general opinion held by the populace concerning them may be gathered from a letter addressed by Don Juan Abril, Spanish Vice-Consul, early in January, 1845, to the Captain-General of Puerto Rico:

"The selection of the Cabinet," he says, "has not been particularly happy; it may be that circumstances justify the selection of some of the members but there are others whom nothing can justify. . . . In the midst of our many necessities, what we feel most of all is the lack of men

capable of solving through their own capacity the great
number of our problems."

Pending a decision as to the most effective means of procuring some European protectorate, Santana determined
to strengthen his position by seeking the recognition of
the United States. For that purpose Dr. José Maria
Caminero, of Carrié correspondence fame, was sent in December, 1844, to Washington to attempt to obtain during
the last days of President Tyler's Administration official
recognition of the new Republic from Secretary Calhoun.
Dr. Caminero's mission appears to have impressed Mr.
Calhoun favourably as being in line with the policy of the
Southern States which he had so long sustained in the
United States Senate. The Secretary of State suggested to
the Spanish Minister in Washington, Don Angel Calderón
de la Barca, that the United States, France and Spain
should recognize the new Republic, as a means of preventing the further spread of negro influence in the West
Indies. The suggestion of Mr. Calhoun, however, does not
appear to have met with favour at the Spanish Court, and
no further step was taken towards the recognition of the
new Republic until the Administration of President Polk
came into being in March, 1845.

Secretary Buchanan, who had learned that Dr. Caminero
had stated to the Spanish Minister in Washington that the
Dominicans were desirous of obtaining a Spanish protectorate, determined to send a special agent to the Dominican Republic to advise him of the conditions which
existed there, and in particular to ascertain whether the
prospect seemed hopeful for the Dominicans to maintain
their independence against the ever threatening danger
from the western portion of the island. Mr. John Hogan

GENERAL PEDRO SANTANA

Marqués de las Carreras

was selected for the task and arrived in Santo Domingo in December of 1845. His investigation of conditions was of the most perfunctory nature. In a despatch to Secretary Buchanan,[1] he indulged in florid eulogies of the geographic position, fertility and history of the Dominican Republic, but made scant reference to the ability of the Santana Administration to maintain itself in power. He estimated the population as being at that date approximately 230,000, of whom he claimed 100,000 were Caucasian, 40,000 negroes, and the rest mulattoes. The financial situation of the Government does not appear to have been precarious, since Mr. Hogan reported that while the expenditures caused the Republic by the intermittent war with Haiti had obliged it to incur a debt of more than a million dollars, the indebtedness had already been wiped out, with the exception of some $250,000, from the annual receipts of the treasury. Mr. Hogan likewise expressed his firm opinion that the French and British Government, "our natural enemies," were engaged in a policy of opposing recognition of the new Republic by the United States.

In accordance with his instructions, Mr. Hogan addressed a note to the Minister of Foreign Relations requesting on behalf of his Government a report upon the form of the Dominican Government, and likewise all information which would tend to throw light on the ability of the nation to maintain its independence. Mr. Hogan surmised in his note that the presence in the Republic of so large a proportion of the coloured race would tend to weaken the efforts of the Dominican Government in its struggle against Haiti. This criterion was not shared by the Minister, who advised the American Agent that

[1] Mr. Hogan to Secretary Buchanan received October 4, 1844.

"It is worthy of note that among the Dominicans pre-occupations regarding color have never held much sway. . . Even the very Dominicans who once were slaves have fought and would again fight against the Haitians because its Government was so evil and so oppressive that it could not obtain the support of any class." [1]

In closing his communication to Mr. Hogan, Señor Bobadilla, with a blithe disregard of the secret negotiations which were being conducted at Santana's instance to obtain a French protectorate, declared, "When a people desires to be free, no earthly power can impede it."

Neither Dr. Caminero's efforts in Washington, nor Mr. Hogan's recommendations, were sufficiently strong to convince Buchanan of the desirability of recognizing the independence of the new Republic before satisfactory assurances had been received that Santana's negotiations for obtaining a European protectorate, which were known to him, would be unsuccessful. Dr. Caminero consequently returned to Santo Domingo, having succeeded only in purchasing munitions and clothing for the army, and in arranging for the minting of copper currency for general use in the Republic. Prior to his return, Mr. Hogan had already left the capital.

During the first months of his administration, Santana occupied himself, so far as the continuation of the war with Haiti made it possible, with the organization of his Government throughout the country. At his instance, the Congress passed legislation creating tribunals of the first instance and one court of appeals, providing at the same time for the observance of the Napoleonic Code. Primary schools were opened in all the larger cities and towns, as well as high schools in Santo Domingo and Santiago. The

[1] Don Tomás Bobadilla to Mr. Hogan, June 19, 1845.

budgetary system was introduced, by which the salaries of governmental officials were fixed in many instances in excess of what they are in modern times, the salary of the President being set then at $12,000 per annum, and the salaries of his ministers at $3,600. That Santana believed in a paternal form of government was soon made very plain to his fellow-citizens. Decrees of the most stringent nature were promulgated, providing for government regulation of even the most innocent activities of the populace. On January 21, 1847, a decree was issued compelling the Comandantes de Armas and the Alcaldes Comunales in each commune to visit every house within their jurisdiction to ascertain the profession and means of livelihood of the inhabitants; all vagabonds were given eight days within which to find some honest means of earning their living, at the end of which time, if they had not found it, they were to be set to work for a period of three months on public construction for the Government. Games of chance and amusements were prohibited except from six o'clock in the evening of the day preceding a holiday until nine o'clock in the evening of that holiday. No goats might be kept within the limits of any city. No citizen was permitted to move from the city to the country, nor from one locality to another, without previously obtaining permission of the Jefe Superior Político and the Alcalde Comunal of the commune in which they were living. Finally, in the interest of education, each head of a family was obliged to place at least one of his children in the public schools.

The iron hand of the first President was likewise not long in showing itself. Claiming that he had discovered a plot against the Government, Santana celebrated February 27, 1845, the first anniversary of the country's independence, by the execution of Doña Maria Trinidad Sánchez, aunt of General Francisco Sánchez, and of several others of the liberals still remaining in the capital, on the pretext that they were traitors to the Republic which they themselves had been so largely instrumental in creating.

While appearances may have suggested that General Santana was occupying himself solely with plans for the strengthening of his own administration, and with the drafting of regulations governing the activities of his fellow-citizens, the cardinal feature of his policy, that of obtaining a protectorate from a foreign power, was never far removed from his thoughts. As soon as he perceived that the assurances received from France were illusory, he lost no time in turning to Spain.

The Spanish Cabinets, which were at the time alternating in power with cinematographic rapidity, were being constantly pressed by the Spanish authorities in the West Indies, notably the Conde de Mirasol, Captain-General of Puerto Rico, to make no commitments which might prevent the Spanish Government, should it later desire to do so, from regaining the authority over the Dominican provinces which it had formerly held. The Spanish representatives in Paris and in London were consequently instructed to ascertain whether France and England would interpose objections should Spain determine to extend her authority once more over Santo Domingo. Satisfactory assurances having been received, General Santana was duly apprised by emissaries from the Conde de Mirasol that the moment might be propitious for commencing negotiations with the Spanish Queen.

Toward the end of February, 1846, a division of six Spanish warships, under the command of Don Pablo de Llanes, appeared in the harbour of Santo Domingo.

Whether popular objection proved too strong, or whether the opposition of General José Joaquín Puello, recently appointed to the Cabinet, proved preponderant in the advice rendered Santana by his Ministers, is uncertain, but the visit of the Spanish fleet had no more definite result than the announcement made by Santana that the Spanish Government had at the time no purpose of recovering its former colony, and that the Dominican Government had been officially advised that Spain was disposed to recognize the independence of the Republic. The visit of the Spanish fleet had at least the concrete advantage, from Santana's point of view, of offering him a pretext for sending without further delay an embassy to Europe for the ostensible purpose of obtaining recognition of the Republic from Spain, France and England.

Confident that no Dominican better suited as his envoy could be found than the instigator of the reactionary policy which he himself was pursuing, Santana appointed, in April, 1846, Buenaventura Baez, together with José Maria Medrano and Juan Esteban Aybar. The envoys were provided with published instructions to go first to Madrid, where they were to negotiate a treaty of recognition with Spain, and when that had been accomplished, to proceed, for the same purpose, in turn to Paris and to London, and with confidential instructions to obtain a protectorate if possible.

Armed with letters of introduction from the Conde de Mirasol, the embassy arrived in Madrid in the summer of 1846. To his surprise, Baez did not find upon his arrival at the Spanish Court any patent desire on the part of the Spanish Government to reassume the responsibilities in Santo Domingo which had previously caused the Spanish Government so many difficulties. During fourteen months the Dominican representatives remained in Madrid, urging upon each succeeding Spanish Cabinet the desirability of extending at least immediate recognition to the Dominican Republic. By October, 1847, they had succeeded in obtaining assurances from Cortaza, the Spanish Premier at the time, that Spain would recognize the independence of the Dominican Republic, and would grant the Republic its protection with all the strength of the forces at its command, official announcement to this effect to be postponed until the authorities in the other Spanish West Indies had been informed of the decision reached. But when Cortaza's Ministry fell a few days later, and when the new Ministry of the Duke of Valencia did not share, apparently, in so positive a fashion the determination expressed by Cortaza, Baez determined to seek better fortune in Paris. He therefore notified the Spanish Government that the Dominican representatives were leaving Madrid, assuring it, at the same time, that in the opinion of the Dominican emissaries the bonds uniting Spain and her former colony were eternal, and that the affection of the Government of Santana for the mother country could not be impaired.

Before the negotiations in Madrid had reached their close, Secretary Buchanan, his interest quickened by what he had learned of them, determined to send another agent to Santo Domingo to ascertain whether the new envoy coincided in the recommendations made by Mr. Hogan for early recognition of the Republic's independence, and to discover whether the project for the Spanish protectorate had proceeded in fact so far as was believed by some of the American diplomatic representatives abroad. Mr. Francis Harrison was selected for this purpose and reached Santo Domingo in March, 1847. Since recognition had not yet been determined upon, Mr. Harrison, while appointed Commercial Agent of the United States, was not provided with personal letters addressed to General Santana and to the Minister for Foreign Affairs by President Polk and by Secretary Buchanan. This omission caused both offense and disappointment, which was officially communicated to Mr. Harrison by General Ricardo Miura, appointed by General Santana Minister for Foreign Affairs after a dispute between the President and Tomás Bobadilla had resulted in the latter's temporary exile from the country.

Shortly after his arrival Mr. Harrison transmitted his first impressions to Secretary Buchanan:

"The country is, so far as I can ascertain, prospering. The depression of their currency is principally affecting foreign merchants, while benefiting native shopkeepers, planters, and woodcutters, who being always in debt to the merchants have cancelled the same with the depreciated paper. The principal part of the irregular army has been allowed to return to their small farms and wood cuts. They will in consequence have a good crop of tobacco, and the mahogany is becoming more plenty. Relative to their finances, they have in circulation $3,000,000 in their paper currency, which is now at an appreciation of eleven currency for one dollar Spanish. In the treasury is $50,000 Spanish money, but very little currency. The pay of the soldiers per month is $4 and an additional $7.50 for rations, which is not always paid and when not paid is considered as so much saved to the nation." [1]

After his official conversations with the members of the Government, Mr. Harrison made a trip overland from Santo Domingo to Puerto Plata, informing himself with considerable thoroughness of the conditions which existed

[1] Mr. Francis Harrison to Secretary Buchanan, March 31, 1847.

in the interior of the Republic. Upon the conclusion of his trip, he communicated again with the Secretary of State:

"From the City of Santo Domingo to Cotuy, the country is almost uninhabited. The beautiful savannas, which were formerly covered with cattle, are now but thinly spotted by the same. On the road I passed twelve persons. La Vega is a town of about 1800 people. The buildings are comfortable huts, the earthquake of 1843 having destroyed all the houses that were of stone and bricks. In the District of La Vega are stationed 400 military, and there is in the National Guard of that District 1600 men. La Vega is noted for its beautiful women, many of whom have a remarkable regularity of feature and form. Santiago, which previous to the earthquake was principally composed of Spanish built stone and brick houses, all of which were, including the massive built churches, destroyed by that event. It is partly rebuilt, having now many comfortable brick houses and contains at present about 4,000 inhabitants. The country between Cotuy and Santiago, including the districts of Moca and Macorís, is in a good state of cultivation, producing, besides ground provisions for consumption, all the tobacco that is exported from the Island. It is the agricultural district of the Dominican Power, the people being generally industrious. In this district reside the principal part of the white population that are not inside the walls of Santo Domingo. The cultivation on this side of the Island has much improved during the last five years and bears a favorable comparison to the neighborhood of the City of Santo Domingo, the country outside of the walls of that city being, for want of cultivation, a perfect wilderness. On the south side, under the immediate eye of the Government, the condition of matters and things in general, instead of progressing is retrograding." [1]

[1] Mr. Francis Harrison to Secretary Buchanan, May 10, 1847.

Mr. Harrison's term of office in the Dominican Republic was not destined, however, to be of long duration, for he died of yellow fever, which was raging throughout the West Indies at the time, a few months after his arrival in Santo Domingo, and Mr. Jonathan Elliott was thereupon appointed Commercial Agent in his place. An estimate of the commercial depression which existed at the time may be gathered from the following remark addressed by Mr. Elliott to Secretary Buchanan some months after his arrival: "There is very little for an agent to do here, I having had only three schooners in six months." [1]

The dispute with Bobadilla and the exile of the latter from the country brought with it a general reorganization of Santana's Cabinet, and towards the end of the year, 1847, a new Cabinet was appointed as follows: Secretary of Justice, Public Instruction and Foreign Affairs, General Ricardo Miura; Secretary of Finance and Commerce, General José Joaquín Puello; Secretary of Interior and Police, Colonel Juan Esteban Aybar, who was to assume office upon his return from his European mission; Secretary of War and Marine, General Manuel Jiménez. The divergence which had existed between the views of the President and those of General Puello regarding the advantages to be obtained from a Spanish protectorate had already given rise to considerable friction. Puello was consequently believed by many of the President's satellites to be identified with the policy of the liberals, and no sooner had he entered the Cabinet than intrigues began against him. The intrigues proved to be successful in less time, presumably, than even their authors had dared to hope, since barely a month after the new Ministry had been installed, General Santana accused General Puello of plotting a military uprising against

[1] Mr. Jonathan Elliott to Secretary Buchanan, August 2, 1848.

the Government. Brought before a military commission, he was sentenced to death, and on December 23rd, with two others, was summarily executed. The vacancy thus created in the Cabinet was filled to Santana's entire satisfaction by the appointment of Dr. José Maria Caminero, of whose loyalty to the reactionary policy Santana could have no doubt.

But even though, by means of execution and exile, Santana had been able to obliterate all domestic opposition to the policy which he pursued, it appeared impossible for him to persuade either France or Spain to assume definitely the responsibilities which he urged upon them. Unsatisfactory economic conditions, as well as the repressive policy of his Government, had succeeded in causing, during the four years of his Administration, a smouldering and sullen discontent throughout the country, which, although it had not broken out in open flame, was yet constantly increasing. Congress, moreover, appeared to Santana to be deviating from the path of utter submission which he had traced for it when he first entered the Presidency, by insisting that the administration of the finances of the Republic, entrusted by the President to Dr. Caminero after his appointment to the Cabinet, was far from satisfactory, and seemed desirous of sharing with the Executive the decisions as to the financial policy to be pursued.

If Santana was disheartened by the opposition of the Congress, he was frankly dismayed by the success of his Minister for War, General Jiménez, in partially organizing a conspiracy, the object of which was to force his chief to resign the Presidency in his favour. During Santana's brief absence from the capital in the Seybo where he was recovering from an illness of some months' duration, all the

troops favourable to the President were removed from
Santo Domingo, which was garrisoned by others whom
Jiménez had found means to suborn. Upon Santana's
return he found the time had passed when he could have
withstood the demands of some of the members of his
Cabinet for his resignation.

Basing his resignation, however, upon his dispute with
Congress, General Santana announced his decision to retire
from the Presidency, hoping that he would be recalled to
power by his fellow-citizens in the not far distant future.

On July 31, 1848, he appointed a new Cabinet composed of Don Felix Mercenario as Secretary of Interior
and Police, and Don Domingo de la Rocha as Secretary of
Justice, Public Instruction and Foreign Affairs, retaining
Dr. Caminero as Secretary of Finance and Commerce and,
necessarily, General Manuel Jiménez as Secretary of War
and Marine. Four days later, on August 4, 1848, General
Santana presented his formal resignation to the Cabinet,
which, under the Constitution, assumed control of the
Executive power. He himself left the capital at once and
proceeded to his estancia, El Prado, in the Province of
Seybo, where he determined to busy himself with the
care of the cattle and the hogs which he raised there
in large numbers until such time as the necessities of the
Government might again demand his attention.

3.

On September 4, 1848, the Congress, convoked by the
Cabinet for that purpose, elected Santana's Secretary of
War, General Manuel Jiménez, as President of the Re-
public. On September 8th, General Jiménez took the oath
as President before the Congress, retaining without change
Santana's last Cabinet. Expectation was general that with

the retirement of Santana, Jiménez, who was known to be indolent by temperament and incapable of the high-handed policy of his predecessor, would permit the exiled liberals to return to Santo Domingo; but when it was seen that he had apparently no intention of deviating in this respect from the policy laid down by Santana, Congress took it upon itself, by a decree of September 26th, to proclaim a general amnesty, mentioning specifically General Duarte and the other exiled members of the Trinitarios. Once this was done, the Congress believed that its responsibilities were over, and in October adjourned, having first, however, adopted the remarkable resolution of granting extraordinary powers to President Jiménez until its next session.

General Jiménez appears to have lacked every qualification necessary for the Presidency. He was utterly lacking in executive ability, and was neither interested in the promotion of any program for the development of the country's commerce, nor even disposed to take measures to ward off the ever increasing danger of Haitian invasion which had been imminent since March, 1847, when General Faustin Soulouque had obtained control of the government in the neighbouring Republic. Jiménez's sole interest in life after his inauguration appears to have been cock-fighting. According to Mr. Benjamin E. Green, who was later appointed American Commissioner by President Taylor, "His whole time was spent in cleaning, training, and fighting cocks, it being frequently necessary to send acts of Congress and other official papers to the cock-pit for his approval and signature. Under his rule, everything fell into confusion, which state of things was soon made known to Soulouque and incited him to the invasion of the Republic." [1]

[1] Mr. Benjamin E. Green to Secretary Clayton, September 27, 1849.

Jiménez, who had been with difficulty induced by his Cabinet to leave the pleasures of cockfighting for a sufficient length of time to make a brief official journey through the Cibao, was finally persuaded, at the end of December, 1848, to decree general mobilization throughout the Republic, all Dominicans from twelve to sixty years being called to the colours. Fortunately for the country, the indolence and indecision of the President were not sufficient to prevent such patriots as General .Ramón Mella, who had returned to Santo Domingo under the decree of amnesty, and General Duvergé, from amassing a considerable body of men near the Haitian frontier in the Province of Azua, and consequently when the long-threatened invasion of the Haitians took place early in March, 1849, sufficient forces were at the disposal of the Government to interpose some opposition to the onward sweep of the Haitian armies. The Dominicans, as ever, fought bravely, but their numbers were not sufficient to check for any considerable period the far superior numbers of the Haitians, nor had they in their possession sufficient ammunition to maintain their position for any length of time. The initial defeats of the Dominicans caused panic throughout the Republic, and the fear of an imminent siege of the capital was general in Santo Domingo itself. The situation in the city is described by Mr. Jonathan Elliott in despatches to Secretary Buchanan:

"The greatest consternation and alarm prevails here. The President of Haiti, Soulouque, is within two days' march of this city with 10,000 blacks. He declares extermination to all whites and mulattoes and has beaten the people of this Republic in every battle. My house is already filled with frightened females. . . . The Haitian army are close to us. Almost all of the foremost merchants have packed up their goods and shipped them to the neighboring islands before leaving with their families. The town is filled with women and children from the country and famine is to be apprehended. . . . The President has told me that it is his intention to set fire to the place in case they cannot hold out against the Haitians." [1]

It was only after repeated urging that Jiménez could be prevailed upon to go himself to the scene of hostilities in Azua, but his presence there seems to have done little to better the situation or to calm the general apprehensions, since upon his return to the capital he found that the Congress, under the leadership of Buenaventura Baez, had, on April 3, issued a decree calling upon General Santana to come to the assistance of the Government with all of the forces which he might obtain in the Province of Seybo. To this decree the President opposed the most strenuous objection, but finally was obliged to give way, and reluctantly despatched Santana, almost unattended, to Baní.

On the way Santana picked up 350 to 500 men. As soon as it became known that Santana had been called out by the Congress, the soldiers who were scattered all over the country seeking their homes, after their initial defeats, returned to join him, so that in a short time his name alone had brought together the dispersed army, and Santana soon found himself at the head of some 6,000 men. From Baní Santana marched to Sabana Buey, operating in conjunction with the forces under the command of General Duvergé. In engagements at El Número and Las Carreras, the Dominicans succeeded in routing completely the Haitian armies, which fled in utter disorder across the

[1] Mr. Jonathan Elliott to Secretary Buchanan, April 13, 1849, and April 24, 1849.

frontier, razing to the ground as ever all evidences of civilization with which they came into contact, and leaving the town of Azua in ashes.

On January 21st, 1849, the long-sought-for recognition had been officially extended to the Dominican Republic by the Governments of France and England. The imminent danger in which the capital had been placed prior to the return of Santana to the command of the Dominican armies had afforded Buenaventura Baez an unlooked-for opportunity to attempt once more to force upon the nation the protectorate of France. The French warship *Elau* had anchored in the port of the.capital on April 17th, and Baez, calling the Congress together in secret session on April 19th, succeeded in persuading his panic-stricken colleagues to pass a resolution beseeching the French Government to accept a protectorate over the Republic. A copy of the resolution was entrusted to the French Vice-Consul, M. Place, who embarked the same night on the *Elau* for Port-au-Prince. There he ascertained that the French Consul-General in Haiti was unwilling to assume the responsibility upon his own initiative of accepting the proposal; and an employee of the French Consulate in Santo Domingo who was sent at the same time to Paris found, to the dismay of Place, that the French Government had no apparent intention of acceding to the Dominican proposals.

The resolution of the Congress did not remain long secret from the British Consul, recently arrived, nor from the American Commercial Agent. Sir Robert Schomburgk, the British Consul, was in fact so alarmed by the report that he addressed immediately a note to the Minister for Foreign Affairs inquiring whether the Dominican Government intended that the Republic should remain free and independent. On April 24th he was advised, notwithstanding the fact that the Government was then still awaiting a reply from France to its proposals, that the Dominican Republic would undoubtedly continue in the full possession of its independence and sovereignty.

As the result of the control which Baez had succeeded in obtaining over the Congress, relations between Baez and the President soon reached the breaking point. For the time being, all idea of maintaining the independence of the Republic appears to have been abandoned by the leading men in the country. The doctrines of the liberals were in the discard. Baez's predilection for France was now evident to all; while Santana's efforts to obtain the protection of Spain had long been rumoured. Deserted by the major portion of his army, which was now under the command of Santana, and in open opposition to the Congress, which was under the sway of Baez, Jiménez determined to attempt to secure assistance from the United States. In May, 1849, the American Commercial Agent communicated the following information to Secretary Buchanan:

"The Haitian army under Soulouque has been beaten and routed at all points. A special messenger was despatched by French steamer from here to St. Thomas and from thence to France bearing despatches asking that Government to accept and confirm the protectorate. Lord Palmerston's purpose is to oppose the aid to be given by the French. The British Consul, Sir Robert Schomburgk, also offered to obtain the aid of England. The object of both parties is to get possession of the Bay of Samaná, one of the finest in the West Indies, of fine resources for a naval depot either in time of peace or war. The President requested a private interview with me, asking me for the protection of the United States and if I thought the United States would allow this Republic to annex itself. I think it probable that a delegation will be sent from here to Washington, whose object will be to obtain the recognition of their independence by our Government." [1]

Events were proceeding with too great rapidity, though, to have permitted assurances from Secretary Clayton to have been of much avail to the President—even had they been forthcoming, Jiménez was doomed.

On May 12th, the Congress summoned the President before it to request from him an explanation of the lack of preparations made by the Government to repel the Haitian attack. In the course of the discussions which ensued revolvers and swords were drawn, without the occurrence, however, of any casualties, and on the following day the Congress, protesting against the "coercion" of the Executive, removed to San Cristóbal. Santana, emboldened by the assistance which Baez was rendering him in the Congress, now also, on May 19th, broke openly with Jiménez, and marched upon the capital where Jiménez had surrounded himself with the very small number of persons who still remained loyal to him. On May 29th, after a capitulation had been agreed to by Jiménez, through the intervention of the British and French Consuls and the American Agent, Jiménez resigned his office, and fled from the capital on a British vessel for Curaçao.

On the following day, Santana, with his victorious army, entered the capital as Dictator, signalizing his return to power by throwing immediately into prison all the citizens who had forced his own resignation and who had supported Jiménez during the last days of the latter's administration. On July 4th, the Dictator summoned the electoral colleges to assemble on the 25th of the same month. The

[1] Mr. Jonathan Elliott to Secretary Buchanan, May 2, 1849.

colleges filled the vacancies which existed in the previous Congress, and the new Congress, under the Presidency of Buenaventura Baez, inaugurated its sessions on July 5th.

The following day, General Santana appeared before the Congress to resign the extraordinary powers granted him by the Congressional decree of April 3rd, when Baez seized the opportunity, as President of that body, to offer him, in the name of the Congress, "the assurances of its highest gratitude for the important services which he had rendered the Republic, freeing it at the same time from civil war," and terming Santana "in the name of a grateful nation, a precious instrument chosen by Heaven itself" to defend the people in their march towards civilization. Immediately thereafter, the Congress elected Santiago Espaillat as President of the Republic, Santana receiving 31 votes and Baez 12, to the 45 cast in favor of Espaillat.

Santiago Espaillat, head of one of the most prominent families of the Cibao, was too far-sighted to be lured, however. With the army under the complete domination of Santana, and the Congress responsive to Baez, the President installed under such conditions would soon be crushed between the millstones of their consuming ambitions. When word was brought to him of his election to the Presidency, Espaillat refused to accept the precarious honours—and persisted in his refusal, notwithstanding the urging of the northern provinces which were desirous of seeing a resident of the Cibao in the Presidency.

Santana, who had by now, although his egotism and the lustre of his recent victories combined to blind him, some faint apprehension of the danger which the increasing prominence of Baez might constitute to his own ambitions, and some perception of the corroding greed which dominated Baez, had hoped to find some figurehead to place in the Presidency whom he could retain there so long as he saw fit. Espaillat, a man of honour and position, who would have obtained the loyal support of the entire Cibao, would have suited Santana eminently. Espaillat's obstinate determination to refuse the Presidency caused the Dictator to face a far less agreeable solution. Baez, representing that his own activities in the Congress had been responsible in great measure for Jiménez's downfall, claimed the Presidency for himself since Santana had already announced his own unwillingness to return to office—and to this contention the Dictator could raise no valid objection.

Perhaps also various other considerations had weight. Santana undoubtedly believed that his own control of the army implied his control of the President. Baez's heritage of African blood, which permitted the coloured elements to feel that they were not excluded from participation in the Government, might prove an added safeguard to the whites in the event of a new invasion from Soulouque's dominions. Finally and most weighty of all, Santana was highly dubious of the outcome of the French protectorate project; were he to permit Baez to assume entire responsibility and incur among the protectionists the odium of disappointing the expectations which the project had excited, might Baez not be definitely eliminated as a possible contender for his own position as supreme arbiter of the country's destinies?

Baez was consequently elected in the place of Espaillat, and the Congress adjourned thereafter—not, however, before it had granted Santana the title of "Liberator of the Fatherland," and the more practical—and incidentally more remunerative—title of General-in-Chief of the Armies of the Republic.

4.

On September 24, 1849, Colonel Baez was inaugurated President of the Republic before the Congress. Better qualified, through no small natural ability and by virtue of his education in Europe, than most of his compatriots, and afforded, by his recent diplomatic missions, the opportunity to gauge more accurately than his predecessors in the Presidency the temper of the European Powers toward his country, all his advantages were nullified by his unrivalled cupidity, against which the interests of his country never had weighed, and never would weigh, in the balance.

Slight of stature, with long shrewd nose and small shrewd eyes, flowing mustache, and the "Burnsides" affected by the Victorian dandies, he showed in his person but faint evidences of the African strain he inherited from his mother, save in the texture of his hair and the grayish tinge of his skin. That he lacked personal magnetism is evident. Senator Sumner said that one of his friends had been impressed by Baez as "the worst man living of whom he has any personal knowledge." [1] And while that impression may have been caused by prior prejudice, Baez never succeeded in capturing that unreasoning support from the masses which more despicable characters even than he have often been granted. He was no military hero—in fact his record is bare of military exploits. Yet for nearly thirty-five years of the nation's history, through the unworthy ambitions he was able to engender in others, and by the intrigues of which he was a past master, he maintained himself ever present as the most powerful—and the most pernicious—influence in the Dominican Republic.

With considerable acumen, immediately after his

[1] Speech of Senator Charles Sumner of Massachusetts, delivered in the U. S. Senate, March 27, 1871.

installation in the Presidency, Baez made use of the manoeuvre which he was to utilize so often in the future: an appeal to the patriotic sentimentality of the Dominican people. He announced, in grandiloquent terms, a program of government which, had it been declared with sincerity and carried out with determination, would undoubtedly have cured many of the ills from which the Republic was already suffering. He stated his fixed purpose to reform the army and, in particular, to inaugurate that system of discipline which it had previously lacked; to revise the monetary system of the Republic by creating a metallic standard which would prevent the disastrous fluctuations in exchange; to simplify and better the administration of justice, and to obtain the modification along determined lines of the Constitution of the Republic; to establish a municipal and a rural police; to reform the system of public instruction; to stimulate the development of the agricultural resources of the land, to open roads, and to encourage foreign commerce; to call to public office the able men of all political parties with regard solely to their integrity, energy and ability; and finally, to assure the peace of the Republic by obtaining the protection of some strong European power.

From the patriotic viewpoint, all provisions but the last in this program of administration sounded well. Unfortunately, the last was the only provision in which Baez was sufficiently interested to turn to it his attention. His Cabinet, announced two days after he assumed office, was composed of Manuel Joaquín Del Monte as Secretary of Justice, Public Instruction and Foreign Affairs; José Maria Medrano as Secretary of Interior and Police; the President's former colleague on his European mission, General Juan Esteban Aybar, as Secretary of War and Marine; and

the famed Trinitario, General Ramón Mella, as Secretary
of Finance and Commerce, who, with rare ingenuousness,
accepted office in the belief that his presence would facilitate entrance into the public administration of the men
who had upheld the doctrines of the liberal party. General
Santana announced his loyal support of the new Government, making it incidentally entirely plain that his voice
had been instrumental in determining the selection of Baez
by the Congress as President of the Republic.

While the administration of President Baez was still in
ignorance of the French Government's determination to
reject his proposals for the French protectorate, Mr. Benjamin E. Green, who had been appointed Commissioner
in the Dominican Republic by President Taylor shortly
after his inauguration, had arrived in Santo Domingo. It
is very clear from Mr. Green's first letters to Secretary
Clayton that the United States Government was desirous
of avoiding the complications which might ensue from the
installation of a European protectorate over the Dominican
Republic, and it is further clear that Mr. Green himself,
inoculated with the imperialistic fever recently spreading
in the United States as the result of the acquisition of Texas
and the still more recent war with Mexico, was not averse
to obtaining for his own Government a protectorate over
the new Republic, or to negotiate the annexation of the
country should it prove feasible.

While on his way to Santo Domingo, a journey which
in those years occupied the better portion of two months,
he sent Secretary Clayton a private letter from Havana.
Notwithstanding the fact that his observation of conditions in Cuba had been limited to a stay of ten days, spent
entirely in the quarantine station at Havana, Mr. Green
wrote that nine-tenths of the Cubans desired annexation

to the United States. He continued, "Many are anxiously looking to the United States for the initiative of annexation. Any such step on the part of our Government or people will be hailed with delight by the whole creole population of the Island." [1] His hope of increasing the dominions of the United States was enhanced by the conditions which he found upon his arrival late in August, 1849, in Santo Domingo:

"On the flight of Jiménez, the late President, of which you will have heard before this reaches you, the administration of affairs was placed temporarily in the hands of General Santana. An election was then had, and Santana declining to be a candidate, Buenaventura Baez, late President of the Congress, was chosen President and will be installed in a few days. The ceremony is only delayed for the arrival of General Santana who is at present in the interior. . . . Baez . . . is supposed to be in the interest and under the control of the French Consul. . . . The French party . . . is composed of a very few individuals and is not likely to become a popular party as many suspect. . . . France would be pleased to see Haitians in possession of the whole Island . . . as in such case the Haitians might be able to make some satisfactory arrangement of their indebtedness to France. . . . England and France desire above all things to get possession of Samaná. . . . This Government will not hesitate to grant it for a term of years or in perpetuity to whichever will negotiate and guarantee a treaty of peace with Haiti so as to enable them to go to work and recover from the poverty to which the long war has reduced them. I have no doubt that they would prefer to make such an arrangement with the United States. . . . I have to request that you inform me by the earliest opportunity how far our Government will

[1] Mr. Benjamin E. Green to Secretary Clayton, July 21, 1849.

be willing to interfere between this Government and Haiti to bring about that result by negotiation or otherwise, and whether, if offered to me, I may accept Samaná as a consideration for our giving notice to the Haitians that they must cease to molest this people." [1]

Shortly after this despatch was written, Mr. Green's hopes were raised still higher by the fact that the Cibao provinces, opposing the "rapprochement" with France desired by Baez, and believing, as did General Santana at the time, that the hope of assistance from Spain was illusory, addressed, on September 25th, a petition to General Santana beseeching him to recommend to the Government the initiation of negotiations with the United States for the purpose of obtaining American protection, or even American annexation. In his reply to the petition, General Santana expressed his determination to support this plea, and Mr. Green's satisfaction must have been still further increased by the fact that the Secretary for Foreign Affairs, the following month, officially requested the French Consul to hasten the reply of his Government to the Dominican request for a protectorate, in order that, should the French reply be in the negative, the Dominican Government might not be prevented from addressing itself for a similar purpose to the Government of the United States. In fact, on October 3, 1849, Señor Del Monte, on behalf of President Baez, had already inquired officially of Mr. Green "whether the Government of the United States would take the Dominican Republic under its protection, or, what they would prefer, annex them." Mr. Green, who was as yet without positive instructions from Secretary Clayton, was constrained to limit his answer to the statement that the Government of the United States

[1] Mr. Benjamin E. Green to Secretary Clayton, August 27, 1849.

would prefer to see the Dominican people maintain their independence, and that the best protectorate the Dominicans could obtain would be through recognition of their independence by treaty with the United States. The American Commissioner's conventional reply caused President Baez himself, two days later, to withdraw from the advanced position taken by his Minister, since he advised the American Commissioner that he himself had always been in the vanguard of those who wished to place the Dominican provinces in the possession of France; alleging a belief that France, having been more concerned for many years past with the affairs of the Island, would be more ready to give effective aid in case of necessity.

At the same time, Mr. Green reported he was informed by Sir Robert Schomburgk that he had just received instructions from Lord Palmerston that British interests and commerce were not sufficiently involved to justify the expense of a British protectorate over the Dominican Republic, and that the British Government had so stated in reply to the Dominican Government's application for protection against Haiti. Sir Robert Schomburgk added that the British Government had no desire to obtain possession of Samaná, "except with a view to preventing the French from obtaining it"; and the British Consul added, angered, Mr. Green reports, by the opposition of the President to the ratification of the commercial treaty negotiated by the British agent during the Jiménez régime, "Baez's opposition to the provision in the proposed treaty with Great Britain stipulating free trade in favour of English subjects, (an article designed to prevent governmental monopolies), is explained by his desire to establish a tobacco monopoly as the basis of a loan to be obtained in France, in which plan he is personally interested."

On October 20th, Mr. Green was informed by the Minister for Foreign Relations that the French Government had refused to agree to assume a protectorate over the Dominican Republic owing to the opposition of the British Government. The danger of the French protectorate having therefore been removed, Mr. Green lost no time in recognizing officially the existence of the Dominican Government by presenting his credentials as American Commissioner. His act was welcomed by the Dominican authorities, who, Mr. Green reported, realized that the public presentation of his credentials would encourage the people "who were disheartened by the refusal of France to accept the protectorate, and by the consequent danger of a renewed invasion from Haiti." Baez, jockeying as ever, made the recognition of his Government by the United States a leverage in his continued negotiations with the French agent. In a further despatch to the Secretary of State, Mr. Green states—

"Del Monte and Baez were the first projectors of a French protectorate, on which project they have staked their political reputation, and consider its failure as fatal to their own influence and importance. They had the idea of making this country a colony of France as antecedent to the first movement for throwing off the Haitian yoke. They have clung to it for six years, in a great measure owe to it their present position, and will abandon it with great reluctance." [1]

The support given by General Santana to the petitions from the Cibao urging his approval of the project of an American protectorate began necessarily to be galling to the Francophile President, whose irritation caused him to

[1] Mr. Benjamin E. Green to Secretary Clayton, October 24, 1849.

warn the American Commissioner that the activities fostered by General Santana were most displeasing to him. Notwithstanding his knowledge of the special reasons for the urgent interest which Baez had in obtaining the French protectorate, Mr. Green could not restrain himself from arguing that the motives of France when she first favoured the protectorate were hardly such as could be relished by a Dominican patriot. He advised the President of his conviction, from certain negotiations of which he was informed, that the sympathies and interests of France were with the Haitians; that France would probably be obliged to maintain her refusal to accept the Dominican protectorate owing to the determined opposition of England to the scheme; but that should France intervene even only as mediator between Haiti and the Dominican Republic, it would be solely with a view to effecting some arrangement by which the Dominicans would be forced to assume a portion of the Haitian debt, and then once more submit to Haitian domination under the guise of a federal reunion.

Mr. Green was well aware that President Baez had taken pains to conceal from public knowledge in Santo Domingo that this very scheme was then being urged upon the French Government by Haitian agents in Paris, who in turn were supported by the powerful influence of the "Institut d'Afrique." In his despatch to the Secretary of State, Mr. Green reports, commenting upon his conversation with Baez, that

"the cruelties of the Haitians toward all who spoke the Spanish language have given such force and universality to the feeling in favor of the whites in the Dominican Republic that it is not uncommon to hear a very black negro, when taunted with his color, reply: 'Soy negro, pero negro blanco' [1]." [2]

In the late autumn of 1849, while continuing to press for a reconsideration by the French Government of the proposals for the French protectorate, upon which his hopes were staked and in which his personal financial interests, through the hoped-for tobacco monopoly, were so involved, Baez deemed it necessary to encourage the populace by making some outward demonstration of energy, and to forestall, if possible, for a breathing space, the invasion of Soulouque, by taking up the offensive against Haiti. Such vessels as the Dominican Government could command were armed and sent to Haitian waters to prey upon Haitian shipping, and to dissipate, if possible, the concentration of Haitian forces on the coast near the frontier. Owing in large part to the fact that the Dominican vessels were commanded by a French officer, Colonel Fagalde, whose constant intemperance rendered him incapable of giving intelligible orders at crucial moments, the Dominican expedition resulted in greater disaster to the Dominicans themselves than to their Haitian adversaries.

The expedition had, however, the desired effect of postponing for the time being the invasion of Dominican territory by Soulouque, who had by now created himself the Emperor Faustin I, and whose ambitions, with the assumption of imperial dignity, were ever increasing. The Emperor Faustin had in view not only the subjugation of the Dominican provinces but also the extension of Haitian sovereignty to the adjacent islands, to which his spies and agents had already been sent. Early in Jan-

[1] "I am a negro, but a white negro."
[2] Mr. Benjamin E. Green to Secretary Clayton, October 24, 1849.

uary, it became known that a Haitian named "Jacinthe" had been arrested by the authorities of St. Thomas for attempting to foment disturbances among the negroes. When his papers were investigated by the police, it was learned that he had sent to the Haitian Emperor a plan of the island of St. Thomas, with full information regarding the garrison, and had advised Faustin that it would be easy for the Haitians to capture the City and obtain possession of the Island. At the same time, it was learned that the Emperor had also been advised that the house of Rothschild and Company was furnishing arms and ammunition to the Dominicans from St. Thomas.

The ambitions of the Haitian Government, as evidenced by the divulgence of the St. Thomas conspiracy and by more positive proof of an impending invasion of the Dominican provinces, caused Mr. Green to advise his Government that should the United States desire to conclude a treaty with the Dominican Government, the Emperor Faustin should at once be notified that unless he desisted from further molestation of the Dominican people, the United States would intervene by force of arms, on the ground that continued war between the Dominicans and Haitians was devastating the Dominican Republic and endangering the independence of the country, and was directly damaging to commercial relations between the Dominican Republic and the United States.

On January 20, 1850, M. Chedeville, the chancellor of the French Consulate in Santo Domingo, who had been for eight months in Paris attempting to induce his Government to accept the protectorate, returned to Santo Domingo unable to obtain any satisfactory reply to the Dominican proposals. Baez, constrained to accept the inevitable, now determined to seek another form of protection against the Haitian plans of conquest. Heeding the ever increasing pressure from the Cibao, and, more powerful yet, the voice of Santana, he was induced to invite the mediation of the United States. According to Mr. Green, the fact that a Spanish squadron, hovering off the harbour of Santo Domingo for several days, had been supposed by President Baez and his Cabinet to be a Haitian fleet, proved an even stronger motive in determining the request for American intervention. At all events, on January 24, 1850, the following note was sent by the Minister for Foreign Affairs to Mr. Green:

"HONORABLE SIR:

"I am charged by my Government to communicate to you that, desirous of putting an end to the cruel war which we have maintained against the Haitians since the moment of our glorious separation, we would see with pleasure the intervention of the powerful Anglo-American nation which you represent to obtain peace, which is so necessary to the moral and physical progress of our country; it being well understood that we will preserve always our nationality and independence as a condition sine qua non of any agreement with our enemies.

"With sentiments of the highest consideration, I am, etc.,

M. T. DELMONTE
Minister of Justice, Public Instruction and
Foreign Relations."

The appeal to the United States was strongly supported by all the members of the Cabinet, who had by now definitely abandoned the hope of obtaining a French protectorate, although Baez, encouraged by the appointment to the French Ministry in 1850 of Ferdinand Barrot, a brother of the Adolphe Barrot who, as French Commissioner to Haiti in 1843, had originally devised the protectorate project with Baez, deluded himself that the scheme might now receive greater support in Paris.

The request for American mediation was at once opposed by the French and British representatives; in the opinion of Mr. Green, because of the desire of their respective Governments to see the Haitians victorious and in possession of the eastern end of the Island. The attitude of Sir Robert Schomburgk left no doubt in the American Agent's mind that his instructions were dictated by a very strong bias in favour of the Haitians; and the dilatory policy of the French was due, he claimed, to the insistence of the Haitian Government that it could not continue to pay the charges on its French debt unless it obtained possession of the revenues from the ports of the eastern end of the island. Pressing for the conclusion of the pending treaty with England, Sir Robert Schomburgk intimated to President Baez, early in February, that were the treaty proposed by him, inclusive of the article prohibiting monopolies, to be signed by the Dominican plenipotentiary, the intervention of Great Britain would be offered to the Dominican Government with a view to preventing further Haitian invasions.

Baez thereupon informed Mr. Green that he had positive information that the Haitians were prepared to invade the Republic at an early date, and that he, naturally enough, desired to know what the United States Government proposed to do in response to the Dominicans' plea for assistance. To this Mr. Green replied that he had already urged his Government to intervene but was unable as yet to give any positive assurances as to what responsibilities it would in fact undertake. Baez, under constant pressure from the French and British agents to call upon France and England for their mediation, rather than upon the United States, and alleging that action by the latter Government might be too long delayed to prevent the anticipated invasion, determined that the best solution of his difficulty was to invite the mediation of the three powers conjointly. Consequently, identic notes, similar to the note already addressed to the American Commissioner, were despatched on February 22, 1850, to Mr. Green and to the French and British Consuls.

In May, 1850, Mr. Green was instructed to proceed to Port-au-Prince. No decision had been reached by Secretary Clayton whether the United States should join with France and England in the projected intervention, and no reply was made to the Dominican request. But the American Commissioner's sympathies appear by now to have been strongly enlisted on the side of the Dominican people, since he admired the courage with which they were prepared, single-handed, to repel the threatened attack upon their independence, and the splendid tenacity with which, despite the unworthiness of their rulers, they were attempting to solve their domestic problems. Ascertaining upon his arrival in Port-au-Prince that two American firms, Messrs. B. C. Clark and Company, of Boston, and Messrs. Ropier and Company, of New York, had engaged to send vessels with provisions and army supplies to assist the Haitians in attacking the Dominicans, he urged the Secretary of State to take prompt action to prevent the planned infraction of the neutrality laws of the United States.

What was far more dangerous, Mr. Green learned, was the fact that the Emperor Faustin had forestalled the official intervention which France and England had by then agreed to undertake, by obtaining from the French and British Consuls in Port-au-Prince the transmission to the Dominican Government of the terms of peace which the Haitian Emperor was willing to propose. The terms were such as Mr. Green had feared the European Powers would favour. As soon as he learned of these proposals, Mr. Green returned hastily to Santo Domingo. There he was advised by the President of the full extent of the ignominy which the acceptance of such terms would entail:

"1. The Dominicans were to acknowledge the authority of the Emperor and to raise the Haitian flag;

"2. In return therefor, Faustin would promise to appoint none but Dominicans to office within the limits of Dominican territory, and would confer titles of nobility upon Generals Santana and Baez, the former of whom would remain as military, and the latter as civil, governor of the 'Eastern Department';

"3. He would likewise confer titles of nobility upon such other Dominicans as the Dominican Government might indicate, and would appoint several Dominican citizens members of the Senate in Port-au-Prince;

"4. He would station no troops within the limits of Dominican territory, and would permit the Dominican authorities to maintain their army and navy in the same state of efficiency as existed at that time."

Before the American Commissioner's return to Santo Domingo, the Dominican Government, although fearing to offend the mediating Powers, had made its position plain:

"As the Dominican Government has requested the mediation of the three great Powers, England, France and the United States of America, no negotiations on this subject can be begun before the certainty of the acceptance or rejection of the said request shall have been obtained.

"In the meantime, let it not seem strange to you to see us making the greatest preparations to repel our enemies, as we have heretofore done, even when less able than now, if they still persist in invading our territory." [1]

The sudden death in the summer of 1850 of President Taylor, which brought with it the appointment of Daniel Webster as Secretary of State by President Fillmore, resulted in the recall of Mr. Green. In his last despatch to the Department of State, he expressed his well founded fears for the safety of the Dominican people should the United States refuse to intervene in their behalf, and advised the new Secretary of State that the Emperor Faustin had sworn "by the soul of his mother, that he will not leave a chicken alive on Dominican soil." In reporting upon the course of his mission, Mr. Green stated that he had obtained the confidence of General Santana and of the latter's loyal follower, General Abad Alfau, but that while he had sought to establish the most cordial relations with President Baez he had the best of reasons for believing that he was the enemy of the United States. Mr. Green may not have been wrong in his conjecture that Sir Robert Schomburgk, availing himself of the fact that General Baez was of mixed blood, might well have increased his prejudice against the United States by enlarging upon the manner in which the coloured race was treated in so great a portion of the territory of the United States at that time.

Upon the refusal of the Dominican Government to entertain the proposals proffered by Faustin, the latter obdurately refused for some time to assent to the mediation of the French and British representatives. Upon

[1] Señor José Maria Medrano, Minister for Foreign Affairs, to Sir Robert Schomburgk, British Consul, April 30, 1850.

receipt of this information, general alarm manifested itself throughout the Dominican territory. The general apprehension is pictured in despatches of the American Commercial Agent:

"The feelings of the people here, their hopes and dependence, rest entirely upon being noticed by the United States. These hopes have been raised by Special Agents sent out here. I have learned, through Sir Robert Schomburgk, that the United States has agreed, in conjunction with England and France, to mediate between this Republic and the so-called Empire of Haiti through their respective consuls. This, added to Mr. Green's having been here eight months and it being well understood that he came here with powers to recognize this Republic and make a treaty and living here without entering into any negotiation, has destroyed the confidence which this Government have heretofore had in me. After both the Governments on this Island had complied and assented to the mediation of the three Powers, the Emperor Soulouque marched his men and committed depredations upon these people. The French and English Consuls here jointly made a protest against this movement. Rather than permit the Consuls of France and England to stand forward in the cause of humanity and republicanism more than myself as the representative of the United States, I alone made a similar protest and shared with them the expense of sending the same to Haiti, which cost me $84, which I hope will be refunded me by my Government.

*   *   *   *

"All that this people ask for is peace with the Haitians. They have nobly sustained themselves for seven years as a republic without involving themselves in debt. They have fought well and bravely; have left their families to support themselves, while they, without pay, without medical attendance, without food and almost naked, have willingly marched and fought for the cause of liberty. While they hold the implement of agriculture in one hand to raise crops which it is doubtful they can reap, they are obliged to keep the sword in the other. To this I have been witness."

* * * *

"In regard to the mediation between this part of the Island and that of Haiti, I learn from authentic sources that England and France have determined to blockade the ports of Haiti in consequence of Soulouque's refusing to come to an armistice of ten days. The policy of the French is this. The Haitians owe to them a large sum of money, which they never can pay so long as they continue at war with these people. The policy of the English to sustain the negroes in the Antilles is well known, and the interference on their part is more for the protection of Haiti against certain supposed expeditions and to oblige them to work and improve their part of the Island." [1]

5

With the advent of Daniel Webster as Secretary of State, the policy of the United States took definite shape. Secretary Webster's sympathies were strongly enlisted on the side of the Dominicans. He refused to countenance the policy of indifference to the sufferings of the struggling Republic which Secretary Clayton had pursued notwithstanding the repeated protests of his Commissioner. Determining, soon after he took office, that the only effective method for maintaining the stability of the Dominican Government lay in joining France and England in a joint mediation, he announced the acceptance of the responsibilities entailed, and later caused the appointment as Special Agent by President Fillmore, in the first days

[1] Mr. Jonathan Elliott to Secretary Webster, July 13, September 29 and November 30, 1850.

of the new year, 1851, of Mr. Robert M. Walsh, who was instructed to proceed immediately to Port-au-Prince to join the representatives of France and England in their efforts to secure, if not a definite peace, at least a suspension of hostilities for a long period between Haiti and the Dominican Republic.

To govern the conduct of his negotiations, Mr. Walsh was handed by Secretary Webster, before his departure from Washington, the following instructions:

"Department of State
Washington, 18th January, 1851

CONFIDENTIAL
To R. M. WALSH, Esquire,
Sir:

"Although in the letter of the Department of this date you are directed to be governed in your proceedings in St. Domingo by the views expressed in the instructions of Sir Henry L. Bulwer to Mr. Usher, yet as the latter may conceive those instructions to warrant him in demanding from the Dominican Republic in behalf of the Emperor Soulouque, concessions which, if yielded, would, it is believed, trench upon the just rights of that Republic, and would therefore render insecure any peace which may be established between the parties, it is deemed advisable to advert to those points, in order that you may endeavor to resist them so far as you can compatibly with the main object of your mission.

"It is probable that Soulouque may require an extension of his dominions so as to include a part of the territory formerly belonging to the Spanish quarter of the Island, but now embraced within the territory of the Dominican Republic. This pretension will, it is presumed, be set up on the ground that the population of the French part of the Island is much more numerous than that of the Spanish part, and yet that the number of square miles embraced by the former is considerably less than that embraced by the latter. There might be some weight in this pretension if the difference between the areas of the territories of the parties respectively were greater than that which actually exists; if the boundaries between them were not naturally good; or if the population of Soulouque's dominions were inconveniently crowded or were likely to become so within any appreciable time. As the reverse of all this, however, is believed to be the truth, you will object to any extension of Soulouque's territory. If, however, a treaty of peace should be concluded between the parties, the boundary should therein be defined so as in future to leave no cause of dispute between them respecting it.

"If, also, the Emperor Soulouque, should require from his adversary any concession of a humiliating character, such as the hoisting of his flag at the City of Santo Domingo, even temporarily, you will oppose it as being incompatible with the actual state of the contending parties, and as being certain to leave a rancorous feeling in the bosoms of the Dominicans, dangerous to the perpetuity of peace. They have shown much gallantry in expelling the Haitians in 1844 and in repulsing the subsequent attempts to resubjugate them. From the information in possession of the Department, it is believed that they desire peace, not so much through any consciousness of inability to maintain their independence, as from a wish to cultivate the arts of peace and thereby develop the vast and almost virgin resources of their part of the Island. The mode of warfare adopted by the Haitians, impelled as they have on former occasions been, not by the lust of dominion only, but by their savage antipathy to a different race, is shocking to humanity, denounced by international law, and cannot claim any sympathy from civilized communities.

"The Department understands that one of Soulouque's

pretexts for bearing arms against the Dominicans is, that unless he can reestablish Haitian authority in their territory, he cannot, without the revenue which would then be collected in their ports, resume the payment of the Haitian debt to France. There is some cause to apprehend that this pretext has not been without influence in the French Councils adverse to the Dominicans. It is difficult, however, to understand why it should have made any impression, especially when it is considered that the Ordinance of Charles X in 1825, by which the independence of Haiti is recognized upon the condition of their paying 150,000,-000 francs to France, expressly confines that recognition to the French part of the Island.

"I am, Sir, very respectfully,

Your obedient servant,

DANIEL WEBSTER."

Mr. Walsh arrived at Port-au-Prince on board the U.S.S. *Saranac* on February 2, 1851. Immediately after his arrival, he obtained an audience with the Emperor:

"The courtyard was filled with troops in rather motley attire, who saluted as we passed, and the hall of reception was crowded with ministers and generals and other dignitaries who made quite a glittering show. Soon after our entrance, the Emperor made his appearance in a costume which, though rich, was not in bad taste, preceded by shouts of 'Vive l'Empereur' from his courtiers, and we were then presented in due form. He seemed at first decidedly embarrassed, as if he did not know what to say or do. . . . On being informed that the *Saranac* would leave in a day or two, he manifested not the least chagrin. The truth is, the big ship in the harbor is not a pleasant spectacle to his eyes. It is a pity the commander cannot protract his stay here, as the presence of the steamer would materially assist our negotiations. Faustin I is stout and

short and very black, with an unpleasant expression and a
carriage that does not grace a throne. He is ignorant in the
extreme but has begun to learn to read and write and is
said to exhibit commendable diligence in his studies.
Energy and decision are his most important traits and no
soft feelings are likely to interfere with their full display
when occasion calls them forth. . . . It is stated that one
of the chief causes of the Emperor's intended expedition
against the Dominican Republic is his desire to be crowned
in the City of Santo Domingo." [1]

On February 7, 1851, Mr. Walsh addressed a note to
the Duke of Tiburón, the Haitian Minister for Foreign
Affairs, in which he made the following declarations:

"The Government of the United States, having determined to coöperate with the Governments of England
and France in bringing about the pacification of this
Island, has sent me as its agent for that purpose. It believes
that the only proper way to accomplish it is for the Government of Haiti to acknowledge the independence of the
Republic of Santo Domingo, that independence having
been now so long maintained as to prove the impossibility
of its being overthrown by the power of this Empire, and
in consequence to establish its claim to general recognition.
Any further prosecution of the war, therefore, is abhorrent
to the dictates of humanity and reason and injurious to
the interests of neutrals. . . . The principle is now fully
established that the actual possession of independence for a
reasonable time entitles a nation to be acknowledged as
sovereign. This is a principle which the American world
established as consecrated and must ever be upheld . . .
The best interests of the Haitian Empire demand the recognition of Dominican independence . . . In every point of
view, therefore, the Government of the United States en-

[1] Mr. Robert M. Walsh to Secretary Webster, February 5, 1851.

tertains the conviction that it is incumbent upon the Emperor to recognize the independence of Santo Domingo."

Upon receipt of this note, the Haitian Minister called upon Mr. Walsh in order to declaim a set speech which he had prepared in advance, in which the Minister maintained that the island was one and indivisible in accordance with the "designs of nature," and also that as the Haitian Constitution declared that the Dominican Provinces formed a part of Haiti, the Dominican people had no right to withdraw from that connection. Mr. Walsh, although it must have been difficult for him to reply gravely to such logic, succeeded in limiting himself to stating that the designs of nature were not necessarily good titles in law, and that the proclamation as a fact of what did not exist, by no means called it into being; for the Constitution of 1806 referred to by the Duke of Tiburón was promulgated by Haiti long before the juncture of the two parts of the Island had been effected.

Previous to Mr. Walsh's arrival, the French and British Agents, in conjunction with the Commercial Agent of the United States in Port-au-Prince, had succeeded in obtaining from the Emperor Faustin a truce of two months, with one month's notice of the renewal of hostilities. They had continued to urge upon the Emperor a definitive peace, but, finding that impossible, had proposed a truce of ten years on December 19, 1850. When Mr. Walsh arrived in Port-au-Prince, no answer to the joint proposal had yet been given by the Haitian Government. Finally, on March 3, 1851, the Haitian Minister informed Mr. Walsh and his French and British colleagues that no official answer could be given by the Haitian Gov-

ernment to their insistence upon the recognition by Haiti
of the independence of the Dominican Republic, inasmuch
as it involved a breach of the Constitution. The three
agents protested at this palpable attempt to promote further delay, remarking that even if Constitutional difficulties existed, they had nothing to do with the declaration
of a formal truce. The only reply which this protest
elicited was the statement by the Minister that "His Majesty will do nothing without consulting the Senate, his
first duty being to God and to observe the Constitution."
Mr. Walsh, in his report to Secretary Webster, stated that
it was only with considerable difficulty that he and his
colleagues could "keep their faces straight" upon receiving
this answer.

The Haitian Government, to postpone matters further,
and to involve the foreign representatives in long drawn
out discussions, appointed four commissioners to confer
with them. On March 6th, the three agents had their first
and only interview with this commission. They were then
notified that the Emperor had summoned the Chambers
of Congress to assemble on March 21st, to consider the
weighty questions involved.

During the course of the protracted negotiations, Mr.
Walsh does not appear to have been without diversion:

"The birthday of the Emperor was celebrated a few days
since . . . At the reception, various toasts felicitating His
Majesty were pronounced by the representatives of different deputations. To all of them, he made replies which
might have been comprehensible if they had only been
audible. But he is so embarrassed upon such occasions, besides having a natural defect of speech, that his remarks
rarely succeeded in crossing the threshold of his lips. His
knowledge, moreover, of French is slight; the only lan-

guage, if it may be dignified by that epithet, with which he is familiar being the creole patois of the country. To the few words of compliment which I addressed him, he looked a brief response, but that was all as far as my ears could ascertain. . . . His diffidence is reported to be the result of an intense consciousness of his own deficiencies combined with a dread which is always haunting him of ridicule. . . . He is approaching threescore and ten although he does not in the least represent that age. The vigor of his frame and color of his hair do not betray the passage of even fifty winters. His peculiar sensitiveness was the cause of the enmity which for some time rankled in his breast against the mulattoes, who, on his election as President, despising his apparent imbecility, made him the butt of all sorts of jests—an enmity which on the 16th of April, 1848, was somewhat appeased by the slaughter of many of the most prominent of his yellow compatriots. The Empress and his daughter, the Princess Olive, were seated near him during the levee, but not on the platform which supported his chair of state. The former is a very ordinary black woman in appearance, and the latter, a child of about ten years old, does not bid fair to surpass her mother in personal charms. . . . There was a great display of plumes and gold lace. . . . Two of the maids of honor of the Empress, who had absented themselves for some reason which was not considered good, were arrested by her orders and sent to different places in the country to expiate their crime in solitary punishment." [1]

On the day preceding the assembling of the Haitian Congress, Mr. Walsh, wearied by the interminable conversations which resulted in no definite commitment, delivered an ultimatum to the Haitian Minister for Foreign Affairs. He insisted upon an immediate reply to the

[1] Mr. R. M. Walsh to Secretary Webster, March 3, 1851.

demand of the three Powers for pacification of the Island, and stated that, "he would warn the Haitian Government for the last time, in the most earnest and emphatic manner, against any attack upon the Dominican Republic. It may be sure that any attempt of the kind will only result in disaster to itself." [1]

On the following day, the Emperor attended the opening of the session of Congress:

"The ceremony of the Chambers was performed with all possible parade . . . His Majesty and suite were robed for the occasion in costumes just arrived from France, making such a display as I have never seen rivalled except at Franconi's in Paris, and certainly none but theatrical magnificoes would venture to exhibit such varicolored and glittering splendor in any other metropolis however imperialistic. The toilette of Soulouque himself was quite wonderful, especially the chapeau with its half dozen feathers of different hues." [2]

The deliberations of the Haitian Congress, completely under the domination of Faustin, had no positive result, as Mr. Walsh had anticipated, and on April 23rd he was forced to report to Secretary Webster that the Haitian Government positively rejected a truce for ten years or a definitive peace with the Dominican Republic, and had proposed as an alternative that prior to a settlement the Dominicans must recognize the sovereignty of Haiti. The sole benefit of practical result obtained by the joint mediation was the promise on the part of Faustin to abstain from hostilities until England, France and the United States had been officially informed. But the intervention

---

[1] Mr. R. M. Walsh to the Duke de Tiburón, Haitian Minister for Foreign Affairs, March 20, 1851.
[2] Mr. R. M. Walsh to Secretary Webster, April 8, 1851.

of the three Governments was also productive in convincing the Emperor of the impossibility, for the moment, of obtaining possession of the eastern part of the Island, although, to assert himself, Faustin compelled Congress to declare that it was not competent to take any step which would result in the modification of the Constitution of 1806.

In the first days of May, Mr. Walsh traveled to Santo Domingo on the French warship *Cocodrile,* accompanied by the French Consul-General in Port-au-Prince. Prior to his departure from the Haitian capital, he communicated to Secretary Webster his opinion of the conditions existing in the Haitian Empire, which, while it may be prejudiced, presents a vivid picture:

"The Haitian Government, in spite of its Constitutional form, is a despotism of the most ignorant, corrupt and vicious description, with a military establishment so enormous that while it absorbs the largest portion of its revenue for its support, it dries up the very sources of national prosperity, by depriving the fields of their necessary laborers to fill the towns with pestilent hordes of depraved and irreclaimable idlers. The treasury is bankrupt. . . . The population is immersed in Cimmerian darkness that can never be pierced by the few and feeble rays which emanate from the higher portions of the social system. The influences of civilized life—the influences of religion, literature, science, or art—they do not exert the least practical sway, even if they can be said to exist at all. . . . The press is shackled to such a degree as to prevent the least freedom of printing and people are afraid to give utterance, even in confidential conversation, to aught that may be tortured into the slightest criticism of the action of the Government. . . . The ultimate regeneration of the

Haitians seems to me to be the wildest Utopian dream." [1]

Upon Mr. Walsh's arrival in Santo Domingo, he delivered to Señor Medrano the following personal letter from Secretary Webster:

"To His Excellency
    The Minister for Foreign Affairs
        of the Dominican Republic.
"Sir:
    "Allow me to introduce to Your Excellency Mr. Robert M. Walsh, who visits the Dominican Republic as a Special Agent of the United States for objects which he will in due time make known to Your Excellency. He is aware of the interest which we take in the prosperity of that Republic, of our strong desire to cultivate its friendship, and to deserve it by all the good offices which may be in our power. He is also aware of my zeal to promote these by whatever may depend upon my ministry. I have no doubt that Mr. Walsh will so conduct himself as to merit your confidence, and I avail myself with pleasure of this occasion to offer to Your Excellency the assurance of my most distinguished consideration.

                          DANIEL WEBSTER
"Department of State,
Washington, 18th January, 1851."

The terms of Mr. Webster's letter created the most favourable impression upon the Cabinet. Mr. Walsh reports the President as saying that while his Government was gratified to hear that the Emperor of Haiti promised not to make war, it was naturally disappointed to learn that he would not consent to make peace; and that Baez expressed the utmost confidence in the ability of the

[1] Mr. R. M. Walsh to Secretary Webster, April 8, 1851.

Dominican people, unassisted, to repel an invasion, and assured the American Agent of his gratitude for the good offices interposed in his Government's behalf by the United States.

In summing up his impressions for Secretary Webster's benefit, Mr. Walsh declared that although the mediation relieved the Dominicans

"for the time being of apprehension of attack, it did not allow them to lay aside their arms and devote themselves to the pursuits of peace; and they expressed the strong hope that the three Powers would continue their inter-position until the independence of the Republic had been secured. That result can only be accomplished by coercing the Haitian Government. All persuasion and argument are thrown away on it; all sense of duty and justice and right is merged by it in sanguinary ambition and avaricious self-ishness. The Dominicans will listen to no terms which do not establish their national sovereignty which they have so long and so successfully defended. They would prefer total extermination, as they declare and as their conduct demon-strates, to falling again under the atrocious despotism which they have shaken off, and every consideration in the interest of justice and of humanity demands that their independence should be placed on a secure and permanent basis." [1]

Mr. Walsh's mission being limited in his instructions to four months' time, he was obliged to leave Santo Domingo immediately after the presentation of his credentials to the Dominican Government.

6.

The practical failure of the efforts of the mediating powers in attempting to force upon the Haitian Emperor

[1] Mr. R. M. Walsh to Secretary Webster, June 10, 1851.

a truce of at least ten years with the Dominican Republic caused Baez to realize that the country must, for the time being, at least, depend upon its own resources in warding off the imminent attack from Haiti. In the spring of 1851, he called to arms a large number of troops from the eastern Provinces, at whose head General Santana marched to the capital. For the time being the mobilization resulted in nothing more concrete than a great military parade outside the walls of Santo Domingo, but the steps taken by Baez were seen, the following autumn, not to have lacked justification. By the middle of September, the Emperor Faustin had again assembled a very large armed force, with headquarters at Ounaminthe across the Massacre River from Dajabón.

General Santana, unwilling to acquiesce calmly in any military decisions reached by Baez, moved, on his own initiative, a correspondingly large body of Dominican troops to the Province of Monte Cristi; Baez thereupon despatched large forces from the capital to the frontier, and with his staff sailed around the island to the scene of the anticipated hostilities. But the speedy mobilization of the Dominican troops rendered possible by the activity displayed by the Dominican authorities proved to be sufficient to dissuade the Haitian Emperor from the intended invasion. Faustin withdrew his troops from the frontier in brief order and returned to Port-au-Prince, where he received, in December, two months after the activity displayed by the Dominicans rendered any foreign intervention unnecessary, stern warning from France and England that those two nations were determined to enforce respect for the independence of the Dominican Republic.

By the year 1852, the constant interference of Santana

in the affairs of the Government began to prove almost intolerable to Baez. It became impossible for the President to take any determined action regarding the organization of the army, under his nominal control, without the prior assent of the ex-President, and Santana even insisted upon the submission to him of all questions involving the foreign policy of the Republic. After the ratification of the treaty with France signed May 8, 1852, Baez despatched General Abad Alfau to Port-au-Prince to attempt to negotiate directly with the Haitian Emperor the peace which the latter had been unwilling to conclude at the behest of France, England and the United States. The negotiations proved fruitless; and since the step taken by Baez proved distasteful to Santana, the President was obliged to make, as he did also upon several other occasions, an expiatory pilgrimage to El Prado to explain matters to Santana and receive assurances that the latter's displeasure would not be pressed to such a point as to prevent Baez from serving out his Presidential term. Baez was not yet able to assert himself.

Owing to the pressure of public opinion, which was convinced at the time that Santana was effectively the liberator of the Republic and the proven defender of the nation's independence, Baez was compelled, notwithstanding his evident reluctance, to approve, before the expiration of his term of office, a decree of the Congress granting Santana not only a golden sword suitably inscribed, but likewise a grant of $16,000 pending such time as the finances of the nation permitted the Republic to place at his disposal a yearly pension for the remainder of his life. It was, in fact, painfully evident to Baez that Santana had obtained such an effective control over the army and was so strongly supported by the mass of the people that his own continuance in the Presidential chair depended solely upon the whim of the "Liberator" of the Republic.

Two months prior to the termination of Baez's term of office, on December 18, 1852, the Spanish man-of-war, *Isabel Segunda,* arrived at Santo Domingo, bearing on board the Spanish historian, Don Mariano Torrente, who had been sent to the Republic by General Cañedo, then Captain-General of Cuba, as his Special Agent. To avoid diplomatic or local comment, Torrente appeared first in the guise of the vessel's purser, later as an itinerant explorer. But the masquerade was soon discontinued, since shortly after his arrival he was publicly welcomed into the Cathedral by the entire chapter of the clergy with the Archbishop at their head. To make Torrente's mission sufficiently significant the Prelate is reported to have remarked, upon pointing out to the visitor the Spanish arms, still fixed above the High Altar:

"Look there, Sir, dominating everything, is the noble shield of the glorious Spanish arms, preserved by the unanimous respect and affectionate veneration which the Dominican people ever bear for your country. There we keep it as a reminder of better days and as a symbol of our hope for a happier and more tranquil future!" [1]

After such a tribute the Spanish Agent was not astonished to have the President, who, forced to abandon the French protectorate project, was only too desirous of cutting out the ground from under Santana's feet by obtaining the sympathies of Spain on his own behalf, approach him on the subject of annexation. On this subject, however, Torrente was not authorized to speak, and in reply merely pointed out that Spanish recognition would doubt-

[1] General de la Gándara "Anexión y Guerra de Santo Domingo."

less be hastened should the Dominican Government assume as a portion of its national debt the amount of the claims held by those Spanish subjects whose properties had suffered confiscation during the Haitian Occupation, and should the Republic volunteer to negotiate a commercial treaty with Spain, in which Spain were accorded most-favored-nation privileges.

Torrente's insinuations bore fruit rapidly, although he himself remained in the Republic but a brief period. As a final bid for Spanish favour, in his farewell address to the Congress, which had assembled January 26, 1853, and had at once elected the "Liberator" President of the Republic, Baez urged the national legislative body to adopt in every particular the proposals advanced by Torrente.

7.

On February 15, 1853, General Pedro Santana again took office as President of the Republic, and on February 27th, the tenth anniversary of the Republic's independence, a general celebration was held. *El Progreso* of March 6, 1853, contains a glowing account of the festivities:

"Great was the enthusiasm which the public showed in celebrating the memorable day of their glorious independence; the day upon which they broke the chains of slavery and showed themselves to the world triumphantly demonstrating their liberty and presenting an example to all nations of how strong the political determination of a people may be.

"The decorations, the music, the illumination, and above all the joyful acclamations had been announcing since the previous evening that the populace filled with joy was celebrating their remembrance of a memorable day.

"There dawned the day of the 27th of February. Great crowds filled the streets and squares of the City and the beat of the drums, the sound of the military music, and the salutes of the cannon made perfect harmony with the general animation. At eight o'clock in the morning appeared in the Plaza de Armas the Liberator, the President of the Republic, followed by a great number of attendants, reflecting in his visage the modesty which is innate in him, and accepting the honors which he so well deserves with the same expression with which he confronted adverse fate on more than one occasion. A moment before entering the holy Cathedral, where a solemn Te Deum was to be celebrated, he addressed the following allocution to the people and to the Island:

" 'Dominicans! I was in retirement in my home given up to the care of my family and enjoying, moreover, the tranquillity which has been existing for some time in our beloved country, when the voice of the people, which is for me the first of all laws, called me by suffrage to preside for the fourth time over the destinies of the Nation. . . .

" 'The advantage of preserving complete harmony in our diplomatic relations is incalculable and I shall make every effort to see that it shall never be interrupted. I realize, moreover, that we should likewise enter into contact with other foreign powers and in accordance with this conviction, I sent to some of them, in my earlier four-year period of administration, diplomatic agents with instructions designed to that end. I believe it possible to obtain it, and to unite our interests with others through treaties of friendship and commerce, and to that purpose I will dedicate a portion of my administrative efforts. . . . I value justly the helpful influence which the intervention of powerful friendly nations can exert over the destinies of the Republic in their decision to protect our sacred cause by intimating to the Haitian Government that it must cease in its impudent and impracticable pretensions to dominate this territory.—I shall now conclude, but listen to me well. If, notwithstanding the mediation of the friendly nations; if, notwithstanding their noble and just desires, the Haitian chief were to persist in arming his legions and with them march against us, you need never be alarmed. Remember that already a thousand times have we defeated his impudent attempts and punished with death his temerity; and finally, count upon the strength of my arm, as I count upon the strength of yours, and believe unfalteringly that I shall always be disposed to sacrifice my life in defending our dear country.

" 'Long live religion, national union, independence and the Dominican Republic!' " [1]

The return to power of Santana was received with approval by the great mass of the people, which was convinced that the "Liberator" was its mainstay against Haitian assaults; even the remaining members of the old liberal party welcomed his inauguration; and General Francisco Sánchez, notwithstanding his enforced retirement from active political life, addressed a congratulatory message to the President through the public press.

The day after his inauguration, Santana appointed General Pedro Eugenio Pelletier Secretary of Foreign Affairs, Justice and Public Instruction; Don Miguel Lavastida Secretary of Interior and Police; Don Francisco Cruz Moreno Secretary of Finance and Commerce; and upon the refusal of General Felipe Alfau to accept the portfolio of War and Marine, his brother, General Abad Alfau, was appointed to that position.

Further light is thrown upon the general situation in the country after the inauguration of Santana, and in particular upon the international relations of the Government, by despatches from the American Commercial Agent:

[1] *El Progreso,* Santo Domingo, March 6, 1853.

"The object of Mariano Torrente, who recently came here in the Spanish steamer *Isabel Segunda,* was to form an alliance with this Government. They offer to land here a Spanish force of 5,000 men in case difficulties should arise with the United States and the proposition has been favorably received. He also went to Haiti to make the same propositions.

"The French are also intriguing for favor here. They are building a steamer for this Government and are completely to man, equip, and furnish everything except the hull, for which this Government have paid them $45,000. The French Consul General, M. Raybaud, is shortly expected here and I believe one of his principal objects is to make a secret treaty of alliance with this Government, as it is well known here that they have requested a military force from France, the greater part of which is to be placed at Samaná.

"According to Article 210 of the Dominican Constitution, the President has absolute power to do as he chooses without consulting Congress. Consequently he need not make public his acts.

"Today, Mr. Juan Abril embarked for Havana, via St. Thomas, to negotiate with the Governor-General of Cuba in regard to the propositions made to this Government.

"It is very probable he will come to Washington to make propositions. His departure and mission has been kept very secret. Should this gentleman arrive in Washington to propose a treaty and should the Government be disposed to enter into negotiations, it would be well to make me acquainted with the same, as I have some suggestions to make which will be of great importance to the Government.

"I earnestly request that the President will not send any more Special Agents here. It has done no good, but to the contrary, a great deal of injury to our interests. . . . Spain is making some alliance with this Government to protect them against the Haitians and more particularly to prevent any large emigration to this part of the Island from the United States. . . . General Santana told me in a conversation that he intended to send a mission to Washington to obtain a recognition of this Republic and make a treaty. . . . The country at present is in such a wretched state and no disposition in the people to work under any circumstances that unless a large emigration come here, it is impossible for this Republic to sustain itself." [1]

As soon as Santana had firmly established himself in the Presidency and had obtained convincing proofs of the general popularity which, for the time being, he enjoyed throughout the Republic, he determined to eliminate from the political scene the two elements which had caused him disquiet during the preceding four years. The first was the clergy, whose intervention in political matters had increased during the Presidency of Baez; the second was Baez himself.

Brusquely ordering the aged Archbishop, Don Tomás de Portes e Infante, to appear before the Senate, Santana accused the prelate of fostering dissatisfaction among the people with the civil authorities, and ordered him, without mincing words, to take the oath of allegiance to the Constitution. The Archbishop at first refused, but upon being confronted with an order exiling him from the Republic should he continue in his refusal, he at length gave in and took the oath required of him. The agitation caused the Archbishop, who had reached an advanced age, to lose his mind, and the speedy exile of those more influential members of the upper hierarchy who had refused to follow the example of their superior by obeying the commands of the President, left the direction of the

[1] Mr. Jonathan Elliott to Secretary Marcy, March 7, 1853, and May 3, 1853.

Church in the hands of such submissive clerics that the President was caused no further uneasiness. As soon as this step had been accomplished, Santana turned his attention to Baez, who had retired to his estates in Azua.

As the first step in his campaign against the man whom he now had valid reason to fear as a potential rival, and whose attempt to supplant him in his championship of the Spanish policy was a further motive for his elimination, Santana commanded his spokesmen in the Congress to draw up a scathing reply to Baez's farewell address. The reply was well drafted, and its effect was only diminished by the fact that the Congress had previously passed a resolution expressing its high appreciation of Baez's accomplishments. In the reply dictated by Santana, the representatives declared that the sole benefits occasioned the nation during the Presidency of Baez were those for which Santana alone was responsible; that it was by his insistence alone that they had been rendered possible, and that had it not been for Santana's utmost exertions, the administration of Baez would have resulted in general disorder. The Congress claimed that, far from leaving the national treasury in a satisfactory condition, as he had alleged, Baez had left it empty, and that his recommendations to the Legislative Body to assume as a part of the national debt the claims of Spanish subjects, would, if carried out, prove ruinous to the nation.

After sufficient time had elapsed to enable Santana to ascertain that the charges formulated against Baez by the Congress were generally welcomed, he called together, on July 3, 1853, all the civil and military authorities of the capital to a general meeting in the Palacio del Congreso, outside of which the troops had been marshalled as if for a military parade. Thereupon, the President read a manifesto addressed to the Dominican people. Commencing his address with the declaration that his acceptance of the Chief Magistracy was solely due to his belief that by that method only could he save the nation from utter disaster, the irascible "Liberator" speedily plunged into a long drawn out and detailed arraignment of Baez: Baez had been opposed from the outset to the patriotic revolution of 1844; as soon as the revolution had broken out, Baez had despatched an Agent from Azua to the President of Haiti warning him of the rebellion, and giving him full information of the movements of the revolutionary troops; Baez, as recently as 1849, had undertaken clandestine negotiations with leading Haitians, from whom he had received financial support which he had later, as President of the Republic, repaid from national funds; Baez had at various times offered the support of the Dominican Government to Haitian revolutionaries, and had even attempted to facilitate the entrance into the Republic of Haitian troops; Baez had proposed to Santana, when the former had decreed mobilization of the national forces in 1851, that they combine in overthrowing the Constitutional Government of the Republic and form a joint dictatorship—and although Santana, as he said, had scornfully rejected the proposal, Baez would, on subsequent occasions, have carried it into effect had he not feared that Santana's opposition would render its success impossible.

The pent-up accumulation of jealousy, the remembrance of all the intentional and imagined slights of the past four years, burst forth and ended in a vulgar tirade. Baez the conspirator—the arch-traitor—the assassin— the scorn of every true patriot; the old "Liberator" stood before the members of his cabinet, who cringed

before an outburst of fury of which they had not for
years seen the like, before his Generals in their gold lace
and all the assembled dignitaries, spent with rage. At the
end of his harangue Santana's mood changed—he admitted his responsibility for the elevation of Baez to the
Presidency, and told his listeners he hoped the frank con-
fession of his earlier error would obtain him the forgive-
ness of his fellow-citizens. But he lost little time in simu-
lated, or at least vain, regrets. Declaring that the safety
of the Republic demanded it, he announced that he had
determined to avail himself of the prerogatives vested in
him by Article 210 of the Constitution to decree the perpetual exile from the territory of the Republic of Buenaventura Baez.

As they left the Palace and walked past the assembled
troops in the Plaza de la Catedral, Santana's auditors must
privately have formulated to themselves the query they
dared not make openly—why had Santana elevated to the
Presidency a man whom he had long known guilty of the
grossest treachery to his own country? That unanswerable
question, which must ever remain as the most positive
impeachment of Santana's own sincerity, was soon publicly propounded to the Dominican people in a manifesto
published by Baez in St. Thomas, to which refuge he had
succeeded in escaping from his home in Azua, before the
"Liberator's" emissaries could seize him. Unfortunately
for his own reputation, Baez appears to have been utterly
unable to disprove the detailed charges made against him
by Santana, and although, with habitual cynicism, he
claimed that the sudden outbreak of Santana was due to
the vigour with which he himself as President had opposed
Santana's constant requests for the advance of public
moneys for his own private uses, it is doubtful that his

reply to Santana gained for him any measure of sympathy from the fellow-citizens whom he was now publicly accused of having attempted to betray.

As soon as the Congress had served Santana's purpose by affording him the pretext for his arraignment of Baez, and had satisfied the President's desires by largely increasing his salary and the salaries of the members of his administration, as well as by granting him the unlimited powers which he demanded, Santana commanded the Legislative Body to adjourn, with which behest it meekly complied. He thereupon directed his attention once more to the foreign relations of the Republic.

8.

In the spring of 1853, assurances had been received from England and France that the policy of the two powers in guarding the independence of the Republic would be maintained. More interested, though, in procuring the attention of Spain, Santana selected no less prominent an emissary than the former "Trinitario," General Ramón Mella, as his representative in Madrid. Mella's instructions as Confidential Agent, though limited to the direction to interpret to the Spanish Court the affectionate regard of the Dominican people for Spain, and to take such steps as might be necessary to ensure the "tranquillity and the future of the Dominicans," afforded him necessarily considerable latitude in his negotiations with the Spanish Ministers. Upon General Mella's arrival in Madrid, his conversations with the members of the Spanish Cabinet turned to the oft mooted question of "protecting the independence of Santo Domingo," but the Spanish Government, fearful, as it stated, of "awakening the jealousy of the United States and of

alienating the sympathies of the Cuban slaveholders,"
appeared no more anxious to assume the responsibilities
which an actual protectorate would demand than it had
when approached in former years by Baez and his colleagues. Mella impressed upon the Spaniards, with considerable skill and still greater logic, that mere recognition
of the Dominican Republic could not have the effect
feared, and concluded by declaring that should Spain persist in her refusal to recognize the Republic, the Dominican Government would be forced to negotiate with some
other nation an agreement which would guarantee the
protection of its independence, and in fact, he assured
the Spanish Minister of State, the greatest embarrassment
of his Government at that very moment consisted in
refraining from the negotiation of such an agreement
with the United States. But his repeated efforts proved
fruitless, and General Mella was forced to leave Madrid
and return to Santo Domingo, having secured none of
the assurances desired by his Government. The attention
of Santana was now, as a last resort, turned to the possibility of securing protection from the Government of the
United States, which had recently despatched to the
Dominican capital another Special Agent in the person
of General William L. Cazneau.

General Cazneau had been appointed Special Agent of
the United States by President Pierce on June 17, 1854.
The new Agent of the American Government had already
had a varied career. Born in Boston and educated in
Massachusetts, he had removed to Texas while still a
young man. He had there participated in the events
which resulted in the annexation of the Texan Republic
by the United States, and had there gained his title of
"General." But his subsequent career in the new state was

such that he was obliged to leave his home at Eagle Pass at short notice in 1853, and cast about for new means of employment. Learning by chance of the general situation in the Dominican Republic, he succeeded in interesting Governor William L. Marcy of New York, who was soon to take office as Secretary of State under President Pierce. Secretary Marcy, who was thoroughly imbued with the doctrines of Stephen Douglas, so often proclaimed in his speeches, which declared that the "manifest destiny" of the United States provided for territorial expansion to the south, and particularly in the direction of the West Indies, pondered the advantages offered by annexation of Santo Domingo. One may picture the Secretary, leaning back, arrayed in the faded dressing-gown which he wore in his home, redolent of the snuff in which he indulged in too copious quantities, emphasizing his points with his favourite red bandana while the Texan General expounded the desirability of the Dominican Republic.

Whether President Pierce at first shared the view to which Marcy soon was led, that eventual annexation of the Dominican Republic should be undertaken, is uncertain, but he too was speedily convinced.

The great figures so long responsible for the direction of the foreign relations of the United States—Daniel Webster, John C. Calhoun, John Quincy Adams, Henry Clay, who had ever fostered the growth of the new Republics to the South—had now vanished. For a while such policy as there was with regard to the Latin American States was a policy far from noteworthy for its adherence to the tenets of international morality. "In 1852, Greytown, the principal port of one of the Republics of Central America, was bombarded and burned by a naval force of the United States, on the flimsy charge that its inhabitants had infringed the rights of the Transit Company. No reparation on our part has ever been made for this wanton and brutal exercise of power . . . the career of the filibuster Walker: first in Sonora, Lower California, then in Nicaragua, where at last he was driven into Rivas, and taking shelter on board the U. S. sloop-of-war *St. Mary's*, was brought to New Orleans, but only to receive sympathy, and not punishment, for his piratical achievements. Mr. Buchanan was loud in deprecating such crimes, but could find no authority for punishing the criminals." Walker's "acts nevertheless ineffaceably stained the character of our country. . . . With Paraguay we had some difficulty . . . which caused us to send a formidable naval expedition there with threatening demands. Will she ever forget or forgive us? . . . Our attitude towards Cuba . . . sometimes our private citizens propose to take it by force at their own risk and expense. . . . We withdrew our Minister from Peru in consequence of the seizure of two American vessels illegally loaded with guano; . . . Peru has paid no damages and loves us little; . . . The Brazilian Government was not permitted to mediate in the war against Paraguay." [1] And it was in the light of a policy, or lack of policy, which had made such conditions possible, that Secretary Marcy caused the appointment by President Pierce of the Texan adventurer as the Special Agent of the United States in Santo Domingo, with instructions to obtain by treaty a foothold in the Republic.

If the purposes of the United States were open to criticism, the contemptuous disregard by the European Powers of Dominican sovereignty at the time General Cazneau

[1] From a speech by Senator Justin S. Morrill, delivered in the U. S. Senate, April 7, 1871.

was despatched to Santo Domingo, may be learned from contemporaneous despatches of the American Commercial Agent in the Dominican capital:

"Two French subjects arrived here from Haiti, and this Government suspecting them to be spies or suspicious persons obliged them to leave the country. For this the Government have been forced by the French Consul and a French steamer of war to pay $2,800. Not content with this, the French Consul required of the President to expel from office the Secretary of the Treasury, the Governor of this City, and the Comptroller of the Customs House, giving as reasons that one Colonel Mendez, who has been receiving the sum of $2,000 per annum to drill the troops, had been grossly offended. This the Government has refused to do. The Secretary of State has been despatched to France, as well as the Secretary of the French Consul, to settle the difficulty there. I have good reason to believe that the intention of the French is to overthrow the present President of the Republic, General Santana, a man of liberal principles, and place ex-President Baez again in power, a mulatto who most cordially hates Americans and all that is American, and is purely a Frenchman in his heart. It would be well to send immediately a vessel of war to this port, by which time I shall have authentic information of what I have stated. . . . Mariano Torrente, of Cuba, is now in Europe assisting this movement of the French to govern this Island. I had an interview with President Santana this morning, who seemed very downhearted and expressed his regret that the United States would not recognize this Republic the same as other nations had. He requested me to ask you if you would receive a special plenipotentiary to negotiate a treaty." . . .

"The French are using all their endeavors to overthrow or destroy this little Republic. The headquarters of their operations is at St. Thomas." . . .

"I have learned that the French Consul General of Haiti is to arrive here on or about the 25th of December. His coming bodes no good for this Republic. Yet another messenger was despatched by this Government to Puerto Rico to ask Spanish protection. In my former despatch, I mentioned that one had been sent to Madrid. I think it proper now to mention that if these applications to Spain fail, which I have every reason to believe they will, this Government and people will solicit the protection of the United States." [1]

France was hoping to effect some arrangement satisfactory to the Haitians which would assure the payment of her claims against Haiti. To accomplish this under Santana seemed impossible, and her efforts were therefore directed towards securing Baez's return to power. Great Britain, desirous of preventing the French from obtaining any foothold in Dominican territory, and not desirous itself of increasing its burdens in the West Indies by assuming a protectorate, had determined to offset French influence by proclaiming its intention to assist the Dominicans in preserving their independence, only so long, however, as the policy of opposing Haitian pretensions did not prove disquieting to its negro subjects in the West Indian colonies. Spain, long resentful of the support afforded by the United States to her revolted colonies in Latin America, and fearful lest the American Government might foster revolution in her remaining colonies in the West Indies, was not minded to incur added responsibilities by undertaking the Dominican protectorate unless it were necessary to do so in order to forestall such an attempt on the part of the United States. That Spain

[1] Mr. Jonathan Elliott to Secretary Marcy, November 27, 1853, November 30, 1853, and December 13, 1853, respectively.

and France during these years had a secret understanding as to the policy to be pursued by them towards the Dominicans is undoubted, and that policy was largely based upon the growing animosity of France to the spread of British influence throughout the world. The policy laid down by Daniel Webster in his instructions to Mr. Walsh was a policy which would have resulted in maintaining the independence of the Dominican Republic, and would have preserved the integrity of Dominican territory against any intrigues fostered by the European Powers through Haiti. Unfortunately, the death of Webster in 1852, and the subsequent change of policy of the American Government caused by the exigencies of domestic politics, reversed completely the attitude of disinterested assistance originally adopted towards the Dominican Government.

CHAPTER II

SANTANA AND BAEZ

1.

TO the stranger arriving in Santo Domingo in 1854, few evidences of material progress since the days of the Haitian Occupation could have been discernible. The capital was still a city of barely 15,000 inhabitants crowded within the old Spanish walls. The palaces, monasteries and churches built in the years of Spain's glory still were standing, but many of them were fast falling to ruin and for years had not been used. The streets were still unpaved, and in the months of the rains presented an almost impenetrable morass to the pedestrian. In the neighbourhood of the Cathedral, and in the streets back from the river-front, the wealthier citizens had their residences, while the shacks of the poor clustered on the cliffs facing the sea, or sprawled along the hillsides towards the suburb of San Carlos, which as yet was a waste expanse outside the city walls, occupied only by a few of the more daring. "Horses, donkeys, sheep, pigs and goats wandered freely about the Puerta del Conde and other portions of the City," [1] but the municipal authorities, notwithstanding the occasional pleas of the local press, took small pains to keep the streets and squares cleared for the city's human inhabitants.

On the days when a schooner arrived, certain activity could be noted along the wharves and in the tiny village of Pajarito across the Ozama River. But for long days on end the capital maintained unbroken the tranquillity of its every-day existence, varied by the occasional interruption of a band of horsemen clattering into the city from

[1] *La Acusación*, Santo Domingo, December 4, 1856.

142

the Cibao, a rare performance in the theatre, the rumour of invasion from the Haitian frontier, enough to bring the women panicstricken to the streets, or the return of the "Liberator" with his escort from El Prado.

Beyond the walls of Santo Domingo, towards San Cristóbal, Baní and Azua, towards the blue mountains of Bonao and Cotuy, or across the Ozama towards San Pedro de Macorís and the distant Seybo, where now lie miles of cane fields and pasture land, there then stretched an endless vista of waste or brush. The plantations of colonial days had long since been swallowed up by the ever-encroaching vegetation of the tropics. The roads to the north, once well-travelled, were now mere trails, through which, in the rainy season, horses and mules must flounder to their withers. The journey from Santiago to the capital, made speedily, took three days; but intercourse between the Cibao and the south, except upon official business, was rare, and travel not always safe. "There is little security for property and persons; every person who travels carries his sword and pistols." [1]

Commerce was stagnating, although from the southern provinces mahogany, lignum vitæ, and dye-woods were still exported, and Puerto Plata still shipped such tobacco as the Cibao provinces could produce, to Hamburg. But the constant mobilizations of the past years, which had taken, time and again, the peasant from his land, leaving his crops to rot in the ground, and the ever-present danger of renewed invasion from Haiti, had killed initiative, and had arrested the progress of the agriculturist at the moment in the nation's history when the fostering and stimulation of agriculture were most urgently demanded.

But to the eyes of General Cazneau, who had been

[1] Mr. Jonathan Elliott to Secretary Marcy, March 11, 1854.

despatched to Santo Domingo by Secretary Marcy early in the winter of 1854, it seems that the picture which the Republic presented could hardly have been more satisfying.

Cazneau's first despatches after his arrival in the Republic miss no opportunity.

"The situation of the Dominican Republic is peculiar in that none of the American Republics have by treaty recognized its independence, and since it is forced to depend upon the good will of France and England for the temporary relief afforded by the existing truce with Haiti, the negotiation of a treaty with the United States will naturally be welcome." [1]

The negotiations of General Mella in Madrid were of no importance.

". . . while it may be the local belief that General Mella's mission is for the purpose of negotiating the return of the Dominican Republic to its old allegiance to Spain, Santana's ruling policy is indubitably the creation of the Dominican Republic as an independent American power, preferably under the protection of the United States . . ." [1]

So much for the broader aspects of international policy; now for the more detailed report of material advantages. The soil is unimaginably fertile—mines of gold, silver, copper, coal, are omnipresent. Timber concessions, salt concessions, railroad concessions, public utility concessions, every variety of concession is displayed before the supposedly dazzled eyes of President Pierce, available for American citizens, if only an American protectorate is negotiated and General Cazneau sent to negotiate it. No military force would be required from the United States.

[1] General William L. Cazneau to Secretary Marcy, January 23, 1854.

"Eight thousand Dominicans are always in arms for immediate service . . . once a week the whole available population is mustered for drill, a certain proportion being
drafted in rotation for military duty . . . the Republic
has artillery and 30,000 stand of arms, all purchased in the
United States since 1844 . . ." [1]

Finally, and this argument was conclusive,

". . . the re-election of General Santana, and his return
to power for an indeterminate period, makes it a most
propitious time for establishing *close relations* between the
United States and the Dominican Republic." [1]

During the weeks of General Cazneau's first visit, General Santana was fully occupied in forcing through the
Legislative Bodies the revised form of the Constitution
which he had long had under consideration, but not too
occupied to discuss with Secretary Marcy's Agent the purposes of the latter's journey. The conversations between
the two were so satisfactory that Cazneau was able upon
his return to Washington in the spring to take with him
in draft form a treaty, approved by the Dominican President, for submission to the American Government.

The new Constitution, finally approved after acrimo-
nious discussion in the Congress on February 25, 1854,
made various fundamental changes in the early Constitution of the Republic. The Consejo Conservador, now
termed the "Senate," was increased to a membership of
ten, two senators representing each province; and the
Tribunado, now termed the "Chamber of Representatives," was composed of twenty members, each province
being accorded a representation of four members. Changes
in the judicial system were introduced, and the Vice

[1] General William L. Cazneau to Secretary Marcy, February 12, 1854.

Presidency was created, the Vice President to be elected for a term of four years, two years after the President's election. Among the transitory provisions was one providing that Santana should hold office for two terms, that is, until 1861. Over the protests of the President, the famous Article 210 of the original Constitution was suppressed, and the discussions to which the suppression gave rise created such friction between the Executive and the Legislative authorities that the President, ten months after the new Constitution had been sanctioned, was led to demand its drastic revision, as the result of which both Legislative Bodies were consolidated into a single chamber termed the "Permanent Senate," composed of two representatives from the provinces of Santo Domingo and Santiago, and one from each of the remaining provinces, each Senator to hold office for six years. Civil liberties were harshly restricted, and the Chief Executive not only finally obtained the dictatorial powers which he desired, but likewise obtained the increase in his own tenure of office of two terms of six years each, dating from April 1, 1855. Prior to this final revision of the Constitution, Santana, who had attempted to induce General Felipe Alfau to accept the Vice Presidency, was forced, upon Alfau's refusal, to offer it to General Manuel de Regla Mota, who took office at the end of August, 1854.

Upon his return to Washington, General Cazneau found he had sown seeds in fertile ground. President Pierce by now shared the views of his Secretary of State that the "manifest destiny" of the United States encompassed the Dominican Republic.

The draft agreed upon in principle by the Dominican President and Cazneau was thereupon revised by Secretary Marcy to conform in general with other commercial treaties negotiated by the United States, with the significant modification that the motive for the negotiation of the treaty was expressly stated in the 27th article of the proposed instrument, namely, the acquisition of a strategic tract as a coaling depot in Samaná Bay. General Cazneau was ordered to return to Santo Domingo to obtain the formal agreement of the Dominican Government to the treaty as re-drafted in the Department of State, with these final instructions: while a mile square of territory for the coaling depot in Samaná Bay was sufficient, care was to be exerted in obtaining for the Government of the United States for an indefinite period all rights of authority and control over it, at an annual rental of not more than two or three hundred dollars; the possession of this tract by the United States, it should be pointed out by the American Agent, would give stability to the Dominican Republic; should the depot not be granted, and the other provisions desired not be obtained, the United States Senate would be unlikely to ratify the treaty, and the President of the United States might not even under such circumstances be willing to submit it to that body for its approval; lastly, the negotiation should be accomplished speedily, and the ratification of the Dominican Government should be procured prior to General Cazneau's return with the signed treaty to the United States.

General Cazneau reached Santo Domingo for the second time on July 18, 1854. At the time of his arrival, since General Santana was absent from the capital on one of his periodical visits to El Prado, the Executive Power was in the hands of the Vice President. Presenting his credentials to the Minister for Foreign Relations, Don Juan Nepomuceno Tejera, who was at once summed up by

General Cazneau as "a man of American ideas," the American representative sent a message to El Prado requesting the presence of the President in the capital. Santana amiably complied with the request, and returned in post haste to Santo Domingo, naming, upon his arrival, the Minister for Foreign Affairs and General Juan Luís Franco Bidó, Senator from Santiago, as Commissioners to commence official negotiations with the Agent of President Pierce.

General Cazneau was charmed with the cordiality of his reception. He at once wrote Secretary Marcy that the only possible obstacle to his success in concluding the proposed treaty entrusted to him was the vague dread on the part of the populace of the real intentions of the United States, which Cazneau was sure was solely due to the propaganda of the European Consuls, who had alleged that the United States intended to seize Dominican territory, set aside the native whites, and enslave the blacks; and that while Santana and the members of his Cabinet, of course, held different opinions, it might be difficult for the administration to resist the active prejudice of the general populace.[1]

This "active prejudice" was naturally enough increased by the precipitancy of Captain George B. McClellan, who had accompanied General Cazneau to the Republic on the U.S.S. *Constitution*, in proceeding with a survey of Samaná Bay prior even to the commencement of negotiations with the Dominican Government. The news of McClellan's surveying operations and his announced opinion that the United States should establish its coaling depot in the harbor of Carenero Chico, and should obtain for that purpose the control as well of Levantados Bay,

[1] General William L. Cazneau to Secretary Marcy, July 24 and August 8, 1854.

were at once reported in Santo Domingo, to the alarm of
the European Consuls and to the delight of the opponents
of General Santana, who raised the cry that the United
States intended to annex the country, and that General
Santana was conspiring to betray the coloured population
into slavery.

Immediately the French and British Consuls joined
forces in opposing Cazneau's negotiations. On August
18th, Sir Robert Schomburgk advised Santana, in the
name of his Government, that Great Britain was decidedly opposed to the negotiation of any agreement between
the United States and the Dominican Republic which
might provide the United States with a coaling depot on
Dominican soil, representing the intention of the United
States as an attempt to create a permanent naval establishment within Dominican territory. The British Consul
was materially aided in his campaign by Theodore Stanley
Heneken, a British concession seeker residing in Schomburgk's house, who had become a naturalized citizen of
the Republic and had recently been elected a member of
the Dominican Congress. The official protests of Schomburgk and the intrigues of Heneken in the Congress
dampened considerably the early enthusiasm for the
American treaty manifested by Santana, since, in view
of the critical condition of the negotiations with
Haiti, the definite withdrawal of England from her
continued mediation would, the President feared, have
serious consequences. In fact, Santana believed that the
action of the British Consul afforded proof of the desire of Great Britain, once peace with Haiti had been
concluded, to force a reunion of the Republic with
Haiti.

But negotiations continued unchecked, and on September 7th, General Cazneau was able to report that all the articles of the proposed draft had been agreed upon. September 8th was set by Santana as the date for the signing of the treaty. Early that morning the British war vessel, *Devastation,* arrived in port. At seven o'clock in the morning and again at noon, the British and French Consuls obtained audiences with the President and his Cabinet. The European representatives, supported by this display of force, declared that were the Dominican Government to conclude the proposed treaty with the United States, France and England would at once withdraw their protection from the Republic, the implication being that the Emperor of Haiti would in that contingency refuse to conclude peace, and would at once commence hostilities against the Dominicans. On September 9th, Santana informed Cazneau that the opposition of the European Powers was so strong, and the threat made so powerful, that it was impossible for his Government to sign the treaty originally agreed upon were the provisions providing for the rental of Samaná retained in the document. The President suggested that the treaty be modified in such a manner as to avoid giving France and England any pretext for subjecting the Dominican Republic to Haiti, and should then in that revised form be signed "before England and France should have time to ripen their plans for endangering the existence of the Republic." [1] Finding Cazneau acquiescent, General Santana shifted the burden of responsibility from his own shoulders by retiring again to the tranquillity of El Prado, and on October 5th the modified form of the treaty [2] was signed by direction of the Vice President. Immediately thereafter, the Congress

---

[1] General William L. Cazneau to Secretary Marcy, November 23, 1854.
[2] Appendix A.

was summoned in extraordinary session to meet November 1st, to consider its ratification.

Fearful lest they had been outwitted, the British and French representatives sent for reënforcements. In response to the summons, on October 27th, Maxime Raybaud, the French Chargé d'Affaires at Port-au-Prince, arrived in Santo Domingo, having been preceded by the British war steamer, *Buzzard,* which in turn was joined by a French war vessel. Believing themselves now in a position to dictate rather than to threaten, Sir Robert Schomburgk, on October 28th, addressed a formal note to the Dominican Government. He apprised the President of the disapproval of her Majesty's Government:

"October 28, 1854.
"Señor Ministro:

"I am instructed by the Earl of Clarendon, Her Majesty's Secretary of State for Foreign Affairs, to inform the Dominican Government that Her Majesty's Government learned with surprise that notwithstanding the advice offered by the representatives of the mediating powers, which could have no other object than to promote the safety and welfare of the Dominican Republic, the President has thought proper to negotiate a treaty with the United States by which both the safety and welfare of the Republic will be greatly and immediately endangered.

"England and France have on more than one occasion interfered to uphold the independence of the Dominican Republic when that independence was threatened by a neighbouring power, and they had a right to expect that the arrangements contemplated by this treaty should not have been made without their knowledge and sanction, particularly with a power which has hitherto refused to acknowledge the independence of the Dominican Republic and the suddenness and peremptory character of whose present proceedings must cause well founded suspicions of its ulterior object.

"The undersigned avails himself, etc.

ROBT. H. SCHOMBURGK."

As the result of these menaces and the show of force practically demonstrated in the harbour of Santo Domingo before the eyes of the citizens of the capital, no quorum appeared in the Congress, and the Vice President hesitated to transmit the treaty for ratification. The British and French representatives were still not satisfied, however. M. Raybaud took it upon himself to advise members of the Senate that he had come to Santo Domingo for the purpose of blocking the conclusion of the treaty and that his Government would prevent it by force if necessary; Sir Robert Schomburgk traveled to the interior of the Island, and holding a series of meetings with the inhabitants of the northern provinces, particularly the residents of Samaná, he advised the Dominican people that ratification of the treaty implied their enslavement by the United States.

Cazneau himself seems by now to have been desirous of postponing the attempt to secure ratification until more favourable circumstances might arise, since on November 24th he notified Señor Tejera that he withdrew for the moment the treaty from the consideration of the Dominican Government.[1] But the American representative was too late, since Santana, aware of the gravity of the situation, doubtful whether effective protection from the United States would in fact be forthcoming, and intimidated, with the almost superstitious dread of European Powers which ever beset him, by the demands of the British and French Consuls, had returned to the capital

[1] General William L. Cazneau to Secretary Marcy, December 6, 1854.

and had secretly advised Sir Robert Schomburgk and Raybaud that he would satisfy their demands by submitting the treaty to the Congress with such modifications and amendments as the European agents might indicate, confident that the American Government would reject the treaty in such form. Consequently, on November 27th, the Dominican Minister for Foreign Affairs replied to General Cazneau's notification of withdrawal by stating that unless General Cazneau desired to abandon negotiations altogether, the Dominican Government possessed the legal right to submit the treaty to the Congress for its consideration. On December 3rd, the treaty was submitted to Congress with "offensive mutilations and additions inserted upon the margin of printed copies of the treaty in the handwriting of the British Consul," [1] and on December 5th, the treaty was ratified with these amendments.

The humiliation of Santana had been accomplished, and the "manifest destiny" of the United States had suffered a setback, but the French and British Consuls were not yet content. Not satisfied with the fact, as Mateo Perdomo, who was an influential member of the Congress, declared, that "no Congress existed since the day when the French squadron arrived, since its members had been threatened with force and could not act freely under such circumstances," Sir Robert Schomburgk and the French Vice-Consul, Darasse, addressed, on December 14, 1854, a joint note to Santana. They stated that before France and England could determine whether they would press for the conclusion of a long truce between the Dominican Republic and Haiti, they desired to ascertain whether the Dominican Government would formally obligate itself

---

[1] General William L. Cazneau to Secretary Marcy, December 6, 1854.

never to sell, lease, grant or alienate in any way any portion of Dominican territory, particularly that surrounding Samaná Bay, to any foreign Government; never to accept any foreign subsidy or hypothecate any portion of the national revenues; never to diminish the sovereign jurisdiction of the Republic nor to permit any foreign Government to establish any naval depot on Dominican territory; never to conclude any treaty with any foreign power for special privileges other than those already granted, "nor to negotiate a treaty with any nation which could not afford the same rights and privileges to all Dominicans regardless of their color." In response to the demand of the two Consuls for an immediate reply, Santana was obliged to afford the assurances demanded, although the assurances so conveyed were not contained in the guise of the secret convention anticipated by the French and British Governments.

2.

Cazneau's mission had terminated disastrously, and although he attempted to palliate his failure by advising the Secretary of State that the treaty with the objectionable modifications had been ratified by the Congress while it was in session as a Constitutional Convention and that consequently its ratification was null and void,[1] even Secretary Marcy realized that his Agent's usefulness was for the time being at an end. Cazneau consequently returned to the United States for a significant series of interviews with some "American capitalists," and then went back again to Santo Domingo where he had purchased in the capital's suburb, San Carlos, the "Estancia Esmeralda," a luxurious plantation. Perhaps his efforts to feather his

[1] General William L. Cazneau to Secretary Marcy, December 23, 1854.

own nest might prove more successful than his attempts to increase the dominions of the United States.

The revelation of the ambitions of the United States proved a stronger argument in persuading the Spanish Government to accord official recognition to the Republic than all of General Mella's eloquence, and at the end of the year, 1854, a Spanish Consul arrived in Santo Domingo, who busied himself, as soon as his exequatur had been granted, in registering innumerable Dominicans as Spanish subjects. Santana, whose faith in his own powers appears for the moment to have been shaken by the failure of his negotiations with the United States, raised no objections to these proceedings, perhaps in the belief that the policy pursued by the representative of Spain might be indicative of a change of heart on the part of the Spanish Government.

In any event, in the first days of the new year, 1855, he retired once more to El Prado, where he awaited the popular verdict upon the *coup d'état* which the final revision of the Constitution had in fact created. Santana had not long to wait. On March 25th, an abortive attempt at revolution in the interest of Baez, headed by Generals Pelletier and Duvergé, took place in the capital. The President, who had been advised of the conspiracy before the authorities in the capital obtained wind of it, reacted as if to a tonic, and immediately captured and executed the leaders of the plot in the eastern provinces. The chief conspirators in the capital, captured by the Vice President, were later sentenced to exile or to long imprisonment, although the Trinitario, General Francisco Sánchez, who had at the last moment participated in the conspiracy, succeeded in obtaining asylum in the British Consulate. General Cazneau, back again in the capital as a private citizen, continued to favour Secretary Marcy with the benefit of his advice:

"The revolution attempted by Baez was inspired by the British and French Consuls and when it was put down the leaders of it were at once granted refuge by the European consuls. England and France are coöperating with the negro party headed by Baez to convert the whole island into an African dependency. None of the negro leaders were executed (with the exception of five taken by President Santana in the interior), since the death sentences pronounced by the courts were modified as the result of the intervention of the European Consuls, sustained by a naval demonstration." [1]

Throughout the period of the Cazneau negotiations, the French and British representatives in Port-au-Prince had lost no opportunity in impressing the Emperor Faustin with the danger which would threaten his own domain should a slave-holding power such as the United States obtain foothold on the Island. The alarm which they occasioned His Imperial Majesty was destined to have graver consequences than the European agents had probably anticipated, and the value of the much vaunted "protection" of France and England must have been questioned by Santana, when, in the last days of November, 1855, the Haitian Emperor commenced his greatest, and what was fortunately destined to be his last, attempt to reconquer the Dominican provinces.

As soon as the danger was actively apparent, Santana moved with admirable despatch. Realizing from past experiences that it was useless to attempt to protect the smaller towns along the Haitian frontier, the President established a large force in Azua, and marched an approximately

[1] General William L. Cazneau to Secretary Marcy, June 9, 1855.

equal number of troops to Guayubín to oppose the advance of the Haitian armies, which numbered some 30,000 men. The Emperor Faustin pursued the usual plan of attack. His forces were divided into three separate armies; one to proceed through the Cibao, one through the southern portion of Barahona, and the central army, commanded by Faustin himself, to overcome the anticipated Dominican resistance at Azua. The Dominican outposts were, as had been expected, obliged to retreat, in comparatively good order, however, before the black flood that was rolling up over the country from the west. The Dominican armies, which had responded to the call to arms as one man, under the command of Santana, supported by the ablest officers of the Republic, inflicted a decisive defeat upon the southern armies of the Emperor at Santomé on December 22, 1855. On the same day, the northern armies of the Haitians were defeated even more decisively at Cambronal. These two preliminary victories were followed up by others, and by the end of January the Haitian defeat had become complete. Loss of life on both sides was great, but the Haitians' losses were far in excess of those which they had inflicted upon the Dominicans.

The last Haitian refugees straggled across the frontier to Ounaminthe on January 27th, where they were granted the recompense of an inspiring address from the Emperor Faustin, who, declaring that the invasion had been undertaken with the assurance that it would be supported by the great majority of the Dominicans, inveighed against Dominican ingratitude in bitter terms. Faustin concluded his proclamation with the following words, which it may be hoped was sufficient reward for the Haitian soldiers, who had been called to arms at the moment when their crops were being harvested and who were consequently returning to a year of famine: "Fly back to your homes with your heads raised high, since you have accomplished your duty."

As soon as Santana had assured himself of the reëstablishment of order throughout the frontier provinces, he returned on March 6th to the capital at the head of his victorious army, receiving a welcome from the citizens of the capital, which from its sincerity must have proved more grateful than the artificial acclamations which the Liberator had so often concerted for himself in the past.

3.

The exigencies of the local political situation and his military duties as commander of the Dominican army in the war with Haiti had not caused Santana to overlook the international problems which confronted his administration, nor had his momentary acquiescence in the demands of the European Consuls in the autumn of 1854 caused the President to abandon final hope of an arrangement with the United States. In May of the following spring, the American Commercial Agent was able to report that Santana had expressed a desire to renew negotiations:

"In a recent interview with President Santana, he expressed the hope that the negotiations for a treaty with the United States would still be pending. The United States can have all they desire here. The Spanish treaty has been concluded. I have not yet got a copy. The principal item is 'that they are not to permit strangers to hold any part of this territory'." [1]

The encouraging reports from Mr. Elliott and the confidential suggestions with which General Cazneau contin-

[1] Mr. Jonathan Elliott to Secretary Marcy, May 5, 1855.

A RIVER OF THE CIBAO

ued to deluge Secretary Marcy, brought a new ray of hope to the Washington Administration's otherwise darkening horizon. But the Secretary of State was well aware that the Senate, which was then wholly under the domination of the Southern States, would never acquiesce in the modifications inserted in the Treaty of 1854 by the Dominican Congress at the behest of the British Consul. Did not the amendment to Article 3 specifically provide that all Dominican citizens in the United States, regardless of their colour, were to be accorded treatment similar to that enjoyed by American citizens? Mr. Elliott was therefore enjoined to insist upon the omission of any such modification as this of the original draft, since "the safety and peace of the Southern States require this exclusion." [1] Should the Dominican Government concede these alterations, the American Government would be eager to conclude negotiations.

No sooner had negotiations once more been taken up, and the agreement of the Dominican Government been obtained to Secretary Marcy's stipulations, than the opposition of the European Powers again made itself felt:

"As this Government agreed that they would recede from their proposed amendments to the treaty, I made overtures to them on the 3rd of December to negotiate the same. At this time a sudden invasion of the Haitians stopped all the business of the Government. I have this day received word from President Santana, who has been all the time with the army, that he will be here in a few days, when the treaty shall be immediately attended to and concluded as soon as possible. . . . The treaty will pass substantially the same as that proposed by William L. Cazneau. They desire to make a separate convention regarding

[1] William L. Marcy, Secretary of State, to Jonathan Elliott, American Commercial Agent in Santo Domingo, October 9, 1855.

Samaná when the country is more tranquil. The Haitians publicly accuse Santana of wishing to give this Island to the Americans. Also Mr. Segovia, Chargé d'Affaires and Consul General of Spain, has arrived to join English and French Consuls in opposition to our having a naval station here." [1]

But Santana's position was for the moment far more securely entrenched than it had been two years before. The resplendent victories of the Dominicans over their Haitian adversaries, accomplished by their own unaided efforts, had dispelled for the time being all further fear of attack from Faustin. The indifference of France and England during the struggle which the Dominicans had fought for existence, had proved the vanity of the promises of protection of the two European Powers, and had convinced Santana that either France was conniving at his own overthrow by Haitian arms in order to place Baez in the Presidency, or else that the two Powers had secretly agreed to the extension of Haitian sovereignty once again over the Dominican Provinces. Finally, Santana's personal prestige in the Republic was greater than ever. The Liberator had once more earned his right to his title.

Consequently, the protests of the British and French Consuls, supported as they now were by their Spanish colleague, fell upon deaf ears, and on March 11, 1856, Don Tomás Bobadilla and Don Jacinto de Castro were instructed by the President to sign the new version of the Treaty of Peace, Commerce, Navigation and Extradition between the United States and the Dominican Republic proffered them by the American Commercial Agent. The Treaty was at once ratified, on March 27th, by the Senado Consultor.

[1] Mr. Jonathan Elliott to Secretary Marcy, January 16, 1856.

While appreciating to its full extent the temporary strength of his position, General Santana was still timorous of entering into any arrangement regarding Samaná, and advised the American Agent that a separate agreement providing for the rental of a coaling depot in the Bay would be entered into by his Government in the near future. Mr. Elliott reported that the increasing hostility of the British, French and Spanish Consuls had prevented the President from ceding the United States the desired depot in the Treaty of Peace and Commerce:

"The Consuls of Spain, England and France have made strong opposition to our having any treaty whatever with this Republic. The treaty as it now reads is substantially the same as that signed the 5th of October, 1854. It does not express all that was desired but is the best that I could make under the circumstances at the present time." [1]

All memories of past discord between the European Powers, as soon as the treaty with the United States had been ratified by the Dominican Congress, were merged in an outburst of hostility against the American Government, increased no doubt by resentment at the success with which the Dominicans had been enabled to repel unaided the attack from Haiti, and the realization that promises of British or French protection would not in the future be rated very highly. The American treaty, simple as its provisions appeared to be, was believed to have secret clauses incorporated in it, and caused bitter attacks to be made upon the policy of the United States in the public press of England, France and Spain, particularly in that of their West Indian possessions. The success of the Dominicans in maintaining their independence was termed "an

[1] Mr. Jonathan Elliott to Secretary Marcy, March 22, 1856.

attempt at revolution," and the Americans were charged with having rendered the Dominican Government the assistance necessary in carrying this "revolution" to a successful termination. An editorial published in the *Daily Advertiser* of Kingston, Jamaica, is sufficiently indicative:

"The Dominicans, aided by our revolutionizing neighbors, the Americans, have given battle to the Emperor Soulouque; His Imperial Majesty had to save himself by flight and there was the greatest disorder throughout the Island. Despatches were immediately sent off to the commodore on this station, which was the occasion of the recent visit of the French man-of-war, *L'Acheron,* and her immediate departure was for the protection of English and French interests in that place . . . It is well known that the Americans some time ago proffered their aid to the Dominicans and not long since it was freely expressed in the American papers that a naval force was to leave for Samaná, which arrived there . . . The effect of this revolution, if the Americans are really engaged in it, will no doubt terminate seriously. England and France will not tamely allow such a violent proceeding, as they are both as greatly interested in the balance of territorial possession in the New World as they are in the balance of power in the Old. The Monroe Doctrine, which the Americans have been the first to start, will be carried out on this—for if they are allowed to occupy Haiti they will most surely concentrate an immense body of troops there and eventually descend upon Cuba, and if America holds Cuba and Santo Domingo, in the event of a war with England, of what use would be Jamaica to the Parent Country. The question is fraught with importance and is another link in the chain that is to draw England, France and America into a bloody war." [1]

[1] DAILY ADVERTISER of Kingston, Jamaica, Tuesday, April 10, 1856.

The terrifying rumour that the United States was already gazing with covetous eyes upon Cuba and Puerto Rico, in addition to the reported American attempt to secure the annexation of the Dominican Republic, had been sufficient to cause the Spanish Government to modify its original attitude of aloofness towards its former colony, and resulted in the negotiation in 1855 of a commercial treaty between the two countries. A new policy was determined upon, and to carry it out, that astonishing individual, Don Antonio Maria Segovia, was sent to Santo Domingo as the Consul General of Spain.

Segovia, whose prior career in the Spanish Consular Service and modicum of note as a "littérateur" had puffed him with an altogether overweening sense of the importance of his new rôle, had been led to believe by the Spanish Minister of State that the article in the new treaty with Spain, whereby the Spanish Sovereign renounced all her former rights in the former colony and specifically recognized the independence of the Republic, would prove so gratifying to the Dominicans that Santana would no longer be tempted to heed the siren voices of the American Agents.

The Spanish Consul was the more chagrined consequently when, upon his arrival, Santana, who was still engaged in the pacification of the frontier provinces, gave no indication of his appreciation of the fact that so important an emissary as Segovia had arrived in Santo Domingo. The President ignored the Spanish Consul's existence, and Segovia was forced to present his credentials to the Vice President. But the sense of slight was rapidly changed to one of injury when Santana, whom Segovia had been charged to invest with the Grand Cross of Isabel la Católica, not only failed to hasten to the capital to receive the decoration, but actually ordered General Regla Mota, the Vice President, to receive it in his stead.

The self-conceit of the Spaniard had received already a severe blow. But when he was apprised, after the President's eventual return to Santo Domingo, that a treaty with the United States had actually been concluded, his indignation had no bounds. The signal ingratitude of the President, after receiving such proofs of the Spanish Government's benevolence—Segovia had carefully overlooked the earlier twelve years of Spain's contemptuous neglect—had by now fully convinced the Spanish Consul that Santana was no fit person to exercise the Presidency.

Casting about for a remedy, Segovia had no need to wait long for suggestions. The partisans of Baez, who one by one had returned to the capital, had lost no opportunity of making evident their profound affection for Spain. They had dined the Spanish Agent, had presented him with scrolls bearing long lists of the names of the Spanish sympathizers, had caused crowds to gather before the Spanish Consulate to cheer the appearance of Spain's worthy representative, and had emphasized the importance of each act of indifference on the part of Santana. Baez, they pointed out, had in his last public address made overwhelmingly plain how different his feeling was towards Spain—how desirous of being guided by the Spanish Government. What a change in the situation there would be, should the Spanish Government favour the return of Baez to the Presidency!

Segovia lost no time in taking the hint. The provisions of Article VII of the treaty between the Republic and Spain afforded an excellent opportunity for accomplishing his purposes. This article provided that Spaniards residing in the Dominican Republic who had adopted Dominican nationality, could recover their former nationality, as could their adult children, during the year subsequent to the ratification of the treaty; those who had been residing without the Republic could recover their Spanish nationality during the two years following. Segovia proceeded to open the registers of "matriculation" in his Consulate, registering not only such individuals as were included within the elastic provisions of the seventh article of the Spanish Treaty, but likewise any other individual able to pay the fee of two dollars demanded for the privilege of obtaining Spanish citizenship.

The opponents of the Government at once availed themselves of the opportunity of obtaining protection from the Spanish Consul so that they might the more freely oppose Santana. The President, determined as he had always proved himself to be in matters of internal policy, once more made evident his inborn dread of open rupture with any European Power, and limited his protests against Segovia's activities to notes addressed to Segovia by his Minister for Foreign Affairs, or to representations to the Spanish Government through his diplomatic agent in Madrid. Mr. Elliott's indignation at the proceedings was swelling throughout the summer:

"A difficulty arose as to the meaning of Article VII of the Spanish treaty, and it was agreed to await the decision from Spain, but all at once the Spanish war steamer *Blasco de Garay* and bark of war *Gravina*, anchored off this port and the Spanish Consul begins issuing certificates of citizenship to all who chose to ask them and in this way will make a large number of Dominicans, mostly blacks, Spaniards, as they are glad to get out of military service. The Haitians can then easily enter . . . The Spanish Consul did all he could to stop our making a treaty and it is

very evident that this calamity has fallen on this Republic
by reason of that treaty. His object is to crush the Republic
and have it handed to the Haitians who do not permit foreigners to hold property or do business in their own name."

＊ ＊ ＊

"Señor Antonio Maria Segovia, Spanish Chargé
d'Affaires, from the very day of his arrival, began speaking
to all the members of the Dominican Government concerning the injury that the ratification of the American
treaty would cause to Spain and urged the Executive to
reject it. He then requested delay in the negotiation of the
treaty to permit him to go to Port-au-Prince to notify the
Emperor Soulouque to vacate that portion of the Dominican territory occupied by Haitians, offering to the Dominican Government a Spanish loan and to create the
means of forming a purely Spanish immigration, but
President Santana would not listen to it. After the signing
of the treaty, he urged the Dominican Government to
withdraw it or to refuse to ratify it and as a means of
accomplishing that he proposed a Spanish protectorate, a
quantity of troops and a good navy and the assumption of
responsibility by Spain for the attitude of the Dominican
Government towards the United States. He then declared
to Santana that the Spanish Government would far prefer
securing Dominican territory for the Haitians than for it
to be under American influence. The Spanish Chargé
d'Affaires is now endeavoring to undermine the Republic by
granting Spanish citizenship to individuals in the Dominican Republic, not only those born after Spain abandoned
the territory but also to Dutch, American, and French who
have become naturalized Dominicans. He has sent agents
throughout the country assuring people that their attain-
ing Spanish nationality will secure them from danger and
freedom from military service, that gold and silver from
Spain will abound in place of Dominican paper money by

a change of sovereignty and that by such change they can be free of the despotism of Santana and the members of his Government of white persons. The result of these reports is that the adherents of the Government are constantly decreasing and that the Government itself is now hardly strong enough to defeat the plans of revolution of Baez, who has openly declared his intention of having a colored government. The Spanish Government has fostered a formal plan to destroy the Dominican Republic. The Spanish Chargé d'Affaires obliged the Dominican Government to hoist the Spanish flag on July 17th, and salute the Spanish vessels of war in the port, and then forced them to repeat the salute and obliged the Secretary for Foreign Relations personally to apologize to him and to his officers 'for not treating Spain with more respect.' He is also about to establish a newspaper here to be called *Isabel Segunda,* for the purpose of advocating the re-assumption of Spanish sovereignty. Certain destruction awaits this Republic if the United States do not immediately and energetically interfere, as this Government are paying very high prices and spending all their means to keep their troops under arms. . . . The United States can make any convention that they desire with this Government. We can have naval stations where we choose on our own terms and in case of necessity depend on assistance from these people—if we only take some interest in them." [1]

The lack in the recently negotiated treaty of the provision—the all-important provision in Secretary Marcy's eyes —for the lease of the Samaná territory, had caused the American Government to grow decidedly lukewarm towards the Dominicans. Not even the urgent appeals of his Commercial Agent could persuade the Secretary of State "to take some interest in them," and he regarded the

[1] Mr. Jonathan Elliott to Secretary Marcy, July 5 and 19, 1856, respectively.

subsequent rejection of the Dominican treaty by the American Senate with complete indifference. The ratification of a mere commercial treaty was not likely to further the realization of the "manifest destiny" of the United States.

Santana, who had continued to countenance meekly the open opposition of the Spanish Consul and the activities of the Baecistas which the latter fostered, unconvinced by the shrewder of his counsellors who, like Bobadilla, were certain that the jealousies between the foreign Powers would render impossible any determined assault by a European nation upon the sovereignty of the Republic, at the first intimation of the withdrawal of American support determined to abandon the struggle, trusting that his countrymen would soon insist upon his recall to power. By the spring of 1856, he had decided to resort to the same manœuvre which had been successful once before. Retiring to El Prado, he announced his decision to resign the Presidency, and forced the Senado Consultor, on May 26th, to accept his resignation, leaving the Vice President, General Regla Mota, to assume the Presidency in accordance with the Constitution then in force.

4.

General Regla Mota, suddenly called upon to assume the Presidency in moments far more critical than those in which he had hitherto, during the temporary absences of Santana, been obliged to direct the administration, at first attempted to maintain a firm control of affairs. The weakness of his character and his lack of popular support rendered his task hopeless.

In the program of administration which he announced to the Senate, General Regla Mota attempted to temper the hostility of the Spanish representative by an obsequious reference to the desire of his administration to maintain the most friendly relations with the Spanish Government. But Segovia was not to be satisfied with any such empty professions of friendship. Surrounded by the opponents of the Government, who were able with impunity to continue their attacks upon the administration in the sheet, *El Eco Del Pueblo,* directed by Don Manuel Maria Gautier, Segovia laid his plans for the immediate return to power of Buenaventura Baez, whom he had visited in St. Thomas and from whom he had obtained satisfactory assurances that were Baez to become President, the policy of the Dominican Government might readily be dictated from Madrid.

Segovia now threw aside all pretense of conforming to the customary rules of diplomacy. Announcing publicly that Buenaventura Baez was "the sole man capable of restoring tranquillity and of governing the Republic in peace and prosperity," he obtained the coöperation of the British and French Consuls, who were nothing loath, in forcing General Regla Mota to propose to Santana that he effect a reconciliation with Baez and agree to the latter's return to the country:

"Yesterday, Santana's reply was received stating that if the Government thought the return of Baez was really indispensable to the country and that his supposed influence would not only reconcile the local disturbances but also cause the Spanish Consul to cease his hostile intentions towards his unhappy and unprotected country, he would agree to the return of Mr. Baez; that whilst yielding to the determination of the Spanish Consul, to whom he attributes the exigent proposal, he tendered his resignation as commander-in-chief of the Dominican army. His resignation was read in the Senate and it created a most extraordinary sensation as it is interpreted to show how much he disapproves of the step. Santana said, after reading the official despatch received from this Government, 'This is what I am reduced to after having signed the American Treaty, and what have I gained with the friendship of the United States? Not even a vessel of war to investigate matters, and Baez once here, adieu to all American projects or conventions.' The Vice President and his brother, General Felipe Alfau, who is a member of the Senate, told me . . . 'We are resolved not to have any further engagements with the United States unless they are accompanied by means of defense . . . The Dominicans know their duty as a nation, but are not sufficiently strong to repel Spain whose Consul is the cause of our having written for the treaty. . . . If the United States Government intends securing its interests in this country, there is no time to be lost as it is a common report that the Spanish Government will land an armed force here to meet the Americans." [1]

Declaring that a war between the United States and Spain was inevitable in the near future, and that it would better suit Spain to meet the Americans in the Dominican Republic as the field of battle rather than in Cuba,[2] Segovia obliged Regla Mota to summon the Electoral Colleges to meet September 22nd, to fill the vacancy existing in the Vice Presidency and to send at the same time an invitation to Baez, who was still in St. Thomas, requesting him to return immediately to the Republic. Baez was to return to the Presidency through the Vice Presidency:

"A letter was written to Mr. Baez, who is now in St. Thomas and has been there since 1852 awaiting a favor-

[1] Mr. Jacob Pereira, Acting Commercial Agent, to Secretary Marcy, August 7, 1856.
[2] Mr. Jacob Pereira to Secretary Marcy, August 7, 1856.

able opportunity to return here, acquainting him with the fact that Santana was disposed to reconcile matters with him provided he would agree to return to the country as a private citizen, respect its laws, and promise not to put himself at the head of any party . . . As the Spanish Consul has all along evinced a deep interest in imposing Mr. Baez on the country, there is no doubt in my opinion that Mr. Baez will readily submit to the most humiliating conditions, particularly as he is aware that the Spanish Consul has already paved the way for him to reach the Presidency —this naturally will be effected by means of a revolution to overthrow the present administration, as the Spanish Consul is determined to have Baez at the head of affairs, (he is a mortal hater of Americans), that will mar the progress of American projects until he can destroy effectually the Dominican nationality." [1]

The sole hope of General Regla Mota and the supporters of Santana lay in some effective demonstration of sympathy by the Government of the United States. On July 18th, Segovia, accompanied by the British and French Consuls, obtained a secret interview with the President and his Cabinet, in the course of which they demanded the withdrawal of the treaty with the United States, stating that their countries "would never permit the people of the United States to have a foothold in the Dominican Republic," and on the following day, Perdomo, the Secretary of Foreign Affairs, was obliged to sign a letter drafted by Segovia himself, addressed to the American Secretary of State, requesting the withdrawal of the treaty with the United States from further consideration.

As a last resort the President requested the American Commercial Agent, Mr. Elliott, to go in person to Wash-

[1] Mr. Jacob Pereira to Secretary Marcy, August 14, 1856.

ington to urge upon the American Government the necessity of affording the Dominican Government some support should they desire to maintain their treaty in force. Mr. Elliott was authorized to offer to the American Government not only any location in the Bay of Samaná which the United States might desire for a naval depot, but any other commercial advantages they might require, "on the condition that the United States will guard the Dominican Government against any of the consequences thereof." [1] On August 2d, Mr. Elliott left for Washington, but he proved unable again to interest President Pierce or Secretary Marcy, nor was he able to induce them to consent to any effective action in compliance with the pleas of the Dominican Government.

Deprived of all hope of the American support upon which they had once confidently counted, Regla Mota and Santana were helplessly obliged to give in to the force of the circumstances which Segovia had created. The return of Buenaventura Baez to the Republic was preceded by the return of the swarm of his office-seeking brothers, cousins, and other relatives, to whom amnesty had reluctantly been granted by the Government at Segovia's behest. Immediately after his return, in accordance with the plans elaborated by the Spanish Consul, Baez was elected Vice President of the Republic. On October 6th, Baez, attended by the President, General Regla Mota, and the sole remaining member of Regla Mota's Cabinet, took the oath of office before the Senate, asserting that now that he was "named to that high office by the omnipotent will of the people" he found himself too overcome by his feelings of gratitude to be able to express them in words.

The time was now ripe for the last step. Consequently,

[1] Mr. Jonathan Elliott to Secretary Marcy, September 10, 1856.

General Regla Mota, who had long since abandoned hope of withstanding the plans of the Spanish Consul, resigned the Presidency on October 8th, leaving Baez once more in the Presidential chair.

Segovia had been signally successful in obtaining as President of the Republic a man of whose docility he could be certain. But his modesty was commendable. Greeted after the inauguration of Baez as President by a cheering throng of the President's partisans, Segovia protested that the merit for this accomplishment was not his alone, but should in fact be shared by all; and that "his small merit in having availed himself of favorable circumstances did not deserve such high praise" since he had only "carried out the desires and instructions of his Queen in working for the liberty of the Dominican people."

He soon found a new field for his talents by increasing the already general unpopularity of the American Government in the Republic. Segovia, who had already distinguished himself upon various occasions by encouraging street crowds to gather before the American Consulate and threaten that they would tear down the American flag and destroy the American coat of arms, now incited public attacks on all Dominicans who had favoured the negotiation of the American treaty. Don Domingo de la Rocha, the father-in-law of Mr. Elliott, and one of the first Senators to vote for the American treaty, was among those singled out for assault, and had it not been for the opportune assistance offered by the Captain of the British war vessel *Tartar*, Mr. Pereira, the Acting Commercial Agent of the United States, and his family, would probably likewise have fallen victims to the rabble incited by Segovia.[1] Having dictated the President's inaugural ad-

---

[1] Mr. Jacob Pereira to Secretary Marcy, November 22, 1856.

dress, which declared that Baez would ever be vigilant to prevent the ambitions of any foreign nation from impairing the sovereignty and independence of the Dominican Republic, Segovia soon spread the rumour that the American Government was sending vessels of war to Santo Domingo to force upon the Dominican Government the exchange of ratifications of the American treaty. Whether Baez believed the report, or whether he more probably desired to further Segovia's policy of increasing hostility against the United States, he in fact gave orders early in November for the fortification of the capital and even mobilized troops in Samaná to ward off the imaginary attack.

The antipathy of the Baez administration to everything American was made evident in many ways. Mr. Pereira reported to Secretary Marcy that he had been invited by the President to an official dinner, served at five o'clock in the afternoon, at which all the members of the diplomatic corps were present.[1] At the close of the interminable function, through which the guests had sweltered, Baez proposed the healths of the Emperor of France, Queen Victoria, and Queen Isabel II, but the health of the President of the United States was ostentatiously omitted; and Mr. Pereira's indignation was increased by the reported remark of General Baez that no power could induce him to drink the health of the "President of the Filibusters." The autumn of 1856 must have been a disagreeable time for American citizens, and in particular for the American Consul.

"On October 30th, St. Andrew's Day, whilst the people were carrying on the old Spanish custom of pitching eggs about the town, a gang of the matriculated or Spanish

[1] Mr. Jacob Pereira to Secretary Marcy, November 22, 1856.

party determined to avail themselves of that occasion to pitch eggs filled with some fetid substance against the sign and eagle attached to this agency." [1]

Apparently the incident of the "pitching of the eggs filled with some fetid substance" caused even the President to realize that it was time to call a halt, since on November 6th, he addressed a proclamation to his fellow-citizens requesting them to cease "once for all, all individual manifestations, and above all, offensive cries, which defame a cultured people and in which our adversaries take delight." The President likewise took occasion to assure the people that his Government had taken efficacious measures to protect the country against any attacks, domestic or foreign, and that were it necessary, they might be well assured that they could count upon the support of "friendly allies."

Segovia had placed Baez in the Presidency, and had created such general hostility to the United States that he feared no longer the possibility of a resumption of negotiations with the American Government. It was now time to proceed with the final elimination of Santana. At the suggestion of the Spanish Consul, the President lost no time in filling all the public offices with members of his own innumerable family, and failing them, with his supporters, and in forcing the resignation from the Senado Consultor of such Senators as had been identified in the past with the Liberator. As soon as a properly submissive Senate had been organized, heeding the advice proffered by Segovia and reiterated by *El Eco Del Pueblo,* Baez came to the conclusion that the institution of the Vice Presidency provided an unnecessary complication, and deliberately ignoring the provisions of the Constitution,

[1] Mr. Jacob Pereira to Secretary Marcy, November 22, 1856.

refused to proclaim General Juan Esteban Aybar, elected
to fill the vacancy caused by Baez's own succession to the
Presidency, Vice President of the Republic. There was
now little doubt that Segovia, through Baez, could govern
the Republic as he saw fit. A new newspaper, appropri-
ately entitled *La Acusación*, had been founded in the capital for the sole purpose of attacking Santana. The first
number, published November 20, 1856, made plain the
policy of the sheet:

"It is now time to hasten the disappearance from the
earth, as he has already disappeared from the political
scene, of the Monster who has openly declared himself the
enemy of humanity and with whom the Nation never can
again reconcile itself. Let the Government know, from
today on, that it has no great political program to settle;
that it has no important passions which it must satisfy, but
rather that it is under the obligation of punishing many
crimes, of avenging the blood of many martyrs slain by the
bestial caprice of a despot who by his own acts has placed
himself without the law." [1]

A week later, the scope of Segovia's program was somewhat enlarged by the call, published in *La Acusación*, to
all citizens of the capital to assemble to discuss the following two questions:

"Is it in the interest of the Dominican Republic to invoke
the protection of Spain, France and England in the event
that it is threatened by some aggression?

"Is the continuance of General Santana in the country
dangerous to the security of the State?" [2]

---

[1] *La Acusación* of November 20, 1856, published in Santo Domingo: Editor,
Juan E. Jiménez.
[2] *La Acusación* of November 27, 1856.

Needless to state, when the suggested mass meeting had assembled, the two theoretical questions propounded by Segovia met with a unanimous affirmative.

The Senate did not delay long in seeing from which quarter the wind blew. Accepting first of all the resignation of Santana as commander-in-chief of the Dominican armies, which it had earlier refused to accept, it proceeded on December 1, 1856, to cancel the lease for fifty years of the Island of Saona granted General Santana on May 26, 1856, in recognition of his public services. Few doubted the impending fate of Santana. Mr. Pereira, himself of Dominican origin, feared the worst:

"There is little doubt . . . of the horrid end that good man will have in this unhappy country if he allows himself to be impeached. Santana is yet on his farm, where he awaits quietly the result of his forced reconciliation with President Baez . . . Let me implore you, Sir, not to abandon our people. All ask for protection from the United States and I cannot doubt but that you will send here a couple of vessels of war merely to look on and see that no injustice is committed against our citizens or their property." [1]

The Senate finally, notwithstanding the insistence of Don Pedro Tomás Garrido and Don Carlos Baez, Senators from Santo Domingo and La Vega, that Santana be impeached, limited itself to passing a resolution granting Baez full powers to deal with Santana as he saw fit. The outbreak of slight disturbances in Neiba, speedily put down, which it was claimed, without the shadow of proof, Santana had directly incited, gave the President the opportunity he sought. He ordered General José Maria Cabral to proceed with a body of troops to El Prado, and Santana

[1] Mr. Jacob Pereira to Secretary Marcy, November 29, 1856.

was arrested and brought to the capital on January 8th. At midnight on the 11th of January, 1857, the Liberator was placed upon the Dominican schooner *Ozama,* and after being later transferred, through the influence of the French Consul, to the French Frigate *Iphigénie,* finally succeeded in reaching St. Thomas, the refuge of so many Dominican exiles.

5.

Amazingly enough, the vengeance which Segovia had succeeded in inflicting upon Santana was directly responsible for his own downfall. The Dominican Agent in Madrid, carrying out the instructions sent him prior to Baez's inauguration, had been pressing for some months upon the Spanish Government the necessity of reaching an agreement restricting the interpretation to be given to the notorious Article VII of the Spanish Treaty, through which Segovia had been able to build up "a bastard state within Dominican territory." The Spanish Cabinet, desirous of meeting, as it thought, the wishes of the Dominican Government, and apprised as well by intimations from France and England that the Spanish Consul in Santo Domingo had been interpreting the treaty in such a manner as to give offense to the French and British Consuls, determined to disavow the actions of Segovia, and suddenly recalled him. Baez was thrown into utter consternation. Were his strongest supporter, the man who had brought him to the Presidency, to be shorn of influence, how could he maintain his own position? Dismissing immediately the Dominican Chargé d'Affaires in Madrid, he reached the extraordinary decision of appointing the recalled Spanish Envoy as his own agent at the Spanish Court, to request the Spanish Government to agree that the treaty be given the exact interpretation

against which the Dominican Government had been protesting, and at the same time he notified the Government at
Madrid that far from disapproving the actions of Segovia,
the Dominican Government viewed his removal from the
Consulate with the deepest regret. Baez's efforts proved to
be vain, however, since the Spanish Minister of State, the
Marqués de Pidal, refused either to reappoint Segovia as
Spanish Consul or to receive him as Agent of the Dominican Government, and Baez was constrained to limit himself to employing Segovia as his secret agent in fruitless
negotiations with the Government of Haiti.

The loss of Segovia forced Baez to the realization that
to remain in power he must from now on depend solely
upon his own resources. To obtain large quantities of ready
money became at once a prime necessity.

At the time of Baez's return to the Presidency the
financial situation of the Government was by no means
disastrous. There was comparatively little paper in circulation. The chief cause for complaint in commercial circles
lay in the fact that the greater demand for paper at the
time of the annual harvesting of the tobacco crop in the
Cibao caused a considerable fluctuation in its exchange
value, resulting in the increasing introduction into the
northern provinces of large quantities of foreign gold and
silver, with which foreign business houses preferred to pay
their obligations. This condition, which might readily have
been remedied had the Government sincerely desired to
find a solution of the problem, provided Baez with an
excellent pretext for obtaining the quantity of ready
money which he required, and likewise with the opportunity to strike at the commercial leaders of the Cibao
who were hostile to his administration. In a message to
the Senate on April 13th, the President called attention to

the constant fluctuation in the value of the national paper prior to the harvesting of the northern tobacco crops, and expressed the opinion that this evil should be remedied by authorizing the national Government to issue larger quantities of paper money, which it was alleged could be retired from circulation as soon as the tobacco crop had been harvested, his recommendation being based upon the conclusion that this operation would maintain the national paper at a stable rate of exchange.

In accordance with these recommendations, the President was authorized by the Senate, on April 20th, to issue immediately $6,000,000 of paper money, and by a resolution of May 2nd the powers of the President were so increased that Baez was enabled to issue altogether $18,000,000.

As soon as the printing-presses had manufactured sufficient quantities of paper money, the leading members of the Baecista "ring," as well as the British, French and Spanish Consuls, were permitted to obtain large amounts at a figure far below the nominal rate of exchange, and like the President himself, sent agents throughout the country to buy up the tobacco or other crops in exchange for the new paper; the produce so purchased was then resold to Europe and paid for in foreign gold. The "ring" made money, but panic set in before more than a small percentage of the quantities of paper money amassed had been unloaded. The "papeleta" or paper dollar shot down in value. While the national currency circulated at sixty or seventy "papeletas" to one silver dollar when Baez returned to power, the new paper depreciated so rapidly that the exchange rate soon became 2,000 to one, and ultimately reached 3,000 to one.

The planters of the Cibao, and in fact all the leading

business men of the Republic, with the exception of those to whom the favours of the President had been granted, were immediately faced with ruin. The President attempted to quiet the situation by calling to a conference some of the leading residents of the Cibao, but the subterfuge proved singularly unsuccessful. Indignation meetings were held, and on July 7th, the political and military leaders in the Cibao provinces proclaimed themselves in open rebellion against the Government. On that night, in the historic fort of San Luis in Santiago, a series of resolutions were drawn up disavowing the authority of the Government in Santo Domingo, and declaring that Baez had usurped the Presidency, since the Constitution of 1854 had stipulated that a period of six years must elapse before a citizen could be re-elected as President of the Republic, and that as Baez's first term had only expired on February 27, 1853, he could not have been constitutionally re-elected before 1859.

The leaders of the revolt, Don Benigno Filomeno de Rojas and Generals José Desiderio Valverde and Domingo Mallol, at once formed a Provisional Government. General Valverde was selected as its President, with de Rojas as Vice President, and these were assisted in the administration by the most prominent leaders of the north, including Don Ulises F. Espaillat, Don Pedro Francisco Bonó, and Don Antonio Hernandez. The revolt spread like wildfire throughout the Republic, notwithstanding the announcement by Baez, calculated to impede revolutionary contagion, on July 10th, that the revolution was the work of only a few turbulent spirits and was opposed by the country at large. Government troops sent from the capital by Baez to quell the revolution soon ascertained the contrary, since they were defeated after a few preliminary skirmishes, and by the end of July the Provisional Government had gained the support of the entire Republic with the exception of Santo Domingo and Samaná.

To a decree of the Provisional Government issued July 26th, declaring the impeachment of Baez on the ground that he had usurped the Executive Power in open violation of the Constitution, the Senate in the capital replied on July 30th by a grant to the President of $50,000 "in payment for damages occasioned his property during the Governments of Santana." Already, by the first of August, the capital was surrounded by revolutionary troops whose command the Provisional Government had entrusted to General Juan Luís Franco Bidó. The capitulation demanded by the revolutionary general was contemptuously rejected by Baez, who ordered repeated attempts made to dislodge the besieging forces from around the walls of the city. It is possible that the revolutionists, discouraged by Baez's success in maintaining himself in the capital, and the Baez partisans who had reason to appreciate the general unpopularity of the administration, might have reached during the month of August some agreement providing for the resignation of the President and the retention by the members of the Government of their loot, had the situation not suddenly radically changed.

General Santana, who had been awaiting the course of developments in St. Thomas, and who had at first been somewhat dismayed by the charges levelled in the revolutionary manifesto of the Santiago Government against his own conduct in his various administrations, finally determined to return to the Republic together with General Regla Mota and the others of his closest followers who had been sharing his exile. Reaching Santiago towards the end of August, he at once petitioned the Provisional Government to appoint him commander-in-chief of the forces which were attempting to overthrow the Government of his detested adversary. The Provisional Government, while it had no illusions concerning the danger which might result from placing Santana in such a strategic position, was, however, so disheartened by the ill success of its armies in reducing the capital, and appreciated so fully the great popularity which Santana enjoyed among the military element in the Republic, that it at length gave in, and permitted Santana on the 18th of September to take over from General Franco Bidó the command of the besieging forces.

The advent of Santana spurred the members of Baez's Government on to still more determined resistance. The certainty that surrender would imply their own imprisonment or death at the hands of the Liberator added an incentive to their defense of the capital. Moreover, the British, French and Spanish Consuls, who envisaged the prospect, should Baez fall, of losing all hope of enriching themselves through the redemption of the paper money of which they still had masses in their possession, now became more active in their support of Baez, and actually procured from the French and Spanish Governments officers to assist in the defense of the city, and to direct the operations of the Government's artillery.[1]

For months the siege continued. By the end of the year, 1857, famine had broken out in Santo Domingo, where the greatest suffering existed for lack of food, since, although Baez could from time to time obtain provisions by sea, all roads leading into the city were shut off. Desertion from the besieged forces was constant. By the beginning of December, the American Commercial Agent reported that

[1] Mr. Jonathan Elliott to Secretary Cass, April 21, 1858.

the number of men supporting Baez in the capital had dwindled to 400, while the number of the forces sustaining the siege totalled at least 6,000.[1]

Throughout the winter of 1858, the situation remained approximately the same, with little change beyond the gradual reduction of the number of the defenders of the capital, and the success of the Provisional Government in crushing the last vestiges of Baez's support in Samaná. By devious financial operations, in the course of which Baez mortgaged properties of the Government, including even the Government Palace, the President was enabled to obtain vessels from neighbouring islands with which he attempted unsuccessfully to blockade Puerto Plata and other strongholds of the revolutionaries.

In the meantime, the Provisional Government, while concentrating its efforts upon the attempt to obtain the surrender of the capital, had not been idle along other lines. A Constitutional Convention, assembled in Moca on December 7th, had agreed upon a new Constitution, satisfactory to the Cibao in that it declared the future capital of the Republic to be the City of Santiago, which established both universal suffrage and direct elections. The Moca Constitution, which was signed February 19, 1858, was drafted along exceedingly liberal lines and was doubtless in no small part inspired by the political theories of one of the leading men in the history of the Republic, Ulises F. Espaillat, who had long been preaching progressive doctrines of government. A transitory provision of the Constitution entrusted the selection of the first President and Vice President under the new Constitution to the Constitutional Convention itself, and General Valverde and Don Benigno Francisco de Rojas were confirmed in

[1] Mr. Jonathan Elliott to Secretary Cass, November 23, 1857.

the offices which they already held, taking the oath of office on the 1st of March, 1858.

The beginning of the summer months disclosed a desperate state of affairs in the capital. Pestilence had broken out, and the nights were hideous with the lament of the mourners and the creaking of the wheels of the death-carts. Famine had for months been taking its toll from the weak, and from the numbers of the poor who could not obtain their portion of the wretched donkeys that were slaughtered for food, nor share in the rare provisions reaching the city by sea. Even the European Consuls were ready to urge Baez to surrender. But the majority of the President's supporters, in mortal dread of the vengeance Santana would impose, refused to permit Baez to give in.

When news of the appalling situation in Santo Domingo reached General Cass, who had the year before been appointed President Buchanan's Secretary of State, he determined to despatch an American warship to the Dominican Capital to take such measures as might be necessary to protect the American Agency, and to bear supplies to the starving Americans resident there. On May 26th the *Colorado* arrived in the port. The commanding officer, Commodore John M. McIntosh, realizing as soon as he arrived that the continuation of the siege was solely due to the well-grounded fear of the Baecistas of the general persecution in which Santana would undoubtedly indulge, offered his services as mediator upon the understanding that the lives of the capital's defenders must be guaranteed by Santana. Consequently, although the Santiago Government protested bitterly at the leniency of its terms, a form of capitulation was at length signed on June 12, 1858. The capitulations provided that the Presi-

dent should resign his office and leave the country, while
Santana obligated himself to refrain from persecuting any
of the supporters of the Baez administration. As soon as
the capitulations were signed, Baez, with the members of
his Cabinet, fled from the capital on a Government vessel
to Curaçao, and Santana, once more at the head of victorious troops, entered Santo Domingo on June 13th. The
year-long siege was ended.

6.

The revolution left the country prostrate. Commerce
had dwindled to such an extent that during the entire year
only two American vessels had reached the port of Santo
Domingo, and only two foreign schooners had left the
capital for the United States. No agricultural produce
had been grown, except in the Cibao, where the tobacco
crop was barely one-tenth of that previously harvested.
The public treasury was empty, government property
had been mortgaged by Baez, and the Republic was
flooded, notwithstanding the precautionary decrees of the
Provisional Government, with quantities of paper money
not worth the paper upon which it was printed. The surrender of the capital, moreover, accomplished little in paci-
fying the Republic. No sooner had Santana entered the
city than he commenced to chafe at the restrictions imposed upon him by the Provisional Government. Little
time elapsed before recriminations commenced between
the southern and eastern provinces and the provinces of
the Cibao, which had, for the first time since the independence of the country, constituted a government responsive
to their own interests and desires. The inhabitants of the
south and east, claiming that their efforts alone had been
responsible for the final overthrow of Baez, refused to

agree to the preponderance of the representatives of the Cibao in the Santiago Government, and far less to the removal of the capital from the south to Santiago.

On July 27th, a commission of prominent citizens of Santo Domingo, among the names of whom one may find without surprise those of Don Tomás Bobadilla, Don Juan Nepomuceno Tejera, and General Abad Alfau, waited upon General Santana to advise him that the provinces of the south conferred upon the Liberator full powers to reëstablish immediately the Constitution of 1854, in place of the Constitution of Moca which "catered solely to the interests of the Cibao," and besought him to maintain public order, and to reach an agreement with General Valverde which might guarantee the interests of the entire nation.

Santana assured the members of the commission that while he was entirely disposed to leave the Republic and return to exile, should the interests of the nation demand such sacrifice on his part, he believed that the Dominican people commanded his presence in the Government, and he could not refuse to heed their call. Appointing, on July 30th, a Cabinet of secretaries composed of well tried supporters, he awaited the reaction of the Cibao Government to the trend which events had taken.

Although General Valverde soon ascertained that the public enthusiasm which had acclaimed his Government outside the Province of Santiago during the revolution against Baez, had been created rather by the general detestation of Baez than by the popularity of the Santiago administration, he was not at first inclined to give in to Santana, particularly in view of the loyal support which the inhabitants of Santiago continued to lend him. Santana soon became impatient, and sending troops from the capital towards the north under the command of General Abad Alfau, forced the towns through which his troops marched to declare themselves favourable to him. La Vega, Moca, and San Francisco de Macorís withdrew their allegiance from the Santiago Government, and finally, as the result of increasing desertions from his own forces, General Valverde accepted the inevitable and tendered his resignation as President of the Republic on August 28th. Santana's troops entered Santiago on September 1st, and with this, the Liberator's authority was generally recognized throughout the Republic. The members of the Santiago Government, profiting by previous experience, left the country as soon as they could find means to do so.

On September 23rd, Santana, who had proceeded to the Cibao to assure himself that effective means were being taken by his subordinates to crush all potential opposition, returned to Santo Domingo, where the populace accompanied him to a Te Deum in the Cathedral to give thanks for the return to power of the Liberator, whom so short a time before they had sped upon his way to exile. The Constitution of Moca was revoked, and that of 1854 was proclaimed in force, and decrees were issued at the same time providing for the election of a new Senate as well as for the election of the President and Vice President of the Republic. On January 31, 1859, General Santana, who had naturally enough been elected President by a great majority, was inaugurated as President of the Republic for the third time, and his close supporter, General Abad Alfau, was elected to the Vice Presidency.

7.

In the month of October, preceding the inauguration of the President, General Santana received the visit of M.

Maxime Raybaud, for many years French Consul General in Port-au-Prince, and prime leader among the European Consuls who had forced Santana to abandon the original treaty of 1854 with the United States. M. Raybaud, who had already been deprived of his office as Consul General by the French Government, made himself popular upon his arrival in Santo Domingo by announcing that the purpose of his visit was "to view with my own eyes the depths of the misery to which the Dominican Republic has been brought." While this was announced as the ostensible reason for his visit to the Dominican Capital, Santana was not long in ascertaining that Raybaud came as the secret agent of the Emperor Faustin, who had been encouraged to believe, well aware as he was of the economic devastation of the Republic, that the moment might be opportune to recover through diplomacy that domination of the Dominican territory which he had proved signally unsuccessful in recovering by the force of arms.

On October 2d, Raybaud addressed a very lengthy communication to Santana, conceived in the most patronizing tone, calling attention to the progress and prosperity enjoyed during the previous ten years by the Haitians, which he alleged was the envy of all thinking Dominicans. He pointed out the fear of the great majority of the Dominican people of being placed at the mercy of the United States, "a people possessing not only a different religion, but who are also actually humiliated in having even a chance contact with any individual suspected of having African blood." He dwelt upon the manifest inferiority of the Dominican Republic, and claiming that the Dominicans were utterly incapable of maintaining their own independence, Raybaud asserted that the present moment offered the last favourable opportunity which the Dominican Government would have to obtain its welcome back into the Haitian fold. In conclusion, he advised Santana that the situation was clear; that should the President oppose a friendly union with Haiti, the Dominican Republic would either be absorbed by the United States or be forced at once into a disastrous war with Haiti, as the result of which the Dominican Republic would be treated as conquered territory.

Upon receipt of this letter, Santana caused its immediate publication, and one may imagine his delight at this opportunity for revenge upon the man who as Consul General of France had been able to inflict the most bitter humiliation of his political career. Sending Raybaud his passports, he had him marched immediately to a waiting vessel, upon which the Emperor Faustin's agent was obliged to return to the territory of his employer.

It was an extraordinary chapter in diplomatic history, that last mission of M. Maxime Raybaud to Santo Domingo, only explicable in that Raybaud believed his successful bullying of Santana when Consul General of France, successful only because of Santana's dread of complications with the European Powers, had procured him such personal influence over the President that he could continue to dictate to him in his new rôle of secret agent of the Haitian Emperor.

The incident had, however, a result of the gravest import. The allaying of popular apprehension resulting from the resolute attitude adopted by Santana, and from the overthrow of Faustin's Government by General Geffrard, which had created a Republic in Haiti with Geffrard as its President, afforded Santana a breathing-space in which to negotiate once more the foreign protectorate, without which he had become convinced the nation could not maintain itself, and without which he felt he himself could not remain in power during the latter years of his life. For there was no doubt that the Liberator was feeling the weight of his increasing years. He was by now approaching the age of seventy, and the many campaigns in which he had seen service, and the vicissitudes of his long career, made increasingly welcome to him the moments of tranquillity at El Prado. His own increasing infirmities made him more than ever anxious to obtain through a foreign protectorate that comforting assurance of his retention of control which he realized that he himself could not much longer ensure by his own efforts.

The oft repeated, and unsuccessful attempts during the past fourteen years to incline France towards assuming new responsibilities, and the lurking suspicion that France's policy was committed to the interests of Haiti, did not tempt Santana to waste any time in negotiations with France. There remained two alternatives—the United States and Spain. The popular prejudice which Segovia had succeeded in creating against everything American, and his own bitter experiences in 1854 and 1856, had well nigh convinced Santana that there was little help to be expected from the North Americans. He was not willing to abandon hope altogether, however. Moreover, the fear of American intervention might well prove the strongest argument in negotiating for a protectorate with Spain. To sound the ground, Santana informed the American Commercial Agent, immediately after Raybaud's dismissal, that while Constitutional difficulties might render it impossible for the Dominican Government to cede exclusive jurisdiction over the Bay of Samaná to the United States, the Government would readily facilitate its purchase, or its rental on a long lease, to private owners.[1]

At the same time, Santana, in accordance with the powers granted him by Article 35 of the Constitution of 1854, granted a concession to a company formed by British and French capital, ceding the company the right to work all the mines in the Republic, the company to pay 1,000,-000 francs within three months and to commence operations within three years, the Dominican Government to receive 10 per cent of the gross returns. A few months later, Santana likewise granted a French company a concession ceding all the guano and wood upon the public lands of the Government, the Government to receive 1,000,000 francs for the privilege, and to obtain likewise from the company the construction of stipulated public works. These two companies, believing that the value of their concessions would be enhanced, and their shares more readily sold in the United States, were the Dominican Government to obtain recognition by treaty from the United States, suggested to Santana that an envoy be sent by him to Washington to negotiate the treaty which the British and French Governments had been so active in opposing four years before. Santana consequently despatched to Washington as his envoy Don Antonio Delfín Madrigal, with confidential instructions to secure a commercial treaty from the United States.

8.

The stage was now set for Santana's real objective, the negotiation of a protectorate from Spain. So early as October 21, 1858, the start was secretly made. In a long communication addressed to the Spanish Govern-

[1] Mr. Jonathan Elliott to Secretary Cass, October 14, 1858.

ment at Santana's instance by his Minister for Foreign Affairs, the Spanish Government was informed that the motive of this note was the President's desire to give the Spanish Cabinet a truthful account of the recent history of the Republic, and of the actual conditions there existing. Protesting his desire to retire to private life, from which only the treachery and disastrous administration of Baez had called him, Santana dwelt upon the relations of the Republic with Haiti and narrated in detail the constant intrigues of the Haitian Government, of which he claimed Raybaud's mission was a flagrant example. The constant dread of Haitian aggression was, Santana advised the Spanish Ministers, the cause of such unrest that it made economic prosperity impossible in the Republic. He denied as an absurd rumour the possibility that the United States would again consider the annexation of the Republic, since the Dominican people had no ties of race or religion with the North Americans, admiring merely "their ability in industry, their activity in commerce, and the kindly disposition which they manifested" in their relations with the Dominicans, qualities which the Dominicans had reason to admire as well in many other peoples. The intrigues of Haiti, Santana concluded, constituted the chief problem which the Dominican Government was called upon to face, and he desired to know whether the Spanish Government, by virtue of the second article of its treaty with the Republic, would effectively impede any Haitian attempt to impair the territorial integrity of the Dominican Republic, since in that article the Spanish Government had declared its desire that the Dominican provinces should always remain under the control of the people inhabiting them.

The reply of the Spanish Government, despatched on

February 23, 1859, must have proved far from satisfactory, since it limited itself to the expression of the belief that with the recent overthrow of the Emperor Faustin and the inauguration of Geffrard as President of a new Haitian Republic, the fear of any invasion of Dominican soil from Haiti was materially diminished, and in formal terms expressed the hope of Spain that the Dominican Republic would continue happy and prosperous, and the assurance that Spain would never remain indifferent to any attempt to diminish the independence of the Dominican Republic.

Santana was naturally not content with this reply. On May 20th he appointed General Felipe Alfau as his Special Representative at the Spanish Court, with instructions to obtain from the Spanish Government solemn assurances that it would maintain the independence of the Dominican Republic and the integrity of its territory; protection in the event that the independence of the Republic or the integrity of its territory were ever threatened; and money and artillery with which to provide for the fortification of the Bays of Samaná and Manzanillo; together with the promise to facilitate the employment by the Dominican Government of Spanish officers to train its army, and the agreement to foment the immigration into the Republic of Spanish settlers. General Alfau was authorized, should he obtain these assurances, to obligate the Republic to offer the Spanish Government such concessions as it might desire, and to undertake that the Republic would enter into no treaty or alliance with any other nation, and would neither lease nor alienate to any other power, public lands or waters pertaining to the nation.

The instructions to Alfau were rendered more peremptory by the unexpected problems with which Santana's

Government was suddenly faced. In addition to the demand of the Danish Government that the Republic indemnify the owners of vessels seized and sold by Baez during his last months in the Presidency, which resulted, when Santana expressed reluctance to assume responsibility for the piratical acts of his predecessor, in a threatened blockade of Dominican ports, the Government was involved in a far graver complication.

With an empty treasury and with a country exhausted by the long drawn out revolution, Santana's Government had found itself unable to redeem at its face value the great quantities of paper money issued by Baez, and had consequently, for the purpose of instilling confidence, issued a decree, on May 5th, 1859, providing for the redemption of the so-called "papeletas" at a rate somewhat higher than the previous market rate. At once the European Consuls, who saw their hopes of amassing riches thus suddenly dispelled, publicly announced that the Government's decree, which had fixed the value of the Dominican paper at 2,000 to one Spanish dollar, was null and void so far as the subjects of the countries which they represented were concerned. Addressing a note, astonishing in its insolence, even from those agents who had so long been able to force their will upon Dominican Governments, to the Minister for Foreign Affairs, the Consuls demanded that the Dominican paper be redeemed at a figure far higher than that fixed by the terms of the decree. The Minister for Foreign Affairs, with unexpected temerity, returned the communication, stating that he could not consider transmitting a note couched in such terms to the President. Once more the Consuls sent the objectionable letter to the Minister, and once more the Minister returned it. At this juncture, the Consuls requested the coöperation of the American Commercial Agent, Mr. Elliott, believing that their position would be strengthened should their attitude be endorsed by all the members of the Consular body. The American Commercial Agent, who had no such personal interest in the speculation as had his European colleagues, by instruction of his Government refused his support.

The Consuls of France, Great Britain and Spain thereupon announced their decision to suspend all intercourse with the Dominican Government, and demanding their passports, left the country. Santana, who had been absent from the capital, was now faced with a situation peculiarly disquieting to him, and returning at once to the capital, issued, on May 27th, a decree stating that the subjects of the three powers whose Consuls had left the country remained under the special protection of the Dominican Government.

The country was now in such a state of misery as it had never previously experienced:

"The treasury was utterly bankrupt. There was no coined money of any kind to be seen in circulation. The entire Republic was filled with paper currency, which in its intrinsic worthlessness and rapid depreciation could only be compared to the 'Continental money' of American Revolutionary days." [1]

All trade in the Cibao, which had fallen into the hands of a few European merchants, was stagnant, and the farmers and tobacco growers throughout the country, discouraged by their experiences during Baez's administration, had refrained from planting crops. During the month of May only one brig in ballast and one small schooner half laden entered the port of the capital. The lack of any com-

[1] Mr. Jonathan Elliott to Secretary Cass, May 21, 1859.

mercial treaty between the United States and the Republic
obliged American vessels entering Dominican ports to pay
extra tonnage dues. As a result, little American shipping
came to the Republic, and American citizens were obliged
to do their freighting under European flags. Business with
the United States had been constantly decreasing, and by
the summer of 1859 there was only one American commercial house doing business in the entire Republic.

Receiving word of the economic distress in the Republic,
a condition always likely to create dissatisfaction with the
Government, and learning of Santana's difficulties with
the European Powers, Buenaventura Baez, who, after his
flight from the capital had been residing in the United
States, hurriedly journeyed to Curaçao, which he selected
as a favourable vantage ground from which to concert a
revolution against Santana. Many of his supporters had
quietly returned to the Republic, but Baez himself preferred to direct operations at a safe distance. Signs of his
activity were soon apparent. An insurrection against the
Government, of slight importance and speedily crushed,
took place in the spring of 1859. A more serious conspiracy to obtain control of the capital was disclosed the
night of Santa Rosa, August 30th, which likewise proved
unsuccessful, owing to the energetic measures adopted by
the Vice President, who had been left by Santana at the
head of the Government. Among the ringleaders of the
plot was General Francisco del Rosario Sánchez, by now
transformed into one of the most pernicious partisans of
Baez. Sánchez and his fellow-conspirators were seized and
exiled, and General Alfau at the head of his troops
marched to Azua, where the revolution which had simultaneously broken out in the border provinces was soon
put down. As soon as a number of executions and decrees

of exile had diminished the ardour of the Baecistas, Santana again temporarily assumed control of affairs, but owing to a return of the illness from which he suffered during the remaining years of his life, speedily returned to El Prado, leaving General Alfau once more in control of the Executive Power.

By returning so speedily to his retreat in the Seybo, the Liberator had relinquished the helm in time to avoid the arrival on November 30th, of the British, Spanish and French warships which were bringing back to the capital the indignant Consuls, who had obtained instructions from their Governments to act conjointly in forcing a settlement of their grievances against Santana's administration. The first three days were passed in the exchange of correspondence between the Consuls and the authorities whom Santana had left in çontrol to bear the brunt of the dispute. Don Miguel Lavastida, the Secretary of Foreign Relations, at first protested his satisfaction at the more courteous terms in which the new demand to modify the decree of May 5th was worded, but insisted upon the inability of his Government to comply with its stipulations, and utterly refused to consider the humiliating salutes of the foreign flags exacted. Thereupon, the benefit of Alfau's negotiations in Madrid was made apparent by the significant withdrawal of the Spanish Consul, who refused to press further for the exaction of the salutes demanded, although he continued to join his French and British colleagues in the demand that the Government's decree be amended so that the paper money should be redeemable at 500 to the Spanish dollar, rather than the 2,000 to the Spanish dollar previously fixed. The French and British authorities refused to follow the example of the Spaniard, and threatened to use force to obtain compliance with all of their demands. Lavastida thereupon resigned, and Dávila Fernandez de Castro, who replaced him, by instruction of Alfau gave in. After the multitude of salutes demanded by the war vessels had been fired, the Consuls disembarked, and on December 13th, the decree providing for the new rate of redemption was issued by the Government.

9.

The negotiations of Señor Madrigal in Washington had not proved productive of any concrete results beyond perhaps inducing unwary American investors to buy shares in the French companies which had urged his despatch. The mission, however, proved intriguing to Secretary Cass. The Secretary of State decided to avail himself of the services promptly tendered him by General Cazneau, who had reached the conclusion during the years he had spent in his "Estancia Esmeralda" since the termination of his earlier mission, that it would be difficult for him to negotiate in the United States the sale of the concessions which he was acquiring from the Dominican Government, should no treaty be concluded between the Republic and the American Government. Gullible as the American investor might be, General Cazneau was doubtful whether his fellow-citizens would invest much capital in a country with which their own Government had no treaty relations. Early in April, 1859, to his satisfaction, he received again the coveted appointment as Special Agent of the United States:

"You have been appointed Special Agent of this Government to the Dominican Republic," he was instructed by General Cass, "and you will receive herewith a letter to the Minister for Foreign Affairs of that Government accrediting you in your official character . . . You are

especially desired to report the situation and probable
stability of the Government, upon the prospects of trade
in the production of the country, upon the security and
protection of foreigners, and particularly of American
citizens, and whether there is any special subject which
demands the interposition of this Government . . . Circumstances may favor the negotiation of a commercial
treaty with that Government. You will direct your inquiries to this subject and report such information as you
may obtain, together with your own views, when the
matter will be submitted to the President for his direction." [1]

While General Cazneau was directed particularly to
obtain a satisfactory settlement of the claims of certain
American citizens whose property had been confiscated
without compensation by Baez, he was instructed that

"It is far from this Government's wish to seem to take
advantage of the exigencies of the Dominican Republic to
press these reclamations to a settlement."

On June 14th, Cazneau returned to Santo Domingo
from Washington, and presenting his credentials to the
Minister of Foreign Affairs, had immediately thereafter a
confidential interview with General Santana. Cazneau, as
ever, was persuasive:

"The Baez party which aims at placing the supreme
control in the hands of the negroes, was defeated and
driven from the City in July, 1858, after sustaining a
siege of eleven months. Its leaders relied on the sympathy
of England and France . . . At present, the Cabinet, Congress and Courts are filled by white men . . . The restoration of Baez or the annexation to Haiti, strongly but se-

[1] Secretary Cass to General William L. Cazneau, April 7, 1859.

cretly urged by France and England, would sweep them out en masse to be replaced by blacks selected from the class most bitterly opposed to American interests." [1]

Convincing arguments, these, to be addressed to a Democratic administration the year before the outbreak of the Civil War!

"The Baez party, which is seeking annexation to Haiti as a means of excluding the white race from the Island, had concerted a general revolt to take place in all the districts simultaneously. The attempt was postponed in consequence of the appearance of the American Commissioner" . . .
"The leading members of the Cabinet and Senate are very anxious to obtain treaty recognition from the United States. President Santana would now propose it but for his morbid dread of a failure, which he firmly believes would precipitate the downfall of the Republic." [2]

It is singular that such arguments did not convince President Buchanan of the desirability of concluding immediately and on any terms a treaty with the Dominican Republic, particularly after the President had received the following plea in which Mrs. Cazneau supported her husband's representations:

"I entreat you, in justice to your own family and in behalf of this isolated young State, not to leave the Dominican Republic much longer out of the pale of United States recognition. Up to this time there has not been a day that I have not been on a sick-bed or waiting and watching by the side of fever stricken members of my family . . . but in all times and under whatever circum-

[1] William L. Cazneau to Secretary Cass, July 2, 1859.
[2] William L. Cazneau to Secretary Cass, October 17 and December 13, 1859.

stances the ruling thought is to accomplish well the duties before us, whatever they may be." [1]

The negotiations of General Alfau in Madrid, which continued throughout the summer and autumn of 1859, at length resulted, notwithstanding the fact that the danger of Haitian intervention had been greatly diminished by the five year truce between the Dominican Republic and Haiti agreed upon in February, 1859, in extracting from the Spanish Government, one by one and ever reluctantly, the assurances which Santana had instructed his envoy to demand. By the beginning of March, Cazneau reported that Santana had received word from General Alfau that the Spanish Ministry was disposed to accede to the plan of a protectorate over the Dominican Republic.[2] In fact, only a few weeks later, Santana determined that the time had come when he might do away with subterfuge, and with long-protracted negotiations with the Spanish Court, and addressed a letter directly to the Queen:

"In the Palace of Santo Domingo,
April 27, 1860.

"My Great and Good Friend:

After Divine Providence favored me with your powerful assistance in bringing peace to this people, brought low by civil war; when the same protection had made it possible to regain the friendship of other nations alienated by the evil government which installed itself by surprise; when at length a truce of five years was concluded with the enemy who disturbs our tranquillity, I have felt myself under the obligation of securing that which still remained to make this same people happy—confidence in the future.

[1] Mrs. William L. Cazneau to President Buchanan, October 17, 1859.
[2] General William L. Cazneau to Secretary Cass, March 4, 1860.

Seventeen years of continuous disquiet have taught us that
our political situation would condemn us to pass through
the long series of tribulations which our brothers on the
South American Continent are experiencing, if indeed we
were not first swallowed up by some powerful state which
coveted us.

"Such a situation destroys the confidence which a strong
and just government might otherwise obtain; it destroys
all hope of utilizing the natural riches of our soil which
would give promise of so much under more favorable circumstances, and obliges him who today is responsible for
the happiness of the people to seek a brighter future under
a condition of affairs which would be more lasting and
stable. Our origin, our language, our religion, our customs,
our sympathies finally, incline us to seek to find that
stability in a more perfect union with her who was our
mother than the union which now exists, and assuredly
never will a more favorable opportunity present itself
than the opportunity which actual conditions offer us
today. The sentiments of love towards the Spanish Nation
. . . have sprung to new life, thanks to the noble and
generous conduct which the Spanish Nation has adopted
towards us and the loyalty with which the Republic has
known how to awaken it. Moreover, the influence with
which Heaven has blest me over a people which I have led
to victory during seventeen years has increased through
the peace which I have been able to bring to them in the
civil struggles which I had not, either directly or in-
directly, been responsible for. Would, therefore, Madam,
this not be the opportune moment to draw more closely
the bonds which unite both peoples? If, when this opportunity has passed, there were to come another one of those
political upheavals to which new republics find themselves
so easily exposed—what then would be the result of that
combination of circumstances when perhaps my more than

sixty years, my sufferings, and perhaps even death itself might have deprived me of the ability to offer my services to the Republic?

"If Spain then has, as I am convinced, an interest in avoiding such a contingency, I and the great majority of the Nation are disposed to adopt whatever measure may be fitting to assure the happiness of the Dominican people and the interests of Spain in her American possessions. The Consul whom Your Majesty has deigned to send to this Republic has obtained by his worthy conduct our affection and esteem, and without doubt has informed the Government of Your Majesty of the sentiments with which all we Dominicans are inspired towards your Royal Person. I, Madam, the representative of the Dominican people, and the personification of those sentiments, have sent to Your Majesty's Court a plenipotentiary to manifest these sentiments with even greater force. These sincere demonstrations of our respectful affection, those proofs of our undoubted inclinations, will induce, I have no doubt, Madam, your Royal Heart to favor those who were your sons. In that hope, I offer my sincere wishes for your prosperity and for the prosperity of the kingdom whose government is entrusted to your hands.

"I repeat the expression of these feelings of regard, and I remain—my Great and Good Friend—

"Your great and good friend,
"PEDRO SANTANA." [1]

10.

While there remains no record of the Queen's reply, Santana's direct appeal bore speedy fruit. By June, the assurances obtained by Alfau were already in process of realization. On June 30, 1860, Cazneau was obliged to report that although there was, in his opinion, a visible

[1] General Pedro Santana to the Queen of Spain, April 27, 1860.

growth of good will and confidence towards the United States in every direction, "the project of a Spanish protectorate appeared to be in active process of realization":

"The Spanish and Dominican Governments have entered into an understanding to garrison this Republic with 10,000 Spanish subjects and to place the standing army under the instruction of Spanish officers. About 1,500 persons have already arrived and three more vessels are under Government contract loaded exclusively with Spanish subjects to be permanently settled here. The immigrants are to remain under the protection of the Spanish flag. The whole movement is conducted in a quiet systematic manner which proved a careful prearrangement." [1]

On July 31st, the situation was even more clearly defined:

"On July 28th, a Spanish war vessel arrived directly from Cadiz with 100 citizens of the better class on board— engineers, teachers, and professional men. Arms and ammunition were likewise landed and a large number of Spanish officers. Another Spanish war steamer is to follow immediately with 350 more. Dominican territory will thus form a link of security for Spain between Cuba and Puerto Rico." [2]

Events were now marching rapidly to their inevitable conclusion. Santana commenced to call to him one by one his leading military supporters throughout the Republic, informing them of the end he had in view, and concerting with them the measures to be taken, once the announcement of the Spanish protectorate could be made public. He had already received assurances of the hearty co-

[1] General William L. Cazneau to Secretary Cass, June 30, 1860.
[2] General William L. Cazneau to Secretary Cass, July 31, 1860.

operation of the Spanish authorities in Cuba and Puerto
Rico, and on October 12th had held an interview at San
José de los Llanos with General Pelaez de Campomanes,
assistant to the Captain-General of Cuba, in the course of
which arrangements were determined upon for the procedure to be adopted so soon as the Spanish Government
could be forced to undertake the protectorate, or, as Santana believed more desirable, decree the annexation of the
Republic. For the Spanish Ministry in Madrid was more
than ever reluctant at this late stage in the comedy to
commit itself.

Although Don Pedro Ricart y Torres, Santana's new
Minister of Finance, was sent with Don Mariano Alvarez,
the Spanish Consul, to Havana at the end of October to
inform General Serrano, the Captain-General of Cuba,
that both Santana and Vice President Alfau, with the support of the whole Cabinet, "certain of the unanimous
desire of the people," had definitely determined to incor-
porate the Republic in the Spanish Monarchy, with the
hope that "during the glorious reign of Isabel II, by the
free and spontaneous will of the Dominican people, the
favorite island of Isabel I might again become a part of
the Spanish Dominions," the Spanish Government still held
off. In fact, as soon as he was advised by an agent from
Havana of this latest and insistent message from Santana,
General O'Donnell, leader of the Liberal Union, and
Spanish Premier at the time, replied to General Serrano, on
December 8th, that the Government of Her Catholic
Majesty had not yet been fully convinced that, should the
step be taken, internal difficulties might not arise which
would place Spain in an excessively embarrassing position,
particularly with regard "to the other nations of the New
World." Consequently, Serrano was instructed that the

Spanish Government desired to postpone consideration of the annexation of the Dominican Republic, while continuing "to support the Government of General Santana, and any other Government guided by the same policy, with all the means at its disposal." Serrano, however, was authorized—and this was all the latitude which Santana and his Spanish supporters needed—in the event that he became convinced that the postponement of its decision by Spain might permit the United States to further its own reported ambitions, to accept the annexation of the Republic without delay. It was merely stipulated as an indispensable prerequisite in such an event, "that the act be, and appear to be, completely spontaneous in order to safeguard absolutely the moral responsibility of Spain,'' and it was further specified that no Spanish troops should be landed on the Island "until the authorities and the people had proclaimed the annexation in a solemn and unanimous manner."

Madrigal's mission to Washington, and the fortunate coincidence of Cazneau's second mission to Santo Domingo, had long since been used by Santana as the means of convincing the Spanish authorities in the West Indies that the United States was only too desirous of securing the advantages which Spain was so dilatory in accepting. So far as the will of the people was concerned, that was a matter which Santana assured Serrano would not cause any trouble. Steps had long since been taken to assure the control of the Republic by his agents, and should any citizens be so ungrateful as to protest against the benefactions which the Liberator was providing for them, Santana could assure the Spanish authorities that he had effective means at his disposal to quiet them. A few did effectively protest against the rumours which by now were current, notwithstanding the secrecy with which Santana had enshrouded his negotiations. General Ramón Mella raised the cry of alarm. Public apathy was so great, however, that his protests were futile, and his immediate imprisonment by Santana caused little, if any, public agitation. His fellow Trinitario, General Francisco Sánchez, who was then in exile in St. Thomas, in printed warnings secretly circulated, likewise called upon his fellow-countrymen to rise to defend their liberties. But the long identification of Sánchez with the interests of Buenaventura Baez, and, more in particular, the fact that Sánchez, by one of those strange inconsistencies with which Dominican history is replete, was seeking, at first with some assurance of success, assistance from the Haitian Government of Geffrard in overthrowing the Dominican Government, made it unlikely that his cry would stir the popular imagination. Almost alone, with only a few others here and there throughout the country, Don Fernando Arturo de Meriño, the Vicar-General of the Church, braved the wrath of the Liberator, and even dared to proclaim in an address which he delivered in the presence of Santana and the Spanish authorities who had congregated at the Te Deum in the Cathedral on February 27, 1861, the seventeenth anniversary of the independence of the Republic, "True patriotism is the first of a citizen's duties, and the foundation of the stability of the Nation." But these few voices raised were of no avail in awakening the people to the impending change in their condition, nor in convincing them that their independence was at stake.

Throughout the winter of 1861, plans were completed for the proclamation of annexation, and the Spanish Government, at length convinced by Serrano of the necessity of heeding Santana's pleas, agreed upon March 18th as the day upon which the incorporation of the Republic in the Spanish Monarchy would become effective.

During these months, the American Special Agent, while well aware of the impending plans, appears to have made no further effort to offset them. The retirement of Secretary Cass in December, 1860, may have proved disconcerting, but it is more probable that the Texan General was far more dismayed by the impending struggle in the United States, and believed that it would be more profitable for him to remain on close terms with Santana. He made little comment regarding the approaching annexation to Spain beyond remarking:

"Four-fifths of the Dominicans, without distinction of class or color, are intensely dismayed at the prospect of a return to the Spanish yoke." [1]

General Cazneau, presumably, had likewise other affairs to attend to. Perhaps the business which Mr. Joseph W. Fabens—that gentleman who was to be so closely allied with him in the future—was now advertising in the Dominican press as having its headquarters "in the old custom-house in front of the Atarazana Gate," was already occupying much of his time.

The Special Agent found time, however, to object to the very evident opposition of the American Commercial Agent to the approaching annexation. Mr. Elliott, who had already alienated the sympathy of Santana's Cabinet by objecting in strenuous terms, not unnaturally, to an editorial published on August 5, 1860, in the *Correo de Santo Domingo,* written by Don José Maria Gafas, a Captain in the Spanish Army, which referred to the United States as "the refuge for all the criminals of the

[1] General William L. Cazneau to Secretary Black, January 11, 1861.

world," and who had observed that "a repetition of the scenes of 1856, when this Consulate and the American flag were grossly insulted, would not again be overlooked," continued in his tactless criticism of Santana's policy.

As soon as he was advised that Santana had requested his recall, he wisely inferred that "General William L. Cazneau appears to be my enemy and is mixed in this business." [1] General Cazneau had already deplored, in communications to the State Department, the interest manifested by Mr. Elliott in furthering the activities of emigration associations from the United States.[2] He now complained:

"Mr. Jonathan Elliott has permitted himself to contract such habits of intemperance that he has become altogether unfit for his post. President Santana has directed the Minister for Foreign Affairs, Don Pedro Ricart y Torres, to address a note stating that the conduct of Mr. Elliott, and his fatal vice of intemperance make it impossible for him to maintain the good relations desired by both Governments. Mr. Elliott has made seditious and criminal harangues from his balcony, in the loudest voice his lungs could compass, inciting the colored class against the Government and offering to lead the negroes to massacre the Canary Islanders whom this Government have brought from Venezuela. Mr. Elliott is endeavoring to convince the negroes that these people have come to enslave them . . ." [3]

An individual who could express any sympathies for the coloured race was naturally, in the opinion of the Texan General, unfit to hold the position of American Commercial Agent, and Secretary Cass so evidently shared Caz-

[1] Mr. Jonathan Elliott to Secretary Cass, August 20, 1860.
[2] General William L. Cazneau to Secretary Cass, March 4, 1860.
[3] General William L. Cazneau to Secretary Cass, September 10, 1860.

neau's opinion that he appointed, a few days prior to his own resignation, a protégé of Mr. Slidell, Mr. William Richmond, to replace Mr. Elliott. Unfortunately for Cazneau, however, Mr. Richmond's Confederate connections caused the cancellation of his appointment by President Lincoln before he had started for his post.

By the beginning of the year 1861, as soon as the date for the proclamation of annexation had been agreed upon by the Spanish Government, and as soon as a grant of $500,000 had been obtained, and a sufficient number of Spanish officers had arrived in the capital to take command of the Dominican troops, General Santana, who, by decree of the Senado Consultor, had been invested with temporary dictatorship, announced to his agents in all parts of the Republic that the formal proclamation of annexation to Spain was to be announced in Santo Domingo on March 18th, and simultaneously in all the other important towns and communes of the Republic. On March 17th, the citizens of the capital awoke to find the walls of the houses and the doors of the public buildings covered with copies of a proclamation commanding them to assemble on the following day in the Plaza de la Catedral.

The events of that historic day are graphically described in the first number of the *Gaceta de Santo Domingo,* the official organ of the new Colonial Government, published on March 21, 1861:

"Editorial

"Long live the Queen!

"The glorious Spanish flag, that symbol of civilization which for more than three centuries waved over our towers and fortresses, has been raised again in this Antillian Island favored by Isabel I, loved by Columbus, and from now on under the protection of Isabel II, the Magnanimous, today once more our august sovereign.

"As the result of this event the Dominican people have seen the realization of their most fervent hopes and of their most real and noble aspirations and in truth, the act in which there took place the solemn proclamation of our political transfer could not have been more spontaneous nor could have satisfied more fully the sincere desires of this people.

"From dawn of Monday, the 18th, the day set for this change to take place, great crowds kept circulating through all the streets of the Capital, which made evident that some great event was soon to take place: at seven in the morning the Plaza de Armas was invaded, one can truthfully say, by every class of individual, and a little later the troops of the garrison of this City began to arrive, *all without arms,* and accompanied by their respective generals and officers. The valiant General Pérez, Comandante de Armas of the Capital, arrived later followed by his estado mayor to view the interesting picture which the scene presented; but as yet there was noted the absence of the illustrious leader of the Dominicans and of his loyal and sapient counsellors whom all awaited with eagerness, as if in the impatience which all were feeling in that moment there existed the general desire to hasten the realization of their cherished hopes. Finally His Excellency appeared, with the brilliant following composed of his Ministers, Senators, Generals, resplendent officers, all the municipal bodies, and all the other personages of distinction who were to be present at the proclamation, and a little later His Excellency presented himself on the principal balcony of the Palace of Justice, from which, as the result of the frank and spontaneous expression of the will of the people and of the infinite number of petitions which the people had sent him, declaring himself definitely in favor of the incorporation of this part of the Island in the Spanish Monarchy, he addressed, in a loud and clear voice to his fellow-citizens, a fervent allocution . . .

"When His Excellency concluded, loud cheers re-echoed: the music of the military band accompanied the voices of the multitude and a salute of 101 shots gave notice that there was now waving from our fortress and public edifices side by side with the Dominican flag the glorious banner of Castile, symbol of salvation, under whose protection and beneath whose shadow all invoke heaven that we may see rewarded with a government of peace, equality and justice the immense sacrifices which this heroic people has for so long been dedicating in its efforts to regain its liberty.

"Immediately afterwards, all went to the Holy Cathedral where there was held a solemn Te Deum as a sign of gratitude to the Almighty who has granted us so many benefits in the midst of our tribulations, but before the Te Deum was solemnized, we saw with pleasure that the Most Illustrious Monseñor Gabriel B. Moreno del Cristo at the foot of the altar steps standing in front of the Most Excellent Don Pedro Santana, addressed to him the expressive discourse which is published in these columns.

"Thus has been briefly indicated the manner in which our political transfer has been effected, a unique example in the history of other countries, but not so in our country which has already given to all unique examples of perfect fidelity and love at all periods, and which, far from being led astray by false illusions, sees and feels the reality of things. May Divine Providence sanctify this splendid union in which both peoples should rejoice, and may we all be today, as we always have been, true Spaniards as sons of that noble nation which gave to us our origin and whose glories, achievements and virtues are likewise deserved by us.

". . . The great importance of the allocution of Don Pedro Santana, the noble sentiments which are reflected in it and the tremendous enthusiasm with which the crowds gathered in the Plaza de Armas heard it and welcomed it, proved beyond the shadow of a doubt how spontaneous the movement has been, as well as the well deserved confidence which the illustrious defender of our country's liberty inspires in all of us."

The allocution of Sanatana, which merited such appropriate praise from the Spanish editor, forms a sardonic climax to the history of these first seventeen years of Dominican independence—years during which the aspirations of the Dominican people, who had sacrificed their lives, their blood, their treasure, their all, to preserve their liberty, were ever betrayed by the two despots who had imposed themselves upon the nation.

"Dominicans! It is not many years since that my loyal and consistent voice reminded you, in presenting to you the reform of our political constitution, in these words, 'Our national glories, the heritage of the great and noble people to whom we owe our origin.'

"In making them so truly manifest my sentiments, I thought as well that I was the faithful interpreter of your own, and indeed I was not mistaken. My own policy was then forever indicated, but your own has gone even further than my fondest hopes believed.

"Many and spontaneous petitions of the people have come to my hands, and if, yesterday, you had granted me extraordinary powers, today you yourselves are hoping that that which your loyalty has ever desired may indeed become fact. Religion, language, beliefs and customs, all we maintain unaltered. Not, however, that there have not been those who have attempted to take from us such precious gifts; and the nation which has given us so much is the same nation which today is bending its arms like a loving mother who recovers her child lost in the shipwreck in which its brothers have perished.

"Dominicans! Only the ambition and the resentment of one man have alienated us from our mother country; in later days the Haitian dominated our lands, but our national valor drove him out, and the years which have passed since then to all have spoken for themselves.

"Shall we permit ourselves to lose the elements upon which we can count today which are so dear to us although they may not be strong enough to assure our own future and the future of our children? Before that may take place, before we see ourselves in the state in which those other pitiful republics find themselves, forever involved in civil war in which are sacrificed valiant generals, statesmen, numerous families, considerable fortunes and innumerable unhappy citizens, without the way being found to make themselves stable and strong, rather than that such a day should dawn here, I, who ever sought your safety; I, who aided by your courage have defended foot by foot the lands on which we stand; I, who realize how urgent are your needs, wish you to hear the Spanish Nation and look well at what she offers us.

"She grants us the civil liberty which her own people enjoy and guarantees to us our personal liberty and therefore removes the danger of our losing it; she assures to us our prosperity, recognizing as valid all the acts of the Republic; she offers to bear in mind and to reward all cases of merit and will not forget services which have been devoted to the country; finally, she brings peace to this soil where so many combats have taken place, and with peace she brings the benefits of peace. Yes, Dominicans, from today on you can rest from the weariness of war and you can occupy yourselves with tireless energy in assuring

the future of your sons. Spain protects us, her flag waves
over us, her arms will repel our enemies; she is not unmind-
ful of our labors and jointly we will defend them, forming
one people and one family, as we always have been. Together we will pray before the altars which that same
nation erected, before those altars which today she will
find as she left them, intact, spotless, and still crowned
with the shield of her national arms, her own castles and
lions, the first standard which Columbus at the side of the
cross raised in these unknown lands in the name of Isabel
I, the Great and Noble Catholic, the august name, which
the actual sovereign of Castile inherited as she likewise fell
heir to the love of the inhabitants of this Spanish Isle. Let
us raise the flag of her monarchy and proclaim ourselves
loyal subjects of our Queen and Sovereign! Long live Doña
Isabel II! Long live liberty! Long live religion! Long live
the Dominican people! Long live the Spanish Nation!"

CHAPTER III

1.

ON February 11, 1861, Abraham Lincoln commenced the long journey from Springfield to Washington to undertake the heaviest task with which any President has been confronted. The South was defiant, menacing, aggressive; in the North public opinion was hopelessly divided, the extremists advocating immediate rupture, the great mass favouring compromise at any cost so long as war might be averted. In his inaugural address the President made the course he had marked for his administration plain beyond doubt: "I . . . consider that in view of the Constitution and the laws, the Union is unbroken; and to the extent of my ability, I shall take care, as the Constitution itself expressly enjoins upon me, that the laws of the Union be faithfully executed in all the States . . ." He besought those who threatened the Union: "In your hands, my dissatisfied fellow-countrymen, and not in mine, is the momentous issue of civil war. The Government will not assail you. You can have no conflict without yourselves being the aggressors. You can have no oath registered in heaven to destroy the Government, while I shall have the most solemn one to preserve, protect and defend it . . ." The preservation of the Union was the goal upon which all of Lincoln's hopes were set, to the attainment of which all his energies were to be expended. No other matter could be taken into consideration. In his own words, "Let us do one thing at a time, and the big things first."

The initial non-resistance of the administration, although it was criticized with scorn by the Northern

217

extremists, created alarm among the members of the Confederate Government at Montgomery, who realized the general reaction which had set in throughout the revolted states, and feared that the conciliatory patience demonstrated by the President would win over great numbers in the seceded states, and cause the prestige and authority of the Confederate Government to vanish. For a few weeks there was outward peace.

To the brilliant Senator from New York, William H. Seward, whom Lincoln had appointed, as his chief rival for the Presidency, his Secretary of State, the opportunity was ripe for a desperate experiment. Were the public mind in the North and in the South to be diverted from the acute danger of imminent civil war to the threat of war with a foreign enemy, any enemy, Europe at large if need be, would not the common patriotism of the country rally at the cry of foreign aggression, and the disease of domestic discord be purged in the struggle for self-preservation against the common foe?

The constant encroachment of the great Powers of Europe upon the American hemisphere during the preceding years, against which Buchanan had but feebly protested, and which had evidenced a most flagrant and contemptuous disregard for that basic principle of the foreign policy of the United States formulated by John Quincy Adams and proclaimed thirty-five years before by James Monroe, afforded the pretext sought by the Secretary of State. There were the continued attempts of France and England to increase their supremacy in Central America; the joint expedition of France, Spain and England to obtain by an armed demonstration from President Juarez a settlement of the claims of their nationals against Mexico, which paved the way for Louis Napo-

leon's disastrous adventure in Empire building in the
Americas; ultimately, the Spanish occupation of the
Dominican Republic, of which a special messenger sent
in haste from Santo Domingo by the American Commercial Agent had just informed Seward.

The project of the Secretary of State, crystallized into
the memorandum entitled "Some Thoughts for the President's Consideration," was transmitted to Lincoln early
in April. The President was urged immediately to send
"agents into Canada, Mexico and Central America to
rouse a vigorous continental spirit of independence in this
continent against European intervention"; to insist upon
an explanation "categorical and at once" from France and
Spain of their now only too evident designs upon Mexico
and the Dominican Republic; to demand similar explanations from Russia and England of their proceedings on
the American continent; and finally, should, as was inevitable, only unsatisfactory explanations be obtained
from France and Spain as to what already was in each
case a "faît accompli," the President was called upon to
"convene Congress and declare war against them."

But the serene determination of Lincoln to concentrate
all the powers of the Government upon the preservation
of the Union was not to be diverted by a policy which in
other circumstances might not have lacked justification.
His logical intellect could see no wisdom, when any chance
spark might kindle the blaze within the house, of deliberately lighting the conflagration of its exterior. And in
fact only a few days elapsed before the Government at
Montgomery, fearful that unless "blood were sprinkled in
the face of the Southern people they would be back in
the old Union in less than ten days," [1] ordered the attack

[1] James G. Blaine, "Twenty Years of Congress."

on April 12th upon Fort Sumter which lit the flame of the Civil War.

The bellicose despatches proposed by Seward were consequently modified by Lincoln's intercession into protests addressed to the European Governments against the activities they had displayed in the American continent. But the counsel of Seward, soon made public, was in great part responsible for the wave of antipathy to the Union which rolled over Europe at the outbreak of the Civil War, and greatly enhanced the sympathy for the Confederate cause, for which various powerful motives already had existed in England and in France. In Spain it quickened into fever heat the resentment against the Government of the United States to which the long-continued sympathy demonstrated to the Latin American Republics, the suspected hunger for the remaining Spanish colonies, and finally the "Ostend Manifesto" had given birth.

Moreover, conditions which obtained at the time in Madrid were such that small heed would have been paid in any event to the American protest against the open violation of the Monroe Doctrine, formally reported some months later to the Cortes by the Minister of State, Calderón Collantes. For there was a fast increasing belief in Spain in the year 1861, that the renaissance of the Spanish Empire was at hand. It was a belief which the Liberal Union, "that group of all the disillusioned," [1] had carefully nurtured, and it was upon a policy of imperial aggrandizement that the party leader, General O'Donnell, Premier at the time, had staked his political fortunes. The war with Morocco, which O'Donnell had waged to the successful conclusion of the capture of Tetuán, from which he had taken his title as Duque de Tetuán, had

[1] La Gándara "Anexión y Guerra de Santo Domingo."

created the wildest enthusiasm, not only in Spain itself but in the Spanish colonies as well. The Spanish people, beguiled by the fantasy that a return to the glorious days of the Empire was dependent solely upon the acquisition of some scattered territories, were well sheltered by their political mentors from the practical realization that conditions abroad and at home would render the emulation by Spain under Isabel II of the exploits of the great Emperor or of his son altogether impracticable. For in Spain itself social and political conditions were at the low ebb of their rankest decadence, over which the recent military exploits in Morocco could barely throw a gloss. The country seethed in the midst of the social revolution which all the years of the nineteenth century could not resolve.

At the head of the State there still reigned for a few more turbulent years Isabel II: "immensely stout, and with the most good-natured face in the world, she was certainly nothing to boast of in elegance of manner or dignity of deportment. . . . always acting on the impulse of the moment, obeying her own will in all things, instead of being guided by any fixed principle of action." [1] Engrossed primarily by the demands made upon her by her long series of favourites, among whom O'Donnell had a conspicuous place, and by the care of the increasing number of her royal progeny, she abandoned affairs of state to the Premier of the moment, who not infrequently mingled his official privileges with those of a more intimate character. The Queen "had no idea of what is meant by ruling over a nation, and made no attempt to do so, well or ill. She carried out the formal functions to which her position condemned her with a sort of resigned ennui.

[1] From a letter of Lady Louisa Tenison, 1852.

But she never really grasped the meaning of the conflicts
that went on around her, she never realized the play of
forces, the struggles of ideas, the supreme interests which
it was in her power to decide. . . . Indifferent to the
great questions of state, incapable of even knowing
whether she was taking the side of Liberalism or Abso-
lutism, she was very sensitive to personal influences. A
man who acquired power over her could attract her
either way." [1]

Surrounding the Sovereign was the horde of office-seekers, each, save for rare exceptions, seeking the Queen's
favour as a means of furthering his own ambitions. Espar-
tero, Narvaez, O'Donnell, Escosura, Prim, González Bravo
—a long line, alternating in power. Beyond the Ministers,
the army, ever-dissatisfied, undisciplined, heeding the
voice of the highest bidder for its support. And so far
removed from the Crown that its voice was inaudible,
the great body of the common people, drifting towards
any leader from whom it thought to obtain a betterment
of its abject misery.

It was for such a Sovereign and for such a Government
that Santana sacrificed the dearly-bought independence
of his country. And through the force of circumstances,
except for the formal protest ultimately made by the
Government at Washington, and for a few words of caution tendered by the British Cabinet, there was but one
Government to raise an outcry against the perpetration
of the annexation to Spain. On April 6th, Fabre Geffrard,
the President of Haiti, registered the protest of his Government "solemnly, and in the face of Europe and
America, against any occupation by Spain of Dominican
territory" and declared that the Haitian Republic would

[1] The *New Review*, London, 1869.

never recognize the annexation, and would reserve to itself the right to employ any means within its power to assure its own best interests.

2.

It is open to question whether the bulk of the Dominican people themselves would have shown any determined resistance to the project of annexation, had they been afforded the opportunity of so doing, before they were confronted with the accomplished fact, in March, 1861. The exhausting struggle of the seventeen years of independence, the ever constant menace of invasion from Haiti, the continued exile of the liberal leaders, which had removed from the political scene the voices which had first roused the nation to respond to its pristine ideals, had all contributed to the gradual decay of the earlier devotion to the concept of liberty; and the passion for independence had become merged in an overwhelming desire on the part of the agricultural and commercial classes for peace, and the material benefits which it was imagined peace must bring. The recurrent dictatorships of Santana and Baez, with their prompt annihilation of anything which even remotely resembled independent thought, had stifled at its outset the growth of any public opinion in the Republic. In fact the tremendous percentage of illiteracy, and the lack of any press, save the sycophant sheets created solely for the purpose of fawning upon the Government, or more rarely for the purpose of upholding the claim of some rival for the Presidency, would, even under far more favourable conditions, have rendered the growth of public opinion, as distinguished from partisan fervour, impossible.

As it was, under the almost feudal system which prevailed, the ignorant masses followed unhesitatingly the opinions evinced by their local "caciques" or chieftains, and even in the larger towns the poorer classes followed like sheep the dictates of the petty leaders to whom, for one reason or another, they were addicted. Santana once said to a Spaniard, after the annexation had been completed, "I have made you an immensely valuable gift, for I have given you a people without journalists and devoid of lawyers." And Santana understated the truth. For the immense majority of the Dominican people were not yet vocal; they responded as yet unswervingly to the commands of their leaders. Betrayed, they were still obedient to the "caciques" whom Santana had suborned to serve his own purposes. And it was only when the utter ignominy of their plight at length became plain to them, that the ideals of liberty and freedom, instilled into the souls of his fellow-countrymen by Duarte and those of his companions who were worthy of the task, instinctively maintained at all costs in the wars with Haiti, caused the masses, ignorant as they were, to rise in their might and cast from them the yoke which their unworthy rulers had placed upon their necks.

The Spanish Premier, even in those months when he foresaw, as he thought, the disintegration of the American Union into factions whose jealousies between themselves would ever prevent their making common cause against the European attempts at territorial expansion in the New World, was still cautious. Notwithstanding the imperial policy to which he was committed, he was reluctant to assume responsibilities which might entail vast expenditures without commensurate returns. It was his chief lieutenant, General Francisco Serrano y Dominguez, whose eminence in the Liberal Union had gained for him the chief office in the gift of the Spanish Crown outside the Premiership itself, the post as Captain-General of Cuba, who prevailed upon his chief to take the risks entailed in the annexation of the Dominican Republic. General Serrano, whose acclaim as the "handsomest man in Spain" had doubtless been of avail to him in becoming the first of his Queen's favourites many years before, and in thus rivaling the distinction accorded his superior, was likewise a man of considerable brilliancy and of inordinate ambition. He was not to be deterred from increasing the dominions of Spain in the West Indies and safeguarding the colonies of Cuba and Puerto Rico, by the sober considerations of his chief, nor by the potential opposition of America, particularly as he was advised by his agents that the Confederacy would interpose no objection to the addition of another colony to Spain's slave-holding dominions in the West Indies.

But the explicit instructions of O'Donnell that the annexation of the Dominican Republic would not be undertaken before the Spanish Government had received the expression of the unanimous consent of the Dominican people, which must be obtained before Spanish troops were landed, could not be overlooked either by Serrano or Santana.

Santana's intention had originally been that the annexation to Spain should be proclaimed in all the communes of the Republic on March 18th, the day upon which it was announced to the citizens of the capital. His plans, however, had miscarried. By March 15th there was no evidence that the Dictator's agents in the more remote provinces had completed the arrangements required. Santana's impatience to be able to advise Serrano that the farcical pretense of obtaining the "unanimous consent of the Dominican people" had been carried out, caused him, early on March 15th, to send special messengers to his agents throughout the Republic with the most urgent instructions, which covered every detail in the proposed ceremonial.

"The Proclamation is to be made immediately; the Spanish flag is to be raised; a solemn notarial act of the ceremony is to be written, which must be signed by all the people present who know how to write, and the names of the persons who do not know how to write are to be included in it . . . As soon as the flag has been saluted with twenty-one guns, the 'comandantes de armas' are to be notified . . . The proclamation should be made as early as possible in the morning, so that the Dominican flag need not be raised . . . A Te Deum is to be sung and the civil governor of the Province is to address an allocution to the public, to explain the guarantees and the advantages which the annexation implies . . ."

A few hours after these reiterated instructions had been despatched, the Dictator received the announcement that in Hato Mayor, where Colonel Manuel Santana, his son, was Provisional Governor of the Province, the proclamation of annexation had been made on March 12th, before a gathering of ninety-five persons congregated in the church. Although the announcement had anticipated the date fixed by six days, Colonel Santana's letter to his father must have been peculiarly gratifying:

"Hato Mayor, March 12, 1861.
"My dear Papa:—
". . . I have received your instructions with the greatest enthusiasm and joy since in this manner we will be freed from this condition of poverty and calamity, and I

can assure you that at no time could [the annexation] have been better received than now, for already the people desired any arrangement at all which would improve our situation, and so it is that here in Hato Mayor, as in the Seybo, everybody has manifested the greatest enthusiasm and contentment and since they have had explained to them so very clearly the advantages which will be brought to the whole Republic and to each individual, all have sworn with the greatest good faith to accept joyfully the splendid arrangement that the Republic is now to become a Spanish province. . .

"I can assure you that here and in the Seybo and in Higüey, from what General Michel has told me, there isn't the slightest sign of discontent, but on the contrary, all have declared that they would have desired the flag to be raised before now.

"At any rate, I have made to them the most persuasive arguments which were within my power.

"All your family were well. I hope that you preserve your health.

Your most affectionate son,
M. G. SANTANA."

But notwithstanding the urgency of Santana's orders, the announcement of the annexation was not made in such important towns as Monte Cristi, Guayubín and Puerto Plata until as late as March 26th.

The President's fear that some unforeseen event might yet arise to prevent the consummation of his project induced him to wait no longer than March 18th, the day upon which the annexation had been proclaimed in Santo Domingo, to issue a decree providing that the laws and general regulations which had been in existence in the Dominican Republic were to continue in effect, except for such as provided for the exercise of sovereignty, until

they were revoked or modified by the Spanish Queen.
On the following day, a further decree was issued providing that until the Spanish Government had reorganized the local administration, the four Secretaries of State
in Santana's Cabinet would continue to attend to the
public business of the new colony.

The first days in the capital, while Santana was still
awaiting word of the "unanimous support of the proclamation of annexation" from the remote towns, were
replete with celebrations. The senior officer among the
Dominicans in the garrison of the capital, Colonel Juan
Ciriaco, invited such Spanish officers as had already arrived
in Santo Domingo, as well as his Dominican fellow-officers,
to a banquet in his residence. After a series of toasts to
the "brotherly love with which the Spaniards and Dominicans today regard one another," the whole gathering, no
doubt somewhat exhilarated by the banquet, accompanied by the military band, marched through the streets
of the town, pausing before the residences of Santana
and General Alfau and other notables of the city to
address congratulatory speeches to them. According to
the *Official Gazette*, "joy was universal." Two days later,
the Spanish officers invited their Dominican colleagues to
a similar banquet in the Casino de Colón, and after this
entertainment had been concluded, the guests once more,
again accompanied by the military band, proceeded to
parade through the streets of the city, "which they kept
on doing until a late hour of the night."

Upon the receipt by Santana of the notarial acts prepared by his subordinates in the communes, which he
believed would be proof conclusive to Serrano of the
unanimous desire of the Dominican people for the Spanish annexation, the official accounts of the reception of

the proclamation throughout the Republic were despatched to Havana. Thereupon orders were immediately
issued by the Captain-General of Cuba, whom it had not
been difficult to convince that O'Donnell's instructions
had been complied with, for a considerable body of troops
from Puerto Rico and from eastern Cuba to embark at
once for the neighbouring island.

By the middle of April, a large number of troops had
already arrived. Some one thousand men were transported to Samaná, which the Spanish authorities had
determined immediately to fortify. A considerable number of troops were likewise sent through the Province of
Azua to garrison the outposts along the frontier, but by
far the greater number of the acclimatized troops from
Cuba and Puerto Rico remained temporarily in the capital. By the early summer, General Serrano had sent altogether some six thousand Spanish soldiers to Santo Domingo, and Santana was enabled to announce that a
garrison of 10,000 men was to be maintained, and that
twelve vessels of war were temporarily to be anchored
in Dominican harbours.

Once Serrano had taken the steps necessary to insure
the retention of the former Republic, the Spanish Premier
was informed that the Dominican people had unanimously
accepted the annexation with every sign of rejoicing.
General O'Donnell was now faced with an accomplished
fact. Overcoming his initial reluctance, he advised the
nations of the world, through the Spanish representatives
abroad, that the Spanish Government had been forced to
undertake the annexation of the Dominican Republic,
without any purpose of derogating its sovereignty or
independence, solely in order that the Dominican provinces should no longer be exposed to the possibility of

invasion by an enemy people. Three weeks later, on May 19, 1861, the Spanish Queen signed the decree, later submitted to the Cortes, officially proclaiming the annexation. Santana's palpable anxiety was relieved on June 16th when an emissary from General Serrano announced to him officially that Isabel II,

"obeying the magnanimous impulses of her heart, had deigned to heed the wishes expressed by the faithful inhabitants of the Spanish portion of Santo Domingo, and had consented to permit the former colony to return to the bosom of the fatherland, forming from now on an integral portion of the Spanish Monarchy."

Returning post-haste to the capital from Azua, where he had gone in company of several officials on a visit of inspection, Santana announced to the Dominican people in a proclamation published June 22nd, that the Queen of Spain had deigned to consent to the annexation of the Spanish portion of the Island of Santo Domingo, which acquired thereby the status of an integral province of the Spanish Monarchy.

So the last step in the program was successfully taken. And the Dominican people, without being afforded the opportunity of passing upon the annexation project through a plebiscite, or by the submission of the project to the Senate or to the courts, having given their supposed "unanimous consent" at the ceremonies so carefully staged in advance by Santana, became officially Spanish subjects, and residents of a remote colony of the Spanish Crown.

3.

But although Santana, now appointed upon Serrano's recommendation Captain-General of the new province, had announced to the Spanish Government that peace and tranquillity existed throughout the colony, the reverse was the case. Barely six weeks after the proclamation of annexation, the first organized revolt against the transfer of sovereignty had taken place. On the night of May 2nd, a group of discontented Dominicans led by Colonel José Contreras had succeeded in obtaining possession of the military stronghold in Moca. The insurrection was doomed to be short-lived, since the Captain-General, at the head of a body of his devoted Seyban troops, immediately marched upon Moca, and capturing the ringleaders of the rebellion, summarily executed them. The ruthless severity displayed by Santana, entirely in keeping with the arbitrary policy which he had followed during the years when he was responsible to no other than himself, was condemned by the majority of the Spanish officials, and notably by the new Lieutenant-Governor of the Province, General Pelaez de Campomanes, as being contrary to the conciliatory course which the Spanish Government should pursue, particularly in that by such measures the impression would necessarily be created abroad that the annexation by Spain of her former colony had been accomplished through conquest rather than as a result of the alleged desire of the Dominican people themselves.

While the executions ordered by Santana effectively curbed for the time being the semblance of revolt within the colony, it quickened rather than diminished the activities of the Dominican exiles in Haiti, who had not abandoned the campaign undertaken prior to the annexation. A guerilla warfare had been effectively maintained for some months along the frontier by General José Maria Cabral and General Francisco del Rosario Sánchez, who still hoped to restore Baez to power, and who had received in their operations effective assistance from President Geffrard. Of a sudden, the President of Haiti, intimidated by the increasing levies which were constantly arriving in Dominican territory from the neighbouring Spanish colonies, determined to withdraw his support from the revolutionaries. As soon as the change in the situation became known, Cabral suspended activities, leaving General Sánchez to continue the campaign by himself. Lured into ambush, Sánchez and his chief supporters were captured at El Cercado by the troops sent in pursuit by General Santana, and were brought as prisoners to San Juan, where they were there executed on July 3rd, without even the bare formalities of military law, by the direct order of the Captain-General. If the executions at Moca had proved distasteful to the new Spanish authorities, the military assassinations at San Juan were far more disquieting. The indignation of General Pelaez at the action of his superior reached such a pitch that he addressed vigorous protests directly to the Spanish Government, and raised a doubt in the minds of the authorities in Madrid whether the unlimited confidence which they had been led by Serrano to have in Santana, as a man indispensable in the Government of the colony, had not in fact been misplaced.

The flicker of revolt, the Spanish Government determined, was primarily caused by the arrogant proclamation of the Haitian President, without whose assistance, they believed with reason, the Dominican rebels could not have successfully waged their revolutionary campaign in the border provinces. With such insolence Serrano proposed to deal speedily. To the dismay of Geffrard, who had seen many threats made in past years by the great

Powers, but who had never before seen such threats materialize into effective action, the Haitian Government awoke on July 10th to find a Spanish fleet anchored in the harbour of Port-au-Prince. On board was General Rubalcava, who proceeded to demand of the Haitian President immediate recognition of the annexation by Spain of the Dominican Provinces, an indemnity of $200,000 for the damages caused Dominican property by Haitian armies, and a positive guarantee that the Haitian Government would in the future maintain a patrol along its boundary so that no further revolutionary attempts upon Spanish authority in the Dominican portion of the island could again be effectively undertaken by Dominican exiles on Haitian soil. Geffrard was successfully intimidated into complete acquiescence in the Spanish demands, and although it is recorded that only $25,000 was actually paid in lieu of the total indemnity required, the energy displayed by Serrano upon this occasion was sufficient to check the Government of Haiti for some years to come.

4.

Enheartened by the easy success of his emissary in curbing the hostility of Haiti, Serrano decided the time had come for him to make a personal inspection of the colony which he above all other Spaniards had been chiefly instrumental in adding to the dominions of Spain. Apparently confident that upon his arrival he would be overwhelmed with demonstrations of popular esteem, and rejoicing in the prospect, he was at the same time vaguely disquieted by the reports reaching him of the increasing friction developing between Santana and the Spanish officers subordinate to him, and solicitous by his personal intercession to remove the causes thereof. "With two magnificent warships, laden with the innumerable effects required upon a ceremonial voyage, surrounded by a resplendent escort adequate to the dual dignity of his person and of his rank, the Captain-General of Cuba appeared" on August 6th "in the harbor of Santo Domingo, where there awaited him disillusions of the kind which even the most optimistic spirit can neither deny nor even mitigate, since they are accompanied by strong and lasting personal impressions. The personal inspection of all that which was contained abstractly and with a certain mythological mystery in the word 'annexation,' the sight of the reality in all its nakedness, must have quenched his enthusiasm and caused his hopes to vanish. . . . In proof of it, his visit which was to have been of considerable duration, was cut short to the number of days necessary for the Te Deum, a couple of banquets, and a ball." [1]

The first and greatest shock occasioned the punctilious Captain-General of Cuba was the absence of his colleague of Santo Domingo from among the group of officials awaiting his arrival upon the dock. Serrano's impression that all was not proceeding harmoniously in the administration of the colony was thus speedily confirmed. In fact while the visiting dignitary was proceeding in state to the Cathedral, where the multitude assembled by the military officials was to give thanks in a solemn Te Deum for the honour conferred upon them by his visit, the Captain-General of Santo Domingo, alleging a sudden indisposition, was swinging back and forth in a hammock upon the balcony of his residence only a block away, sulkily meditating upon the better days, for the change in which he himself had been primarily responsible, when there were no superior authorities to question his actions, and

[1] La Gándara "Anexión y Guerra de Santo Domingo."

no upstart Spanish subordinates who dared to protest against the measures which he saw fit to take. For the disagreements between Santana and his Dominican satellites and the ever-increasing number of Spanish officials, which had commenced with the protests of General Pelaez against the military executions ordered by his superior, had undergone a rapid growth. The resentment among the Dominicans had already struck deep roots.

For a brief period Serrano's diplomacy improved the situation. Bearing in mind the old fable of the mountain and Mohammed, he called upon Santana as soon as the ceremonies of his public welcome had been completed. Concealing his astonishment at being received by the Captain-General of Santo Domingo "bare-foot, and clad only in a country-man's shirt and linen pantaloons," he assuaged Santana's irritation temporarily, upon ascertaining that the appointment of Spanish officials to posts coveted by many of the Dominican's followers had been a chief contributing cause of the difficulty, by assuring him that the Spanish Government would thereafter give the lion's share of lucrative appointments to the Dominicans indicated by Santana. The latter was so far mollified that upon the following day, his sudden illness entirely cured, he presented himself, still arrayed in peon's dress, which formed a striking contrast to the ceremonial uniforms of the brilliant escort accompanying Serrano, in the Government Palace, to be installed officially as Captain-General of Santo Domingo, and to take the oath as Knight Grand Cross of the American Order of Isabel la Católica.

5.

If Serrano's brief visit temporarily appeased the irascible Captain-General of Santo Domingo and his insatiate band of sycophants, it had no such beneficial effect upon the rank and file of the Spanish Queen's new subjects. Already among the men of note in the northern provinces of the Cibao, who had at first inclined to the belief that any change in their condition must be for the better, discontent was rife. Gradually the epidemic spread, gained headway with each new cause for dissatisfaction, captured the leaders in the southern provinces who at first were more readily dominated by the Government at the capital, and when it had finally permeated the lower classes, incited at length by their own peculiar grievances, the smouldering opposition to Spanish rule broke into the blaze of concerted revolt which eventually destroyed utterly the last vestige of alien control.

The causes for popular discontent were fundamental, manifold and cumulative.

In the words of General Gándara, the last Spanish Captain-General of the colony, who for personal reasons was not over-partial to the policy pursued by his Government:

"There existed complaints . . . to which Spain was not in a position to attend, since similar vices in the Spanish Government itself lacked attention; . . . There were others which the proximity of the other Antilles made it difficult, if not impossible, to remedy; there were others finally, and by far the greater number, which our statesmen utterly failed to comprehend, and of which they did not grasp the importance, and for that reason they were disregarded. . . . The original oligarchy of Generals and merchants ruling Santo Domingo was replaced by another of Spanish officials; all the evils in administration were rendered worse rather than better, and the sole panacea offered by Spain to her new colony, that system of centralization and monopoly which was governing us ourselves, instead of tending to placate and captivate, was far more likely, as proved to be the case everywhere, to foster discontent, and to provoke those terrible crises of modern society which terminate upon the field of battle." [1]

In the instructions which Santana had given his agent at the Spanish Court when it was at length believed that annexation would be undertaken, the Dominican President, appreciating better than any other the bases which would be likely to win popular approval for Spanish Government, had stipulated that the Cabinet of Madrid must agree to enter into certain obligations respecting the Dominican people. These stipulations, readily accepted by the Spanish Ministers, were:

1. That individual liberty be guaranteed, and that slavery be never again established on Dominican soil.
2. That the Dominican Republic be considered as a Spanish Province, and enjoy as such the same rights.
3. That the greatest possible number of those men who had rendered important services to the country since 1844 be given public employment, especially in the army, and that these might continue to be employed by Her Majesty.
4. That as one of its first measures, the Government of Her Majesty decree the amortization of the paper money actually in circulation in the Republic.
5. That the validity of the acts of the successive governments of the Dominican Republic since its birth in 1844 be recognized.

Of these specific obligations, which Santana believed constituted the sum of the material requirements of the

[1] La Gándara, "Anexión y Guerra de Santo Domingo."

people once peace was assured, only the first and the fifth were actually carried out.

At the outset the Spanish officials were loud in their promises of the benefits which annexation would confer upon the colony. The ports were to be fortified and enlarged. The peninsula of Samaná was to be fortified in such manner that complete control would be obtained over the Mona Passage, and the town of Santa Barbara de Samaná itself was to be immediately increased to the size of an important commercial center, with the most liberal municipal charter ever granted by Spain. Steam communication was to be established between Santo Domingo and the other Antilles, post offices were to be installed in every commune, roads were to be constructed between all the principal towns, and telegraph lines were to be laid. The courts were to be reconstituted, and the tariff was to be reformed so as to stimulate Dominican commerce. Sanitation was to be undertaken by experts.

As the months sped by and not only the general assurances of reform failed to materialize but even the specific obligations entered into by Spain were not carried out, the very munificence of the promises so glibly made reacted against the Spanish authorities.

The first signs of dissatisfaction were noted among the military elements, when Spanish officers were one by one appointed to positions of importance in the colonial troops, and the Dominicans, forced to make way for them, were retired upon a small percentage of their former pay. The experience of the Dominican military authorities was soon after shared by the civil officials. From Spain, Cuba and Puerto Rico there poured a stream of hungry office-seekers, to whom O'Donnell and his colleagues were gladly offering the lucrative positions they could not find for them elsewhere. To satisfy them the native office-holders were gradually removed, and Santana himself had difficulty in obtaining, when a Royal Audiencia was established by a decree of November 21, 1861, the appointment of such trusty supporters as Don Tomás Bobadilla and Don Jacinto de Castro as Magistrates of the Crown. Within a brief period the Dominican people saw the national pay-roll augmented from the small figure of the latter days of the Republic to the immense total of $3,500,000, when the yearly revenues barely produced half a million dollars, and saw eighty per cent of the salaries granted reverting to the Spanish "carpet-baggers."

The resentment of the office-holders was soon equalled by that of the commercial and agricultural classes. Believing at first that the assurance of peace would cause the immediate increase of prosperity, they found the reverse to be the case. With the outbreak of the American Civil War commerce with the United States was necessarily cut off, and the increasing discrimination evidenced against foreign business for the purpose of favouring commerce with Spain, had the immediate effect of closing to Dominican products the best markets they had previously possessed in Europe. The Dominican merchant soon found to his cost that the reform of the tariff benefited solely the Spanish exporter and would ultimately strangle Dominican trade. The gravest cause for discontent, however, in that it implied the inevitable ruin of many who had legitimately obtained quantities of Dominican paper, was the constant postponement of the agreement of the Spanish Government to redeem the paper money in gold or silver at a fixed rate. Not until two years after the date of the annexation was the work of redemption commenced, and the redemption, if it can be so termed, was undertaken by replacing the Dominican "papeletas," which had been issued in denominations of $2, $5, $10, $20, and $50, with paper notes of worse quality than those they replaced, in issues of fifty cents, $2, $5, $15, and $25, or with copper coin. The entire Dominican issue of $50 notes the Spanish authorities, without justification, declared counterfeit, and announced its repudiation. There was no action of the Spanish Government which created more bitter antagonism, or more thoroughly demonstrated the corruption of the standards of the Cabinet at Madrid.

There were other causes, equally potent, however, for the increasing ferment of unrest. The enforcement of the Spanish penal code, with all its heritage of the dark ages, was intolerable to a people which had enjoyed the benefits, which shone by contrast, of the more enlightened Napoleonic Code. The Spanish penal code, among its other retrograde provisions, instituted severe punishments for the observance of religious rites other than those of the Catholic Church. To the Dominican people, to whom religious liberty had been a cherished principle, notwithstanding the fact that they were in their immense majority devout Catholics, the restrictions now imposed were repellant, and were rendered doubly so by the attitude displayed by the new Spanish Archbishop, Don Bienvenido Monzón y Martín.

Archbishop Monzón soon proved himself to be, in his utter failure to grasp the necessity of conciliating public opinion, a worthy colleague of most of the Spanish officials sent by O'Donnell to the colony. The Dominican clergy, who had at first eagerly welcomed, with few exceptions, the transfer of sovereignty, were soon thrown into consternation, not only by the fact that Spanish priests

were fast replacing Dominicans in the more important
posts in the gift of the Church, but also by the action of
the prelate in undertaking to control their private lives,
which were in some cases notoriously lax. The success of
the Archbishop in eradicating the "heretical" Methodist
churches which had been founded many years previously
by American immigrants, and his subsequent altercation
with Santana, who refused to turn over the papers and
secret archives of the Masonic Order to the Archbishop
for his inspection, and advised the prelate to attend to his
own concerns, since masonry "was not a fit business for
an Archbishop to meddle with," fanned popular discontent as well as that of the clergy. It remained for the
Archbishop to force the native priests to abandon the
practice of accepting fees for their parochial services, and
content themselves with a beggarly monthly stipend, and
the immense power which the Dominican clergy was able
to exert was at once directed not only against their religious superior, but against every semblance of Spanish
control as well.

Finally the resort of the Spanish authorities to the levy
of greatly increased taxes upon the impoverished inhabitants of the colony to meet the ever-increasing expenses
of the occupation provided the last straw upon the back
of the already sorely over-burdened populace. After little
more than two years the disastrous result of the Spanish
experiment was clearly shown in reports of the American
Commercial Agents:

"It is now nearly two years that this part of the Island
has been under Spanish rule and as yet it remains in the
same miserable state as formerly. I neither hear of nor see
any improvements . . . The small amount of money in
circulation is that which the troops (only 3,000 men are

now alive) spend from their pay. Living and all articles
of necessity are excessively high. Spain has already expended $2,000,000, and is now wasting $100,000 a month
. . . All foreign produce imported now pays a duty of
30%; Spanish products in Spanish vessels pay only 9%
. . . [1] The arbitrary levies and taxes which have been
forced upon the people of this Island to support a gang
of idle Spanish officials have so disheartened the people
that the majority have abandoned their farms and wood-
cuts, and have allowed their plantations to overgrow with
weeds . . . commerce is dead . . . there is an almost
total suspension of exports, and ruin has come to the
merchants of the Island." [2]

If the Spanish authorities so soon succeeded in causing
the ruin of the colony and in awakening the burning
hostility of all classes, they obtained by their policy even
more speedily the violent antipathy of the foreign residents, many of whom had been among the first to
welcome the advent of Spanish rule. To none was the
hostility of officialdom more heartily displayed than
towards the resident Americans. According to the American Agent, "the Spaniards here are no friends of the
United States, and almost without exception lean towards
Jefferson Davis and his bogus Southern Confederacy.
Nothing has pleased them more than to hear of the defeat
of our army and as they hoped, the ruin of the United
States." [3]

But hatred for the American Union was demonstrated
in more practical fashion than in the mere expression of

[1] Mr. Jonathan Elliott, Acting Commercial Agent, to Secretary Seward, January
13, 1863.
[2] Mr. William G. W. Yaeger, American Commercial Agent, to Secretary Seward,
October 2, 1863.
[3] Mr. William G. W. Yaeger, Commercial Agent, to Secretary Seward, September 28, 1863.

the hope of its defeat, or in the confiscation of the churches of the American Methodist negroes. On July 28, 1862, the *Alabama*, built in a British shipyard and manned with British seamen, had slipped quietly down the Mersey to commence the long series of its depredations upon the shipping of the United States. Within two months its ravages in the Caribbean had driven the major portion of the Union vessels from those waters. In the ports of the colony the raider found a ready refuge. On January 28, 1863, anchoring in the roadstead of Santo Domingo, the commander of the Confederate steamer, Commander Ralph Semmes, put ashore the crews of two Union sailing vessels which he had sunk between Santo Domingo and Haiti. Welcomed by the Spanish authorities, the *Alabama* plied sometimes for weeks within the territorial waters of the colony, taking occasional refuge from the American men-of-war concentrated at St. Thomas, in some sheltered port of the Dominican colony. The protests of the American Agent were fruitless, and his indignation appears to have been divided between the Spanish authorities for their breach of neutrality, and the commanders of the Union men-of-war, to whom he had sent repeated word of the raider's whereabouts. "So long," the Agent reported to Secretary Seward, "as they could lay in St. Thomas, and the officers indulge in iced juleps and cocktails, they cared nothing about the *Alabama*." [1]

6.

By the end of the year 1861 Santana clearly foresaw that unless a radical change took place in the policy of the Spanish Government, disaster was inevitable. Discon-

[1] Mr. William G. W. Yaeger, Commercial Agent, to Secretary Seward, October 10, 1863.

tent against the occupation was increasing dangerously, not only among the better educated elements of the populace, but among the lower classes as well. His own indignation at the treatment accorded him was unbounded. For a few brief months after the visit of General Serrano his wishes had been generally met, but as time went on the Captain-General found his recommendations entirely ignored, and his own supporters not only passed over in favour of Spanish office-seekers, but also upon the rare occasions when Dominicans were offered preferment, his most bitter opponents, the partisans of Baez, received appointment by recommendation of General Pelaez, the Lieutenant-Governor, whose relations with his chief had now become those of open hostility. The climax came when Santana's two remaining Dominican Secretaries of State, Dávila Fernández de Castro and Miguel Lavastida, were removed from office early in January, 1863, without the prior knowledge of the Captain-General.

With the impetuous temper characteristic of him, Santana despatched immediately his resignation to the Queen, believing undoubtedly that the announcement of his resignation would be received with such consternation in Madrid that not only would the Spanish Government insist upon his retention of authority, but that it would likewise provide him with the ample powers which he had formerly held as Dictator of the Republic, and accede to his pleas for the removal of the Spanish officials, whose constant meddling in the administration of the colony had now become altogether insupportable. Basing his resignation upon the conventional ground of ill-health, he did not lose the opportunity to magnify his own accomplishments:

"A strong and well organized administration extends throughout the country, and promises to improve its condition. Forces on land and sea, and even more the glories which the nation is acquiring in all quarters, act as a guaranty against foreign menace; everything has changed; all has improved; all, finally, has obtained that character of progress which assures a successful future."

During the preceding months, however, the Spanish Ministers had commenced to feel that Santana was by no means so indispensable to their purposes as they had at first been led to believe. Serrano himself had been disillusioned. Consequently, Santana's resignation was promptly accepted, on March 28th, 1862. Although the pill was gilded by the grant of the title of Marqués de las Carreras, the rank of Senator of the Kingdom, and a life-pension of $12,000, Santana's mortification was intense and his dismay unassumed, when he at length realized that his hope of retaining indefinite control of the country was now irretrievably shattered.

But he was unwilling to permit his fellow-subjects to perceive his chagrin. In a farewell address he assured them that "already their fortunate fate was securely written in the book of destiny; their families have a safe home; their properties a strong arm to defend them"; and impressed upon them that "union, respect of the law, affectionate submission to the authorities, love of order and devotion to their daily tasks" were the means of permitting them to enjoy the fruits of his tireless efforts of the past eighteen years to promote their well-being. On July 20, 1862, Santana installed his successor, General Felipe Rivero y Lemoyne, as Captain-General, and retired to meditate upon the perversities of fate at his beloved estancia, El Prado.

7.

The Spanish Government was incredibly inept. Among all the masqueraders of the Liberal Union, desirous as they were of playing the rôle of empire builders of the nineteenth century, the sole leader who demonstrated a spark of capacity, Serrano, was soon to leave the Antilles to pursue his fortunes as Duque de la Torre in the wider sphere of opportunity of Spain itself. The incapacity of the Spanish Cabinet, already evidenced by the utter failure of its Premier to grasp what were in reality the simple requirements of the situation in Santo Domingo, was strikingly emphasized by the character of its appointees to the new colony.

Of all the prominent officials sent by Spain to Santo Domingo, General Rivero is perhaps the outstanding figure for the crass stupidity which he consistently displayed during the fourteen months of his rule as Captain-General. Born in Caracas, his outlook on life was bounded by the narrow limits of the colonial environment in which he had grown up. Through petty intrigue he had now reached, as Captain-General of the Spanish province, the apex of his ambitions. Quite ignorant of the fundamental necessities of the situation with which he was now called upon to deal, he attempted at first to palliate by means of conventional phrases the very practical discontent which was smouldering in the hearts of the Dominicans, and as soon as he discovered that words would not solve the problem, he resorted to the other alternative of a weak character, and attempted to stamp out by sheer brutality the dissatisfaction which was rife.

No sooner had he entered office than he proceeded at once to heap upon the Dominican people a mass of petty restrictions and limitations of the personal freedom which they had formerly enjoyed, which brought home to each individual, far more intolerably perhaps than the broader and already existing causes of unrest, how obnoxious the Spanish administration actually was. Severe penalties had already been imposed upon those partaking in the seemingly innocent pastime of playing cards in the taverns and cafés, the only amusement besides cockfighting generally existing in the monotonous lives of the Dominican poorer classes. Additional decrees were promulgated on September 20th and October 15th by General Rivero, which greatly increased the resentment of the laboring classes. The first obliged the country people to transport from one district to another the equipment of any troops or officers who might pass their way, thus obliging the farmer to leave his home for days at a time at the option of any passing Spanish officer. The second was a series of regulations governing sanitation, religion, morality, and the upkeep of houses, streets, and country roads, all unadapted and inadaptable to the requirements and needs of the Dominican people. A third decree of January 12, 1863, obliging each householder to remodel his house in accordance with the theories of the Captain-General, was an attempt to force the already impoverished inhabitants of the country to spend uselessly sums they had no means of obtaining.

If the policy pursued by the new Captain-General was already creating for the Spanish troops a potential enemy in each Dominican, an equally formidable antagonist had already appeared among them, for yellow fever had broken out. Before Rivero's arrival, the dread enemy had already thinned the ranks; after his arrival it increased its ravages:

"On July 1st, 1,000 troops arrived from Havana. Of the 5,000 troops previously landed, only about 300 remain, all the rest having died of yellow fever, and of those left between twenty and thirty are dying daily. On account of the rainy season and the filthy condition of the City, there is no hope for an abatement of the fever." [1]

During the next five months another thousand died, and the soldiers who had come from the garrisons in Puerto Rico and in Cuba, and who were believed to be acclimatized, were buried by the hundreds in Dominican soil. The holocaust was so appalling, the signs of general discontent among the Dominican populace so formidable, and the mutterings of mutiny among the Spanish troops so disconcerting, that Rivero took alarm:

"On the night of the 30th of September, a meeting of the highest Spanish authorities was held at the house of Governor-General Rivero, when it was agreed to advise General O'Donnell and the Spanish Government to abandon the Island." [2]

But General O'Donnell, holding his position in Madrid against increasing odds, could not stultify himself by admitting to the Spanish people that the hopes of a new empire with which he had beguiled them had so speedily vanished, and issuing orders that more conscripts be drafted from their vineyards or their olive groves to be poured into Santo Domingo, where they would die even more rapidly than their brothers, who had already undergone exposure to the tropics in Cuba and Puerto Rico, he rendered inevitable the struggle of the next two years, which was to result in the gravest tragedy for Spain and in the utter desolation of the colony which had been so briefly restored to her.

[1] Mr. William G. W. Yaeger to Secretary Seward, July 3, 1862.
[2] Mr. Jonathan Elliott, Acting Commercial Agent, to Secretary Seward, October 3, 1862.

By now the storm was breaking. An attempt at rebellion, which was put down, in the first days of February, 1863, at Neiba, was followed by a more threatening revolt which broke out on February 24th, when General Lucas de Peña, leading a small body of Dominican patriots, captured a Spanish detachment at Guayubín. Martial law was immediately proclaimed by Rivero, who sent an urgent message to the Marqués de las Carreras in his retreat at El Prado to join the Lieutenant-Governor, General Carlos de Vargas, in stemming the tide which was flooding the Cibao. Before Santana reached the decision to comply with the request, the revolution had been proclaimed in both Moca and Santiago, where the Dominican flag was once more hoisted. But the early attempts at revolution proved temporarily unsuccessful. The better drilled and better armed Spanish troops succeeded in dispersing the revolutionaries, who were mostly armed solely with machetes. Such of the rebels as could escape, fled into the impenetrable brush of the frontier provinces, and those of their leaders who had been captured were shot without a hearing on April 17th, notwithstanding the appeals and the petitions which came both from the foreign Consuls and from leading Dominican citizens. Had it not been for the general amnesty proclaimed by the Queen at the request of the Spanish Cabinet, on May 27th, more executions would have followed, and the remaining captives from the revolutionary forces would have been condemned to work as galley slaves in chains in Cuba, "some for twenty years and others for ten years, and a few of those of lesser importance in the streets of Santo Domingo in the chain-gang." [1]

The lull afforded by the amnesty was of short dura-

[1] Mr. William G. W. Yaeger to Secretary Seward, April 6, 1863.

tion, and resulted principally in granting the opportunity to the leaders who had escaped, among them notably General José Cabrera, General Pedro A. Pimentel and General Benito Monción, to perfect arrangements with the Haitian General, Sylvain Salnave, who had commenced a revolt in the north of Haiti against Geffrard, for support in their efforts to dislodge the Spanish authorities.

On August 16th, the revolution broke out once more at Capotillo, where a small body of Dominicans under the leadership of Cabrera and Monción surprised a Spanish detachment and utterly routed it. And this time the revolution was not to be quenched by the energy of Santana, nor by the brutality of the Spanish officers; it was destined to continue until the last Spanish soldier had been driven from Dominican soil.

The reports from the American Commercial Agent were now constant:

"A state of martial law has been declared by General Rivero. The revolutionists attacked General Hungría, the Governor of Santiago; his bodyguard were mostly slain but he himself escaped. They next attacked Guayubín, where all the Spanish soldiers were killed and the town destroyed. The whole Cibao has risen in arms and they are killing and driving the Spaniards before them. . . Over one-half of the officers and men of the Spanish garrisons in the northern part of the Island have been killed or wounded, and two-thirds of the garrison in Santo Domingo have died from yellow fever during the present month. The total number of Spanish soldiers is under 3,000 men and at least one-third of them are in the hospitals. The Government is engaged in building fortifications around the Capital since the Spanish force in the Capital is less than 1,000 able-bodied men. General Rivero has appointed a military tribunal in Santiago with full powers to pass sentence upon any revolutionists brought before it." [1]

"The revolution has been gaining strength daily and every district nearly has declared against the Spaniards. In several parts of the Island where there were but few Spanish troops, the commanders called together the Dominicans and supplied them with arms and ammunition with the intention of marching to La Vega and Santiago to crush the revolution, but as soon as the Dominicans had the arms in their possession, they slaughtered the Spaniards. The few Spanish soldiers and residents who escaped fled to the Capital. Moca has been burned to the ground."

"Five hundred Spanish troops have arrived in Santo Domingo from Puerto Rico to protect the palace and the City.

".   .   .   .   .   . [2]

"Spain's Governors in Macorís and Cotuy, Dominicans by birth, succeeded in reaching the Capital bearing each a passport issued them by the revolutionists. The passport states 'The Dominican Republic still lives. Liberty or death, and a war of extermination to all Spaniards and their blood.'

"General Santana is now in the Capital where he awaits the arrival of additional Spanish troops to lead them against the revolutionists." [3]

"Owing to the fact that no Spanish troops arrived, General Santana obtained 500 Dominicans from the neighborhood of San Cristóbal, and with 1,000 Spanish troops, on September 15th, crossed on the rope ferry the Ozama

[1] Mr. William G. W. Yaeger to Secretary Seward, August 31, 1863.
[2] Mr. William G. W. Yaeger to Secretary Seward, Sept. 6, 1863.
[3] Mr. William G. W. Yaeger to Secretary Seward, Sept. 14, 1863.

River marching towards Santiago by the Monte Plata road, the shorter road being impassable owing to the floods.

"Santiago has been totally destroyed. Some 2,000 troops reaching Puerto Plata from Havana, with the local garrison, totaling in all 3,000, marched towards Santiago taking six days to arrive there. General Buceta, the Spanish Commander of the Cibao, who had taken refuge in the fort with about 1,000 men and taking the revolutionists in the rear, enabled the Spanish forces from Puerto Plata to cut their way into Santiago. The Spaniards thus regained possession of the City, but immediately afterwards the Dominicans attacked them from all sides and the Spaniards were forced to take refuge in the fort of San Luis. The Spaniards refusing to surrender the fortress, the Dominicans burned the City to the ground, when the Spaniards agreed to capitulate. The terms of the capitulation were that the Spanish troops were to leave everything in the fort together with their own arms, but contrary to their agreement, they blew up the powder magazine and retained their arms. At this the Dominicans were so incensed that notwithstanding their agreement to give the Spanish troops free passage, they fell upon them and only one-half succeeded in returning to Puerto Plata. About 6,000 rifles have thus been obtained by the revolutionaries.

"General Santana with his army has been checked at Monte Plata and is there awaiting reënforcements."[1]

"When the news reached here that the districts of Bánica, San Juan, Neiba, and Azua in the west had declared against the Spaniards . . . the Government became so frightened that at midnight, with a strong guard, they took from their beds thirty-six of the most respectable and influential men in the City, handcuffed them, and marched them on board of a small schooner, sending them as

[1] Mr. William G. W. Yaeger to Secretary Seward, September 21, 1863.

prisoners to Puerto Rico, without one cent in their pockets or even a change of clothing . . . Among them were several foreigners, some who have been merchants in this City for ten and fifteen years. Among the number arrested is Joaquín Delmonte, a merchant of this City, who had resided some years in the United States and received his first naturalization papers. The Government has also arrested three of the principal priests . . . and sent them as prisoners to Havana. As the Spaniards have been routed and driven from every town, hamlet, and district in the interior and have now been obliged to take refuge in this City and Puerto Plata, there is no limit to their arbitrary rule . . . At Samaná, they had over 300 Spanish convicts in the chain-gang, murderers and felons of the worst kind, who had been sent there from Spain, and as this motley government needed troops, the chains were taken from these convicts and arms put in their hands. As these men were condemned to the chain-gang for life, they will no doubt, with these arms in their hands, and free from their chains, make good their escape to teach the poor Dominican the villainy of a Spanish convict." [1]

"The Dominican revolutionists have obtained possession of Puerto Plata and hoisted the Dominican flag. They gave the Spaniards and their families time to embark. While this was going on, a Spanish man-of-war arrived and when the Spaniards were embarked, the Spanish war vessel began firing upon the City and the whole City was destroyed by fire." [2]

"On Sunday, October 4th, the Spanish troops and the Chinese laborers employed by the Spanish authorities, pillaged all the stores and private residences in Puerto Plata. This was sanctioned and encouraged by the Spanish officers

[1] Mr. William G. W. Yaeger to Secretary Seward, September 28, 1863.
[2] Mr. William G. W. Yaeger to Secretary Seward, October 10, 1863.

present. On October 5th and 6th the same individuals set fire to the stores and dwellings of the City." [1]

"The refugees from Puerto Plata were brought to the Capital. Many poor families have been put on shore at this City without shelter, food, clothing or friends, and it is heartrending to see these poor women and little children wandering through the streets exposed to the broiling tropical sun or the rain, not knowing where to go or to lay their heads. The public buildings and churches are used as barracks and hospitals for the troops.

"A large number of wounded soldiers have been sent to Puerto Rico. Two steamers left today filled with sick and wounded. All the families who had the means left Puerto Plata for the neighboring islands after Santiago was destroyed. There is now not a town or district which has not pronounced for the revolution. San Cristóbal has declared, and the ferry at the Haina River has been taken possession of by the Dominicans, preventing the Spanish troops from the Capital from marching to San Cristóbal. Samaná has been burned. Two steamers were despatched this morning for Azua and Baní to bring here the troops and their families. In the east at Monte Plata the revolutionists are attacking Santana, who has been fighting for the last ten days. Living is enormously high. The few old goats around this City and its outskirts are being brought up and killed, and those who can afford it get some as a favor at from thirty to fifty cents a pound. . . . The people of San Carlos, numbering about 1,500 inhabitants, have been ordered by the Government to move into the City. The chain-gang of Dominican prisoners has been employed for two weeks in cutting down the trees within one mile of the City walls and for the last three days they have had over 1,000 men employed at the same work. The whole

[1] From an affidavit forwarded by Mr. Arthur Lithgow, American Vice Consul in Puerto Plata, to the Department of State.

village of San Carlos is to be destroyed so as to erase all protection to the enemy." [1]

"Five steamers have arrived bringing troops and families from Azua. The Spanish authorities spread the rumor throughout that province that 30,000 Spanish troops were soon to arrive to lay waste the whole Republic and that the citizens of Azua who remained in their homes would be treated as rebels. The Azuans were consequently frightened into abandoning their homes in that province and to take passage as refugees on these Spanish steamers, from which they have been landed in Santo Domingo City without shelter, food or clothing. Every house in the City of Azua has been abandoned and most of the country people have fled. The Captain-General has sent his own family to Puerto Rico for safety. Santana is still held at Monte Plata where his retreat has been cut off. Attempting to give battle to the revolutionists at Yamasá all his baggage, mules, horses, guns, ammunition, provisions, together with two Spanish generals and about 100 Spanish troops were captured. He has sent for reënforcements from the Capital day after day but his messengers are generally taken before they reach the City. Two hundred troops, with one cannon, were sent to his relief, but they only got five miles from the Capital when they were captured or killed. The Spaniards are fortifying the walls of the City and they are afraid to venture one mile out on the Guibia road." [2]

In the midst of the struggle, as soon as it became evident that the first scattered attempts at revolt were fast merging into the supreme effort to end Spanish occupation, amid the still smoking ruins of Santiago, a Provisional Government of the Dominican Republic was once

[1] Mr. William G. W. Yaeger to Secretary Seward, October 10, 1863.
[2] Mr. William G. W. Yaeger to Secretary Seward, October 19, 1863.

more constituted. On the 14th of September, 1863, in one of the few houses which still stood after the conflagration, a small group of citizens proclaimed, "Before God, the world, and the throne of Spain," that the Dominican Republic had been restored. By popular acclamation, General José Antonio Salcedo, who had figured prominently in the initial battles of the rebellion, was chosen President of the Provisional Government, and Don Benigno Filomeno de Rojas, who had already figured as Vice President in the Santiago Government of 1858, was once more selected to hold his previous post. Don Ulises F. Espaillat was called upon to direct the foreign relations of the new Government, and Duarte's companion, General Ramón Mella, joined the administrative Junta together with other prominent citizens of the Cibao, among them Don Pedro Francisco Bonó and Don Sebastián Valverde, all of them long identified, so far as conditions had made it possible, with the spread of liberal doctrines in the Republic.

The Provisional Government, on September 23rd, addressed a proclamation to the Spanish Queen, detailing the motives for the rebellion against her Government's authority and begging the appointment of plenipotentiaries by Spain to agree with the Provisional Government upon the bases of a treaty of peace which might put an end to the conflict. The petition obtained no reply, as might have been anticipated, but had presumably some effect in inducing the Spanish Cabinet to listen more attentively to the counsel of General Carlos de Vargas, the Lieutenant-Governor of the colony, who had gone to Madrid and had remained there for some months urging modification of the policy which the Spanish Government had been pursuing, and the conciliation of the Dominican people. Vargas was finally successful in obtaining the approval of his recommendations, and received himself the appointment as Captain-General in the place of Rivero. His return to Santo Domingo was generally welcomed by those who had not taken an active part in the Revolution, and in line with the new policy upon which he had insisted, his early proclamations endeavoured to dispel the general hatred and bitterness toward the Spanish authorities, and announced the pardon of the majority of the unfortunate Dominican non-combatants who had been exiled from the country by Rivero.

Rivero himself was ordered to leave the capital the day upon which the new Captain-General arrived, and left for Madrid to be tried by court-martial. The reign of terror which the later months of Rivero's administration had produced was reported by the American Commercial Agent:

"Rivero's imbecility, mismanagement, and retaining of such men in office as General Buceta, late Governor of Santiago and the Cibao, have been the cause of this late revolution and the almost total ruin and desolation of this country. General Buceta is a fair specimen of the Spanish tyrant. Being brought up as a jailer and the keeper of felons on the barren island of Ceuta, his training has not been such as would fit him to be the governor of a harmless, free and independent people. His first appointment under this Government was that of Commander at Samaná, where he compelled, at the point of the bayonet, all the people within his jurisdiction to work on the public highway one week out of every three without receiving one cent for their labor. At Samaná there are about 300 American colored people who have resided in this country for some years; also a few English subjects. These poor enslaved people appealed to the English Consul and myself and we protested against such arbitrary and brutal proceedings. We finally succeeded and General Buceta was removed, but instead of sending him to the Island of Ceuta, from where he ought never to have been taken, the Captain-General appointed him Governor of Santiago and of the Cibao, where he made himself still more obnoxious. In Santiago, he would walk the streets early in the morning and wherever he found a house closed he would send his buglers and drummers to turn the people out of their beds. . . . His own guilty conscience would not allow him to sleep and he was determined to deprive every one else of their rest . . . On several occasions, where he passed houses about seven in the morning and found them closed, he would at once order his drummers before the doors, and many a poor woman in her confinement breathed her last under his inhuman and tyrannical mood. Several respectable men of Santiago, whose income was sufficient to maintain them without labor, he took from their houses at the point of the bayonet, marched them to the plaza, and there made them shoulder heavy timbers and carry them around the square until the blood would run from their shoulders. A reign of terror and arbitrary cruelty commenced . . . and a certain Colonel Campello, who was unfortunately appointed to the command of the frontier, committed there the most abominable outrages, robbing property, ravishing women, and shooting in cold blood a number of inoffensive and respectable inhabitants without even the form of a trial." [1]

General de Vargas, who had made friends among the Dominicans while serving as Rivero's lieutenant, and whose efforts to better the condition of the people had gained for him the esteem of many, might earlier have succeeded in postponing, at least, the outbreak of the rebellion, but he had now come too late.

[1] Mr. William G. W. Yaeger to Secretary Seward, October 26, 1863.

8.

During the first weeks after the installation of the new Captain-General there was a temporary lull in the hostilities. It was the expectancy of the Provisional Government, and the belief of the disgruntled elements generally, that the adoption by the Spanish Government of the new policy made evident by the appointment of Vargas, portended its willingness to negotiate an agreement of evacuation. The instructions given the Captain-General, however, contemplated no such eventuality, and Vargas's leading generals, Santana in particular, who interpreted the conciliatory proclamation of their superior as a deplorable evidence of weakness, not only combated the course adopted as stubbornly as they dared, but likewise in their dealings with the populace made emphatically plain the divergence between their own views and those of General de Vargas. As a natural result intense hostility was not long in showing itself again generally against the Spanish authorities, and the Santiago Government, disappointed in its expectations, and ignored by the Cabinet at Madrid, formally declared on December 25th that a state of war existed on land and sea between the Dominican Republic and the Spanish Monarchy. By the same proclamation the accumulated bitterness of the Cibao people was vented on Santana; the "Liberator" was declared guilty of the crime of high treason against his country; he was proclaimed an outlaw, and all officers of the Provisional Government were urged to shoot him at sight.

To General de Vargas, largely ignorant of the manner in which his desires for a milder policy were being deliberately thwarted by his subordinates, the recrudescence of animosity against Spanish rule on the part of the Dominicans, notwithstanding his attempts at conciliation, was only explicable on the ground of gross ingratitude. This belief, gradually engendered in him, and his disappointment at his ill success in obtaining the pacification of the country, which he had assured his Government the adoption of the policy which he proposed would speedily procure, eventually converted his desire for conciliation into a bitter determination to force submission to his authority by strength of arms.

The renewal of the campaign was not marked by any outstanding achievement on either side, however, due to the lack of loyalty to their commander displayed by the Spanish Generals, and the jealousies and increasing rivalries among the revolutionary leaders. For months the exhausting conflict continued:

"The Dominicans are keeping up a continual guerilla warfare and with the rainy season at hand the few Spanish troops left are fast dying. Santo Domingo is a perfect hospital. Three thousand troops sent from the Capital the middle of October to attempt to quell the revolution in San Cristóbal took ten days to fight their way there. Over 500 men were killed or wounded on the way. When they arrived, they found the town deserted. Being obliged to procure their water from the River Nigua, half a mile from the town, they are losing about fifteen men daily in obtaining it. Only 1,000 are left who are capable of doing duty." [1]

"The Spanish troops have been forced to abandon San Cristóbal and have fallen back upon the Haina River. The position which they occupy there is one of the most unhealthy on this Island. A force of 800 men on a Spanish steamer from Cuba arrived at Monte Cristi intending to

[1] Mr. William G. W. Yaeger to Secretary Seward, November 10, 1863.

march to Santiago overland; when a few had landed, the Dominicans started firing and captured 100 prisoners and four boats. The steamer with the troops which were left retired and landed the forces in the fort at Puerto Plata. A few weeks later, two men of war with 1,500 Spanish troops arrived at Manzanillo Bay, intending to land at the mouth of the Dajabón River for the purpose of marching to relieve the Spanish garrison at Dajabón and from there to take the road to Santiago. They were thereupon ordered away by the Haitian garrison and when word of their arrival reached President Geffrard, he issued orders to them that not one Spanish soldier would be permitted by his troops to land. The Spanish men of war consequently proceeded to Puerto Plata and came thence by sea to Santo Domingo." [1]

"The Spanish troops which abandoned San Cristóbal and encamped on the Haina River, with a reënforcement of 1,000 men from the Capital, have marched along the coast to Baní under the protection of the guns of two men of war. The Dominicans abandoned the town after setting fire to it and have fled to the mountains." [2]

"2,300 Spanish troops have reached Azua and the Dominican inhabitants of Azua who had taken refuge in Santo Domingo at the instance of the Spanish officials have been permitted to return to their homes.

". . . General Santana has now been three months at Monte Plata. The Dominicans whip him about twice a week and it keeps the small steamer busy bringing down his sick and wounded and taking up rations and fresh troops. The small steamer ascends the Ozama as far as Yabacao, about fifteen miles, where the Spaniards have established a depot for supplies with a guard of 300 men. From there everything is taken by mules to Santana's army

[1] Mr. William G. W. Yaeger to Secretary Seward, November 25, 1863.
[2] Mr. William G. W. Yaeger to Secretary Seward, December 4, 1863.

some ten miles further. On December 11th, the Dominican revolutionists captured Santana's depot of supplies, obtaining 70 mules, 500 arms, 2 cannon, 60,000 rounds of ammunition, 40,000 rations and 300 prisoners. Santana's men were consequently kept six days with almost nothing to eat." [1]

The position of Santana must by now have appeared desperate even to himself. General Luperón, the negro leader from Puerto Plata, whose brilliant participation in the rebellion had already brought him to a position of high prominence, with a force of eager patriots, now well armed with the arms and ammunition they had succeeded in capturing from their adversaries, was opposing Santana at every step. Time and again, the dwindling force commanded by Santana was defeated by the troops commanded by Luperón. The morale of the Spanish soldiers was fast disintegrating. The orders issued by Santana were often set aside by the Captain-General, whom Santana's opponents among his Spanish colleagues had succeeded in alienating from him.

At the beginning of March, Santana was ordered to abandon his attempt to force his way to the Cibao, to withdraw from the outposts at Monte Plata and Guanuma which he had so long been defending, and to concentrate his troops in Guerra and San Carlos. When he received these instructions the despair of the Marqués de las Carreras had no bounds. With the passing of the months, as the failure of the Spanish troops to maintain their supremacy became more manifest, and the popularity of the Government in Santiago increased, the desertions to the cause of the revolution from among the ranks of Santana's personal supporters had become more numerous.

[1] Mr. William G. W. Yaeger to Secretary Seward, December 28, 1863.

One by one the sycophants of the days of Santana's greatness, the recipients of his favours, were going over to the Provisional Government. The name of even Tomás Bobadilla was soon to be counted among the revolutionists, and the old General felt himself very much alone. When he received word of the order to retreat, which made evident the lack of confidence of the Spanish Government in his capacity, such faith as he had in those of his followers who were still with him, weakened. Accusing them of cowardice and indecision, he complained bitterly to Don Miguel Lavastida, one of the very few who still remained loyal to their old leader.

"I have maintained," he wrote on March 16th to Lavastida, "the two outposts at Monte Plata and Guanuma with perseverance and under the most unfavorable circumstances . . . It was because I realized the necessity of maintaining those two points; because I had an interest in saving the situation, and notwithstanding the obstacles and the difficulties that may have presented themselves I had sufficient energy to overcome all hindrances as they came, ignoring the intimations of my timorous colleagues, dismissing from my side the cowards who could have engendered lack of confidence among the troops . . . General Alfau . . . has once more demonstrated his desire to withdraw from the discouragements and the fatigues which we are all encountering, and has retired to enjoy the tranquillity which he should not dare to attain before peace has been well established in the land of his birth."

But the complaints of Santana were now as fruitless as the protests he despatched to the capital, where the defeats which his troops encountered during the retreat had destroyed the last vestige of Santana's military prestige. The evacuation of Monte Plata permitted the revolutionists to obtain control of passes of the utmost strategic importance, inasmuch as they afforded them free access to the Cibao from the outskirts of Santo Domingo and resulted in the isolation of the Seybo, whither Santana with some two thousand men had retired. The disasters of the preceding months, for which the leaders of the Liberal Union in Madrid threw the blame upon the change of policy sponsored by Vargas, brought about the speedy recall of the latter, who was now stricken with brain fever, to which the disappointments and humiliations he had suffered had no doubt largely contributed. In the stead of Vargas as Captain-General came General José de la Gándara y Navarro, whose severe ability, demonstrated during several years of efficient service in eastern Cuba, encouraged the Spanish Cabinet to hope that the repressive measures, to which it had become thoroughly committed, and which Gándara had instructions to carry out, would bring about the pacification of the colony in short order.

9.

General Gándara assumed office on March 31, 1864. The first words which he addressed to the troops under his command gave notice to all that an implacable foe had arisen to head the struggle against the revolutionists.

"The impenetrable forests, the roughness and the impassability of the roads, the torments of the climate and all the natural and man-made obstacles which we may encounter in our campaign shall not be invincible to us; . . . Soldiers of the Army and of the Reserves, our Queen and our country expect energy in our operations and constancy in our duties until this land shall have been pacified. When this has been accomplished, we shall all have complied with our duty, but in any event, it shall always be said of you that the glory is yours since you can always claim the victory and the honor."

General Gándara lost no time in making preparations to undertake an offensive campaign upon a scale far larger than that which had been previously contemplated, and in this purpose he had the hearty support of the new Captain General of Cuba, General Dulce, who had received orders to support Gándara with all the means within his power. The first step, in la Gándara's opinion, was to establish discipline among all the officers under his command, and with this object in mind, well aware of the resistance his predecessors had encountered from Santana, he lost no time in taking steps to procure either the humble subordination of the Marqués de las Carreras or his downfall, should he resist. He therefore appointed immediately a Spanish General of recognized ability, General Baldomero de la Calleja, second in command to Santana, in order that the latter might be replaced by Calleja in case of necessity. The climax which Gándara had anticipated was not long delayed. Santana, violently incensed by the preference shown to a Spanish officer over the Dominican officers still loyal to him, protested at the appointment. He wrote at once to Gándara, with whom he had already had an interview in which heated recriminations had passed:

"This order of yours appointing a Spanish officer as my lieutenant, when there are many officers of the old Dominican army of equal rank, makes it evident that you lack confidence in them, and this lack of confidence is entirely unfounded since there is no ground for it when it concerns men who are daily giving proof of their loyalty and patriotism . . . When I entrusted this land to Her

Majesty, Queen Isabel II, as its chief, making possible its annexation to the Monarchy, I made an agreement with the Spanish Government in which it was stipulated that equal consideration should be given to the generals and officers of the Dominican army as to those of equal rank in the Peninsular Army, and by virtue of these circumstances it is my duty to raise my protest to the highest authority of the Island when I see that the rights of those functionaries are prejudiced or when their dignity, which is my own, suffers offense, for I will not accept the confidence and the distinctions conferred upon me if these are granted in derogation of the rights of the officers who stand in the same situation as my own."

La Gándara, nothing loath, seized the opportunity to threaten Santana with a court-martial should he persist in the attitude which he had taken. The Captain-General claimed that the old man's criticism of the instructions he had issued were mutinous:

"Your Excellency has forgotten even the most fundamental notion of your position and of your duty, and if through an excess of undeserved consideration I do not in the present case make complete use of the powers with which I am invested, it is to give Your Excellency one more proof, and perhaps the last, of the consideration with which I propose to treat you and to respect the position and the antecedents of Your Excellency. I shall presently give a full account to my Government of the manner in which the Marqués de las Carreras treats, considers and obeys the person whom Her Majesty has honored with royal generosity and upon whom she has conferred her authority to represent her in this distant portion of her dominions. At the same time, I shall advise Her Majesty's Government, as I now inform Your Excellency, that appreciating as I do all the obligations imposed upon me by my command in the honorable mission which has been entrusted to me, and desiring to repay, as I should, such honorable distinctions, I am firmly resolved to maintain the dignity of the position which I hold and the respect which should be shown to my person as the representative of the sovereign authority, and as the commanding general of the army to which Spain has entrusted the honor of her arms before the world and before history. To accomplish it, my first duty, my instant obligation, is to maintain the most severe discipline in the army, and the most complete subordination to my orders and decrees in all that which I deem necessary for better service to Her Majesty. To this discipline and to this subordination, all members of the army should incline, without distinction of classes or of persons, and the Marqués de las Carreras should be the first to submit to them, to give the example to which he is obligated by his position and by his rank. Solely under these conditions am I able to consent and to tolerate that the command entrusted to me, be exercised by me, and only in the event that Your Excellency as the first of my subordinates recognizes these facts can you continue to hold the command with which you are actually entrusted. Therefore, if Your Excellency is not disposed to recognize my authority and to obey my orders, Your Excellency may depute your command to the general appointed as your lieutenant, to which his rank entitles him. I am making this finally very plain to Your Excellency, that should you continue to hold your command, the repetition of another instance similar to the one which gives rise to this communication will cause me, however regrettable it may be, to dictate your removal."

It was Santana himself, his hand shaking with the infirmity of age, his body racked with the disease which,

due to the rigours of the last two years, had made rapid
inroads on his iron constitution, who penned the last
chapter in his own long career. The ingratitude, as he
considered it, of the Spanish Captain-General steeled his
spirit to a final gesture of self-assertion.

"My communication," he wrote, "contained solely
proper criticism made with all good faith and loyalty
. . . in the interest of the service of Her Majesty . . . in
order that more favorable results might be obtained in
combatting the rebellion and in hastening the triumph of
her cause . . . General Santana does not commit acts of
insubordination, and respects every law, both social and
military. If, after having made a voluntary abdication of
the supreme authority of an independent state, through
love and loyalty to the mother country, I had sheltered the
thought of submitting to no authority superior to my own,
I would not have insisted upon resigning, as Captain-
General of the Island, the post which Her Majesty conferred upon me when the former Dominican Republic was
declared to be a Spanish province, nor would I have persisted in presenting my resignation and have submitted
with pleasure to the authority of the new Captain-General
whom the Government desired to appoint. But while I
obey the authority and respect the orders of the Captains-
General, I can do no less than offer to them just and indispensable criticisms when I see that they are committing
errors and are following a policy which may produce
prejudicial results, and that is what I have done with Your
Excellency . . . Your Excellency accuses me in sweeping
terms of harboring subversive intentions and that opinion,
most Excellent Sir, I can do no less than reject with all
the dignity of my honor and of my offended loyalty. The
Marqués de las Carreras cannot, nor does he know how
to, harbor subversive ideas. That opinion might be held

of other generals who do not have my qualities nor my antecedents. I have been governing this country for twenty years, after having been the prime factor in its independence. During those twenty years, I had no other ambition than its well-being and its glory, and it was for that sacred purpose that I undertook its annexation to the mother country, from which I think it should never have been separated. From that moment I committed myself heart and soul to sustain with equal enthusiasm and energy the honor of the Spanish flag and the throne of Doña Isabel II, to whom I had sworn loyalty, holding first the rank of Captain-General with all the rectitude, the conscience, and the responsibility for the laws which the holder of that high position should demonstrate . . . I desire to state to Your Excellency, first of all, that I do not fear your menaces. Your Excellency, with the authority which you hold, can, of course, take any step which you deem prudent, but I, tranquil in my conscience and in the conviction of my own loyalty, can await serenely the verdict of those who may judge me, assured as I am that some day justice and truth will reveal themselves. If I have committed any fault, let me be judged. But I will not suffer menaces . . . General Santana is not threatened, he is judged. In any event, since Your Excellency qualifies my criticisms as mutinous, and since you consider them acts of insubordination, and since I must continue making them to Your Excellency whenever I consider that you take measures which are improper, similar to those which have given rise to these communications, I am entrusting the command of this army to General Baldomero de la Calleja, appointed by Your Excellency my lieutenant, and I am leaving for Santo Domingo, where Your Excellency may dispose of me as you see fit, in order that, if you do so desire, the faults which you attribute to me may be judged."

When Santana had despatched this missive, he handed over the command of his troops to General Calleja, making his arrangements to go to the capital for a final test of strength. Proceeding to El Prado, he sought two days of repose to gird himself for the struggle. On June 8th, the Lieutenant-Governor, General Villar, who saw him at his home, found him sitting in the doorway of his residence, looking out over the fields at his cattle grazing in the shade of the towering mangoes and caobas with which the plains were dotted. Villar was shocked by the old man's appearance. It almost seemed as if his faith in his own destiny had been shattered. Word may have reached him that secret orders had been given by La Gándara that as soon as he arrived in the capital he was to be made a prisoner, and be sent to Cuba to await the decision of the authorities at Madrid.

But Santana was not to leave his country again. On June 14th, the day after he reached the capital, he died suddenly, whether of a stroke or by his own hand has never been definitely established.

Who knows what passed through his mind during those last few hours of his life? The long years when the Haitians ruled over the land, and the secret conspiracies in which he had so often taken part; the first call to arms, when he had collected about him his loyal farmers from the Seybo to march to Azua; the intrigues of Baez; the steady growth of the ambition which tormented him more and more as the years passed by—the vision of a foreign Power which would guard his country and permit him, so long as life would last, to remain the supreme authority; the glories of Azua and Las Carreras, and the cheering crowds as he rode back to the capital so many times at the head of his victorious army; where were those now who had applauded him then? Instead of being the supreme power, the hero of his country, the Liberator of the Fatherland, he was execrated, detested by them all, an outlaw for whose assassination any patriot would receive the thanks of the Dominican people, a defeated subordinate broken by the Spanish Captain-General. The glory of the day when the annexation had been proclaimed and he believed that all his ambitions had been realized; the growth of the cancer of rebellion; the jealousy of his new Spanish colleagues; the nightmare struggle to retain his own supremacy; the humiliation of his last defeats; the contemptuous insolence of La Gándara. Perhaps at the last, his thoughts turned to the sunny childhood days out in the pastures with his brother, Ramón, long before the turmoil and the heat of the later years. Of all the disappointments and torments and frustrated hopes, perhaps those last few hours before death wiped it all from his memory must have been the most bitter to endure.

Villar wrote humbly to General Gándara:

"Taking into account the important part General Pedro Santana has played in this country, the distinguished mark of regard which Her Majesty has deigned to confer upon him, his rank and his position as ex-President of the former Republic of Santo Domingo, believing that I was interpreting faithfully the desires of the Government of Her Majesty, I have given orders that the honors of a Captain General of this province be paid him when he is buried, although I appreciate, of course, that he is not entitled to them; and I have ordered that his remains be buried within the fortress of La Fuerza in accordance with the petition of his family, who fear that the hatred of the factions into which this country is now divided might cause a sacrilegious profanation of his tomb."

10.

By a strange and dramatic coincidence, the last months of Santana's life saw the brief return to the Republic, a wraith from better years, of Juan Pablo Duarte. For twenty years, the hero of the Separation had wandered unknown from one country to another. From Germany, where he had been sent as an exile by Santana, he had journeyed to Venezuela. Penniless and unknown, he had traveled far into the interior of South America, suffering hardships of every description. His family and friends had long since believed him dead. At length, word reached him by chance, in the small village where he had taken refuge on the Rio Negro on the boundary of northern Brazil, that the country to which he had devoted all he held dear in life had been sacrificed by Santana's ambitions to the Spanish Monarchy. Making his way to Caracas, he found there a handful of friends who told him of the revolution and that in Santiago a Provisional Government had been installed. Reaching Guayubín at last, Duarte wrote Don Ulises Espaillat:

"Exiled from my native land by that band of parricides who beginning by exiling the founders of the Republic, have concluded by selling to the stranger the country whose independence they swore to defend against all enemies, I have led during twenty years the nomad life of an exile, without previously obtaining from Providence the realization of the hope I have always fostered in my heart to be able to return one day to my fellow-citizens, to consecrate to the defense of their liberties what still remained of my strength and life. But there came the hour when Judas Iscariot believed that his work had been con- summated through his treason, and there came then for me the hour of my return to my country. God has made smooth my path notwithstanding the many difficulties and risks attendant upon my return. Here I am with four companions in this heroic town of Guayubín, ready to share with you in any way which you see fit all the vicissitudes and struggles which God may yet have in store, in the great task of restoring the independence of the Republic which you have already initiated with such honor and glory."

Espaillat was the sole member of the Provisional Government ready to welcome the hero of the independence of the Republic back to participate in its restoration. The chorus of thanksgiving which arose among the masses when they learned that the idol of twenty years ago had returned to give them new courage in their struggle against the Spanish usurper, aroused universal jealousy among the leaders of the rebellion, whose rivalries between themselves had already assumed formidable proportions. They were by no means disposed to step aside in favour of the man to whom more than to any other was due the founding of the Republic itself. Refusing to agree to the appointment of Duarte to any position of authority within the Government, and equally unwilling to bestow upon him any military command, it was due solely to Espaillat's insistence that the members of the Government could be persuaded to refrain from ignoring Duarte's presence completely. Finally, he was offered a diplomatic mission abroad. At first his indignation at such ingratitude caused Duarte to refuse the mission offered him. At length, however, he accepted it, realizing, readily enough, that his continued presence in the Republic would give rise to such dissension that the task of the restoration would become more than ever difficult. His last words upon leaving, for the last time, the shores of the Republic were these:

"If I returned to my country after so many years of absence, it was solely for the purpose of serving her with my soul, my life, and my heart, preaching as I always have, love among all the Dominicans. It was never my purpose to be a cause for discord nor a motive for dissension."

Forgotten once more by the band of politicians, when he could no longer jeopardize the realization of their own ambitions, as he had been forgotten before, he died some twelve years later, July 15, 1876, alone and utterly destitute, in Venezuela.

11.

Before the death of Santana had removed the sole figure likely to question his military decisions, La Gándara had already embarked upon the campaign which he had conceived before his installation. It was his belief that the capture and occupation of the northern sea-ports of the colony would render it possible to cut off all communication between the Provisional Government in Santiago and the outside world, which would result in the speedy fall of the revolutionary stronghold itself. Once Santiago was taken, the Spanish troops could readily crush opposition in the central provinces and clear the road to the capital in the south. If La Gándara's strategy was theoretically sound, he failed to take into account two overwhelming handicaps under which his men would labour. The first was the lack of adequate preparations to provision the Spanish forces, once they were landed in a devastated region where no supplies could be obtained, and the faulty equipment of the soldiers. The cannon and rifles furnished the forces under La Gándara's command were antiquated and often useless. Even the vessels upon which additional

troops were being sent to Santo Domingo by General
Dulce, the Cuban Captain-General, were unseaworthy.
According to a report of the American Commercial
Agent, "The Spanish war vessels are rotten. An American
engineer in Spanish employ has told me that there are ten
Spanish men-of-war lying in Cuba with their boilers
burnt out, not fit to go to sea. One of the principal Spanish
frigates, the *Blanca*, 51 guns, fired a salute at Port-
au-Prince which so completely disabled her that she had to
proceed at once to Spain for repairs." [1]

The second, and the more formidable, handicap was
the inability of the Spanish troops to withstand the
climate. During the last months of the preceding year,
18,000 troops had been sent to Santo Domingo from
Puerto Rico and from Cuba, making, together with the
troops already on duty upon their arrival, a total of some
21,000 men in occupation of the colony. Of that number,
prior to May, 1864, over 9,000 had died of fever, or had
been sent back from Santo Domingo incapacitated by
wounds or disease. Some 1,000 had been killed in the constant fighting. With the approach of the rainy season,
black water fever and yellow fever had recommenced
their inroads, and an epidemic of smallpox likewise
ravaged the garrisons.

By the middle of May La Gándara was energetically
carrying out his plans. Mustering as many of the troops
left at his disposal as he could remove from the southern
garrisons, together with a force of Dominicans between
the ages of fifteen and sixty conscripted in flagrant violation of the commitment of the Spanish Government at
the time of the annexation, he joined at Manzanillo Bay

---

[1] Mr. William G. W. Yaeger, Commercial Agent to Secretary Seward, January
10, 1864.

a force of more than 6,000 men transported upon a squadron of fourteen warships from Santiago de Cuba.

The first attack in the new campaign was directed against the town of Monte Cristi, gallantly defended by General Benito Monción, who had under him not more than five hundred Dominicans, sparsely armed, with only a few ancient cannon at their disposal. Assistance was hurriedly rendered him by General Pedro Antonio Pimentel and General Juan Antonio Polanco, and this small number of patriots, while eventually forced to abandon the town, were enabled to inflict serious losses upon the immensely superior number of the Spanish troops. In the course of the engagement, the commander of the Cuban expeditionary forces, Field Marshal Primo de Rivera, was severely wounded.

When La Gándara attempted to follow up his initial successes and sought to crush the guerrillas in the waste regions between Monte Cristi and Santiago, he courted inevitable disaster:

"The Dominicans pursued the policy of evacuating every town or village before the Spanish troops arrived, burning or destroying all property so that the Spanish troops are not able to maintain themselves. In addition, the Spanish soldiers are exposed to continual sniping. Mule trains with provisions sent to the Spaniards are almost invariably captured by the revolutionists." [1]

Through the impenetrable cactus brush of the regions now incorporated in Monte Cristi Province, the Spaniards were utterly unable to pursue the revolutionists. Continually losing their way, misled by guides sent for the purpose by the Dominicans, cut off from their provisions,

[1] Mr. William G. W. Yaeger to Secretary Seward, May 18, 1864.

suffering agonies of thirst under the blazing tropical sun, they no sooner encountered a band of the Dominicans than the latter retired, leaving the invaders to continue a pursuit during which their numbers were daily reduced by fever and sunstroke, or by the occasional bullet of the sniper. The guerrilla warfare waged by the inhabitants of the country, they could not withstand. La Gándara, in his despatches to his Government, reported that his campaign, as a result of the victory of Monte Cristi, had gained much moral strength and that

"if the operation of Monte Cristi had been commenced in the year 1863, it would have put an end to the war and would have resulted in the pacification of the Island. Undertaken in 1864, it was the first step towards a similar end, but it required a campaign in the autumn as a necessary complement." [1]

As it was, the Spaniards succeeded only in occupying Monte Cristi and in retaining control of Puerto Plata, and nothing more:

"In Puerto Plata, the Spaniards have been confined to the fort for more than nine months. They have succeeded in taking Monte Cristi at a great sacrifice of men, but from there they cannot advance inland. In addition to the yellow fever, an epidemic of smallpox is raging." [2]

The Spanish commanders in the north were soon compelled to realize that they could undertake no more than to maintain the seaports. In the south their position was equally desperate, notwithstanding the large reënforce-

[1] La Gándara, "Anexión y Guerra."
[2] Mr. William A. Reed, Acting Commercial Agent, to Secretary Seward, July 21, 1864.

ments which the Lieutenant-Governor, left in command of the capital, had obtained:

"Sorties of the Spanish troops from Santo Domingo have been repulsed in every encounter and a convoy of provisions for the troops has to be accompanied by 800 to 1,000 men. Skirmishes occur daily and the stillness of the night is ever broken by the rattle of musketry from the advance guard station half a mile distant from the City." [1]

12.

The fighting continued with considerable activity throughout the summer of 1864. La Gándara, whose confidence in his ultimate success proved at first unshaken by disaster, persisted in his futile effort to break the stubborn resistance of the Cibao provinces by attempting to force a wedge of Spanish troops into the heart of the Cibao. Realizing at last that this was hopeless, he diverted his attention to the increasing activities of the revolutionists in the eastern and southern Provinces; but here likewise his troops met with but slight success, and the successes which they were able to wrest, with considerable losses, were invariably rendered sterile by the continued inroads which disease made upon the armies. By the end of the summer not only had the virtual control of the revolutionaries of the territory adjacent to the northern seaports been successfully maintained, but many of the scattered Spanish garrisons to the east and to the west of the capital had been forced to abandon their positions and concentrate in the larger towns. Troops despatched to relieve outlying garrisons were ambushed along the route of march by the revolutionaries, and throughout October and November the losses suffered were so severe that by

[1] Mr. William A. Reed to Secretary Seward, August 27, 1864.

the latter month the Spaniards had been forced to abandon all points which they had formerly held in the east except the town of Seybo, and in the west they had been obliged to evacuate before the revolutionists and content themselves with holding the capital. By the end of December, La Gándara had been forced reluctantly to the conclusion that pacification of the colony by military force, under the circumstances which existed, was impracticable, and to commence the concentration of his forces in the capital, Samaná and Puerto Plata.

Before this date, however, the Captain-General, forced to appreciate the utter failure of his plans of conquest, and receiving, to his chagrin, repeated reports of the increasing unpopularity in Spain of the effort to pacify the colony, had determined to make the attempt to obtain by diplomatic means that acquiescence in the occupation which his policy of conquest had been unable to secure.

For several months the Provisional Government had vainly sought to obtain recognition or at least the admission of their status as belligerents from the foreign Governments with which the Dominican Republic had had diplomatic relations. The circular note drafted by Don Ulises Francisco Espaillat as Minister of Foreign Relations to arouse sympathy with the Dominicans in their struggle to regain their independence, encountered, as was to be anticipated, but scant response from Europe, and as little from the Government at Washington, which was then in the midst of the dark days of the campaign of 1864. Believing that the most favourable hope for moral support lay nevertheless in the United States, the Provisional Government despatched General Pablo Pujol as its Confidential Agent to Washington. To Seward, eager as he had been to lose no opportunity of hastening the elimination of

European dominion from the American continent, and particularly anxious as he was to see the termination of Spain's occupation of the Dominican Republic, the petitions of Pujol for the moral support of the Government of the United States proved peculiarly embarrassing. When the Governments of Europe had recognized the belligerency of the Confederate States less than three weeks after the proclamation of the blockade of the southern ports by President Lincoln, no voice raised in protest in the United States had been louder than that of the Secretary of State at the "affront" and "act of hostility" to the Union. When, a year later, Gladstone made his famous declaration at Newcastle that Jefferson Davis "had made a nation," and the recognition of the Confederacy by the British Cabinet as the result of pressure brought to bear by Napoleon III seemed imminent, no man in public life in the United States had denounced more vehemently the anticipated announcement of recognition than Seward. Recognition therefore of the Provisional Government at Santiago, or even the admission of its belligerent status, so long as the contest with Spain was not permanently decided and the independence of the insurgents was still inchoate, would necessarily have been regarded, in Seward's own words, as a "hostile act towards the Sovereign State." The Secretary of State was consequently constrained to receive the agent of the Dominican Provisional Government unofficially, and to limit himself in his private conferences with Pujol to personal expressions of sympathy with the revolutionary cause. While the American Government gave, therefore, no formal assistance to the Dominican insurgents, frequently thereafter privileges were conceded them which hardly concorded with the most rigid observance of the national laws of neutrality, as when, the Provisional Government having issued letters of marque, no steps were taken to prevent the outfitting and sailing of several vessels from New York under the Dominican flag.

The return of General Pujol in August from Washington, where, in the opinion of the offended leaders of the revolution, he had accomplished no more than to obtain "promises from President Lincoln," presented the opportunity sought by La Gándara to establish direct contact with the Revolutionary Government. Having already attempted, without result, to spread dissension among the insurgent forces by inducing a group of Dominican generals commanding Spanish troops to address a manifesto to the rebels beseeching them "to put down their arms, and to follow no longer the path of illusion and of error," he sent a secret agent to Pujol immediately after the latter's return from the United States. This emissary was instructed [1]

"to advise him that he would not reject any proposition made by the Dominican Government which would have for its purpose the negotiation of an arrangement which would permit both countries to terminate the war and possibly to negotiate the terms of peace."

The Provisional Government directed Pujol to reply

"that the Spanish Government, guided by the great and elevated principles of humanity and of political necessity, should give a proof of the magnanimity so characteristic of the Spanish people by granting the Dominican people peace and relief, tranquillity and repose."

The exchange of these communications led the Provisional Government momentarily to believe that a cessa-

[1] General Luperón, "Apuntes Históricos."

tion of hostilities might be obtained by negotiation, but the result of conversations had with La Gándara by a commission sent to his headquarters near Monte Cristi by the Provisional Government soon made evident that the Captain-General's sole purpose was to obtain the unconditional surrender of the revolutionaries. La Gándara, in his report upon the negotiations to the Spanish Minister for War, stated that the revolutionary commissioners, while willing to negotiate a treaty of surrender admitting the recognition of the triumph of the Monarchy, insisted upon the recognition of the Republic's independence and the complete evacuation of the Island, although they were disposed to agree to furnish a future contractual obligation to cede no portion of their territory to any other nation, nor to grant to any other country privileges which might prejudice the interests of Spain in the Antilles. Their pretensions, La Gándara reported, he scornfully rejected.

13.

The internal dissensions with which the Provisional Government was filled in the autumn of 1864 undoubtedly gave La Gándara ground for hope that his insistence upon conditions of peace far more humiliating to the Dominicans might eventually be crowned with success. The charge of inertia had long been levelled by many of the revolutionary generals against the head of the Provisional Government, General José Antonio Salcedo. The intrigues against the President were in part caused by Salcedo's lack of military capacity, and were stimulated by the failure of the negotiations with La Gándara, but they were due far more to the desire of the more prominent of the revolutionary chieftains to obtain for themselves the powers which had been vested in the Provisional

President. Jealousy of his superior had for some months dominated General Gaspar Polanco in particular. Availing himself of the continued absence of the Provisional President from Santiago, Polanco finally gathered about him a clique of the dissatisfied. As soon as they deemed the time ripe for action, a meeting of the disgruntled Generals assembled on October 10th in the fort of San Luís in Santiago. A series of resolutions were drafted proclaiming their refusal to recognize any longer the authority of General Salcedo as President of the Provisional Government, charging Salcedo with secret sympathy with the Spanish Government, and with the creation of a dictatorship in his own person in open violation of the terms under which the Provisional Government had been installed the preceding year. The acquiescence of Salcedo in the desire of the Spanish Captain-General to enter into negotiations was the most popular charge which could be levelled against him, and General Polanco concluded his impeachment of the Provisional President with the declaration, intended to gain the approval of the populace in general, that his own presence in the new Provisional Government then proclaimed was the best assurance that the "common enemy" would be summarily expelled from the national territory.

The Provisional Administration was completely reorganized by those responsible for the coup d'état. For the time being, the effort to overthrow Spanish tyranny was forgotten in the struggle which followed the domestic revolution. General Salcedo, whose headquarters had previously been established in Guayubín, still retained a considerable number of loyal followers. Announcing his determination to quell immediately the rebellion against his own authority, Salcedo marched towards Santiago. As soon as the newly organized Provisional Government was informed of the threatened attack, General Luperón was sent to prevent the onward march of the troops commanded by Salcedo, with confidential instructions to obtain from him, if possible, assurances that he would recognize the new state of affairs and consent to a voluntary exile in Haiti until such time as the new Provisional Government had been enabled formally to establish itself. The encounter of Luperón and Salcedo took place in Barrancón. Salcedo was accompanied on his march by his wife, and his lady, according to Garcia, "of little foresight and with a most energetic temper," advised her husband by no means to accept his dismissal from office, but rather to put down by force the rebellion against his authority. Salcedo, evidently lacking the determination of his wife, consented to adopt the counsel of Luperón and agreed to accompany him to the Haitian frontier. General Luperón relates in his account of the occurrence the repeated efforts which he himself made to save the deposed President on his journey to Haiti from assassination.[1] Both in Dajabón and in Mangá, General Monción and General Pedro Antonio Pimentel attempted to seize Salcedo in order to execute him. The situation was finally rendered more serious by the refusal of the Haitian authorities to permit Salcedo to set foot on Haitian soil. At length, Luperón was forced to return with his prisoner to Santiago. The deposed President was later removed from Santiago to Puerto Plata, where he was assassinated by secret orders issued by General Polanco. The murder of Salcedo, whose chief fault appears to have been his incurrence of the jealousy of his rivals, permitted the new Government at least to pose as the sturdy defender of the nation against all attempts on the part of the Spanish

[1] General Luperón, "Apuntes Históricos."

authorities to procure by diplomatic means the victories which they had not been able to secure in the field. For the time being, La Gándara was obliged to desist from his resort to diplomacy.

14.

The ignominious failure of the Liberal Union in Spain to satisfy the hopes of imperial aggrandizement which they themselves had inspired had caused the fall, in the late autumn of 1864, of the O'Donnell Cabinet. General Narvaez, Duque de Valencia, who had succeeded O'Donnell as Premier, instructed La Gándara, as soon as he took office, that the Spanish Government was unwilling to permit a continuation of hostilities in the interior of the colony, and ordered the Captain-General to take no steps other than those necessary to maintain the authority of Spain in the seaports still held by the Spanish troops. The new Cabinet was considering "attentively the general situation in the territory of Santo Domingo, the state of the war, the expenses and charges which its continuation imposed upon the nation, the sanitary conditions existing in the army, and the advantages which the country might hope to procure as a result of the campaign," and had already, upon assuming office, determined "to submit the entire question to the decision of the Cortes upon the approval of which it had to count, inasmuch as the fundamental interests of the State were involved."

The news of the decision which the increasing unpopularity of the war had forced upon the Spanish Cabinet reached the Provisional Government as soon as the Captain-General had been apprised of it. Immediately thereafter, on January 3, 1865, the Provisional Government addressed a plea for peace to the Spanish Queen, through the Haitian Government, which had already been acting as an intermediary between La Gándara and the insurgents:

"Through circumstances which Your Majesty no doubt ignores and which would be exceedingly painful to relate, our liberty and independence were wrested from us and our land annexed to the vast possessions of your glorious monarchy. For barely three years, this people bore impatiently the loss of its dearest and most sacred rights; but the day came when the unanimous will of the Dominican people appealed to God and to their own strength to reconquer their Fatherland, their liberty and their independence. For more than sixteen months, Madam, this small portion of the world has been presenting to the universe the sad spectacle of a struggle which must be afflicting to humanity. Deign to hear, Madam, the voice of a whole people which is addressed to Your Majesty and to the generous sentiments of your great heart, beseeching you to put an end to the struggle and to return to it that which it yesterday had lost. The voice of the people is the voice of God; it is the voice of truth. The Dominican people, with the deepest sorrow, say to Your Majesty: 'Think, Madam, that there where yesterday were flourishing cities today can be seen only mountains of ruins and ashes; that the fields, which recently were filled with crops, today are barren and desert; that their riches have disappeared; that on all sides nothing but devastation and misery can be seen; that desolation and death have taken the place of what was a short time ago animation and life . . . May peace and tranquillity, by your royal command, be restored to the Dominican people, and this concession will ever be one of the most glorious deeds of your reign, for it will be an act of humanity and of transcendent justice."

The appeal of the Provisional Government, if it ever in fact was read by the Sovereign Lady, proved unnecessary, since the Cabinet of Narvaez had already presented to the Cortes, before its receipt, the project of the law authorizing the evacuation of the Dominican colony. The preamble of the project, alleging motives of the noblest humanity for the annexation, undoubtedly afforded cynical amusement to O'Donnell and Serrano, and the other leaders of the Liberal Union:

"This desperate struggle, which occasioned, without compensation, the necessity of spending futilely the public treasure, and of wasting the wealth of the Spanish colonies, had not been brought about by the attempt of former Cabinets to undertake a selfish war of conquest, so foreign to the reasoned, just, pacific and disinterested policy which Spain had for so many years been observing; neither had it originated through the need to repel foreign aggression, opposing force to force at any cost in sustaining the defense of the threatened honor of the nation. Far from it: this struggle commenced immediately after the former Government of Her Majesty had concluded that all the inhabitants of the Dominican Republic were begging, imploring and soliciting with impatience their reincorporation in the Spanish Nation, their former mother, and to become one of her provinces, aspiring to the happiness which Cuba and Puerto Rico enjoyed. . . . The Government, . . . believed in the desire which appeared to inspire the Dominicans and accepted the petition; and advised Her Majesty to agree to the annexation. . . . In that manner two motives, at the same time most noble, most just, and most powerful, were those as the result of which the annexation was undertaken. The first, the right based upon the unanimous will of a people, a right which is indisputable and which already had been consecrated by the common consent of the nations of Europe and of America. . . . The second, the obligation of humanity, the pity towards the unfortunates who beg favor and assistance when they see themselves submerged in a sea of disasters and misfortunes. No other right was asserted by the Spanish Government in taking possession again, as it had in the past, of the Spanish portion of the Island of Santo Domingo: it did not assert the right of recovering what it once had possessed, nor the right of conquest, since both are contrary to the policy of the Government, to the interests of nations, and to the good relations which at all times it has maintained with the independent nations of America . . . Soon, however, fatal signs made themselves manifest that there were lacking the spontaneity and unanimity which should have been the foundation of the annexation. Nevertheless, it was the duty of the Government to assure itself of the general sincerity of those violent protests which several times were repressed. The conflagration spread; it overwhelmed towns and provinces, and extended to the whole territory, and today the Spanish portion of the Island of Santo Domingo presents to the eyes of the civilized world the spectacle of an entire people in arms ungratefully treating as tyrants the same individuals who believed that they had been called to come to them as their saviors . . . The belief that the Dominican people as a whole or even that an immense majority desired and above all insisted upon their annexation by Spain was an illusion: since the struggle there has become general, it no longer has the character of a measure taken to subject a few discontented rebels, but has acquired rather the character of a war of conquest, completely foreign to the spirit of Spanish policy; and even by increasing our sacrifices in order to obtain a triumph we will place ourselves in the sad situation of acquiescing in a complete military occupation filled with difficulties and not free from the necessity of *dangerous explanations;* and even under the most optimistic belief that one part of the population might be favorably inclined to us after our victory, the authorities which might then be established in those dominions would necessarily have to be either little suited to the habits and customs of the natives or very distinct from those which are installed today in our other foreign colonies."

Whether the defeat of the Confederacy, which made imminent those "dangerous explanations" with the United States Government referred to by Narvaez, or the popular disgust with the Dominican campaign, proved the stronger argument, is a matter for conjecture. In any event, the Spanish Cortes supported the Government's policy of evacuation by a large majority, notwithstanding the plea of Serrano, now Duque de la Torre, "to save the nation's honor and the future of Spain's West Indian Colonies."

Before instructions had time to reach La Gándara to undertake that immediate evacuation of the colony which the Cortes had now authorized, the Provisional Government installed by Polanco had in its turn been overthrown. In January of 1865, the towns of the frontier provinces proclaimed a state of rebellion against the Government at Santiago. By the end of the same month, the leaders of the new revolution, Generals Pimentel, Monción and Federico García, had entered the town of Santiago without opposition, and after imprisoning the members of the late Government had appointed a "Junta Gubernativa" under the temporary presidency of Don Benigno Filomeno de Rojas. The chief figures among the new authorities were General Luperón and that expatriated Englishman, Theodore Stanley Henneken, who had ten years before proved of such invaluable assistance to the British Consul, Sir Robert Schomburgk, in opposing the treaty with the

United States. Announcing a determination as strong as that of its predecessor to come to no agreement with Spain other than one based upon the unconditional evacuation of the Island, the new Government proceeded to declare in force the Moca Constitution of 1858, and, after the holding of such elections as the times permitted, installed on March 25th a Constitutional Government of the Republic, at whose head were General Pedro Antonio Pimentel as President and de Rojas as Vice-President.

Proclaiming a general amnesty to all Dominicans in the ranks of the enemy save those who had participated in the act of annexation, those who had accepted positions as Spanish officers, and those who openly opposed the restoration of the Republic, the new President made his policy plain in his inaugural address. "If Spain," he declared, "is disposed to continue the war, we must wage it with all of its terrible consequences; but if she wishes peace in good faith, if openly and sincerely she extends towards us the hand of friendship, we will accept it frankly, we will bury our resentments and inaugurate a new and happy era of peace and concord . . . If I combat, it is for my country, for her welfare, happiness, liberty and independence. My ambition is limited to that, and once those cherished objects are attained, I aspire to nothing further than to withdraw to private life, and to enjoy in the quiet of the domestic hearth the satisfaction of having fulfilled my duties." Announcing at the same time that he had been entrusted with the chief magistracy only until a Constitutional Assembly might convene in the capital within ninety days after the termination of the Spanish occupation, General Pimentel awaited the renewal of negotiations by La Gándara.

15.

For some time, the speedy abandonment of the province had been anticipated. Public expectation was rife. At the end of March, the American Commercial Agent reported:

"It is momentarily expected that the Spanish officials will receive instructions to abandon the colony. Arrangements have already been made with the Dominican Provisional Government for an exchange of prisoners. While no suspension of hostilities has been officially proclaimed, no warlike demonstration on either part has taken place for a month past." [1]

La Gándara's negotiations were initiated in personal correspondence with the Vice President, whom La Gándara described as "having afforded services of the greatest magnitude to the Spanish cause, notwithstanding the fact that he had later become our bitter antagonist." [2] On April 2nd, the Captain-General sent a confidential letter to de Rojas advising him that the Spanish Government had under consideration a project of law as the result of which Spain would doubtless abandon the colony. Declaring that his Government had no desire for vengeance, and that he as the representative of the Queen desired to do everything within his power to carry out his instructions with dignity and chivalry, he requested to be informed whether the Government at Santiago would be disposed to negotiate an agreement, should the moment arrive in which the various questions attendant upon the evacuation of the Island might be settled. A week later the President himself replied that he had no doubt an understanding could be reached. A few weeks later, General Pimentel, who had

[1] Mr. William A. Reed to Secretary Seward, March 28, 1865.
[2] La Gándara, "Anexión y Guerra."

encountered considerable difficulty in conciliating the divergent opinions of his Cabinet, requested the Captain-General to be patient, since his Government was nearly ready to commence negotiations.

While awaiting the decision from Santiago, La Gándara appears to have been exercised by the attitude of the Cibao press, which purported to publish the views of the Government. An article which appeared in the *Boletín* of Santiago on April 30th, raised the indignation of the Captain-General to such a pitch that he could only calm himself by addressing a heated protest to the President:

"I regret having to inform you that my reading of the *Boletín* of Santiago of April 30th has caused me a bad impression. The complaints of Cabral are intemperate; the information of Manzueta is false, and the official comment is not appropriate in view of the present circumstances. I am glad that you did not sign the document and I must express my regret that Señor de Rojas did sign it . . . Never shall I grow weary in lamenting that the Dominicans respond with an offensive lack of confidence and an unjust and disloyal spirit of suspicion to the magnanimous conduct which Spain observed when she came to Santo Domingo, and to the generous policy which she pursues today when she renounces her perfect right to remain in Santo Domingo—her conduct finds no example in history and most assuredly no other nation would have emulated her."

General Pimentel, dominated by Henneken, who was at the time alleged to be unduly partial to the Spanish cause, replied on May 11th in an astonishingly mild tone, declaring that he was sincerely desirous of leading the discussions to conciliatory ground, and assured La Gándara that he would employ all his authority and prestige to dispel exaggerated ideas among the Dominicans, as well as to moderate the tone of the press to which the Captain-General had so bitterly objected.

"There is no doubt," he concluded by saying, "that if we were able to approach one another, we would embrace each other under the shadow of our respective flags . . . Already the hour is striking when Dominicans and Spaniards should put aside their arms to give each other an embrace in which will disappear forever the remembrance of this struggle in the magic cry, 'Long live the Queen and long live the Dominican Republic.' "

On May 9th, the commissioners of the Dominican Government were appointed, and General Pimentel lost no time in notifying the Captain-General of their departure. General José del Carmen Reinoso was, he assured La Gándara, an honourable man of good sense, not exaggerated in his ideas; General Melitón Valverde was a "joven simpático," intelligent and well disposed; Presbítero Miguel Quesada, one of the finest models of the Dominican clergy. The commissioners were empowered to negotiate

"regarding the evacuation of the territory, towns, capital, and all places and cities actually occupied in Dominican territory by the Spanish troops; the exchange of prisoners, and concerning every other matter which may refer to the termination of the war with Spain; negotiating and signing a convention providing for peace in the manner and in the form regarding which they were privately instructed . . . the Government obligating itself to carry out all that its envoys and special commissioners . . . may do by virtue of their letters of credence."

For several weeks negotiations were continued, and the convention which resulted was signed in Guibia on June

2nd by the Captain-General and the three Dominican commissioners. Its terms had been agreed upon, however, before the receipt in the Republic of the information that the Queen of Spain had sanctioned, on the first of May, the law approved by the Cortes revoking the decree of March 19, 1861, which authorized the annexation of the Republic to Spain.

The convention of June 2nd would doubtless not have been negotiated had the Dominican commissioners been apprised in time of the terms of the Spanish decree declaring the abandonment of the Republic, but under any circumstances, the convention to which they had affixed their signatures contained extraordinary concessions to be granted by the Dominican patriots who had so successfully resisted the long continued attempt of the Spanish armies to subjugate them. The convention explicitly recognized the fact that the Spanish Government had obeyed "motives of the highest generosity and nobility" when she had acquiesced in the annexation of the Dominican Republic; that Spain had been entirely within her rights in opposing by the force of arms the restoration of the Republic; the Dominican Government was obligated to declare without effect any decrees which it might have promulgated against any individuals on account of occurrences which had taken place during the revolution, and to offer full protection to any Dominicans who had assisted the Spanish authorities in their efforts to pacify the country. Article IV of the convention provided that the Dominican Government should pay the Spanish Government an indemnity, the amount of which was to be fixed in a subsequent treaty, to cover the expenses of the war, of the government, and of the administration of the colony, as well as to cover all expenditures occasioned by the con-

version of the Dominican paper money, and the cost of
any local improvements which might have resulted from
the Spanish administration or from the investment of
Spanish capital; Spanish vessels were to receive most
favoured nation treatment, and in Article VII it was provided that

"The Dominican Government obligates itself never to
alienate either the whole or any portion of its territory to
any nation or people, and to enter into no convention
which might prejudice Spanish interests in the Antilles,
without the prior agreement and consent of the Spanish
Government."

Finally, special commissioners of the Spanish Government
were to reside in the Republic to see that the provisions of
the convention were carried out, and to protect Spanish
subjects until such time as a treaty of peace and amity
between the two nations had been concluded.

As soon as word reached Santiago of the contents of the
convention there was an outburst of popular indignation.
General Pimentel, forced by the general clamour to disavow the acts of his commissioners, issued on June 12th a
decree which declared that as the commissioners had exceeded their power, and had gravely compromised the
future of the Republic by violating the dictates of the
Provisional Government, the Convention of Guibia was
null and void. At the same time, the President was forced
by his Cabinet to publish a project of a convention which
would be acceptable to his Government, markedly distinct
in all of its provisions from the convention already signed.
The convention as now proposed provided simply that
from the date of the signing of the agreement a state of
peace would exist between the Dominican Republic and

Spain, as the result of which Spain would proceed with the immediate evacuation of Dominican territory. The remaining articles stipulated the manner in which the exchange of prisoners was to be undertaken, provided the assurances that the sick and wounded of the Spanish troops would be properly cared for, and stipulated that compensation would be made for private property confiscated by one or the other of the opposing forces; the commercial treaty of 1855 between Spain and the Dominican Republic was to be renewed until such time as a modification of it might be negotiated, and provision was made that Spanish vessels in Dominican ports and Dominican vessels in Spanish or colonial ports were to receive most favoured nation treatment.

Upon the publication of the draft convention, the Government appointed General José Maria Cabral and General Henneken to persuade the Spanish Captain-General to accept the convention in the form now proposed. But La Gándara indignantly refused to receive the newly appointed commissioners, declaring that the conduct of the Government in repudiating the action of its former commissioners, to whom it had granted full powers, constituted a gross breach of faith. On June 26th, he addressed a communication to Cabral and Henneken declaring the convention of June 2nd entirely valid, and announced his intention of seeing that it was carried out without alteration or modification; the Captain-General further stated that in view of the conduct of the Dominican Government he intended to carry out the evacuation of Dominican territory in the way and at the time he deemed fit, and that pending such time, he would continue the war in any form which appeared to him to be advantageous to the honour and interests of his Government.

The Captain-General, already bitterly opposed to the announced determination of his own Government, and infuriated by what he claimed was the intentional perfidy of the Dominican Government, attempted to make good his threats by the issuance, on July 5th, of the following declaration:

"1. In abandoning the portion of this Island which constituted the former Dominican Republic, spontaneously annexed to the Monarchy in March, 1861, Spain reserves all the rights accruing to her by virtue of such annexation; which rights she will avail herself of in any way she deems appropriate and by any method within her power.

"2. Until the Government of Her Majesty may dispose otherwise, the present war between Spain and Santo Domingo will continue.

"3. Apart from the measures which I may think necessary to accomplish that which is contained in the preceding article all the ports and coasts of the Dominican territory will continue in a state of blockade in conformity with the provisions contained in the proclamations of October 5 and November 7, 1863, which are extended from this date to cover all the ports and coasts of the said territory of Santo Domingo which were not included in the second of the proclamations referred to."

But these menaces could not cause serious alarm to the Dominican Government in view of the fact that the evacuation was already in process of realization. The spite of La Gándara was, however, made evident in more practical ways. All arms and ammunition which the Spanish authorities could not remove upon the fleet of Spanish vessels which had arrived in the first days of July to bear away the Spanish troops, were either destroyed or hurled into the sea; public edifices were wrecked; and finally, the

Spanish officials spread terror among the non-combatants of the capital by embarking upon the vessels a number of civilians, among them women and children, with the announcement that they were to be held as hostages until such time as the Spanish Government was satisfied that the exchange of prisoners had been satisfactorily carried out. On July 11th, the last Spanish forces embarked from the capital, and on July 20th, the Spanish troops which had been delayed in Puerto Plata by the formalities attendant upon the exchange of the last remaining prisoners likewise sailed away. A month later the American Commercial Agent was able to report:

"All is quiet under a Provisional Government." [1]

[1] Mr. Paul T. Jones to Secretary Seward, August 14, 1865.

CHAPTER IV

THE AFTERMATH OF THE INSURRECTION

1.

THE tranquillity which the American Commercial Agent alleged as existing subsequent to the Spanish evacuation was but short-lived. Within a week after the despatch of that reassuring report, Mr. Jones, the Agent, was himself urgently demanding that an American warship be sent "for God's sake" to the Dominican capital to save his life and the lives of the foreign residents. Although the commander of the U.S.S. *Mercedita*, who responded to the call, felt constrained to report that the perils which had so shaken the American Agent were solely those conjured by the alcoholic hallucinations of a man who was "intoxicated, morning, noon, and night," the brief calm with which the exhausted land had at first been blessed, rapidly merged into a condition of anarchy which was to continue, with but slight alleviation, for more than twelve months.

The state of the country was in fact such that any spark might have caused the outbreak of rebellion. The moment required the presence at the head of the Provisional Government of a man strong enough to capture popular confidence, and able to quiet the unrest arising from the state of abject misery into which the people had been plunged by the devastating war for a time sufficiently long to enable constitutional government to be reëstablished. For with the departure of the Spanish authorities, there were neither national Executive, Legislative nor Judicial authorities. The authority of the National Convention of Santiago was local in its character, and to it neither the inhabitants of the eastern or southern provinces, nor those of the capital, were responsive. Unfortunately, the Provisional President, General Pimentel, lacked entirely the qualities and the character necessary to maintain order during such troublous times.

His authority, in so far as it was exerted at all, was repressive and capricious. Such small amount of public monies as his agents could obtain from the Cibao Customs Houses was spent for the gratification of the clique about him, and the soldiers of the restoration, who had sacrificed all they possessed, were obliged to return to their homes and to their abandoned plantations and farms without even the recompense of the small percentage of their pay which they might have obtained under an honest administration. The opposition to the Provisional Government became so violent that in the beginning of August armed outbreaks occurred in the capital and in the west, where the military leaders refused further to recognize the Santiago Government, and proclaimed General José Maria Cabral "Protector" of the Republic. Pimentel, cowed and unable to withstand this early rejection of his authority, resigned his office on August 13th, leaving the field clear to General Cabral.

Cabral, while similar to Pimentel in lacking strength of character and decision, differed radically from him in having at heart, so far as his limited intelligence permitted him to grasp them, the interests of his country. He obtained the immediate support of two widely divergent elements. The first was the liberal group composed of the younger generation which, appreciating Cabral's good intentions, hoped that by installing him in office it might prevent the return to power of the ring of politicians to whom it attributed the downfall of the Republic four years before. The second was the group composed of the

former followers of Santana. While most of these had in
the later days of the revolution deserted their chief to seek
favour from the leaders of the restoration, they feared,
with reason, that they could expect no favours from the
members of the Santiago Government whose antipathy to
the memory of Santana and to all which savoured of him
continued vehement. But the Santanistas feared far more
the return of Buenaventura Baez, at whose hands they had
already ascertained from experience they could expect no
political favours, and might far more probably encounter
imprisonment or exile.

Perhaps the most astonishing phenomenon in all Dominican history is the fact that Baez could still hope to
rally around him popular support. For his course during
the war of the restoration had been pusillanimous to the
last degree. Protesting against the annexation to Spain so
long as he hoped that the early outbreaks against Spanish
rule might cause the evacuation of the colony, he later
went over, body and soul, to the Spanish cause. Through
the connivance of a few of his partisans who had succeeded in gaining the ear of the Captain-General who
followed Santana in office, he persuaded the Cabinet at
Madrid that his own influence in the colony was so considerable that it was worth their while to conciliate him,
and the method of conciliation, it was made evident, must
be material. Receiving as the result of his representations
a liberal subsidy from the Spanish Crown and the honorary
rank of Field Marshal in the Spanish army, he passed the
years during which his fellow-citizens were struggling for
liberty in leading a life of luxurious ease in Europe. As soon
as he became confident that the rebellion would eventually
triumph, and that the abandonment of the colony would
be decreed by the Spanish Government, he resigned with

a patriotic flourish his rank as Field Marshal, and, leaving Europe, took up his abode in Curaçao to manipulate at closer quarters, though still at a safe distance, his own return to power.

Largely due to the manner in which Baez played, through his agents, upon the jealousies and rivalries of the chiefs of the late revolution, the Provisional Government of Cabral fell before many months. One by one the civilians who had rallied about the "Protector" were forced through the pressure of the military chieftains to vacate the posts to which Cabral had appointed them, and the struggle degenerated into the old effort of the followers of Baez to throw out of office the supporters of Santana. At the end of October, General Pimentel, recovered from the panic into which the unpopularity of his own Government had thrown him, and permitted to return to the capital, seized his opportunity and demanded the removal of all those partisans of Cabral who were opposed to Baez's return. Cabral weakly acceded to these demands, and dismissing from office all of his supporters who were known to be antagonistic to the former President, appointed in their stead Baecistas nominated for him by his own opponents. On the same day upon which the National Assembly after much deliberation had finally agreed upon one of the most liberal constitutions which the Dominican Republic has known, the Assembly found itself forced, by the threats of a rabble of armed ruffians brought to the capital from the Seybo by General Pedro Guillermo, an illiterate negro partisan of Baez's, to elect the latter President of the Republic. Acting under similar coercion the Assembly was later forced to agree to the election of a new Congress, composed of Baez's followers, and at the same time Cabral agreed further to stultify himself by proceed-

ing to Curaçao at the head of a commission to beseech
Baez to return once more as President of the Republic.

2.

On December 8, 1865, Buenaventura Baez, heralded by
his own newspaper as "the angel of peace called to fulfill
the patriotic mission of uniting the Dominicans and of
making them truly happy under the protection of a government which will guarantee all their rights," was
inaugurated for the third time as Constitutional President
of the Republic.

That Baez was under no illusions regarding his own
security was evidenced by the fact that far from permitting his fellow-citizens to indulge in pleasing prospects,
as he had been led to do in the past, he painted for them
in his inaugural message the desperate situation of the
Republic. The Government, he advised them, was without
organization in any Executive department; with a floating
debt the amount of which was unknown; shaken by
anarchy, the country was permeated with extravagant
ideas, impracticable and impossible of fulfillment; agriculture was abandoned; commerce was ruined; entire
cities and towns had been wiped out; there was no national
credit and consequently the nation was deprived of the
indispensable means of defense in the case of emergency.
But Baez must have become still less optimistic upon hearing the words of Padre Meriño, who, upon his return to
Santo Domingo at the end of the revolution, had been
elected President of the National Assembly, and in that
capacity had been called upon to announce officially to the
President of the Republic his election. Throughout his
long career, Padre Meriño was one of the few men in the
Republic whose convictions stood foursquare, whose own

ambition for power constituted an unfaltering desire to
utilize such power for the benefit of his country, and who
was never shaken in his beliefs by fear of popular opinion.
By a man with the vision of Meriño, no doubts could be
harboured as to the benefits which the return to power of
Baez might entail:

"Extraordinary things happen in this country," he
warned the President; "your star has once more risen upon
the horizon of this Republic and you are called upon to
occupy again the Chief Magistracy. So unexpected an
occurrence has prostrated with astonishment many who
are now looking at you . . . Speaking to you in the frank
language of truth . . . I shall not avoid saying to you that
you should labor under no illusions, since among a people
like our own, to make use of the expression of an illustrious American orator, 'It is as easy to pass from exile to
supreme power as it is from supreme power to impeachment before the Bar of the Senate' . . . Sincere patriots,
men of principle, all decent citizens, who desire, and are
the only ones able, to give stability to the Government,
are always disposed to support governments which are
progressive and liberal, governments which are truly national. They only refuse their support and leave such
governments at the mercy of their opponents, when they
see them prostitute public interests to private interests,
when they understand that despotism has banished justice
from the seat of power, when, finally, they see in the
stead of the Executive elected to labor for the happiness
of the people a sanguinary tyrant in the Presidential Chair,
a perverse ruler or an audacious speculator who collects a
colossal fortune, robbing the people of the riches which
they have confided to him in order that he may procure
peace, liberty and progress for his country . . . If, during
the Presidential period fixed for you by the Constitution,

you obtain, as I hope you will, the good of the country, the satisfaction will be that of all, but the glory yours in particular."

Very much of a man was Padre Meriño. His intent was clear to all. There could be no doubt as to whom he referred by the "audacious speculator" and the "bloody tyrant." That the sentiment of many in the country was that of the President of the National Assembly was soon made manifest by the fact that on the same day as that upon which General Baez was inaugurated in the capital, a revolution against his Government broke out in Puerto Plata under the able leadership of General Gregorio Luperón.

In the appointment of his Cabinet, Baez made a shrewd effort to conciliate all the groups with which he felt there was even the slightest possibility of establishing relations. Of the Ministers appointed, Don Manuel Maria Gautier, named Minister of Justice, Public Instruction and Foreign Affairs, was the only one upon whom Baez could personally depend. The Minister of Interior and Police, General Pimentel, thus rewarded for his participation in the overthrow of Cabral, had been previously unknown to Baez, who mistakenly believed that Pimentel's appointment would bring with it the support of an influential class in the Cibao. The Minister of Hacienda, Don Pedro Tomás Garrido, had broken away, like many others, from Baez in 1857, and his appointment demonstrated the intention of the President to draw back by the lure of public office all individuals of prominence who had formerly been connected with his party. The remaining member of the Cabinet, the Minister of War, in the person of General José Maria Cabral himself, made plain the desire of Baez to obtain through his appointment the support of the western provinces. In that hope, however, he was likewise to be disappointed.

The revolution so soon proclaimed by General Luperón was speedily suppressed, owing to the inability of the revolutionary leaders in the north to postpone the satisfaction of their own ambitions long enough to make a concerted front against Baez's troops. Urging as a justification this outbreak of rebellion against his authority, Baez thereupon commenced a series of personal persecutions which did nothing to enhance his own popularity. One by one, not only those who had been identified in the past with Santana's party but likewise the principal leaders of the liberal party, who vainly struggled to further the growth of democratic government in the Republic, were imprisoned or exiled. The new elections to the National Congress naturally enough, therefore, united in the Legislative body solely such citizens as were submissive to the wishes of the President, and in that sense the election of the President's half-brother, General Valentín Ramírez Baez, as President of the Senate was significant.

Embarking upon a policy of absolute repression, General Baez brought his power to bear with merciless severity upon all those whom he suspected of revolutionary sympathies. Before six weeks had passed 190 political prisoners from Puerto Plata, Santiago, and Azua, against whom no specific charges had been lodged, filled the prisons of the capital.[1] Baez was, however, speedily forced to the conclusion that he could not gain the support of any of the various groups which he had tried to conciliate, by his inability to retain their leaders in his Cabinet. The rivalry

[1] Mr. Paul T. Jones, American Commercial Agent, to Secretary Seward, April 7, 1866.

between the President and Cabral, terminating in the flight of the latter, brought matters to a crisis. Azua, although so long dominated by the President, rallied to the cry of rebellion at once launched by the fugitive Minister.

"When a portion of the revolutionary army was twelve miles from the Capital, the gates of the City were closed, and a cannon placed in front of the President's palace. The reluctant citizens were called on by proclamation read at the corners of the streets to array themselves in the common defense . . . In two engagements between the revolutionists and the Government, the latter was each time defeated . . ." [1]

Martial law was at once proclaimed, and the submissive Assembly harried into granting authorization to the President to issue $100,000 in paper currency with which to pay off his shoeless, coatless and shirtless soldiery. But stronger measures still were deemed necessary, as the result of the growing symptoms of unrest. Under the lash of compulsion the Congress at length set aside the Constitution of 1865 and replaced it with the Constitution of 1854 by which the President was granted almost dictatorial powers. With the change of Constitutions the stage was set for the advent of mob tyranny.

"On April 22nd, a proclamation was read at the corners of the streets announcing the change in Constitutions. There was no demonstration. The following day, the new Constitution was inaugurated by a parade, the ringing of bells, and the firing of salutes. At midday, all public functionaries were invited to assemble at the palace to proceed from there to the Cathedral to attend a Te Deum

[1] Mr. Paul T. Jones, American Commercial Agent, to Secretary Seward, March 10, 1866.

of Thanksgiving. Two days later . . . General Pedro Guillermo, a favorite of General Baez, rode through the streets, sword in hand, proclaiming 'Death to all merchants opposed to Baez's administration,' and ended up in front of the store of Joaquín Delmonte accompanied by twenty-five ragamuffin soldiers demanding the person of Mr. Delmonte, dead or alive. Immediately all the stores were closed, the streets cleared save by the soldiery. Twelve prominent citizens were at once arrested and imprisoned, among them a priest recently arrived from St. Thomas." [1]

In these days of chaos, the gallant President took no chances as to his own security. Mr. Jones reported him as

"taking every precautionary measure for his personal safety. He now is garbed in military clothes, and every evening at dusk two cannon are placed in front of the palace door, which are removed the next morning." [2]

But all Baez's struggling to retain the Presidency was fruitless. On April 23rd, the principal leaders of the Cibao, charging the President with disregard of his most sacred obligations in setting aside the Constitution of 1865 and with indulging in persecution to satisfy his personal spite, alleging that Baez was conspiring to sell the Republic to France, and accusing him of robbing the national treasury for his individual profit, declared themselves in open rebellion, and a week later announced their support of a new Triumvirate, composed of Generals Luperón, Federico de Jesús García and Pimentel. It was only then that Baez found that his flamboyant Minister of the Interior, with a capacity in treachery and in double-dealing worthy of his chief, had long been intriguing for Baez's overthrow.

[1] Mr. Paul T. Jones to Secretary Seward, April 25, 1866.
[2] Mr. Paul T. Jones to Secretary Seward, April 17, 1866.

The troops of the Cibao supported, although half-heartedly, by the revolutionaries under the command of Cabral in the south, rapidly overcame the Government's resistance and within a few days occupied Moca, La Vega and Cotuy. At this point, General Pimentel, hoping to outmaneuver his colleagues in the Triumvirate, as he had already successfully deceived Baez, deserted Luperón and García and by forced marches appeared alone before the Capital at the end of May. On May 28th, the entrances to the city were forced, and Baez, who had already stationed a Government vessel in the port upon which he hoped to escape in the case of necessity, was obliged to take refuge at midnight, owing to the suddenness of the attack, in the French Consulate, whence he was secretly placed on board a passing steamer and was eventually enabled to reach Curaçao once more.

3.

For the time being, therefore, the partisans of Baez, or the members of the "Red" party, as they were now known, were completely defeated, and the "Blues," the term applied to all the elements opposed to the return of Baez, were in complete control. Unfortunately, however, for the Republic, once the object which all the groups loosely termed the "Blues" had in view had been successfully achieved, there was no common policy to bind them together. In the south, the furtherance of the ambitions of General Cabral was the cause of the rebellion; in the east, the former partisans of Santana had joined the revolution, terrified at the prospect of a continuation of Baez's administration; in the Cibao, popular opinion was pulverized, each group supporting its local leader in the hope that fortune might favour the advancement of that leader to the Presidency. For a time, the state of open anarchy which threatened was postponed by the agreement of many of the revolutionary chiefs upon a pact, signed on July 12th in Jacagua, providing that Buenaventura Baez was deposed from the Presidency and should at no time in the future be permitted to return to office; that until the Dominican people in general elections should select a President all candidacies for the Presidency should be ignored, and that until such time as a President might be constitutionally inaugurated, the Government of the Triumvirate should be generally accepted throughout the country.

On August 10th General Luperón and General García joined the third member of the Triumvirate, General Pimentel, in the capital and immediately decrees were issued providing for the election of a Congress and a President of the Republic. The air was filled with rumours of plots and counterplots. A working agreement was soon entered into by Pimentel and García for the capture or assassination of General Luperón, whose increasing popularity they had good reason to fear. But the latter, realizing that his own hopes of obtaining the Presidency must for the time being be laid aside, succeeded in checkmating his colleagues by publicly suggesting that the Triumvirate be replaced by General Cabral, to hold office as Provisional President until such time as a Constitutional Government might be elected. Pimentel and García, outplayed in their turn, were forced by the pressure of public opinion to agree, and on August 22nd, a decree was issued appointing General Cabral Provisional President, whereupon the members of the Triumvirate jointly agreed to withdraw with their personal followers from the capital.

Now that General Cabral had been returned to power as the result of the rivalry between the three members of the Triumvirate, his election as Constitutional President of the Republic was assured. On September 23rd, Cabral was proclaimed elected by a majority of 4,000 votes over those cast for the other candidates, and as soon as the Constitution of 1865 had, with slight modifications, been once more proclaimed in force, the Provisional President, on September 29, 1866, was inaugurated as Constitutional President of the Republic.

4.

During the years of the Spanish occupation, General Cazneau, that "tenacious adventurer," as he is described by José Gabriel García, had not been idle. A few months prior to the annexation of the Republic to Spain he had entered into partnership with Colonel Joseph W. Fabens, whose activities in Santo Domingo had already been advertised in the local press. Colonel Fabens, like his partner a native of the State of Massachusetts, and, also like General Cazneau, a participant in the activities which had led to the annexation of Texas to the United States, had first emerged from obscurity in 1854, when he had been employed by Secretary Marcy in a diplomatic capacity to investigate the validity of claims against the United States for property destroyed in Nicaragua during the bombardment of Greytown by Captain Hollins. According to Davis Hatch, an American who had obtained, for certain New York interests, a concession in 1864 from the Spanish authorities for the working of the salt mines at Neyba, and whose grievances against Cazneau and Fabens were to be later responsible for the final wrecking of the latter's schemes,

"If Cazneau was the more vicious of the two, Fabens was the more dangerous from his greater cunning and excessive duplicity."[1]

The partners, as is made plain by a confidential letter written March 17, 1861, by Santana's last Minister of Finance, Ricart y Torres, to the Captain-General of Cuba, had made every effort to entrench themselves securely before the annexation officially took place:

"A gentleman . . . who passed through Havana . . . embarked for this City on board the steamer *Cuba*. The object of his arrival, which we supposed might be some claim regarding the guano affair of Alta Vela, is far more important in its nature. This gentleman, together with General C[azneau] and Colonel F[abens] (other strangers, both Americans) spoke with me first and later proposed, in a conference which they had with the President of the Republic, the following points:

"1. To grant a loan to the Government for the sum of $500,000 bearing a small rate of interest and for a long term, the amount of which would naturally be placed at the disposal of the Republic;

"2. To establish a current of immigration, paid for by themselves, to people the Peninsula of Samaná;

"3. In return for these advantages, from the Government they request exclusive privileges to open up the navigation of the Yuna and Yaque Rivers (the two principal rivers of the island); a concession to establish a ship yard, to be undertaken by the immigrants . . . the exploitation of the coal mines and all other mines of the Republic, and a concession covering some leagues of agricultural land on the banks of the Yuna and Yaque Rivers where agricultural colonies may be established . . ."[2]

[1] Howard's "Hatch-San Domingo Report."
[2] La Gándara, "Anexión y Guerra."

While the desired concession was not secured, it was the hope of Cazneau that the relations of intimacy which he had formed with Santana would permit him notwithstanding to obtain other concessions which might be advantageously disposed of in the United States. In this hope he was disappointed so long as Santana remained in power. The early revocation of his appointment by Secretary Seward as Special Agent of the United States no doubt increased the notorious sympathy which Cazneau demonstrated for the Confederacy during the earlier years of the Civil War, and caused him to remain during the first two years of the war in Santo Domingo, trusting that his protestations as a Confederate sympathizer would render the Spanish authorities more favourably disposed towards him.

The partners first availed themselves of the fact that President Lincoln and his Secretary of the Interior, Caleb Smith, were known to favour the colonization of emancipated negroes in the West Indies or in Liberia. As early as December 16, 1862, Senator Wilson of Massachusetts had introduced a bill to abolish slavery in the District of Columbia, which carried with it an amendment appropriating $100,000 to assist in the colonization of former slaves who desired to emigrate from the United States. The bill, finally passed with the express approval of President Lincoln, received the benediction of Charles Sumner as making possible the payment of "a small installment of that great debt to an enslaved race which we all owe." Quick to detect the practical advantages which could be reaped from this hobby of the Abolitionists, Cazneau and Fabens at once formed a company in New York known as the "American West India Company." In the prospectus it was declared that the Company had purchased extensive tracts of land for colonization purposes, particularly with a view to cultivating cotton on an extensive scale by free labour. The colonists, with the assistance of the Spanish authorities, were to be settled on land situated four leagues north of Santo Domingo upon a navigable branch of the Ozama River

"which has the reputation of being one of the most beautiful and healthful spots on the south side of the Island . . . The example and instruction it will afford to other settlers will be of incalculable value to those while constituting the best mode of employing the best classes of free labor in a manner which will insure permanent homes and satisfactory means of livelihood . . . Very favorable arrangements can be made . . . for the introduction of a large number of agricultural homeless laborers from the United States for whom the United States Government feels a responsible interest and who would find there a most desirable home."

Many of the unwary were caught by the elegant verbiage of this alluring prospect, and numbers departed for Santo Domingo. Their experiences were later divulged:

"Upon an investment of short of $4,000 in wild lands in Santo Domingo, Cazneau and Fabens represented that they had property to the value of $2,000,000, the capital of the Company. They sacrificed hundreds of lives by their fake representations; and those who escaped with their lives lost everything. Not one remained. Cazneau and Fabens made small fortunes out of the operation." [1]

The following report of the American Commercial Agent at the time, which recounts a typical instance, would have been enlightening to the Abolitionist societies:

[1] Howard's "Hatch-San Domingo Report."

"About twelve or fifteen immigrants arrived some weeks ago to settle here. They came out under the auspices and persuasions of J. W. Fabens and William L. Cazneau. They all intend to return to the United States by the first conveyance, cursing in their hearts the West India Company of Fabens and Cazneau." [1]

But the experience suffered by Cazneau in the autumn of 1863, when his house and plantations at San Carlos, where he and his wife were living at the time, were completely destroyed by order of the Spanish authorities, evidently led him to realize that temporarily at least his expectations of increasing his fortune in Santo Domingo must be abandoned, and returning to the United States, he undertook, with his partner, the flotation of various other companies, among them the San Domingo Cotton Company and the San Domingo Company, all of them as unlikely as the first wild-cat scheme to prove profitable to the American investor. With the termination of the revolution against Spain, General Cazneau and his partner returned to Santo Domingo in June, 1865, to await the opportunity which they were sure would arise to enable them to profit at the expense of the Dominican people.

5.

The opportunity was not long delayed. During the months he was seeking to recover from the wounds inflicted by the assassins who had murdered Lincoln—a shrunken parody of his former self, sunk in his wheelchair at the State Department, his broken jaw bound to his head—Secretary Seward was labouring to devise the means to repair the havoc wrought to the Monroe Doctrine

[1] Mr. William G. W. Yaeger to Secretary Seward, April 6, 1863.

by the unchecked activities of the European Powers in the years of the Civil War. Upon this aim his singularly uneven abilities were from now on concentrated.

As the first step in the rehabilitation of the Monroe Doctrine in the eyes of the world, Seward believed it imperative that the United States acquire a West Indian naval base, which, he felt, would remove the danger of repeated aggression from Europe in that portion of the American hemisphere. For a while he hesitated between the purchase of the Danish West Indies and the acquisition of the Bay of Samaná. He was at length inclined to favour the latter, alarmed by the report in the autumn of 1865 that the return of Baez to the Presidency of the Dominican Republic was being actively fostered by Napoleon III to smooth the way for the long-postponed annexation to France, but more particularly exercised perhaps by the proposal of the British Government, in July of that year, that the United States concur in a joint declaration of the neutrality of the Samaná Peninsula. This proposal, Seward replied, the American Government, although earnestly desiring that no foreign state attempt to disturb the inhabitants of the Dominican island, could not entertain owing to its traditional objection to entangling alliances. The declaration so proposed, implying as it did European intervention in an exclusively American question, had been broached to both the British and French Cabinets by agents of the Haitian Government, fearful lest the unsuccessful experiment of Spain in Santo Domingo might leave the way clear for the ambitions of some more powerful nation. Consequently Seward determined to lose no further time and to trust to no agents in ascertaining how far the commitments of President Baez to France had actually gone, and to anticipate any European declaration of neutrality by the lease, or preferably by the purchase, of the Peninsula of Samaná by the United States itself. He therefore set sail for Santo Domingo where he arrived January 15, 1866, accompanied by his son, Frederick W. Seward, the Assistant Secretary of State.

Seward's visit appeared a heaven-sent opportunity to General Cazneau and to Colonel Fabens. Welcoming Secretary Seward upon his arrival in the harbour, they availed themselves of the chance presented by the fact that the Commercial Agent, Mr. Jones, incapacitated by his habitual intemperance, was unable to accompany the Secretary of State in his formal call upon the President of the Republic, and offered their services as interpreters during Seward's interview with Baez. While the official paper, *El Monitor*, limited itself to the statement that the interview was restricted to a frank exchange of opinions, "in which our independence, our Constitutional organization, our pending questions with Spain and Haiti, and the recognition of our nationality" were discussed, it added the significant comment that "the details of this interview provided the most satisfactory preliminaries for negotiations tending towards a frank understanding between the United States and the Dominican Republic."

The personal contact which Cazneau had thus been enabled to effect with the American Secretary of State, and the coincidence of his own hope of enhancing the value of his concessions in the desire of Seward to guard against continued encroachment by the European Powers, made Cazneau lose no opportunity to encourage Secretary Seward to believe that the Dominican Government eagerly awaited the negotiation of closer ties with the United States. Within two weeks of Secretary Seward's visit to Santo Domingo, we find Cazneau writing to him:

"I have had several interviews with President Baez on American affairs. He is a statesman and is very anxious to satisfy the Government and people of the United States that he will encourage American enterprise and energy. He is very anxious to carry out your suggestions in relation to more intimate relations with the United States." [1]

On April 11th, General Cazneau wrote again to advise Seward that President Baez had "honored" him

"with several private interviews for the purpose of having an accurate and confidential exposition of his policy conveyed through the Secretary of State to President Johnson. President Baez desires the President to consider it as the unofficial appeal from the youngest of the American Republics to the oldest and the strongest, believing the United States to be the closest friend and protector of those children of the common family who from their geographical proximity are the natural allies of the United States. Haiti, to which the friendly countenance of the American Cabinet is imparting dignity and strength, is of all the States of the world the most completely alien in policy and sentiment, inasmuch as her Constitution excludes the white race from citizenship while the Dominican Republic has invariably pursued a different course. 'The equality of all races before the law' is one of the foundation stones of the Dominican Republic. The Dominicans have, since 1844, been obliged to defend their independence at incredible sacrifices from the constant menace and repeated attacks of Haiti. President Baez believes that the Dominican people having saved the Republic for the American system by their own unaided efforts may justly claim the confidence and sympathy of the United States. President Baez outlines a plan of administration so just, peaceful, and comprehensive that it needs

[1] General William L. Cazneau to Secretary Seward, January 29, 1866.

but to be fairly understood to commend the cordial approbation of every enlightened government and most of all
that of the United States. The President's message to Congress advising the establishment of diplomatic relations
with the Dominican Republic was received with joy. That
has decided the Dominican Republic to determine a policy
of acting as the sentinel state for the United States in the
Caribbean. While President Baez is making overtures to
the President of Haiti for a treaty of peace, Haitian officials
are fomenting rebellion against the Dominican Government, spreading the propaganda that President Baez wishes
to sell the Dominican negroes to the Americans as Santana
sold them to Spain. It is highly necessary to secure the
Dominican territory, *as well as American capital invested
in it*, from the devastating invasions of Haiti." [1]

For the time being, the ambitions of Cazneau and his
partner and the completion of the policy set for himself
by the Secretary of State, were both checked by the overthrow of Baez from the Presidency. Nevertheless Cazneau
wrote again, relating the circumstances which caused the
exile of Baez from the country, and advised the Secretary
that immediately prior to the President's flight from the
capital he had sent for General Cazneau and had urged
him to inform the Secretary of his intention, so soon as he
returned to power, to obtain a treaty of amity and recognition from the United States, and had in particular besought him not to abandon the country "until American
vested interests should be established in vigorous activity,
since he regarded them as the principal means for the
eventual redemption of his country from revolutionary
chaos." [2]

The brief intercourse which Seward had had with

[1] General William L. Cazneau to Secretary Seward, April 11, 1866.
[2] General William L. Cazneau to Secretary Seward, May 30, 1866.

Cazneau evidently led him to believe that the latter might become an effective instrument in carrying out his own purposes, apparently ignorant of the fact that in the carrying out of those purposes Cazneau furthered the satisfaction of his own pecuniary ambitions. Inducing President Johnson to appoint Cazneau as Minister Resident in the Dominican Republic, a special appropriation was thereupon requested from Congress to provide for the expenses of the mission. At this juncture, Davis Hatch, of the Neyba salt mine, whose original antipathy to Cazneau and Fabens had been fanned by the partners' refusal to permit him to approach Seward during his brief visit to Santo Domingo, wrote to Washington setting out in no charitable aspect the previous careers of both Cazneau and his associate, and dwelling particularly upon the fact that Cazneau during the Civil War had openly announced his support of the Confederacy and had at the same time been excessively bitter in his denunciation of Seward himself, as well as of other leading men of the North. When this information reached Washington, Charles Sumner, as Chairman of the Senate Foreign Relations Committee, not unnaturally insisted that the nomination be rejected. Seward, however, remarking merely that Cazneau had "deceived" him, had the nomination withdrawn by the President from further consideration by the Senate.

Notwithstanding the withdrawal of his nomination, General Cazneau continued to communicate with the Secretary of State. In a further letter, he opened up a new vista of alarm to the apprehensions of Mr. Seward by impressing him with the possibility that the Dominican people might become involved in a revolutionary struggle instigated throughout the Spanish Antilles by Haiti for

the purpose of obtaining negro supremacy.[1] Claiming that
had his nomination as Minister Resident been confirmed
he would have been able to retain President Baez in power,
he insinuated that he could be appointed Special Agent,
as he had been in the past, without the concurrence of
the United States Senate and that in that event he could
save the Republic from negro anarchy. He urged Seward
to grant official recognition to the Dominican Government, and claimed that should he only be able to obtain
"periodical visits from American war vessels" he would
feel entirely able to regulate the action of the Dominicans.

At the same time, the situation of the Republic had
given rise to considerable alarm on the part of the Government of President Cabral soon after his inauguration
as President, owing to the outbreak of war between Spain
and Chile. The historian, José Gabriel García, a leader of
the liberals, who had been temporarily appointed by
Cabral Minister for Foreign Affairs, realized that were
the hostilities between Spain and Chile to spread to some
of the other of Spain's former colonies, the neutrality of
the Dominican Government might readily be jeopardized.
On October 18, 1866, García addressed a confidential note
to the American Secretary of State requesting that he be
advised as to the course that the Dominican Government
should pursue in the event that the theatre of the war
between Spain and Chile were to extend to the Caribbean
Sea. García, announcing his belief that the Monroe Doctrine implied that the republican system in the American
continent should not be capriciously attacked and that its
destruction should not be the object of any war undertaken by a European Power, requested some declaration
from the Secretary of State as to the policy which the

[1] General William L. Cazneau to Secretary Seward, October 9, 1866.

United States would pursue in the event that the Republics of Latin-America were attacked by a European Power, or by a combination of European Powers, in order that the Dominican Republic, without going beyond the strict limits of neutrality, might conform its attitude to that adopted by the United States. The reality of the apprehensions of the Dominican Minister was made patent by his admission that he realized that the neutrality of the Dominican Republic might not satisfy Spain's aspirations in the American hemisphere, and that Spain might consequently pretend to derive from the maintenance of such neutrality a pretext for resuming her interrupted war with the Dominican Republic. García asked whether in that event the United States Government would support the Dominican Republic.

Further information which reached Secretary Seward during the autumn of 1866, to the effect that the Dominican Government was desirous of concluding, without further delay, a treaty of amity and commerce with the United States, and finally the definite request, on November 8, 1866, for the negotiation of an agreement whereby the United States Government should furnish practical assistance to the Dominican Republic, led Secretary Seward to the belief that the time was ripe to press to a conclusion the negotiations which he himself had initiated the preceding winter.

6.

On November 8th, the Minister for Foreign Affairs had addressed an official note to Secretary Seward asking whether, in view of the unequal contest which the Dominican Republic had maintained for two years with the Spanish Monarchy, the Government of the United States "would be disposed to advance to it a million dollars in the character of a loan on just, equitable and reasonable conditions." He likewise inquired whether the United States Government

"would also be disposed to give to the Republic, on credit, a number of pieces of heavy artillery sufficient to meet the requirements she has of them, since the artillery which had been in Dominican strongholds before the Spanish War had all been broken up."

On the same day, an official request of the same character, but in more detailed form and with ramifications which the Minister for Foreign Affairs had not cared to put on paper, was conveyed to the new American Commercial Agent, Mr. Somers Smith. Mr. Smith reported [1] that President Cabral had requested him to ascertain whether the United States Government would be willing to grant a loan of one or two millions of dollars to the Dominican Republic, and had added that the Republic preferred to apply for assistance to the United States rather than to any European Power. The Government's need of financial assistance was immediate in that it was necessary to redeem the outstanding paper currency, amounting in all to some $500,000, inasmuch as the Government of Baez had refused to accept it in the payment of customs duties, (notwithstanding the obligation printed on the face of the bills), and it was believed indispensable to retire money in which there was no confidence from circulation, the Government intending to redeem it at 50% of its face value. Mr. Smith was authorized by Cabral to state that the Dominican Government had no other indebtedness with the exception of approximately $100,000

[1] Mr. J. Somers Smith to Secretary Seward, November 8, 1866.

of bonds issued for supplies which were receivable in payment of customs duties. The remainder of the loan, once the paper currency was redeemed, was desired for the purchase of 10,000 stand of approved arms, 100 cannon, a few heavy guns for fortifications, and a small steamer. In concluding his relation of the desires of the Dominican Government, Mr. Smith declared that he had been authorized to offer to the United States as collateral the use of the coal mines at Samaná and the possession of the Levantado and Carenero Keys at the entrance to Samaná Bay, "for such time and for such purpose as might be agreed upon." The request of the Dominican Government, made with the utmost secrecy, met with immediate response from the American Secretary of State.

Selecting his son, the Assistant Secretary of State, Frederick W. Seward, as the representative of the United States in the proposed negotiations, Secretary Seward provided him with detailed instructions as to the course to be pursued during his mission in Santo Domingo. The Assistant Secretary was officially apprised that President Johnson authorized him to conclude a convention with the Dominican Republic for the cession or lease of the strategic portions of Samaná to the United States.[1] He was provided with a draft convention which the Secretary of State had prepared, of which the salient article, Article IV, was as follows:

"The United States shall have the right to fortify and garrison and protect the leased territory aforesaid during the term aforesaid with such fortifications and land and naval forces as the President of the United States may deem expedient and to remove all ordnance, arms and

[1] Secretary Seward to Asst. Secretary of State Frederick W. Seward, December 17, 1866.

military stores that may be placed there during the said lease by the United States; but the Dominican Government may, at its option, purchase the same or any part thereof at a fair valuation to be paid to the United States."

In the event that the absolute cession of the territories desired would be consented to by the Dominican Government, he was to offer as a consideration therefor not more than $2,000,000, payable one-half in cash and the other half in arms and munitions of war, no cession to be acceptable, however, unless made in full sovereignty to the United States. In the event that only a lease of the territory were to be agreed to, the territory was to be leased for not less than thirty years, and in that event the sum of $10,000 might be paid upon the ratification of the convention by the Dominican Government, and after the exchange of ratifications the United States would remit annually as rental the sum of $12,000, either in gold or in munitions of war at the option of the Dominican Government.

In his instructions, Frederick Seward was reminded that during the administration of President Pierce an effort had been made to obtain a lease of the Bay of Samaná, as a coaling station for passenger and naval steamers, but that the activities of Captain McClellan, who had proceeded to Samaná to make a survey prematurely, before definite arrangements had been concluded with the Dominican Government, had given notice of the negotiations to certain European Governments, which had been enabled to thwart the plans of the United States. The Secretary of State added that the intervention of Spain in the Dominican Republic had been caused by the desire of the Spanish Government to prevent the United States from obtaining any foothold in Samaná. Seward's instructions concluded with the warning:

"The proposition now under consideration will not succeed unless caution, secrecy and despatch shall be preserved in carrying it into effect . . . It is deemed indispensable that the convention should be ratified by the Dominican Government before any consideration shall be paid by this Government . . . You will direct your attention to the competency of the Executive for the time being to enter into and ratify the convention or whether the consent of the Dominican Congress to the instrument will be indispensable to its validity. Vice Admiral Porter of the Navy will accompany you . . . His great experience in foreign countries and especially his familiarity with the region you are about to visit will be found useful towards the purpose of your mission."

At the same time, full powers were transmitted to the American Commercial Agent, Mr. Somers Smith, to negotiate the commercial treaty requested by the Dominican Government.

On January 19, 1867, the Assistant Secretary of State, accompanied by Admiral Porter, arrived in Santo Domingo on the U.S.S. *Gettysburg*. General Cabral, who had been absent in the northern provinces, returned immediately to Santo Domingo and negotiations were at once initiated. Upon the day following the President's arrival, the American representatives commenced their conferences with the President and the members of the Cabinet, to whom they had been presented by Don José Gabriel García, the Acting Minister for Foreign Affairs. Referring to the request of the Dominican Government that the United States advance a loan to the Dominican Republic, the younger Seward declared that in the opinion of his

Government a lease or purchase of the Samaná Peninsula appeared more advisable and more advantageous than the suggested loan. He reminded the members of the Dominican Cabinet of the purchase by the United States of Louisiana from France, of Florida from Spain, and of various territories from Mexico as having been productive of friendship and mutual advantage, and insisted that events in Mexico and in Haiti and elsewhere indicated

"but too plainly how difficult it is to preserve independent sovereignty and peaceful relations between two nations one of which occupies the position of creditor and the other that of debtor."

He added:

"The United States has no disposition . . . to enter upon any line of policy which would not assure to the republics of America stability, prosperity and progress." [1]

It was soon evident that the policy which the agents of the American Government desired Cabral to adopt had caused a serious disagreement in the Dominican Cabinet. The Ministers of the Interior and of Finance, Don Apolinar de Castro and General Pablo Pujol, favoured the acceptance of either of the alternatives proposed by the United States, while the Ministers of War and of Foreign Affairs, General José del Carmen Reinoso and Don José Gabriel García, objected to the trend the negotiations had taken. For the moment, Cabral needed time in which to arrive at a conciliatory solution, and General Pujol was consequently appointed Commissioner to prolong the negotiations. In his account of the continued conferences had with the Dominican Commissioner, Frederick Seward

[1] Mr. Frederick W. Seward to Secretary Seward, January 20, 1867.

reported that the Dominican Government manifested a willingness and even a desire to enter into some arrangement with the United States with regard to Samaná which would provide the American Government with a suitable naval harbour and coaling station, but that it was placed in an embarrassing position since it could not, without flagrantly violating the second article of the new Constitution, consent to an absolute cession of any of its territory, and that it had consequently proposed a lease of the Levantado Key which commanded the entrance of the Bay of Samaná, together with the use of the adjacent waters, as well as certain specific privileges on the mainland of the Peninsula.[1] The American representative declined to entertain this proposition on the ground that the Levantado Key and the waters adjacent were commanded by the heights of the Peninsula, and insisted that the United States desired no territory unless they acquired absolute control of it, and unless such territory could be held and fortified against all enemies.

As the result of past experience, it was not unnatural that the Dominican Government had entered upon these negotiations with some degree of distrust, although Seward had emphasized that the negotiations then in progress had not been sought by the United States but had been entered upon at the request of the Dominican Government. While the members of the Dominican Government realized the advantages of the American proposal as a means of protection against foreign aggression, they were reluctant to assume the responsibility of taking a step which they feared would render the Government unpopular. For the bitter memories of the Spanish occupation had been directly responsible for the introduction of the second

[1] Mr. Frederick W. Seward to Secretary Seward, January 22, 1867.

article into the new Constitution, and this article was generally interpreted as making unlawful even a temporary occupation of Dominican territory by a foreign government. Appreciating at length the strength of the opposition to his proposals, Seward recommended that nothing further be done for the time being, suggesting that the matter be held in reserve for future discussion until such time as a way might be found to evade the evident constitutional obstacles.

During the course of the discussions, General Pujol provided Seward with a memorandum outlining what Cabral's Government was then willing to concede. It contained four points:

1. The rental to the United States of the waters of Samaná Bay so that the United States and the Dominican Republic might hold joint sovereignty over them;

2. The sale of lands on the Peninsula to be used by the United States as shipyards;

3. An agreement on the part of the United States to provide the Dominican Republic with the means necessary for undertaking the defense of Samaná Bay;

4. The lease of the Levantado and Carenero Keys.

In his formal reply to this memorandum, Seward stated that an agreement to Point 1 would be contrary to the established policy of the United States to avoid entangling alliances. In regard to Points 2 and 3, he replied that shipyards would be worse than useless to the United States if they could not be protected and defended by American fortifications, and that were the United States to obtain actual sovereignty over the Peninsula of Samaná it could be far more effectually defended than were the United States to be merely permitted to render assistance, in case of necessity, to the Dominican Government. In regard to Point 4, Mr. Seward stated that the lease of the Levantado and Carenero Keys alone would not be sufficient inasmuch as the fortification of these keys could not, owing to their natural position, render them sufficiently strong, nor could fortifications there have sufficient extent.

General Cabral, greatly disturbed by the divergence in the opinions of the members of his Cabinet, was as usual unable by himself to come to a decision. He therefore sought the advice of his ring of supporters, who, apprised of the intention of the National Assembly to pass a resolution proposed by Don Mariano Cestero and supported by the President of the Chamber, Don Juan Bautista Zafra, providing that any public authority instrumental in effecting the cession of any portion of the Republic to any other nation should be declared guilty of high treason, strongly recommended that the President terminate the negotiations. Cabral, therefore, finally stated that owing to the second article of the Constitution, which provided that "no part of the territory of the Republic could ever be alienated," the Dominican Government was unable to enter into either of the alternative agreements proposed by the United States.

For the time being, Secretary Seward was constrained to postpone the consummation of the project; but believing that the reluctance of the Dominican Government to accede to the American proposals was largely due to the fear that the Baez faction might make the acquiescence of General Cabral a plausible ground for another revolution, and realizing that the increasing impoverishment of Cabral's Government might tend to make it later more willing to find a means of granting the suggested lease or cession of the Samaná territory, he instructed the Commercial Agent, Mr. Somers Smith, to continue negotiations. These instructions were in general similar to those issued before to Seward's son, but contained the proviso that the lease of the territory should, if possible, be for a period of ninety-nine years, for which privilege the Commercial Agent was authorized to offer the sum of $1,000,000, payable in annual installments. He was informed that

"as any convention that may be made will require ratification by the Senate of the United States and a law of Congress to carry its stipulations into effect, you will take care that the period allowed for ratification and payment shall embrace sufficient time to prevent any lapse in case Congress should not be in session when it is signed . . . If the convention could be made during the ensuing session of the Fortieth Congress" it would be particularly desirable "in order that it might be immediately submitted to that body for final action before its adjournment."

Mr. Smith was authorized, however, to remit immediately after ratification the sum of $75,000 in case the agreement provided for the sale of the territory, and $25,000 in the case of a lease. In the latter event, the lease was to cover

"the territory known as the Peninsula of Samaná, the Bay of Samaná and the keys known as Levantado and Carenero with all the rights and appurtenances thereto belonging as they have heretofore belonged to the Government of the Republic, the territory . . . to extend from west to east thirty-two miles and to be eleven miles across at its greatest breadth, together with the waters of the Bay of Samaná and all the bays and harbors in said Peninsula and the full and exclusive jurisdiction over the territories and waters aforesaid."

As the months passed by, although President Cabral became more favourably disposed towards the American proposals and transmitted an agreement based upon Seward's later proposals in the first days of June to a secret session of the Congress, the opposition in the Congress became more vocal although a majority was apparently in favour of the project. Secretary Seward at length became disheartened at the long-continued delay, and instructed his agent on May 8th to terminate negotiations and to return all correspondence regarding the matter to the Department of State, in order that no papers referring to the negotiations might remain in the archives of the Agency. Subsequently he notified Mr. Smith of the new developments which had taken place elsewhere in the furtherance of his policy:

"I have now to inform you confidentially that the delay and apparent indisposition of the Dominican Government has rendered it expedient for the United States to open parallel negotiations in other quarters. There is good reason to expect that they will be successful and thus the chief want of the United States be supplied. Those proceedings would not have been adopted if there had been a reasonable prospect of the acceptance of the offer made to Dominica. It is impossible for the United States not to desire to contribute by moral influence to the stability and security of the republican system in Dominica, while the United States are incapable of entertaining an ungenerous thought or design against that Republic. Influenced by those feelings, it has seemed to me that an acceptance of our proposition would be vastly more important to Dominica than to the United States . . . It is possible, but rarely possible, that a proposition by Santo Domingo equivalent to that which we have withdrawn, if her Government should reconsider the question, might come in time to be accepted by us." [1]

The "parallel negotiations" referred to by Secretary Seward which resulted in the treaty providing for the sale by Denmark of the Danish West Indies, checked momentarily all further progress in the negotiations for the cession of Samaná, although the Commercial Treaty between the United States and the Dominican Republic the negotiation of which had been so many times commenced and so often postponed, was finally ratified by the United States Senate on April 30th, and by the Dominican Congress on May 16, 1867. [2]

7.

The disturbances which had distinguished the Provisional Presidency and the "Protectorate" of Cabral occurred with similar and ever increasing frequency during the course of his Constitutional administration. They had broken out, in fact, in localities where the supporters of the "Red" party were powerful, on the day of his inauguration; and although they were at first put down with rapidity, as time passed they acquired increased momentum. The political attacks to which the frustrated negotiations with the United States had given rise became more potent owing to the refusal which Cabral had encountered in his attempt to procure from the Holy See a concordat which would make possible the appointment of Padre Meriño as Archbishop of Santo Domingo. Cabral's resultant loss of prestige, cleverly seized upon by the supporters of Baez as a means of spreading dissatisfaction with the Government, was rendered far more

[1] Secretary Seward to Mr. Somers Smith, July 1, 1867.
[2] Appendix "A."

serious by the fact that in the spring of 1867, the Government of President Geffrard of Haiti, upon whose support Cabral had counted to prevent the outbreak of revolutionary disturbances along the Haitian frontier, had been overthrown by General Salnave, known to be in connivance with Baez. As soon as Salnave came into power, the Haitian Government not only permitted the return to Haitian territory of military leaders of the Baez party, but actually lent the "Reds" effective assistance by placing at their disposal arms, money and ammunition. In Cape Haitien, General Valentín Ramirez Baez soon established his headquarters, and, gathering a considerable number of revolutionary troops, commenced a series of attacks against the Governmental forces near Monte Cristi. These disturbances, which included an unsuccessful attempt to land an expeditionary force composed largely of foreign filibusterers near Monte Cristi in the month of July, succeeded in convincing President Cabral that should he desire to remain in the Government he must either enter into an arrangement with Salnave which would make impossible a continuation of the attacks from the Haitian frontier, or else attempt to resume the interrupted negotiations with the United States. Fearing, as it later was made evident, unnecessarily, the opposition which had broken out against the negotiations with the United States, Cabral determined upon the former alternative as the lesser of two evils. Agreeing to enter into a pact with the Haitian Government for mutual support, Cabral consented to receive a delegation from Salnave headed by L'Instant Pradine and General Ultime LaFontant, and on July 27, 1867, as the result of negotiations between the members of the Haitian mission and the commissioners appointed by the Domini-

can President, a convention was signed providing for perpetual peace between the two Republics, for the mutual
obligation to extirpate revolutionary activities, and for
the settlement in general of all outstanding issues between
the two countries. The significant feature of the convention was, however, contained in the fifth article, which
read as follows:

"Both Contracting Parties assume the obligation to
maintain with all their strength and power the integrity
of their respective territories, and not to cede, pledge or
alienate in favor of any foreign power either the whole
or any part of their territories or of the islands adjacent to
them."

The continuation of Salnave's open support of Baez
brought Cabral speedily to an exact appreciation of the
insincerity of the Haitian Government, and despatching
a vessel to Jacmel to bring back his diplomatic agent, who
had already commenced his journey to Port-au-Prince to
exchange there the ratifications of the convention signed
in Santo Domingo, Cabral reversed his policy completely,
even authorizing the Commander-in-Chief of the Dominican forces to march to the frontier to render support
to the Haitian faction which was opposing the government formed by Salnave.

But even at this point, with the revolution against his
Government spreading throughout the Republic and the
financial resources of his administration at their lowest
ebb, Cabral was still reluctant to resume the attempt to
obtain assistance from the United States. He preferred to
seek financial assistance in Europe. An agent, Jacobo
Herrera, sent to France for the purpose by Cabral, succeeded in obtaining an agreement from the banking house

of Emile Erlanger and Company of Paris, on November 15, 1867, by which the French company was entrusted with the flotation of a loan to net 10,000,000 francs. The Dominican Government was to mortgage the entire customs receipts of the Republic as collateral for the loan, Erlanger and Company to receive a commission payable over a period of twenty-four years of approximately 16% for their share in the project. Cabral's attempt to obtain financial assistance in this manner, however, was frustrated by the opposition of the Congress, which refused its consent to the agreement negotiated.

Cabral now realized that his sole hope lay in the United States. Early in November, by instruction of the President, his envoy, Don Ramón Fiallo, requested the American Commercial Agent to ascertain whether Secretary Seward would be inclined to renew negotiations for the lease of Samaná. This tardy decision of the President was likewise due in large part to the constant propaganda of the more important political leaders in the Cibao, who dreaded the return of Baez to the Presidency, and continually urged the President not to lose the "opportunity to obtain the civilizing current which might turn towards the country should the North American Nation obtain a foothold in the Peninsula of Samaná." Cabral was still hesitant in reaching any final decision as to the offers to be made to the American Government until he obtained definite assurances from Generals Luperón and Pimentel and General Gaspar Polanco that they would support the proposal. Upon receiving the confirmation which he desired, after the increasing spread of the revolution had necessitated the declaration of martial law, Cabral, on December 7th, instructed General Pujol, who had been from the outset one of the sturdiest supporters of the

American project, to proceed to Washington to negotiate the lease of Samaná. Pujol started upon his mission strengthened by the fact that the leaders in twelve of the principal towns of the Cibao had addressed a public letter to the President informing him that the situation was desperate and stating their opinion that unless the Government made an immediate proposal acceptable to the United States, anarchy might ensue throughout the Republic; and by the fact that the early opposition in the Congress to the project had been modified to such a degree that the Congress had confirmed by a large majority his appointment to negotiate in Washington the agreement now generally regarded as desirable by the "Blue" factions.

Secretary Seward, sceptical by reason of the failure of the former negotiations, was not inclined to view their resumption with optimism. He had been incensed at the proclamation issued by Cabral the previous summer which officially declared that the Dominican Government had no intention of negotiating the transfer of Samaná to the United States; and was still more indignant because of the "very extraordinary agreement with Haiti," as Seward termed it, which virtually made public the unwillingness of the Dominican Republic to agree to any of the proposals hitherto made by the United States. In instructions to Mr. Smith, as soon as he learned of the approaching visit to Washington of General Pujol, the Secretary of State announced that it would not be compatible with the self-respect of the American Government to discuss the matter further, unless he were first furnished with authentic evidence that the Government of the Dominican Republic had given their agent full powers to negotiate in its behalf; and that even so, the situation had now changed and the United States could not consent to be a tenant to another foreign Power, since Cabral's convention with Haiti, although not ratified, indicated the concurrence of the Dominican Government in the old Haitian contention that Haiti was directly concerned in any concession made of Dominican territory. Seward's conclusion was frankly aggrieved:

"I do not doubt that the Government of the Dominican Republic will soon come to the conviction that a transfer by that Government of the Peninsula of Samaná to the United States would have been a harbinger of independence and prosperity instead of a danger to that Republic. I regret only that this conviction will come so late. The independent States in the West Indies, in Central America and South America will, in every case, find jealousy of the United States a policy less injurious to the United States than unfavorable to their own security and welfare." [1]

On the 8th of January, 1868, Pujol commenced his negotiations in Washington, communicating the bases agreed upon in principle by the Dominican Government. In the proposal so tendered it was stipulated that the territory desired by the United States might only be leased, but that the lease might run for a period of between twenty and fifty years, the United States obtaining "perfect and exclusive sovereignty and jurisdiction throughout that time over the territories and waters above mentioned." In return therefor, the United States Government was to pay "one million silver dollars down and $300,000 in cash every year during the time the lease might last, as well as such arms and ammunition as were later to be agreed upon, and was likewise to obligate itself to sustain the autonomy of the Dominican Republic, and

[1] Secretary Seward to Mr. J. Somers Smith, Commercial Agent, December 13, 1867.

the integrity of its territory, should any difficulties arise with foreign nations in consequence of such agreement." Ten days later, having received in the meanwhile the counter proposals advanced by Secretary Seward, General Pujol agreed that the lease be extended to cover a period of ninety-nine years, and consented to reduce the total amount of the compensation demanded to the sum of $2,000,000, agreeing to submit any difficulty which might arise regarding the interpretation of the proposed treaty to the determination of the Supreme Court of the United States. On January 20th, Seward replied insisting that the amount of the rental be limited to $1,000,000 in cash and $1,000,000 in armaments, but expressed his willingness to request the United States Senate, in view of the political situation in the Dominican Republic, to agree that $200,000 be paid upon the signing of the treaty and its ratification by the United States Senate, prior to its ratification by the Constitutional authorities in the Dominican Republic. On the following day, the terms fixed by the Secretary of State were accepted by General Pujol on condition that they be likewise approved by the United States Senate.

Although the negotiations in Washington were proceeding with considerable rapidity, Cabral had delayed too long to make any assistance from the United States effective in preventing the overthrow of his own Government. By the beginning of January, 1868, the situation of his administration had become desperate. In the north, General Luperón and General Pimentel, discouraged by the lack of support which they had received from the capital, were obliged to give in before the increasing strength of the revolutionaries, and escaped from the Cibao. In the south, the rebellion had shattered the resist-

ance of the Government and the "Red" forces had succeeded in occupying the territory adjacent to the capital,
including Baní and San Cristóbal. In December, a Provisional Government of the "Reds" had been installed in
Santiago under the leadership of General Hungría, and
by the end of January the authority of Cabral had been
reduced to the uncertain control of the capital itself.
The American Commercial Agent had by now little hope
that the Government of Cabral could maintain itself in
power. His reports during the month of January made
the situation plain:

"The greater part of the country have pronounced
against the Government, but the Government still holds
the Capital and its environments. The troops stationed
without the City were called into the Capital on January
3d and on that night the insurgents commenced an occasional scattering fire which was replied to from the walls.
General Pimentel has arrived and will probably be made
Commander in Chief of the army. The Dominican
schooner of war *Capotillo* has been captured by a Haitian
war steamer near Monte Cristi, this proceeding being due
to the Dominican negotiations respecting Samaná. There
undoubtedly exists a perfect understanding between President Salnave and General Baez to overthrow Cabral's
Government, to sell Samaná and divide the money." [1]

Finally, having lost all hope of being able to sustain his
Government through its own resources, and failing to
receive any word from Pujol that an agreement had been
reached in Washington, Cabral determined to capitulate:

"On January 21st, Santo Domingo surrendered to the
opposition army. No word being received from Señor

[1] Mr. Somers Smith, to Secretary Seward, January 6, 1868.

Pujol, General Cabral lost hope, the appearance of an epidemic of cholera at the same time causing many of the Government troops to desert. Generals Cabral and Pimentel, together with about 150 of the wealthier citizens of the Capital, embarked for Puerto Cabello, Venezuela, and the besieging army took possession of the City today." [1]

8.

On February 12th, General Hungría, the head of the Santiago Provisional Government, arrived in Santo Domingo. His Cabinet resigned three days later owing to the distaste of its members for the policy of persecution initiated by the revolutionary generals. Thereupon a Triumvirate composed of Generals Hungría, Gomez and Luciano was installed, which inaugurated the new régime by casting 100 political prisoners into the jail in the fortress of the capital. Enheartened doubtless by official congratulations from the Haitian Government upon the success of the revolution in overthrowing General Cabral, who "had endeavored to dispose of part of the national territory to foreigners," the Triumvirate sent to Curaçao to bring Baez to the country.

On March 29th, Baez returned once more to Santo Domingo, where he was welcomed with every manifestation of apparent popular delight. He was finally inaugurated on May 2d as President of the Republic, an office which, he announced, he had chosen in preference to that of Dictator, offered to him by the National Assembly. He condescended to accept, however, with every sign of gratification, the title of "Great Citizen" which the Assembly thrust upon him "in the name of a grateful country."

Even before his inauguration, Baez spared no efforts to

[1] Mr. Somers Smith to Secretary Seward, February 1, 1868.

make it evident that he would be glad to negotiate immediately the lease of the territory of Samaná in accordance with the terms agreed upon by Secretary Seward with Cabral's representative. He made it plain that he consented to go still further, instructing one of his satellites, Don Felix Maria Delmonte, to advise the American Commercial Agent, for the information of Secretary Seward, that he would raise no objection even to the sale of the whole Peninsula of Samaná, since the unconditional cession would doubtless reap a far greater financial reward, and with no greater risk attached to himself. He merely stipulated his hope that, in the latter event, the United States would despatch men of war to Santo Domingo and to Puerto Plata to support his Government.

With the change of Government in the Republic, the activities of General Cazneau and his partner, Colonel Fabens, were redoubled. Before Baez reassumed the Presidency, Fabens had reached Washington charged with the double mission of representing Baez and General Cazneau. In the letter of introduction with which the latter had provided him, General Cazneau informed the Secretary of State that Colonel Fabens bore with him "a plan for the complete realization of your patriotic and comprehensive views for the advancement of American interests in these seas." General Cazneau was almost exuberant in his optimism, assuring the Secretary that he was

"fully convinced that if the negotiations be carried out with General Baez and the protection of our flag be extended over any portion of this country, it will not only be hailed with joy and gratitude here but will give to our country a new and extended field for enterprise and a very prolific source of national wealth."

[1] General William L. Cazneau to Secretary Seward, April 17, 1868.

The precarious conditions under which he returned to the Presidency could not be ignored by Baez. With his customary cynicism, he had replied to the words of the President of the National Convention when he informed the "Great Citizen" that

"the majority of the Dominicans believed that with his knowledge, his patriotism, and the coöperation of all good citizens, he would carry out with glory his difficult task and the acts of his administration would distinguish it from the preceding government by the august seal of justice,"

with the statement that he was returning to the Presidency

"without hate in his heart, without gall on his lips, to submit himself once more to the crushing burden which he must assume on Dominican soil, desirous solely of making one last attempt to save his country from its imminent ruin."

The "imminent ruin" which Baez foresaw was not that of his country, which never caused him concern, but the crumbling of his own life-long ambitions, since he realized fully that without support, which he could not find within the confines of Dominican territory, it would be impossible for him to control much longer the followers whom he had so often hoodwinked by the specious promise that his own return to power would bring with it for them days of peace and prosperity. To his limited vision, of which the scope had not widened with the years, although his native shrewdness had been sharpened by the vicissitudes he had undergone, only one resource presented itself, the resource which he had devised in 1843. This solution in another guise was now pressed upon him by Cazneau and his associate, who had small difficulty in convincing Baez that a closer connection with the United States would, in all probability, make it possible for him to regain a preponderant influence in domestic affairs, and at the same time would assuredly, in any event, permit him to share in the profits which would be realized should the protection of the United States be extended over Dominican lands, and thereby make feasible the lucrative sale of concessions in return for good American money.

The solution determined upon by Baez was identical to that reached by Santana seven years before. He determined to follow meticulously the precedent set by his great rival against which he had so long inveighed publicly and privately. The barren state of the national treasury, the ruin of commerce in the Republic, of which the determination of the Government to fix the value of Dominican paper at 400 to one silver dollar gave eloquent proof, the early rise of concerted rebellion made evident by the engagements resulting from Cabral's presence in the frontier Provinces, quickened the President's decision. Within six days after his inauguration, Baez again despatched Delmonte, now Minister for Foreign Affairs, to the American Commercial Agent to tell him officially that the President had determined to accept the proposals made by the American Government for the purchase of the Samaná Peninsula and the waters of Samaná Bay. At the same time agents were sent abroad to attempt to obtain a loan to furnish the funds urgently required by the Government until such time as a definite agreement could be reached with the American Government.

For the time being, no definite response was obtained from Seward, who was by no means ignorant of the unsettled condition of the Republic. Although Baez had announced his determination to refuse the office of Dictator, which the National Convention had tendered him, and had confirmed his refusal by a decree issued on May 18th declaring officially his intention solely to govern as a Constitutional President, his early actions gave the lie to his public assurances, in the opinion of the Commercial Agent.[1]

"As to this country at present being a Republic, it is so only in name. Baez exercises despotic powers."

Persecutions, decrees of exile, imprisonments and executions were constant. For this policy the activities of the leading generals of the "Blue" party gave the President the needed excuse. Before the end of May, General Cabral had already entered Dominican territory from Jacmel, in Haiti. General Luperón and General Pimentel were daily expected to invade the north of the Republic. In the Seybo, revolution had been proclaimed by General Manzueta, and even in Azua rebellion threatened to break out at any moment, notwithstanding the presence in the Province of the President's relatives, Cárlos Baez and General Valentín Ramírez Baez, at the head of a considerable number of Governmental troops. In Haiti, the instability of the Government of Salnave, whose fortunes had been linked with those of Baez, gave cause for constant alarm lest the increasing activities of the Haitian revolutionists headed by Nissage Saget, who had openly espoused the cause of the "Blue" party in the Dominican Republic, might result in the overthrow of Salnave and the creation in Haiti of a government bitterly hostile to Baez and his partisans.

[1] Mr. Somers Smith to Secretary Seward, May 18, 1868.

9.

Consequently, on June 9th, urged on by General Cazneau, and feeling sure that the refusal of the United States Senate to ratify the treaty for the purchase of the Danish West Indies would induce the American Secretary of State to take renewed interest in the Samaná project, Baez once more sent his Minister, Delmonte, to the American Commercial Agent. The proposals now tendered were more extensive than those made the preceding month, and conveyed in great detail. Baez now declared that his Government was prepared to sell the Peninsula and Bay of Samaná for $1,000,000 in gold and $1,000,000 in armaments; he suggested that full powers be sent to the Commercial Agent in Santo Domingo to sign a convention which he also suggested might well be prepared by the American Secretary of State himself; and finally requested that three vessels of war be despatched to the Dominican Republic, one to remain in Santo Domingo, one in Puerto Plata, and one in Samaná, to sustain his Government until the sale had been consummated. The hope was likewise expressed that the American Government might be willing to advance at least a few thousand dollars upon the ratification by the Dominican Government of the convention, to provide for the pressing needs of the Administration. This request was made orally, since Baez feared that should the United States decline the proposal, and the matter be made public, it would prove seriously prejudicial to his own interests.

While awaiting Seward's decision, Baez attempted to strengthen his own position temporarily by the publication of arbitrary decrees declaring that any revolution-

aries landing upon Dominican soil would be shot if captured, and that any vessels bearing them which might be
taken by Government ships would be confiscated. Restrictions upon personal liberty were at the same time
made far more stringent, the Government going to the
extreme of forbidding all Dominican citizens to enter
foreign Consulates no matter what their business might
be. To such an extent was this latter regulation enforced
that even the domestic servants of the foreign Consuls
were not permitted to enter the Consulates without special
permits signed by the President himself. More concerned,
as each day passed, by the inability of his Government to
maintain order, Baez finally sent for the American Commercial Agent, in the early morning of July 18th, to
inform him that General Luperón had joined General
Cabral upon the Haitian frontier for the purpose of
assisting the Haitian revolutionaries in overthrowing the
Government of Salnave, and that in return therefor
Saget's generals had promised help to the leaders of the
"Blue" party in a subsequent attempt to overthrow Baez
as well, upon the understanding that there should be no
alienation of Dominican territory once this had been
accomplished. Hoping to expedite negotiations by utilizing the knowledge he had gained from Cazneau of Secretary Seward's fear of a repeated attempt by the European Powers to infringe the Monroe Doctrine, Baez declared that should the United States provide him with
moral and material support in maintaining his own Government, the sale of Samaná could be carried out at once,
and the question of the compensation therefor, which
depended, as he realized, upon the consent of the United
States Senate, be postponed for future determination; but
that should the United States refuse to accede to his pro-

posal, he would be obliged to make similar proposals either to England, France or Spain.

Notwithstanding the efforts of Baez to preserve entire secrecy regarding his proposals to the American Government, the fact that such propositions had been made was soon generally known. The Department of State was at once flooded with protests. Among the first of them was a protest dated August 1, 1868, which had been signed at Guayubín by Generals Pimentel, Imbert, and Valerio and by Luperón's brilliant lieutenant, Ulises Heureaux, denouncing the sale of Samaná, and calling Seward's attention to the fact that General Baez had already been declared an outlaw by the chiefs of the revolution. This protest was further confirmed by General Luperón himself, who wrote to Secretary Seward from Jacmel on August 9th, declaring that the Dominicans had knowledge of the fact that Baez had sent Colonel Fabens to Washington to negotiate the sale of Samaná, and expressed the hope that the Cabinet at Washington would "scornfully reject the rash proposals of Baez and Fabens." Luperón's protest likewise contained the warning that the party of which he declared himself the head would recognize no act of the Dominican Government carried out subsequent to January 31, 1868.

Paying small heed to the protests with which he was showered both from within and without the United States against the annexation of any portion of the Dominican territory, Secretary Seward finally advised the American Commercial Agent that the proposals of the Dominican President would be held under consideration, and although he had been warned by Mr. Smith that "the speculative characters of Cazneau and Fabens are well known not only here but in the United States" . . .

and that

"they are not entitled to the least consideration on the part of our Government,"

the Secretary of State continued to correspond with Colonel Fabens, who had now been for some three months in the United States representing himself as the Confidential Agent of President Baez. Fabens missed no opportunity of rendering himself agreeable to the Administration. In one of his letters to the Secretary of State he informed him:

"You will be pleased to hear that the friends of Mr. O'Sullivan, who is now enroute to Santo Domingo for the purpose of making proposals to President Baez for the establishment of regular steam connection at the ports of that Island, have purchased two steamers for the line and are now fitting them up in good style for passengers . . . This, I hope, will be the beginning of many American enterprises which will raise to new life the dormant resources of that fertile and beautiful island." [1]

He concluded by saying that he had that day been instructed by President Baez to seek a suitable occasion "to congratulate President Johnson, in the name of President Baez, on the triumph of Constitutional principles shown in the result of the recent impeachment trial."

10.

Whether Secretary Seward's sympathies were warmed or not by this evidence of Baez's interest in the "triumph of Constitutional principles" in the United States, notwithstanding the Dominican's total disregard of them in

[1] Colonel Joseph W. Fabens to Secretary Seward, September 5, 1868.

his own country, his interest was finally aroused by a despatch received from the American Commercial Agent in the autumn of 1868.

In this despatch he was informed that the President of the Dominican Republic desired the President of the United States immediately to publish a decree placing the Dominican Republic under the protection of the United States, and to make the proclamation effective by sending vessels of war to take possession of all the strategic points in the Republic.[1] Such a measure, Baez wished Seward to know, would impart great confidence to the people of the country and likewise to foreigners who might wish to settle there; and since the overthrow of the Monarchy in Spain might lead to fundamental changes in the status of Cuba and Puerto Rico, the proposed declaration might induce many Spaniards to remove from those islands to Santo Domingo once the Republic had been placed under American protection. The assurance was offered by President Baez that should a protectorate be proclaimed by the United States, the Dominican Republic would at once apply for admission into the Union.

"The United States," Mr. Smith concluded, "are invited to take this Republic under their protection and pave the way for annexation by Mr. Baez, who, although President in name, is virtually clothed with dictatorial powers."

This despatch brought forth at length a definite statement from Secretary Seward: [2]

"I have received," he wrote, "your very important confidential despatch of the 24th of October, last. You have

[1] Mr. Somers Smith to Secretary Seward, October 24, 1868.
[2] Secretary Seward to Mr. Somers Smith, November 17, 1868.

communicated to me certain views and wishes which have been expressed to you by President Baez and by his confidential Minister, Felix Delmonte. These views and desires are, substantially, that the United States shall immediately publish a declaration placing the Dominican Republic under the protection of the United States and shall sustain the proclamation by sending vessels of war to take possession of Samaná and Manzanillo Bays and any other points that military strategy may indicate and thus pave the way to annexation to the United States by Mr. Baez, who, although President by name, is virtually clothed with dictatorial powers. You have given me the considerations out of which these views have arisen . . .

"President Baez and his Minister cannot be unaware that the proceeding which they propose, however benevolent its purpose might be, would nevertheless in its nature be an act of war, and that as such it transcends the power of the Executive Government and falls within the exclusive province of Congress.

"In submitting such a proceeding to the judgment of mankind, it would be difficult to distinguish it from the attempt which was made during our recent Civil War by Spain to re-annex the Dominican Republic to her own dominions by means of an illegal arrangement made between the Spanish Government and Santana, then President of the Republic. There would, indeed, be this difference that in the case proposed by President Baez the Dominican Republic would be virtually transferred to and accepted by an American Republic whereas in the other case it was an attempt to subvert a republican Santo Domingo and annex it as a province to one of the ancient European Monarchies.

"It may be doubted whether this distinction would be regarded as a moral justification of the proceedings.

"If, however, we lay that question aside, there still re-

main inherent difficulties in the case. To establish the protectorate in Santo Domingo would be virtually annexation by act of war, not by the consent and agreement
of the people of the Dominican Republic. The Congress
of the United States are always disinclined to foreign
military conquests, perhaps more so now than at any time
heretofore. It seems unlikely, therefore, that Congress
would entertain any other proposition for the annexation
of Dominica than one which should originate with and
have the sanction of the Dominican people, expressed in
a regular Constitutional manner. Nevertheless, the subject
is a very important one and I reserve further consideration
of it until Congress shall have assembled, which will be
on the first Monday in December.

"You may read this despatch confidentially to President
Baez and his Secretary."

To Baez the scruples of Secretary Seward must have
appeared difficult of comprehension. Brushing them aside,
he declared that his Government was prepared to obtain
a national declaration in favour of annexation by popular
vote or by acclamation, or in any form that the United
States might indicate. But,

"It is necessary, however," and this consideration was
evidently far more important, "that the United States send
out to this City at once a vessel of war with a convention
and the sum of $300,000." [1]

Whatever the doubts may have been which had originally existed in Seward's mind as to the justification in
acceding to the proposals made from Santo Domingo, and
in thus sanctioning the perpetration by the United States
of a fraud against which he had violently protested when

[1] Mr. Somers Smith to Secretary Seward, December 19, 1868.

BUENAVENTURA BAEZ

it had been committed by Spain, it is certain that those doubts were overcome. It is equally certain that they were not overcome through any illusion that the will of the Dominican people could be any more fully expressed under the rule of Baez than it had been under that of Santana.

It is probable that the Secretary of State, smarting under the humiliations which the United States had suffered throughout the Civil War in the contemptuous disregard shown by Europe for a policy which it was destined to resent for many years longer, had come to the conclusion that benefits arising from the rehabilitation of the Monroe Doctrine were of greater import to the American continent than was the evil occasioned by the proposed disregard for the "right of self-determination" of the smaller nations of that continent. The reaffirmation of the preponderant influence of the United States in the American continent had been Seward's chief purpose in remaining in Johnson's Cabinet, and to the achievement of that ideal his failing powers had been dedicated. In the carrying out of his determination he had been in great measure successful notwithstanding the obstacle presented by the complete breach in the relations between the President and Congress. Alaska had been purchased from Russia; republican government had been reestablished in Mexico; the treaty right had been obtained from Nicaragua for the construction of an interoceanic canal. By all of these achievements the danger of the increase of European influence on the continent had been greatly diminished. But the keystone of his policy, the acquisition of a coaling and naval station in the West Indies, the strategic value of which at that time appeared convincing to both military and naval authorities, Seward had failed to secure. For the Senate, owing to its bitter hostility to the President, had resolutely refused to ratify the Danish treaty for the purchase of the Danish West Indies.

Presumably the disappointments to which he was exposed by the attitude of the Senate were responsible in some degree for the startling changes which Seward's policy at length underwent. From his original, far-sighted, and logical view that the prevention of the increase of European dominion in the American continent, and the ultimate withdrawal of European Powers from America, was, for the United States, a basic policy, grounded in the need for self-preservation, he swiftly increased the scope of the doctrine to one of frank and radical expansionism. His latter convictions were made known in the extraordinary message sent to Congress by President Johnson on December 9, 1868, less than a month after Seward received the final version of the Dominican proposals:

"The political and social condition of the Republics of Haiti and St. Domingo is very unsatisfactory and painful. The abolition of slavery, which has been carried into effect throughout the island of St. Domingo and the entire West Indies, except the Spanish islands of Cuba and Porto Rico, has been followed by a profound popular conviction of the rightfulness of republican institutions and an intense desire to secure them. The attempt, however, to establish republics there encounters many obstacles, most of which may be supposed to result from long-indulged habits of colonial supineness and dependence upon European monarchical powers. While the United States have on all occasions professed a decided unwillingness that any part of this continent or of its adjacent islands shall be made a theatre for a new establishment of monarchical power,

too little has been done by us, on the other hand, to attach
the communities by which we are surrounded to our own
country, or to lend even a moral support to the efforts they
are so resolutely and so constantly making to secure republican institutions for themselves. . . .

"Comprehensive national policy would seem to sanction
the acquisition and incorporation into our Federal Union
of the several adjacent continental and insular communities as speedily as it can be done peacefully, lawfully,
and without any violation of national justice, faith, or
honor. Foreign possession or control of those communities
has hitherto hindered the growth and impaired the influence of the United States. Chronic revolution and anarchy
there would be equally injurious. Each one of them, when
firmly established as an independent republic, or when
incorporated into the United States, would be a new source
of strength and power. . . .

"It can not be long before it will become necessary for
this Government to lend some effective aid to the solution
of the political and social problems which are continually
kept before the world by the two Republics of the island
of St. Domingo, and which are now disclosing themselves
more distinctly than heretofore in the island of Cuba. The
subject is commended to your consideration with all the
more earnestness because I am satisfied that the time has
arrived when even so direct a proceeding as a proposition
of an annexation of the two Republics of the island of St.
Domingo would not only receive the consent of the people
interested, but would give satisfaction to all other foreign
nations.

"I am aware that upon the question of further extending our possessions it is apprehended by some that our
political system can not successfully be applied to an area
more extended than our continent; but the conviction is
rapidly gaining ground in the American mind that with

the increased facilities for intercommunication between all portions of the earth the principles of free government, as embraced in our Constitution, if faithfully maintained and carried out, would prove of sufficient strength and breadth to comprehend within their sphere and influence the civilized nations of the world." [1]

A letter was at once addressed by Baez and his Cabinet to the President of the United States expressing their profound gratification:

"Most Excellent Sir:

"The Government of the Dominican Republic feels ineffable satisfaction at the ideas expressed by Your Excellency in your last message to Congress in relation to the great political measure that ought to be adopted immediately by the Cabinet at Washington with reference to the future of Santo Domingo.

"We have the honor to say to Your Excellency that the sentiments of a nation were never so well interpreted as they were on that occasion by Your Excellency and that such are the sentiments of an immense majority of the inhabitants of our country, which has been depleted too long by the oppression of anarchy.

"Your idea is preferable to any other policy for this country, as it is highly honorable and is very acceptable to all our people whose hopes and desires are to place themselves under the protection of a powerful sister republic.

"If the honorable Congress will assume the direction of the destinies of the Dominican Republic, we, its people, will hasten to show our gratitude by a frank and open ratification of the Resolution.

"Your Excellency will please accept the sentiments of high consideration, etc., etc.," [2]

[1] President Johnson's Fourth Annual Message to Congress, December 9, 1868.
[2] President Buenaventura Baez to President Johnson, January 8, 1869.

Thus encouraged, Baez considered the possibility, as he informed the American Commercial Agent,[1] of causing the authorities in the different provinces of the Republic immediately to hoist the American flag, and to proclaim by acclamation that they placed themselves under the Government of the United States. Although Baez was advised by Mr. Smith "to wait a little," matters were further pressed by an official communication addressed to Seward by Don Manuel Maria Gautier, who had replaced Delmonte as Minister for Foreign Affairs, requesting that the protection of the United States be immediately extended to the Dominican Republic.

The hostility to President Johnson among the members of the United States Senate and in the House of Representatives was so great that Baez was constrained to realize that no definite steps could be taken until after the inauguration of General Grant. This impression was confirmed when, soon after the opening of Congress, General Nathaniel P. Banks, Chairman of the House Committee on Foreign Affairs, who had submitted a resolution authorizing the President of the United States, with the consent of the Dominican Republic, to extend protection to that Republic, obtained in support of his measure only forty votes. A further resolution, submitted on February 1st by Mr. Orth, a member of the same Committee, declaring the consent of Congress to the annexation of the Dominican Republic, with the consent of the people and Government of that Republic, had been tabled by a vote of 110 to 62. Notwithstanding the fact that Secretary Seward, in an instruction [2] to the American Commercial Agent for the advice of General Baez, had stated that the action of

[1] Mr. Somers Smith to Secretary Seward, January 9, 1869.
[2] Secretary Seward to Mr. J. Somers Smith, February 5, 1869.

the majority in the House of Representatives had been due to the fact that the information in the possession of the movers of the resolutions, regarded as confidential by the Department of State, had not been shared by the majority of the members of Congress, Baez was forced to wait the short period intervening before the inauguration of Grant before taking further action.

CHAPTER V

NEGOTIATIONS FOR ANNEXATION TO THE UNITED STATES

1.

THE Spring of 1869 found Baez confronted with domestic difficulties which appeared well-nigh insurmountable. The financial distress of the Government, which had scarcely been lessened by his recourse to his customary procedure in issuing paper, this time in the guise of "metallic bonds," soon depreciated to twenty cents on the dollar, Baez attempted to relieve by negotiation of a European loan. This loan, known as the Santo Domingo Government loan of 1869, was, Baez stated to the American Commercial Agent, merely a temporary measure to enable his Administration to maintain itself, pending the decision of the United States Government as to the course it would pursue with regard to the Dominican Republic.

The contract first provided for an advance of £757,700 sterling by a group of English bankers headed by Hartmont and Company, to be raised by the sale of Dominican national bonds to the public, or to friends of the syndicate, at prices ranging from 70 to 50 per cent of their nominal value, as the case might be. While Baez attempted to prove his unwillingness to mortgage unduly the resources of his country, by pointing out with pride that he had refused the insistent request of Hartmont to include in the loan contract a lease of the Bay of Samaná for fifty years, as a matter of fact the entire resources of the Republic, both real and hypothetical, were pledged, and the terms agreed to by the President were of so onerous a character as to be almost incredible. The terms of the contract specified that the bonds to be issued were to be redeemable at par in cash after six months' notice, or at par by an accumulated sinking fund after twenty-five years by semi-annual drawings;

"In addition thereto for repayment of the loan and interest thereon, being the first and only lien of the State, the general property and revenue of the Republic were to be liable, and in addition thereto, the Government of the Dominican Republic specially hypothecated the entire proceeds of the receipts of the export and import customs dues of the ports of Santo Domingo and Puerto Plata . . . and in addition thereto the royalties produced from the working and export of guano from the Island of Alta Vela. And the revenues arising from the coal and other mines and minerals as well as the mahogany and other woods from the forests of the Peninsula of Samaná were specially hypothecated for the service of the loan." [1]

While the object of the Government in contracting the loan was alleged to be its desire to secure the construction of highroads and railways, it was perfectly apparent to all that the prospectus was blatantly false, since it was well recognized that Baez had not the slightest intention of constructing either highroads or railways, and desired to utilize the proceeeds of the loan solely for the redemption of a portion of the outstanding paper currency and thereafter for the personal needs of the members of his Government.

As the result of the intervention of the Senate, in this instance less amenable than usual to the dictates of the President, the original contract was later modified to cut the total amount of the loan down to £420,000 sterling, but notwithstanding the attempt of the Senate further to

[1] Mr. Somers Smith, Commercial Agent, to Secretary Fish, 1869.

modify the conditions originally agreed upon by the President's agents, the final contract, as it proved, provided that Hartmont and his associates were to receive "as a commission" £100,000 sterling, while the Government would obtain solely a possible cash advance of £320,000 sterling, and was bound to pay in return for that amount not only the sum of £58,900 annually for twenty-four years, but was likewise obligated to remit for the personal profit of Hartmont and the members of his syndicate, in addition to their original commission, an amount equivalent to the last interest payment due, as payment for "the first year's interest and the cancellation of the loan."

Confiding, apparently, in their belief that their outspoken and repeated protests against the realization of Baez's projects for annexation to the United States would render the incoming American Administration less inclined than its predecessor to further the ambitions of their antagonist, the leaders of the "Blue" party momentarily forgot their differences among themselves and renewed their activities in the early spring of 1869. Raising the cry that the consummation of the annexation to the United States would enslave the negroes in both Haiti and the Dominican Republic, Generals Cabral, Luperón and Pablo Pujol entered into a joint agreement on March 11th at St. Marc, Haiti, under the benevolent auspices of the Haitian revolutionary leader, General Nissage Saget, providing for the continuation of joint support between the Haitian opponents of President Salnave and the leaders of the "Blue" party in the Dominican Republic. The pact was notable, moreover, in that its evident purpose was to prevent further discord between Cabral and Luperón in the event that the revolution which they were then waging should prove successful, since it provided that Cabral and Luperón were each to appoint executive juntas to determine upon a joint policy, the obligations incurred by the two juntas to be subsequently recognized as obligations of the Dominican Republic. The agreement further provided that General Luperón was to proceed to the north to attempt to raise the standard of revolt against Baez in the Cibao, while General Cabral was to continue his operations in the south to strengthen the attacks against the Baez forces already initiated there by General Andrés Ogando. While Cabral's attempt to increase the authority of the revolution in the south proved generally unsuccessful, the campaign of General Luperón, as was to be anticipated in view of his extraordinary qualities, was waged with far more vigour, and had it not been for the odds against him would presumably have met with success.

Gregorio Luperón, destined for some decades to play a preponderant part in determining the destinies of the Republic, was in many ways a unique figure. A negro, born in Puerto Plata in the most humble circumstances, he had, by dint of strength of character and overpowering ambition, early obtained for himself a devoted following throughout the country. In the main self-educated, he had acquired the rudiments of instruction at a mission school in his native city, but his hold on the popular imagination was due in the greatest part to the charm of his personality and to his unfaltering courage. What Luperón has written of himself—

"No man has ever had more control over himself, more strength of will, nor more consistency in his ambitions" [1]—

---

[1] Luperón, "Notas Autobiográficas," Vol. I, p. 82.

may appear to be a flash of almost childlike egotism, but an impartial study of his career will demonstrate that his self-estimate is not wholly unjustified; and while it may not be possible for the student of Dominican history to share to the full the other glowing appraisals which Luperón has written of himself, and one may deplore his venality and his unmasked jealousy of those who obtained the prizes on which his own heart was set, he still remains in his virility, his dominating love of liberty, and his unsurpassed valour, an attractive and at times an admirable figure throughout many dreary years when vacillation, self-interest and sordid ambitions appear to be the dominating characteristics of the Dominican scene.

Luperón had no illusions as to the ability of Cabral to maintain himself unaided against Baez. He moreover felt confident that were the opponents of the Baez Government to enter into a coalition the relatively small forces at the Government's disposal would necessarily have to be separated. For this reason he entered into the pact of St. Marc, but at no time had he any intention of identifying his own struggle for supremacy with the interests of Cabral whom he later termed, in no uncertain phrase, "narrow-minded, stupid and egotistical." [1]

Having purchased through his agents in St. Thomas a small steamer of some 500 tons, which as the *Redbird* had seen service as a blockade runner during the American Civil War, the steamer was re-christened the *Telégrafo,* and raising the American flag, Luperón sailed thereon with forty-five companions from St. Thomas about the middle of May. When the *Telégrafo* appeared in the port of Puerto Plata on June 1st, the Government forces were taken by surprise and for two days

---

[1] Luperón, "Notas Autobiográficas," Vol. II, p. 127.

the city underwent a hot bombardment. Realizing, however, that the approach of additional Government forces
made it impossible for him to maintain his position, Luperón steamed to Samaná. There he was disheartened to
find the populace of the Province were reluctant to
acclaim the revolutionary manifesto addressed to them,
and after intermittent fighting extending over many
days, the *Telégrafo* was overtaken by two Government schooners towed into position by the steamer
Tybee, an American vessel owned by the firm of Spofford, Tileston & Company, of New York, which was running from New York to Santo Domingo, under a lucrative
concession granted some time previously by Baez. In the
engagement which ensued, several shots from the *Telégrafo* grazed the American steamer, and heeding the
counsel of his friends Luperón fled to the southern coast
of the Republic, disembarking his forces to harry the
Governmental authorities at Baní and Azua, and finally
bringing an end to the expedition at Barahona, where the
persistent refusal of Cabral to agree upon a joint plan of
campaign obliged Luperón to abandon his original project,
and to despatch the *Telégrafo* to the Island of Tor-
tola, where it was eventually sold.

2.

The spring of 1869 brought with it likewise, with the
inauguration of General Grant, a new era in Washington—an era when the standards of honesty and decency
in government were to sink lower than they had ever
sunk before, or have ever been destined since to sink.
From all parts of the country the lobbyists, the spoilsmen,
the concession hunters, the seekers of special privilege,
came flocking in. The President, unfitted by prior experi-

ence to meet the exigencies of the situation, surrounded himself in the White House with a clique of officers who had seen service with him, and upon whom he relied, and with the members of a Cabinet composed, with but few exceptions, of as inefficient and untrustworthy officers as have probably ever been appointed to an American Cabinet. Unfortunately for his own good name, and still more unfortunately for the repute of the Government, the individuals upon whom General Grant most relied were too frequently broken reeds. Only a few weeks had passed before the rumour of corruption was rife, and the rumour was destined to grow in extent until successive storms broke in the scandals of "Black Friday," of the "crédit mobilier," and of the "whiskey ring."

In such an atmosphere and amongst such surroundings the hopes and ambitions of Colonel Fabens were bound to prosper. Through his connections in New York an introduction to the President was secured. In addition to his immediate attempt to interest General Grant in the project to annex the Dominican Republic, Fabens gained without delay the coöperation of the Secretary of State, Hamilton Fish, who had replaced Secretary Seward on March 4th. As early as March 9th, Colonel Fabens obtained an interview with Secretary Fish and left with him a memorandum which contained the following salient points:

"The Dominican Government is disposed to enter fully into the American Union as a free and sovereign state and is prepared to assert that the question when submitted to the people will be approved with enthusiasm. Nevertheless it cannot take the initiative. It appears most suitable that the United States Congress, advised of the true situation

of the Dominican Republic, should accept the Dominican
Republic as one of its states;"

and doubtless recalling his own successful efforts at im-
perialism in the past, indicated that the Secretary of State
should take

"The act providing for the annexation of Texas as a
model . . . This done, the execution of all that remains
depends solely on the time which the President of the
United States may take to place the Dominican Government in a position to make a formal declaration."

Within a few days General Banks, the Chairman of the
House Committee on Foreign Affairs, whose sympathy
Colonel Fabens had already gained some months previously, requested that Colonel Fabens be despatched to
Santo Domingo to draft a report for the benefit of the
members of the Committee upon the financial and political condition of the Republic. Colonel Fabens, to preserve
appearances, actually made the voyage, but remained at
Santo Domingo barely thirty-six hours, and upon his
return to Washington presented the Chairman of the
Committee with a report which had been prepared long
in advance alleging that the total indebtedness of the
Dominican Republic was not more than $600,000, and
impressed upon the Committee that the Dominican people as one man were longing for annexation to the United
States. Soon after his return to Washington Fabens again
communicated with Secretary Fish, urging that the
United States take immediate action towards leasing as
a naval station such portions of the Bay and Peninsula
of Samaná as might be required, and adding:

"This can now be obtained of the Dominican Government at an annual cost of $100,000." [1]

Surprised by the apparent reluctance of the American Government to take immediately the action urged upon it, Baez caused his Minister for Foreign Affairs to address a communication to Colonel Fabens to urge greater activity upon him. In his note to Fabens Gautier pointed out that the situation of his Government was precarious in that all the southern and western Provinces with the exception of Azua were already in the control of the "Blue" leaders, and that the revolutionary forces commanded by Cabral, Luperón, and Pimentel were rapidly gaining ground. Gautier complained that no action was being taken in the United States regarding the lease of Samaná, the proclamation of a protectorate, or the project of annexation; that the Dominican Government had requested the sending of a commissioner and two vessels of war; and terminated with the plea:

"The vessels of war have not arrived—neither has the commissioner—why? We know not.

"Now then, on your return to the United States, seek a method of conferring with President Grant and with his influential friends there and expound these views. The hour is propitious and the favorable moment should not be lost." [2]

Stimulated to renewed energy by the complaints of his employers, and more particularly by the fact that President Salnave, emulating his ally in the Dominican Republic, had despatched an envoy to Washington to pro-

[1] Colonel Joseph W. Fabens to Secretary Fish, April 21, 1869.
[2] Manuel Maria Gautier to Colonel Joseph W. Fabens, June 22, 1869.

pose the cession to the United States of the Môle St. Nicolas, and by the alarming information that the revolution in the Dominican Republic had now spread to such an extent that the "Blue" leaders had, by the end of June, obtained possession of San Cristóbal on one side of the capital and of Los Llanos on the other, Colonel Fabens advised the Secretary of State that should any more time be lost, the whole project which he had been sponsoring might have to be abandoned.[1] Urging upon his attention the depredations of the steamer *Telégrafo* (officially declared by the Dominican Government on June 19th to be acts of piracy), and its reported interference with American shipping, Colonel Fabens, on July 9th, succeeded in having a conclusive interview with Secretary Fish. Impressing upon the Secretary the fact that the business with which he had been entrusted by the Dominican Government was so secret that were publicity to be given to the negotiations for annexation they would be thwarted by the European Powers, Fabens expressed the hope that some suitable person might be selected by President Grant to proceed at once as Commissioner to Santo Domingo, and suggested that the person so selected sail upon the *Tybee* on the following 17th of July in order that this agent might at once provide the Secretary with a broad and accurate report of present conditions in the Island. He himself was by no means reluctant to undertake the mission, since he declared in a letter written to the Secretary upon the same date:

"In the matter of Samaná, if you will confide to me the wishes of the United States Government I will use my best efforts to aid in securing their acceptance by the Do-

[1] Colonel Joseph W. Fabens to Secretary Fish, July 1, 1869.

minican Government. Under all circumstances, you may rely upon my hearty co-operation in any plan you may have to propose looking to the honor and welfare of the two countries."

The persuasive arguments of Fabens were moreover supported by a communication received by the Secretary of State from his Dominican colleague:

"The enemies of peace and progress of the country, fearful lest a change be made from this provisional state of affairs which favors so highly their shady projects, have made every effort to overthrow this Government in which they see a menace and a bar to their iniquitous plans. General Gregorio Luperón, a voluntary exile, a man of vindictive spirit and very backward ideas, has declared that the African race shall dominate in this Island and that that race should unite in order to exterminate the other races . . . In this situation, overcoming natural reluctance brought about by the idea of asking too much, my Government has decided to ask most urgently of Your Excellency's Government that like a powerful and philanthropic sister it may be good enough to assist the Dominican Government in its difficulties.

"The acquisition of a steamer of 300 tons, with artillery, munitions, and sufficient coal, would be our salvation, but we could not obtain it except as the result of the munificence of the United States, which sending it immediately might be kind enough to await payment until better times come along, which perhaps would not be far distant.

"I understand, Most Excellent Sir, that perhaps we are asking a great deal, but in the family of nations, as among individuals, there are relationships of proximity, of mutual interest, of hope in the future, which make one their political and social necessities.

"His Excellency [Baez] hopefully believes that our solemn hope will not be defrauded and that this our request will be granted." [1]

Persuaded of the advantages of the annexation project as explained to him by Fabens, attracted by the glory which he imagined would ensue to his Administration by adding to the domains of the United States, and convinced by the favourable reception given the propaganda from the pen of Mrs. Cazneau and other interested persons which such influential papers as the New York *Herald* were publishing with increasing frequency that public opinion was in accord with the opinions which he himself had formed, President Grant definitely committed himself to the annexation program.

The first step consisted in the issuance of instructions to the Secretary of the Navy to use the full power of the American Navy in capturing the *Telégrafo* and its redoubtable crew of forty-five revolutionaries commanded by the "pirate" Luperón, and thus made immediately and practically evident the support which the Government of the United States intended to render Baez and his Administration. In accordance with these orders, the Secretary of the Navy, George N. Robeson, at once wrote the following despatch to Commander Owen of the U.S.S. *Seminole* to proceed immediately to capture the alleged pirate:

"Navy Department, July 10, 1869.
"Sir:
"You will proceed without delay to the Bay of Samaná in the Island of San Domingo and ascertain if there is a steamer there present named the *Telegraph* under the

[1] Manuel Maria Gautier to Secretary Fish, July 9, 1869.

command of one Luperón or officers of his. This vessel has been interfering with American commerce and sailing upon the high seas without legal authority. You are directed to seize her and bring her in to the port of Baltimore . . . You will be particular to bring with the vessel the officers and crew and all papers found on board. Transfer a sufficient number of prisoners to your own vessel to prevent re-capture. . . .

"If you do not find the vessel alluded to in Samaná Bay, search for her along the coast until you find her. If she has fallen into the hands of the Dominican Government or into the hands of a United States or English cruiser you will touch at the several Dominican ports on your way to Key West, where you will proceed to report to Rear-Admiral H. K. Hoff for duty. . . ."

As the next step, in accordance with the urgent request of the agent of the Dominican President, General Grant immediately selected one of his private secretaries, General Orville E. Babcock, as his Commissioner in the Dominican Republic.

General Babcock was provided with full instructions by the Secretary of State:

"The President, deeming it advisable to employ a special agent to obtain information in regard to the Dominican treaty, has selected you for that purpose . . . You will endeavor to obtain full and accurate information in regard to the disposition of the Government and people of the Republic toward the United States, the character of the Government, whether it be military or civil, whether it be stable or liable to be overthrown, . . . You will also ascertain what the debt, foreign and domestic, of that Government may be, how long it may have to run, the rate of interest, and where it is held . . . Generally, any information tending to illustrate the condition and resources of that Republic and the character and influence of those charged with its destinies, will be acceptable." [1]

Sailing on the *Tybee,* whose owners, Spofford, Tileston & Company, had offered free passage to any Agent of the United States proceeding for the purpose of procuring the annexation of the country, General Babcock found himself accompanied by Colonel Fabens, another American adventurer, Mr. O'Sullivan, and Senator Cornelius Cole of California. He was welcomed with effusion upon his arrival by General Cazneau who, in the words of the American Commercial Agent, together with Fabens "never lost sight of him after his arrival." [2] General Babcock first proceeded to Azua, where Baez was engaged in military activities, and then returned to Santo Domingo where he was joined some ten days later by the President. During those ten days General Grant's Commissioner carefully abstained from obtaining any information from the Commercial Agent or from any other sources, limiting himself to absorbing the projects expounded to him by his mentors, General Cazneau and Colonel Fabens. To such an extent did he become subject to their influence that the plight of his fellow-citizen, Mr. Davis Hatch, who had been imprisoned and sentenced to death by General Baez upon the ground that he had offered hospitality to the revolutionary leaders when the *Telégrafo* put in to Barahona, but in reality because of the representations of Cazneau, whose enmity Hatch had incurred when he had prevented the confirmation of the latter's appoint-

[1] Secretary Fish to General Orville E. Babcock, Brevet Brigadier-General, July 13, 1869.
[2] Mr. Somers Smith to Secretary Fish, September 2, 1869.

ment as Minister Resident, left him indifferent, and he refrained from assisting the endeavours of the American Commercial Agent in securing the release of the imprisoned American. The unwillingness of General Babcock to agree to any move contrary to the desires of the partners, whose projects he found so attractive, went still further. The U.S.S. *Tuscarora*, which arrived during the course of General Babcock's visit to provide him, in accordance with the phrase of Secretary Robeson, with the "moral support of its guns," was requested by the American Commercial Agent to proceed to Azua to endeavour to prevent the continued detention or at least the summary execution of Hatch. General Babcock refused, however, to permit the vessel to proceed for this purpose, alleging as a ground for his refusal that he was convinced of Hatch's complicity in the revolution against Baez, and in particular that the Cabinet in Santo Domingo had assured him that Hatch had attempted to mislead public opinion in the United States by openly opposing the project of annexation.

When Baez finally returned to the capital he found the emissary of General Grant entirely responsive to his desires. After brief discussions, at which Cazneau and Fabens were invariably present, the former ostensibly as interpreter and the latter as the friend of the Dominican President, a memorandum or protocol was signed by Don Manuel Maria Gautier, the Minister for Foreign Affairs, and by General Babcock, to prevent, as the latter later alleged, any subsequent divergence of opinion as to the agreements reached by the representatives of the two Governments. The protocol contained the following unusual commitment on the part of an Agent of the President of the United States:

"Orville E. Babcock, aide-de-camp to His Excellency General Ulysses S. Grant, President of the United States of America, and his Special Agent to the Dominican Republic, contracted and agreed in the name and on behalf of the President that he should use all his influence with the members of Congress to popularize the idea of annexing the Dominican Republic to the United States and that he would withhold from them all official communication on the subject until certain of its approval by a majority."

The protocol further required the Government of the United States to remit forthwith to the Dominican Government the sum of $150,000, $100,000 to be in cash and $50,000 in armaments. On September 6th, General Babcock returned to the United States bearing with him this protocol, confident that his efforts would meet with the approbation of his chief.

In this he was not disappointed. Upon his return he ascertained that President Grant and his Secretary of State were disposed to press the annexation proposal to a speedy conclusion.

3.

As the first step in removing all persons from connection with the negotiations who might be suspected of holding unfavourable opinions regarding the project, the American Commercial Agent in Santo Domingo was recalled. He had been unwise enough to have reported to the Secretary of State that Cazneau and Fabens were "speculators who stopped at nothing to bring about their own selfish ends," referring to them as adventurers who were endeavouring to obtain the most valuable localities in the country, and to have remarked

"There has undoubtedly been a strong effort made here

to enlist the sympathies of our Government in favor of the Baez party and against the Cabral party, and if possible to entangle the United States in this revolutionary question. The better policy is not to interfere in the dissensions in this revolutionary country while the permanency of its government is so precarious. The prisons are filled with political offenders and several hundred of the most respectable men in this City are in exile." [1]

It was evident to Secretary Fish that an Agent more amenable would be a more useful tool in carrying out the policy determined upon by the President. His choice fell upon Major Raymond H. Perry, and the latter was, as Senator Carl Schurz later remarked, by one of those "absurd freaks of chance characteristic of our system of civil service, appointed Commercial Agent in Santo Domingo, which required just the opposite of the qualities he possessed," since the apex of Major Perry's ambitions had been his appointment as United States Marshal for the Western District of Texas. Major Perry had had a checkered career while in the army during the Civil War. As the result of one of the many "horse and mule cases," he had been tried by court-martial on charges of peculation and found guilty, and sentenced to be dishonourably discharged; but he had later been restored to active duty and at the close of the Civil War had received an honourable discharge. He had subsequently gone to Mexico where he had served in the ranks of the republicans against the Emperor Maximilian and later, under the orders of General Sheridan, had been on special duty in Louisiana and Texas.

In his instructions Major Perry was advised that General Babcock was to return to Santo Domingo to complete the final negotiation of the treaty of annexation, but that

[1] Mr. Somers Smith to Secretary Fish, September 2, 1869.

since, under the Constitution, General Babcock could not sign the treaty on behalf of the United States while he still retained his rank in the United States Army, Major Perry was to sign the treaty as the President's Agent, although he was in all instances "to govern his course by the advice of General Babcock." The new Commercial Agent arrived in Santo Domingo on September 10th. Four days before Perry's arrival, General Babcock's second set of official instructions had been handed him by the Secretary of State. They were as follows:

"The President having directed you to meet Mr. Raymond H. Perry in San Domingo and to advise with him unofficially as to the execution of the powers with which he is entrusted to conclude a treaty and a convention with the Dominican Republic, and he also having further directed you in case of the execution of such treaty and convention, then as an officer of the army of the United States to take steps to carry out the agreement of the United States contained in said treaty to protect the people of that Republic against foreign interference while the nation is expressing its will and also to protect the interest and rights which the United States may obtain under such convention, I now place in your hands herewith drafts of such a treaty and of such a convention as the United States are prepared to enter into with that Republic . . . You will accordingly receive herewith . . . a draft on New York for $100,000 and also a quantity of arms and ammuntion valued at $50,000, of which a schedule is annexed."

General Babcock was further advised that the Dominican Republic could not enter the Union as a State, since the third section of the fourth article of the Constitution provided that new states might solely be admitted into the

Union by act of Congress, and the Dominican Republic could therefore only be annexed as a territory. Moreover, the loan contract known as the Hartmont loan was to be duly and legally cancelled and the amount of $50,000, received as an advance upon that loan by the Dominican Government, was to be deducted from the sum of $150,000 stipulated by the draft treaty as the amount to be paid by the United States to the Dominican Republic before any convention or treaty was to be signed by the Dominican Government. In conclusion, he was notified:

"The Navy Department will receive orders from the President to place at your disposal in the harbor of San Domingo a force sufficient to enable the United States to comply with their agreement in the proposed treaty to protect the Dominican Republic until the will of its people can be ascertained, and also to receive possession of the territory and waters leased by the proposed convention to the United States. In case of the delivery to the Dominican Republic of the $150,000 and the execution of the proposed convention, the naval officer detailed for that purpose will proceed to Samaná Bay and take actual possession of the lands, coasts, islands, waters, and property leased in the name of the United States. The President enjoins that the fact and the object of your visit to San Domingo, as well as the provisions of the proposed instruments, are to be kept a secret as long as practicable." [1]

On November 18th, General Babcock appeared once more in Santo Domingo, on the U.S.S. *Albany* accompanied by General Ingalls and General Sackett. At the conferences which were at once undertaken with Don Manuel Maria Gautier, appointed as Commissioner by

[1] Secretary Fish to Orville E. Babcock, Brevet Brigadier-General, November 6, 1869.

President Baez by a decree which stated that the appointment was made as the result of the fact that

"Various individuals of importance and note, both of the provinces of the Cibao, as well as of the provinces of the south, interpreting the sentiments and aspirations of the people, have splendidly manifested their desires that the Dominican Republic join its destinies to those of the United States of America,"

Cazneau and Fabens were once more invariably present. For ten days the negotiations continued. At the latter conferences, Baez himself participated in the discussions. At the last moment a delay occurred, the American representatives being unable to ascertain the reasons for the President's unexpected reluctance to sign the instruments upon the provisions of which they were apparently in accord. The difficulty was, however, soon cleared up, since, seizing an opportunity presented by the momentary absence of General Babcock, President Baez made the following statement to General Sackett:

"I will tell you what we want. General Babcock was very kind to us last summer. He sent Captain Queen with the *Tuscarora* to seize the *Telégrafo* and ran her into a place where she was tied up by the English . . . After all of these things, showing great kindness on the part of General Babcock, we should like to make him a grant of land in Samaná." [1]

Since Article VI of the proposed treaty provided that no further grants or concessions should be authorized subsequent to its conclusion, Baez desired to tender this worthy

[1] Howard's "Hatch-San Domingo Report."

recompense before the opportunity for so doing should have passed. While the offer of the President, when it was communicated to him, was rejected with great determination by General Babcock, his scruples did not prevent him from continuing his intimate association with Cazneau and Fabens, who had already procured the great majority of the concessions and grants authorized by the Dominican Government, and who were in a better position to provide President Grant's Agent with satisfactory compensation for his efforts than was the President of the Dominican Republic himself.

On November 29th, the treaty [1] of annexation was signed, as well as the convention [1] providing for the lease of the Bay and Peninsula of Samaná, which President Grant had determined would be ratified by the United States Senate in the remote contingency, as he thought, that the treaty of annexation was rejected.

The difficulties regarding the Hartmont loan were fully disposed of, in General Babcock's opinion, by the following communication which he received from President Baez on December 3rd:

"According to the best information which I have been able to obtain relative to Mr. Hartmont's loan, I am convinced that this gentleman is not in a situation to deliver the balance of the loan at the stipulated time, which is the 31st of this month.

"If, contrary to the information aforesaid, Mr. Hartmont appear at the proper time with the money to fulfill his contract we shall receive it, refraining from making any use of it until instructions reach us from Washington with regard to the matter and until we know whether, in case of our refusing to receive it, the Government of the

[1] Appendix "A."

United States will take upon itself the consequences of such refusal.

"As the contract for the loan expires on the 31st next, it is very important that a final resolution of the Government of the United States reach us before the 15th of January."

Oblivious of the fact that those interested in the Hartmont loan were now to become the most avid supporters of the annexation project, since they realized that annexation would secure their speculation, while it was obvious that any Dominican Government succeeding that of Baez would be reluctant to abide by the usurious terms of the loan contract, General Babcock busied himself with thoroughgoing preparations to carry out the final steps in the annexation program. Proceeding immediately on the steamship *Albany* to Samaná, he there took possession of the Province in the name of the United States. The American flag was hoisted at Samaná and saluted by the local authorities. Colonel Fabens was selected by General Babcock to represent the United States in the town of Samaná, where he was entrusted with the custody of the United States flag, and with various monies and properties belonging to the American Government. The *Nantasket* was ordered to Jacmel, and its commander, Captain Bunce, was instructed to proceed first to Puerto Plata, to fire upon the town in the event of any revolutionary outbreak against the Baez Government, and to inform the Haitian authorities at Jacmel subsequently, that should they render any assistance to Cabral or any of the other leaders heading the revolution against the authority of Baez,

"any hostile steps taken against the Dominican Republic would be considered as an unfriendly act against the

United States Government, as the latter had guaranteed them protection against interference while certain negotiations were taking place."

So far, the plans of Cazneau and Fabens had worked smoothly, and on December 10th, Major Perry was able to inform Secretary Fish that President Baez was "in very good spirits and thus everything is working favorably."

With the parting injunction to Major Perry to use all of his endeavours on the side of annexation and "always to speak encouragingly of it in his communications to the State Department," General Babcock now returned to the United States to transmit to President Grant the treaty which he had been enabled to conclude. To General Cazneau and to Colonel Fabens the prospect could not have been more promising. In a communication to Secretary Fish, Colonel Fabens was moved to expatiate upon the idealistic aspect of the annexation to the United States. Relating his satisfaction at receiving the appointment from General Babcock as Agent of the United States Government in Samaná, he continued:

"The people, both native Dominicans and those of American descent, are well satisfied with the proposed change of sovereignty, and I believe that if a vote were to be taken today on the question of annexation, it would be decided in the affirmative without one dissenting voice. The accounts from the River Yuna, Santiago and Puerto Plata are all highly favorable to the proposed change.

"On the Sunday following the raising of the United States flag, I attended services at the American Wesleyan Chapel. The house was crowded with a well dressed, quiet, and devout congregation, who had come to return thanks to God for the anticipated blessings of a good government about to be conferred upon them . . . the chaplain, Reverend Jacob James, expounding in a clear and forcible manner the character of the great political change about to take place . . . The scene was very touching for the whole congregation of several hundred were responding with tears and sobs of grateful joy."

The sole fault, in fact, which Colonel Fabens could find in the situation to report to Secretary Fish was the fact that there was "no Sunday school among the native Dominican population in Samaná."

4.

Before President Grant had time to present the instruments signed by his Agent to the United States Senate for its ratification, events had occurred which afforded convincing proof to Baez that he must move with rapidity should he wish to maintain his own Government in power. Toward the beginning of December, the President of Haiti, Silvain Salnave, had been obliged by the increasing pressure of the revolutionary forces headed by General Nissage Saget to abandon Port-au-Prince, and hoping, apparently, to effect a juncture with the forces of the Dominican Government in the Province of Azua, had attempted to cross the territory along that portion of the frontier held by General Cabral and the other leaders of the "Blue" party, among them Generals Benito Ogando and Ulises Heureaux. Unfortunately for his projects, the Haitian troops were surrounded and defeated by the troops of Cabral near Neiba, and Salnave and his chief followers were taken prisoner by the Dominican revolutionists. Cabral at once turned over the captives he had taken to the representatives of his ally, Nissage Saget, whereupon

many of the Haitian officers who had accompanied Salnave were executed on the spot and Salnave, being taken
to Port-au-Prince, was summarily executed by General
Saget who, as a sign of his gratitude, even paid a considerable bounty to the Dominican officers responsible for the
capture of his adversary. The death of Salnave and the increased stability which his removal from the scene gave to
General Nissage Saget, who now proclaimed himself
President of Haiti, made it evident that Baez could look
no longer for assistance in Haiti against the increasing
activities of the Dominican revolutionaries in Haitian territory.

Baez therefore directed a cry for assistance to the
Government in Washington. In response to his request,
the American Government despatched immediately to
Dominican waters an additional number of warships, and
by the end of February, 1870, seven American vessels of
war were cruising in Dominican or Haitian waters, their
commanders, by order of the Secretary of the Navy,
directing their operations in accordance with the indication of the President of the Dominican Republic. Rear-
Admiral Poor, in command of the naval detachment,
arrived at Port-au-Prince on the U.S.S. *Severn* on February 10th, and directed by order of President Grant the
following communication to President Nissage Saget:

"Sir:
"The undersigned avails himself of the arrival at this
port of the *Severn,* flagship of the United States North
Atlantic Fleet, accompanied by the monitor *Dictator,*
to inform His Excellency that he, the undersigned, has
instructions from his Government to inform His Excellency that negotiations are now pending between the
United States Government at Washington and the Gov-

ernment at Santo Domingo and that during the existence
of such negotiations, the United States Government has
determined, with all its power, to prevent any interference
on the part of the Haitians, or any other Power, with the
Dominican Government.

"Any interference or attack, therefore, by vessels under
the Haitian or any other flag upon the Dominicans during
the pendency of such negotiations will be considered an act
of hostility to the flag of the United States and will provoke hostility in return."

As soon as Baez was reënforced by this unprecedented
support rendered by the United States Navy, which not
only succeeded in intimidating the Haitian Government
but also prevented the outbreak of any sporadic acts of
protest in the Dominican ports, he proceeded to carry out
the plebiscite to which he had in advance committed his
country. Proclaiming on February 16th that the plebiscite
was to be held on February 19th, he issued the following
decree:

"In view of the manifestations which the people of the
Dominican Republic have been making in different man-
ners concerning their firm resolution to unite their destinies
to the destinies of the great Republic of North America
and to form a part of that powerful union, it is high
time that the Government should take legal steps to assure
itself that the desired purpose is in truth the real expression
of the national will. Bearing in mind that the municipal
authorities are the legitimate representatives of the people
and are called upon to receive the expression of their will
when they, in these crucial moments, resolve through a
plebiscite to determine the important questions which
affect the future destinies of the Nation, and in accordance

with the advice of the Secretaries of State and with the consent of the honorable Senado Consultor, I decree

"From the publication of this proclamation, that the voting booths are to be open in all the provinces, communes and military posts of the Republic in order that the inhabitants may come one by one to cast their votes, expressing definitely their desire to be united to the great Republic of the United States of America and to form a part of its territory and political entity."

On the day the voting commenced, the *Boletín Oficial* published an appeal to the Dominican people indicative of the propaganda which Baez had spread widely throughout the country. The Government paper announced that the United States were in reality a collection of free and independent republics united by a common bond, each state possessing its own religion, language, habits and customs; entirely free to select its own judges, legislators, and municipal officials; and in fact, it was declared,

"it can be said that they govern themselves except when, in affairs in which all the states are interested, the National Congress may take action . . . Santo Domingo gains everything and loses nothing . . . Annexation means salvation because it will oblige Haiti to respect Dominican rights and to maintain a decent conduct and because it will persuade all Dominicans to renounce political disputes." [1]

But the persuasive methods of Baez were by no means limited to newspaper propaganda. Having obtained the despatch of American war vessels to all the important ports of the Republic during the time the voting was

[1] *Boletín Oficial,* Santo Domingo, February 19, 1870.

taking place, he made it known through his agents that any open opposition to the annexation project would meet with imprisonment or banishment or an even more stringent punishment. According to Major Perry, the announcement of the opening of the plebiscite in Santo Domingo was made known by bands of music sent through the streets. Thereupon

"a list was opened in the police headquarters for citizens to register their names. Baez and Delmonte have told me several times that if any man opposed annexation they would either shoot him or send him his passports. They have also told me that it should be a free vote of the people but such has not been the case. There was much feeling throughout the Island kept in check and the people were not permitted to express any opposition to annexation. I have seen Baez himself shake his fist in the face of some of his nearest friends, amongst whom were officers of the army, in Baez's own house, and tell them he would banish them from the Island if they opposed annexation. This conduct on the part of Baez made many who were in favor of annexation opposed to it and also to him. . . . The prisons are filled with political prisoners." [1]

As the result of these tactics it is not surprising that out of a total of some 16,000 votes cast, only eleven were announced as having been cast in opposition to the project, and these were recognized as having been cast at the President's instance by his agents in order to prevent the proceedings from appearing too farcical. On March 16th, the Senado Consultor adopted a resolution declaring that

"The people of the Dominican Republic have demonstrated their desire to be united to the United States of America,"

[1] Major Raymond H. Perry to Secretary Fish, June 7, 1870.

and consequently approved unanimously this determination, considering it "most proper and most efficacious in order that liberty and democracy might be preserved in the country."

On the following day, the Minister for Foreign Affairs, in a communication to Secretary Fish, expressed his belief that the American Government would be as gratified as he at the large percentage in favour of annexation, and assured him that

"The desire is great with which this country almost unanimously is burning to see the conclusion of its annexation to the United States." [1]

Although the constant presence of the American warships had rendered temporarily quiet the revolutionary activities of the leaders of the "Blue" party, a group of foreign merchants and residents of Puerto Plata, among them the British Vice Consul, had contributed the sum of $8,000 to assist Generals Cabral and Luperón in their campaign. When the American Admiral learned of this fact from President Baez, who magnified the report by the statement that General Luperón, "at the head of an army of Haitians was established in Capotillo and was about to invade the Cibao," his indignation knew no bounds. The U.S.S. *Swatara* was ordered to proceed at once to Monte Cristi "to render such aid as it can to the loyal citizens and frustrate, if possible, the aims of Luperón," and the *Nantasket,* at the same time, departed for Puerto Plata

"to inform the people of that place who entertain hostile feelings towards the United States of the determination

[1] Don Manuel Gautier to Secretary Fish, March 18, 1870.

of her Government to protect Santo Domingo and its present administration and to inform them of the naval force in these waters and its instructions to carry out the plans of the United States Government."

Baez and his accomplices, General Cazneau and Colonel Fabens, were enabled, moreover, to find equally firm support in quieting the unexpected hostility suddenly evidenced by the American Commercial Agent, who they had hitherto had every reason to suppose was completely submissive to the instructions which General Babcock had left with him to "write encouragingly to the Department, keeping back facts regarding the election and Cabral's party and the discontent of the people of the Island," and to "stand by Cazneau and Fabens since they represented large interests in the Island in which he participated." [1] Fabens and Cazneau were all the more grieved since Fabens had promised Major Perry that if he proved friendly to Cazneau and to himself "he would have a great opportunity for making a rapid fortune," and the latter had assured the Commercial Agent that he could provide him with "a fine plantation and opportunities to handle money for men in New York City."

The knowledge which gradually dawned upon the American Commercial Agent that the whole annexation project had been hatched by Cazneau and Fabens with the connivance of Baez solely to further their own interests and the interests of General Babcock and his associates, and later the interests represented in the Hartmont loan, for which Spofford, Tileston & Company had recently become the agents, had aroused Major Perry to a deep indignation at the proceedings.

[1] Major Raymond H. Perry to Secretary Fish, June 7, 1870.

At first he had kept his indignation to himself, although he had early broken off his personal relations with General Cazneau. Upon asking President Baez why General Cazneau had so much influence in the decisions which the President reached, Major Perry was answered that it was because General Cazneau was a personal friend of General Babcock, and in direct communication with the President of the United States, and that in the event the annexation project was successfully concluded Cazneau would become a very wealthy man and the first Governor of the Island. That, Baez stated, he knew was the intention of General Babcock. But Perry's distrust reached its culmination when word came to him in April, 1870, that Cazneau and an associate, an American named Schumaker, in open violation of the terms of the sixth article of the treaty signed on November 29th, had with the support of Gautier applied for two concessions from the Dominican Government, the former for a grant of 200,000 acres of land, ostensibly for colonization purposes, and the latter for a concession to build a railroad between Santo Domingo and Azua.

Requesting information regarding the accuracy of these reports, Major Perry was assured by both the President and the Minister for Foreign Relations that no such concessions had been requested, and that they would not be granted should they be requested. Since the American Commercial Agent had first received his information from two members of the Senate, before a secret session of which the concessions were pending, he thereupon addressed a further communication to the President of the Senate, Don Pedro García, asking what truth there might actually be in the matter. Realizing that public knowledge of these proceedings would ruin their chances of success, the President of the Senate was instructed by Baez to reply that the American Commercial Agent should limit himself to addressing his communications to the Ministry of Foreign Relations, and, indignant at the sudden obstacle which the attitude assumed by Major Perry had interposed in his plans for his own financial advantage, the President instructed Gautier to demand the recall by Secretary Fish of his Agent in Santo Domingo. As soon as word reached General Babcock of the interposition of the American Commercial Agent in a matter which, according to the latter, General Babcock and General Ingalls knew all about, since they "had in fact taken copies of the desired concessions with them to the United States," [1] Major Perry was ordered to return to the United States.

In a short interchange of letters which took place before Major Perry's departure from Santo Domingo with General Cazneau, the former stated that he was well aware of the business of Cazneau and Fabens thus far; and added:

"You may rest assured that inasmuch as it lies within my power I shall do all I can to prevent injury or intrigue against the interests of my Government and to defend the name of President Grant, which name I have every reason to fear has already been used by a financial ring for their selfish ends."

In his reply to this arraignment, General Cazneau brushed the matter aside with the statement that the insinuation that President Grant's name had been used by him or by any of his associates for private speculations was too ridiculous for serious notice. Adding that there was not "a candid gentleman in this community who would not treat such

[1] Major Raymond H. Perry to Secretary Fish, June 7, 1870.

a charge as the wild fancy of a distempered brain," he concluded with the statement that Mr. Perry's lack of due official reticence had brought on a "premature disclosure of facts that for the public interest should have been strictly confidential for the present."

Availing himself of the support rendered him by the fact that his partner had been appointed by Baez, in April, as Dominican Minister Plenipotentiary in Washington, General Cazneau reënforced the protestations which he had no doubt Colonel Fabens would make by a communication addressed to Secretary Fish, in which he alleged that his motives in the matter reported by Major Perry had been of the most patriotic character.[1] The whole project had been merely an effort to settle the troublesome border question by settling a line of immigrants from the United States along the Haitian frontier. For that purpose, he claimed he had surrendered to the Dominican Government "a valuable mining and colonization charter," and a new plan had been drawn up "to induce large capitalists having the necessary steamers and other appliances at their command to undertake the accomplishment of our project of border settlements." It was perfectly understood, he assured Secretary Fish,

"in the Baez Cabinet that the whole plan should be submitted to our Government and in no way acted upon if disapproved by President Grant."

Mr. Perry's interference,

"owing to his reckless and violent impulses . . . brought the affair before the public in a partial and dangerous light."

[1] General William L. Cazneau to Secretary Fish, May 17, 1870.

To the Secretary of State, Major Perry could necessarily be no longer a satisfactory Agent, inasmuch as he had by now earned the bitter antagonism of General Babcock, who had, not unnaturally, succeeded in prejudicing President Grant against him. Replying to Major Perry's complaint that he had not been treated by the Department of State with frankness, inasmuch as when he went to Santo Domingo "everything was involved in mystery," Major Perry was advised that his complaint was "an uncalled for and unwarranted charge, totally without foundation and improper to be introduced in an official despatch," and that his compliance with the instructions of General Babcock in not previously communicating the facts regarding the annexation plebiscite which he now reported, was "a subject for regret and a cause for censure," and that while his efforts to prevent the granting of the concessions requested by General Cazneau and his associates "were well intended and would have been approved by the President," his representations towards that end had been made neither in a correct nor tactful manner.[1] It was evident that Major Perry's usefulness was at an end, and he was permitted to tender his resignation some days later.

5.

Notwithstanding the hold upon Congress which General Grant's widespread personal popularity had given him when he assumed office, the project for the annexation of the Dominican Republic, which had by now become the cardinal feature of the Administration's foreign policy, had encountered stubborn resistance. In the President's first message upon the subject to Congress, he had expressed the belief that the Island (having in mind the annexation

[1] Secretary Fish to Major Raymond H. Perry, June 16, 1870.

both of the Dominican Republic and of Haiti) would yield to the United States all the sugar, coffee, and tobacco and other tropical products which the country could consume. The message glowed, in fact, with a series of platitudes worthy the pamphlet of a tourist agency. The President declared that

"The production of our supply of these articles will cut off more than $100,000 of our annual imports besides largely increasing our exports . . .

"With such a picture it is easy to see how our large debt abroad is ultimately to be extinguished. With the balance of trade against us (including interest on bonds held by foreigners and money spent by our citizens in foreign lands) equal to the entire yield of precious metals in this country, it is not easy to see how this result is to be otherwise accomplished . . . The acquisition of San Domingo will furnish our citizens with the necessaries of every-day life at cheaper rates than ever before; and it is in fine a rapid stride towards that guidance which the intelligence, industry, and enterprise of our citizens intended this country to assume among Nations."

Thoroughly as the Administration was committed to the proposed treaty, and notwithstanding the manner in which the President had identified his own political fortunes with its ratification, the great influence of Senator Charles Sumner, the Chairman of the Senate Committee on Foreign Relations, was thrown against it. During the early days of the Administration, Senator Sumner, who had been one of General Grant's strongest backers in his final break with Andrew Johnson, had continued to be one of the strongest supporters of the President, but the honest convictions which he had reached concerning the proposed measure made it impossible for him to continue to coöperate with the leaders of his own party. The result of his own investigations, and his peculiar knowledge of conditions in the Caribbean, had proved to his satisfaction that there existed no spontaneous desire for annexation on the part of the Dominican people themselves, and he had become assured that the stimulus behind the project, apart from Baez's own ambitions, had been the machinations of the ever-increasing group of speculators and promoters headed by Cazneau and Fabens, with whose past careers Senator Sumner was fully acquainted. An even stronger motive for the opposition of Senator Sumner was the implied threat in the policy of the Executive that the annexation of the Dominican Republic would necessarily entail the eventual annexation of Haiti. In the destinies of the negro Republic Senator Sumner was profoundly interested as the foremost remaining member of the New England Abolitionists, whose original and commendatory sympathy with the negroes during the long years of their oppression and slavery had evolved into the fanatical concept of the negro as a superior being fitted by nature to participate instantly in all the higher manifestations which centuries of modern civilization had produced. That the experiment involved in the sovereign Republic of Haiti could be considered unsuccessful or could be arrested by pressure from without was unthinkable; it was a contingency which Sumner would not countenance, and the prospect of the forcible annexation of Haiti was not only a proposition contrary to his own peculiar prejudices but one which likewise was revolting to the spirit of justice with which his character was instinct.

The opposition of the Chairman of the Committee on Foreign Relations should have been sufficient in itself to give the President pause. Execrated in the South, Sumner's prestige and personal popularity were equally widespread in the North.

"His written arguments were the anti-slavery classics of the day and they were read more eagerly than speeches which produced greater effect on the hearer . . His arguments went to the millions.
"They produced widespread and prodigious effect upon public opinion and left an indelible impression on the history of the country." [1]

The opposition of Sumner to the treaty, in which he was joined by many of the prominent Republicans in the Senate—among these Senator Carl Schurz, Senator Ferry, and Sumner's colleague, Senator Wilson of Massachusetts—proved to be sufficient to defeat the project by a wide margin. When the treaty came up for a vote the Administration, instead of obtaining the two-thirds vote required by the Constitution, was able to muster only twenty-eight votes, an equal number of votes being cast against it.

During the summer of 1870, the additional knowledge which came to him concerning the activities of the American promoters of the project strengthened Senator Sumner in his refusal to compromise. In this determination, communications which were repeatedly addressed to the United States Senate both by the leaders of the "Blue" party in Santo Domingo, and by prominent exiles from the Republic such as Mariano A. Cestero and José Gabriel García, had a considerable share. Before long the cry of corruption was raised. Schurz demanded that the thieves in President Grant's Administration should be driven out

[1] James G. Blaine, "Twenty Years of Congress."

of the public service, and imputed to the Administration of President Grant even greater corruption than that with which he had charged the Administration of President Johnson. Before the New Year, Senator Sumner's antagonism had reached such a point that he was publicly asserting that the President himself was financially interested in the proposed deal. In an interview given to the correspondent of the New York *World* in Chicago, Sumner declared that a friend of his who lived in Santo Domingo had told him that the coast of Samaná Bay was staked off into lots marked "Baez," "Cazneau," and "Babcock," and that some of the largest ones were marked "Grant." [1]

Resolved, nevertheless, to overcome the opposition which he had encountered in the Senate by all the great strength which his powers of patronage bestowed upon him, and infuriated by the doubts cast upon his personal integrity, General Grant rushed to the attack. On December 5, 1870, in his annual message to Congress the President declared:

"I now firmly believe that the moment it is known that the United States have entirely abandoned the project of accepting as a part of its own territory the Island of San Domingo, a free port will be negotiated for by European Nations in the Bay of Samaná and a large commercial city will spring up, to which we will be tributary without receiving corresponding benefits. Then will be seen the folly of rejecting so great a prize . . I believe the subject has only to be investigated to be proved."

And he concluded with the recommendation that

"By joint resolution of the two Houses of Congress the Executive be authorized to appoint a commission to

[1] New York *World*, November 22, 1870.

negotiate a treaty with the authorities of San Domingo for the annexation of that Island and that an appropriation be made to defray the expenses of such a commission."

So intense was the opposition that even the most outspoken of the adherents of the Administration feared to permit the measure proposed by the President to be discussed. At length Senator Morton of Indiana introduced a resolution empowering the President to appoint three Commissioners to make a visit of inquiry to Santo Domingo, the Commissioners to have no compensation, although their expenses were to be paid and a secretary who spoke the Spanish language was to be appointed. Even in this form, however, the resolution was hotly opposed. It was then that Senator Sumner delivered his most famous address upon the annexation scheme to the Senate:

"The resolution before the Senate commits Congress to a dance of blood. It is a new step in a measure of violence. Already several steps have been taken and Congress is now summoned to another. . . The object of the resolution, and I will demonstrate it, is to commit Congress to the policy of annexation . . It is a new step in a measure of violence which so far as it has been maintained has been upheld by violence ever since . . As senator, as patriot, I cannot see my country suffer in its good name without an earnest effort to save it. Baez . . is sustained in power by the Government of the United States that he may betray his country . . The Island of San Domingo, situated in tropical waters and occupied by another race . . never can become a permanent possession of the United States. You may seize it by force of arms or by diplomacy, where an able squadron does more than the Minister; the enforced jurisdiction cannot endure . . It is theirs by right of possession; by their sweat and blood mingling with the soil; by tropical position; by its burning sun and by unalterable lines of climate. Such is the ordinance of nature which I am not the first to recognize. San Domingo is the earliest of that independent group destined to occupy the Caribbean Sea toward which our duty is plain as the Ten Commandments. Kindness, benevolence, assistance, aid, help, protection, all that is implied in good neighborhood, this we must give freely, bountifully; but their independence is as precious to them as is ours to us and it is placed under the safeguard of natural laws which we cannot violate with impunity."

Notwithstanding this powerful arraignment and the determined opposition of the antagonists of the treaty, the resolution was finally adopted, although the House of Representatives refused to concur except with the proviso that "nothing in this resolution shall be held, understood or construed as committing Congress to the policy of annexing San Domingo."

That the Presidential Message immediately awakened alarm in Haiti was made evident by the protest of the Haitian Minister in Washington, M. Stephen Preston. Announcing to the Secretary of State that the message of the President had caused him very deep and painful surprise inasmuch as it appeared to him to contain a formal menace to the independence of Haiti, the Minister requested assurances which would enable him to calm the legitimate anxieties of his Government.[1] To his protest the Haitian Minister received, however, no further satisfaction than the frigid statement by the Secretary of State that the message of the President was strictly and exclusively

[1] M. Stephen Preston, Haitian Minister in Washington, to Secretary Fish, December 8, 1870.

a domestic document to which no foreign Power could take exception, and that consequently until the recommendations referred to had become law the Minister's interference in the matter must be regarded at least as premature.[1]

On January 16th, the three Commissioners appointed pursuant to the resolution by the President—all of them of recognized standing, Senator Benjamin F. Wade of Ohio, Andrew D. White, and Samuel G. Howe—arrived at Santo Domingo upon the U.S.S. *Tennessee*. The members of the Commission and their secretary traveled throughout the Republic obtaining such sparse information as they were enabled to gather from the inhabitants, spending altogether approximately two months in the country. As regarded by President Grant, their report more than sustained all that he had said

"in regard to the productiveness and healthfulness of the Republic of San Domingo, of the unanimity of the people for annexation to the United States and of their peaceful character."

In his message of April 5, 1871, transmitting the report of the Commission, the President stated to Congress that the mere rejection by the Senate of a treaty negotiated by the President only indicated a difference of opinion among different departments of the Government, without touching the character or honour or pride of either;

"but when such rejection takes place simultaneously with charges openly made of corruption on the part of the President, or of those employed by him, the case is dif-

[1] Secretary Fish to M. Stephen Preston, Haitian Minister in Washington, December 12, 1870.

ferent. Indeed, in such case the honor of the Nation demands investigation. This has been accomplished by the report of the commissioners herewith transmitted, which fully vindicates the purity of motive and action of those who represented the United States in the negotiations . . My task is finished and with it ends all personal solicitude upon the subject . . I gladly hand over the whole matter to the judgment of the American people. . . . My opinion remains unchanged; indeed, it is confirmed by the report that the interests of our country and of San Domingo alike invite the annexation of that Republic."

In accordance with the suggestion which the President himself had made, the report of the Commission was merely ordered to lie upon the table, and no further action was destined to be taken regarding the treaties which President Grant's emissary had concluded.

General Grant had undergone his first defeat in the Presidency, the bitterness of which was no doubt in part assuaged by his success in at length obtaining the removal of Senator Sumner from the Chairmanship of the Committee on Foreign Relations. Senator Sumner, submitting silently to the indignity inflicted upon him as the result of the voicing of his honest convictions, died soon after. General Babcock, having found his position as Private Secretary to the President so agreeable and so lucrative, retained it for some years longer, until in 1876 an investigation unfortunately undertaken by Benjamin Bristow, the incoming Secretary of the Treasury, disclosed his close connection with General McDonald, the Supervisor of Internal Revenue for St. Louis, convicted of complicity in the frauds perpetrated by the "whiskey ring" in that district. When the scandal become too great for even General Grant to withstand, General Babcock was dismissed as the Private Secretary to the President and promoted to be Superintendent of Public Buildings. Cazneau and Fabens soon thereafter removed themselves from the Dominican stage.

6.

Although the hopes of Baez had by no means yet been stifled by the turn which events had taken, the opposition of the American Congress, which had brought with it the withdrawal of most of the American war vessels from Dominican waters, had encouraged a recrudescence of revolutionary activity. With the early summer of 1871 the western provinces were overrun with Haitian troops openly assisting the scattered forces of the "Blue" party. According to the American Commercial Agent,

"the whole country between Bánica and Cachina was filled with Haitian troops." [1]

Approximately 4,000 of the Government troops were consequently stationed at Dajabón to check the expected advance of three regular regiments of the Haitian army. General Luperón, who had obtained authority from the Haitian Government to impress Haitians in order to form an army of invasion, was momentarily expected to head the expected assault.

Confronted with this emergency, the Dominican Government was placed in an extremely embarrassing position, since the liberal grants which Baez had promptly made from the funds provided by the payment of the first installment of the rental for Samaná under the rejected treaty with the United States, had left him with barely $3,000 in the treasury with which to keep his troops in

[1] Mr. Fisher Ames, American Commercial Agent, to Secretary Fish, June 3, 1871.

the field. Still deluding himself that the treaty of annexation would be ratified by the United States Senate, Baez had refused to accept the proposal of the Hartmont interests to continue payments upon their loan, and when the Department of State, owing to the refusal of the United States Senate to ratify either the treaty of annexation or the convention for the lease of Samaná, was unable to pay the second installment due, Baez found himself without money and without credit. Although Secretary Fish, officially, was still hopeful, as was President Grant, that the treaty of annexation, or the convention signed at the same time, might yet obtain the approbation of the United States Senate, he was unable to take further action beyond that of instructing the Commercial Agent in Santo Domingo to extend for a period of one year the life of the convention providing for the lease of Samaná, which had expired, by the terms of its fourth article, when the United States Senate had refrained from ratifying it within four months from the date of its signature.[1] This act, which was as far as Secretary Fish could go under the circumstances, was hardly sufficient to prove of much assistance to Baez in his difficulties, particularly since the protocol reviving the original convention contained a stipulation that the further obligation of the United States Government to pay the rental agreed upon must depend upon a Congressional appropriation.

On July 17th, brought to the realization that the activities of his former associates, General Cazneau and Colonel Fabens, would no longer be welcomed by the American Government in view of the disclosure of the nature of their participation in the annexation project, Baez addressed a letter directly to President Grant. Referring to the diffi-

[1] Secretary Fish to Mr. Fisher Ames, June 28, 1871.

culties of his Government occasioned by the open hostility of the Haitian forces, he stated:

"I should much regret it if to the warmth with which the propriety of annexation has been regarded in the United States there should now succeed a glacial indifference on the part of your people, since that would cause the general belief here that a solution contrary to the wishes of the inhabitants of this Republic would ensue. It would be sad, if after so many efforts and sacrifices, after so much time employed in the arrangements connected with that grand project, the vanity of one haughty, petulant man and the gratuitous calumnies of the detractors of Your Excellency should triumph at length by preventing Your Excellency from realizing a political program of peculiar utility and one of philanthropy in behalf of a sister people not unworthy of its sympathies." [1]

To this appeal Baez received no reply beyond a bare acknowledgment, and thereafter, lest the American Government might lose interest in the project, President Baez again wrote to President Grant advising him of the appointment of his Minister for Foreign Affairs, Don Manuel Maria Gautier, as Special Envoy to Washington in order that he might advise the Chief Executive of the United States of the "actual situation in the Republic and the stability of the present Dominican Government," and attempt to obtain an amendment to the protocol suggested by Secretary Fish for the extension of the life of the convention for the lease of Samaná.[2] In the opinion of Baez and his Minister, should some satisfactory amendment not be found, the Dominican Government might be forced to

[1] President Buenaventura Baez to President Grant, July 17, 1871.
[2] President Buenaventura Baez to President Grant, Aug. 22, 1871.

return the sum of $150,000 which it had received as an anticipated installment on the first year's rental of Samaná. As an added stimulus, therefore, Baez informed the American Commercial Agent that the Prussian Government proposed to acquire the Bay and Peninsula of Samaná with a view to the eventual annexation of the whole Republic.

The alarm which may have been occasioned the Secretary of State by this evidence of Prussian ambition could not have been long lived, since he was informed within two months that the Prussian proposals had been rejected by the Dominican Government.[1] Notwithstanding his gradual abandonment of hope of obtaining the official protection of the United States Government, Baez was still enabled to stay the increasing tide of the revolution for the time being by resorting to the issuance of additional paper money, since on May 4, 1872, in accordance with his recommendation the Dominican Senate had authorized him to issue $100,000 paper acceptable for the payment of one-fourth of customs duties.

The farce still went on. In his yearly message to the Senate on January 27, 1872, Baez advised that body that upon his recent trip to the Cibao he had been struck by the sincere and cordial reception which had awaited him. He evidenced deep regret that the administration of justice was in such a deplorable condition, adverted to the necessity of the creation of two additional judicial departments in order that the course of justice might be facilitated, and expressed his determination to decree the holding of elections for a Constitutional Convention to revise the Constitution of 1868.

This Constitutional Convention assembled in August, 1872, and revised the qualifications of the electorate, which

[1] Acting Commercial Agent to Secretary Fish, October 27, 1871.

were now fixed so that the voter must possess full civil and political rights, be a resident of the commune where he voted, and be either a land owner, an employee of the Government, an officer in the army or navy, have authority to pursue some profession or to engage in industry, or be the tenant for at least six years of agricultural holdings. Under the presidency of General Valentín Ramírez Baez, the President's half brother, the Convention concluded its labours on September 14, 1872, having first granted the President a term of six years' duration, with almost dictatorial powers, and having created the Vice Presidency, stipulating that elections for the President and the Vice President be held three years apart.

Having succeeded in stemming the disorder within the Republic, and having obtained, by virtue of the new Constitution, the selection as Vice President of a supporter in whom he felt implicit confidence in the person of General Manuel Altagracia Cáceres, Baez felt strong enough to turn his attention towards repairing the damage wrought his ambitions by the definite refusal of the United States to agree to the annexation of the Republic.

7.

On January 2, 1873, Baez addressed a message to the Senate advising it that the necessity for annexation to the United States or for the lease of Samaná Bay and Samaná Peninsula to that country had ceased, and assured the Senators that he regarded it as far more in keeping with the progress of civilization and the true ideals of the Dominican people to enter into an agreement with a private company for the lease of that territory. He therefore transmitted to the Senate a contract which his representative, Don Manuel Maria Gautier, had entered into

with an association composed of various New York
financiers incorporated as the "Samaná Bay Company of
Santo Domingo." Among the members of the Board of
Directors were many individuals of reputed standing and
financial integrity, whose consent to figure upon the Board
of Directors was doubtless accounted for by the terms of
the seventh article of the contract which provided that
the Company could obtain all the privileges, rights and
immunities granted Colonel Fabens in the concession accorded him July 3, 1868.

The proposed activities of the Company were broad and
far-reaching. In general, they were stated to be the furnishing of assistance to the Dominican Republic in order
that it might increase its commerce, establish direct shipping communication with foreign countries, build railroads and other public works and obtain desirable immigration. The Company was authorized to acquire property
of any nature in any part of the world, and by the terms
of Article IV of the contract acquired all the rights,
privileges and immunities granted the United States in the
proposed convention signed November 29th, 1869, as well
as absolute sovereignty over the Peninsula and adjacent
islands in Samaná Bay, the Company being specifically
authorized to appoint all authorities, executive, legislative,
or judicial in the territory. The Company was further permitted to establish a bank of issue, deposit and discount in
Samaná, to build and administer railroads, canals, tele-
graphs and highroads, to utilize free of charge for those
purposes any public lands as well as all timber on such
lands, and to expropriate any private lands in any portion
of the Republic by paying compensation to the owners
therefor after appraisal. Furthermore, for every mile of
railroad or canal and for every three miles of telegraph

line or of highroad constructed within five years by the Company, it was to receive from the Government without cost a square mile of the public lands adjacent thereto, and the Dominican Government obligated itself to accord no concessions in the future to any individual or company without permitting the Samaná Bay Company to determine whether it desired to obtain such privileges itself.

In return for the monopolistic privileges so acquired by the Company through a concession which was to continue for ninety-nine years, the Company was solely obligated to pay to the Dominican Government the sum of $150,000 yearly. By the terms of its incorporation, the Company commenced operations with an authorized capital of $800,000, having the right to issue bonds and stock, provided merely that the total value of the issues should not exceed $20,000,000 in stock and $10,000,000 in bonds. The affairs of the Company were to be entrusted to a Board of Directors who might be citizens either of the Dominican Republic or of any other nation, who were protected in the event of any disagreement between the Dominican Government and the Company by the stipulation that in any such case the disputes were to be referred to two arbitrators, one chosen by the Republic and the other by the Company, and in the contingency that the arbitrators so selected could not agree, the dispute was then to be settled by its submission to some "political personage" in Europe.

On the day following the receipt of the Presidential message, this unique contract was ratified by the Senado Consultor, and on January 4th, the Dominican people were called to a plebiscite to pass upon the contract, which the President in his decree of convocation lauded in the highest terms. By the use of the same coercive methods which had proved so satisfactory three years before, the concession was approved in the popular vote by a majority even greater than that cast in favour of the annexation project. On February 22, 1873, President Baez officially announced that the votes cast in the plebiscite had resulted 20,496 in favour of the contract and only 19 opposed thereto, and that consequently the contract was to be considered in effect as a law of the Dominican Republic.

Frustrated in his early ambitions to make of his country a French province, outmaneuvered by Santana in his later desire to make the Republic a colony of Spain, defeated in the opportunity which he believed within his grasp to annex the Republic as a territory to the United States, Baez had at length been successful in selling the sovereignty of his nation to a group of speculators. It is not impossible that the eminent directors of the Samaná Bay Company of Santo Domingo had learned a useful lesson from the history of those British chartered companies which had in devious ways so often increased the territorial limits of the British Empire.

CHAPTER VI

FROM BAEZ TO HEUREAUX

1.

THE year 1873 marked the recurrence in the Republic of that social and political phenomenon which has periodically made itself felt in Dominican history—a contagious feverish desire to obliterate the past, and to fashion a new era under new leaders and under new auspices. It has ever been a longing dissociated from the selfish aims of the instigators of the revolutions continuously fermenting. It has rather been the result, as it was in the present case, of the utter weariness and disgust of the petty leaders in each community, the formers of public opinion, with the havoc and devastation wrought their country by the rulers foisted upon them. This longing, noticeable at first on the part of a few groups in various parts of the country, gradually infiltrated itself throughout the great illiterate masses subservient to them.

The extremes to which the tyranny of Baez had at length gone, the utter disregard on the part of the "Great Citizen" for life and private property, had no small part now in hastening the eventual climax, but the manifestation even at this time was explicable mainly as a general revulsion of popular feeling against the past and all the tragedy of lost opportunity that the past implied, together with an overwhelming longing for something new, new men, new measures and new ideals; with which feeling there existed the certainty that life in no event could be more unendurable than it had been under the old régime.

This impulse, engendered, as always, in the Cibao, reached its culmination in the early autumn of the year. At first discussed secretly by small groups of prominent

citizens in the Cibao cities, the movement at length became vocal, and included among its chief supporters many
who were prominent as members of the "Red" party. By
the latter it was agreed that Baez must be discarded and
forever. No less radical, the leaders of the "Blue" party
participating in the project made known their willingness
to abandon their chieftains, Cabral, Pimentel and Luperón.
But once these cardinal principles were established, the
rival interests of the antagonistic parties came once more
into play, the prime movers among the "Reds" insisting
that one of their own group should be selected to captain
the struggle for "regeneration," while the leaders of the
"Blue" party remained equally insistent that some leader
identified with their own political interests be chosen for
the task. The former clamoured for General Cáceres, the
Vice President, and the latter resolutely opposed him.

While the dispute continued, at first underground and
later openly, Baez made strenuous efforts to suppress the
opposition which he saw was constantly increasing. Before
it was possible for the President to take effective action,
however, the opportunity was grasped by General Ignacio
Maria González, who had been appointed some time previously Governor of Puerto Plata by the President from
among the ranks of the supporters upon whom he most
relied.

On November 25, 1873, in Puerto Plata, before a great
public meeting called to protest against the tyranny of
Baez, composed of representatives of both parties, General
González proclaimed himself leader of the revolution.
Within a month the feeble resistance which was all that
Baez had been able to interpose was crushed, and on Jan-
uary 2, 1874, Baez resigned his office to the Congress as-
sembled in the capital, and fled from the country.

2.

The avowed purposes of the new government of González could not have been more laudable. Although González, referred to by Luperón as a "general of the dance and of the salon," was accused by his great detractor of being an inveterate schemer and a selfish intriguer, it seems far more probable that he undertook the leadership of the movement for regeneration in all sincerity, his spirit attuned to the eloquent words publicly addressed to him by Don Ulises Espaillat—

"One sole necessity has made itself felt—the belief, the conviction, the need of uniting in one body all parties, of bringing new men to the government . . Those who rejoiced in the anticipation of shedding the blood of the Cibao; those who had composed for their own satisfaction a poem of the anticipated lament of their victims and of the tears of their desolate families; those, finally, who deliriously were seeking blood and more blood were destined to fall without a struggle before the cry of 'Unity, Fraternity and Concord.' "

That González lacked personal ambition cannot be asserted if his subsequent career is kept in mind, but there is no evidence, beyond that attributable to the rancour of his disappointed rivals for the Presidency, to prove that he accepted the Provisional Presidency with other than a wholehearted desire to benefit his country and his people.

The members of the new Cabinet appointed by the Provisional President were men of recognized standing from the Cibao, among them Don Tomás Cocco, Don Ildefonso Mella, and General Pablo Lopez Villanueva, the latter of whom as Minister for War led the victorious troops of the revolution into the capital on January 3rd.

No sooner, however, had the Provisional Government established itself firmly throughout the Republic than the inevitable rivalries between the parties which had supported the revolution began to make themselves apparent. Since he had rapidly come to the conclusion that the popular reform movement of which he was now the recognized leader could only be successfully carried out under a constitutional government with himself as President, González sought to eliminate the sole opposing candidate who had any chance for success in the popular elections which the Provisional Government had decreed. Baez had fled into exile; Cabral, Pimentel and Luperón had been exiled by decree of the Provisional Government. There remained as his sole rival General Cáceres, behind whose candidacy the "Red" leaders had grouped themselves. By dint of tactics which were not altogether to his credit, González finally succeeded in ensuring his own election, after a Constitutional Convention had once more revised the national charter of liberties, and he was consequently inaugurated Constitutional President of the Republic on April 6, 1874.

In his inaugural address the new President reiterated the assurances offered the people when he had assumed the Provisional Presidency—

"To bring peace to the Republic and guarantees to her sons; to respect and to enforce the respect of the rights of all and the freedom obtained by the revolution in November; to ensure the power of the law and the free action of justice; to stimulate progress, industry, and commerce; to increase public instruction and to unite under the national flag all Dominicans."

The measures adopted by the González Government at first evidenced the sincerity of the President's protestations.

An amnesty was declared to all, and invitations were extended even to Generals Luperón, Cabral and Pimentel, who had at first been exiled, to return to the country. All political prisoners were released and liberty of the press and the right of free speech were guaranteed.

One of the first acts of the Government and one destined to increase its popularity, was the cancellation of the concession granted by Baez to the Samaná Bay Company of Santo Domingo on the valid ground that the Company had failed to make its annual payments upon the dates set by the terms of the concession, and had, in fact, expressed its inability to meet those payments by requesting a reduction of the payments due and an extension of the time limit set for paying such installments. For a few months the popularity of the Government continued, evidenced to the satisfaction of General González himself by the manifestations of popular approval which greeted him at first upon his frequent visits to the various cities of the Republic. The President's belief in his own popularity received a rude setback, however, when early in August General Cáceres with a few supporters, comprising largely a number of the disgruntled friends of Baez, attempted to commence a revolution in Santiago. The movement was rapidly crushed, to the satisfaction of the populace in general, but the threat made was sufficient to cause in General González a sudden revulsion of feeling. Fearing, apparently, that his Government had been too liberal, he determined to adopt dictatorial methods, completely overlooking the lesson taught by the disasters which had met his predecessors in office. Adopting the most stringent measures of repression, he formally requested the Congress to authorize a further revision of the Constitution and this time a revision intended to grant greater powers to the President, which, in his own words, should be "more adapted to local necessities."

Once the course of his Administration was set in this direction, González's failure was inevitable. To govern by force rather than through popular support necessarily required greater resources in the national treasury. The President announced his intention of seeking a loan of $3,000,000 in Europe. While the negotiations to this end were in progress, González sought to recoup the Government for the loss of the annual installments which the cancellation of the Samaná Bay contract concession had brought with it. This he accomplished in a peculiar manner.

One of the features of his program of administration and one, in fact, which he was destined throughout his public life to seek to carry out, was the formation of closer economic and social ties with the neighbouring Republic of Haiti. In his inaugural address he had urged the necessity of a treaty of peace and commerce with Haiti. In accordance with this recommendation a Commission was sent by the Dominican Government to Port-au-Prince to negotiate a treaty with the Government of President Domingue, which had recently succeeded that of Nissage Saget. On November 9, 1874, a Treaty of Peace, Amity, Commerce, Navigation and Extradition was signed. Articles I and III provided that solely the Dominican Republic and the Republic of Haiti possessed sovereignty over the Island, and that both parties obligated themselves jointly to maintain the integrity of their respective territories and not to cede, mortgage, or alienate the whole or any part of their lands. They likewise obligated themselves not to solicit nor to agree to the annexation or the foreign domination of any portion of their possessions. Both Governments likewise

GENERAL IGNACIO MARIA GONZALEZ

agreed to negotiate a concession for the construction of a railroad to link the capitals of the two Republics. In addition to these provisions and the articles customarily found in treaties of amity and commerce, there were included, however, the agreement that

"The High Contracting Parties formally bind themselves to establish, in the manner most in accord with equity and the common interests of the two peoples, the boundary lines which separate their actual possessions,"

and a stipulation for the establishment of free trade in return for the yearly payment to the Dominican Government by Haiti of $150,000 over a period of eight years. The loss in the Dominican Government's revenues was thereby recouped, but the proviso for free trade carried with it the economic ruin of the Dominican border Provinces, permitting at the same time the infiltration of great numbers of Haitian emigrants; whereas the phraseology of the provision concerning the boundary lines diminished in the future the opportunity for the Dominican Government to regain the territory on the frontier which it claimed lay within the boundaries of the Spanish colony of Santo Domingo, and which Haiti had occupied illegally, it alleged, subsequent to the Haitian evacuation in 1844.

It is worthy of remark that the conclusion of this treaty met with the formal felicitation of the British Government, which still maintained its original policy of fostering the identification of the interests of the neighbouring Republics. During the weeks preceding the signing of the treaty, the British Minister in Haiti, Mr. St. John, had been actively engaged in the Dominican capital in urging upon the members of the Dominican Government the negotiation of closer economic ties with the Haitian Republic. It was commonly reported that by instruction of his Government he was exerting his efforts in the interests of the Haitian Government with a view to the eventual formal consolidation of the two Republics.[1]

3

Although for a while subsequent to the adoption of the new Constitution upon which he had insisted in the spring of 1875, the new policies adopted by González appeared to meet with success, measures to which the Government had had recourse in the preceding autumn incurred clamorous disapproval. Because of the scarcity of its financial resources, the Government reached the determination in October, 1874, to suspend payments upon its obligations. This implied the discontinuance of the payments which were being made upon many of the revolutionary claims from the Cibao, notably the claim of General Luperón, who had returned to the Republic and who was pressing the Government for the payment to him of some $170,000 which he alleged represented the total of the debts he had incurred in the course of his revolutionary activities during the six years of the Government of Baez. Although Luperón insisted that the President had assured him that the payment of these claims met with his full approval, when the claims were finally presented to the Congress González made evident his opposition to their settlement. The financial policy of the Government met with open opposition, as was to be expected, throughout the Cibao, and prompted the consolidation of the opponents of the Government within the "Blue" party, and added increased strength to the opposition which existed among the Baecistas. The storm finally

[1] Mr. Paul Jones, American Consul, to Secretary Fish, September 11, 1874.

broke when González's Governor of Puerta Plata, General Francisco Ortea, evidenced an excess of zeal in ordering the arrest of General Luperón on the ground of the latter's open opposition to the Government. The leaders of the "Blue" party, even those who had been originally opposed to Luperón, rallied to his support. The "Red" leaders momentarily forgot their differences and joined the conspiracy, and General Gonzáles was left with only a few personal followers to confront the situation. A revolution was speedily proclaimed in Santiago by a political organization of widespread influence somewhat paradoxically known as the "League of Peace." Generals Benito Monción and Ulises Heureaux, together with Don Juan Isidro Jiménez, seized the town of Monte Cristi. General Luperón took possession of Puerto Plata. The revolution rapidly spread through all portions of the Republic.

Notwithstanding the fact that the Congress in the capital had, on February 21, 1876, declared unfounded the charges of corruption, tyranny and treason levelled by the "League of Peace" against the President, General González, realizing that he lacked the means wherewith to withstand the opposition to his Administration which had now become almost universal, determined to heed the advice tendered him by representatives of both the "Blue" and the "Red" factions, and resigned his office. He thereupon entrusted the Executive power to the members of his Cabinet until a new Government could be organized, and prior to his resignation proclaimed the holding of general elections in order that the people might once more be afforded the opportunity of selecting their Chief Magistrate.

On the day following the resignation of the President, General González's Minister for War, General Villanueva,

called upon his fellow-members of the Cabinet to take
measures to protect the city from invasion. This, however,
they declined to do until the Minister for War had surrounded the Palace, where the Cabinet was in session, with
armed soldiery. Alarm guns were fired and intense excitement prevailed in the capital.

"Soldiers and civilians were running through the streets
armed, parents and servants were engaged in gathering
to their houses the school children, and doors and windows of all buildings were hastily closed and securely
fastened, and in fifteen minutes not a solitary individual
was to be seen on the streets except here and there a
belated soldier." [1]

From February 24th until March 7th, General Villanueva
assumed entire control of affairs with the intention of preparing the way for the return of Baez. At length, on
March 7th, realizing that public opinion, and more especially the opinion of his colleagues in the Cabinet, was
overwhelmingly against him, and learning that troops were
marching on the city from east and west, Villanueva concluded to resign and fled from the capital to Haiti. Immediately thereafter the capital city was peacefully surrendered to the control of the leaders of the revolutionary
forces.

4.

The result of the elections of March, 1876, proved that
the general longing for a reform government had not
spent itself as the result of the ill success of the González
Administration. The choice of the populace, guided
thereto, it must be admitted, by the admonitions of

[1] Mr. Paul Jones to Secretary Fish, March 30, 1876.

Luperón, fell upon a man who had never been an active partisan in politics and who had no claim to military glory beyond his participation in the overthrow of Spanish domination. By an overwhelming majority, Don Ulises Francisco Espaillat was elected President and took office in the capital on May 29, 1876.

In many ways one of the greatest men whom his country has produced, Espaillat possessed preëminent qualifications for the Presidency. He had been born in 1823 in Santiago de los Caballeros, where his family, of pure Spanish origin, was long established. A student by nature, profoundly interested in scientific research and in natural history, he was still more attracted by the study of his fellow-men. Lacking fundamentally all love of profit or of power, it had required the appeal to his patriotism, which was the dominating force of his life, to rouse him to prominent participation in the revolt against Haiti, and to the holding of office in the revolutionary Government which overthrew the authority of Spain. Fearless where his sense of right was concerned, unwilling to remain silent when he was faced by the evidences of injustice or corruption, his public arraignment of the dictators and spoilsmen who succeeded themselves in power had brought him repeatedly persecution, exile and imprisonment.

When the call to office came, Espaillat had long since determined the course which spelled salvation for his country—the Republic, he believed, must remain utterly free from all foreign entanglements. In his earlier years a fervent admirer of the United States, the negotiations between Grant and Baez had destroyed his faith in the disinterestedness of American statesmanship. It was to him "the most bitter disillusion," he once wrote,[1]

[1] U. F. Espaillat to General Gregorio Luperón, January 10, 1876.

"—the hope that the small Latin-American peoples might have conceived of the logical protection of a great and powerful nation . . we were now sadly forced to the realization . . that we must in the future live under the shadow of fear and constant alarm by reason of the policy of conquest of the Great Republic. Can you understand how bitterly they have suffered who had thought to find in the United States their perfect ideal of political institutions? Can you appreciate how sad and at the same time how repugnant a spectacle it has been to those who have admired the achievements which have created the political life of that great people to see one of their Presidents negotiating a "deal" with the Government of a small Republic—following the example proffered by a European Monarch, and without even having, as had the latter, for excuse the force of selfish interest?"

In the realm of domestic policy Espaillat's convictions were equally clear-cut. In his own words, "that people which views the exercise of its own rights with indifference, is preparing itself to become enslaved"; and "our 'to-morrow' . . . never dawns, and it is always until to-morrow that we postpone our accomplishments." The prime necessities, and the chief aspirations, of the Dominican people, Espaillat felt confident, were absolute political freedom, an incorruptible and efficient judiciary, and universal education. He saw clearly furthermore that the political system which had prevailed in the Dominican Republic since the date of its independence from Haiti, inasmuch as it was a system of political parties based solely upon the personality of the party leaders, was fundamentally vicious. He was convinced, likewise, and made his convictions public, that no Dominican Government could be stable until the finances of the country had been placed upon a healthy basis—until the resources of the Government were real and not theoretical, and until the national budget could actually be balanced. His concept for the solution of the financial situation lay in economy and in the imposition of legitimate taxation, implying necessarily his determined opposition to the issuance of paper money and the negotiation either of foreign loans or of foreign concessions destined to stifle the natural growth of the national resources.

Espaillat came to office with the approval of all, and what was most important, with the devoted support of such leaders as General Luperón, who was in part responsible for overcoming Espaillat's reluctance to accept the Presidency. That Espaillat had no illusions regarding the inherent difficulties of his task was evident. He realized fully the fact that the popularity he commanded upon his installation would quickly vanish when the Government found itself obliged to impose measures affecting the pockets of its citizens, and that the support of many of the military leaders at first spontaneously tendered him, would rapidly be withdrawn when it was found that the Government had no special favours and no pecuniary privileges to offer them. While the practical side of his nature undoubtedly grasped the well-nigh insurmountable obstacles which confronted him, it was the visionary side of his character, confiding in the latent genius of the Dominican people for self-government, which rendered Espaillat willing to assume the Presidency. His proclamation to the people when he took office makes this plain:

"The time perhaps is not far distant," he said, "when the Dominican people, as exploited and outraged as it has been badly led and badly governed, will heed the voice of reason and render homage to justice."

Naming a Cabinet composed of the ablest men that could be selected in the country—Manuel de Jesús de Peña, Manuel de Jesús Galván, José Gabriel García, Mariano Antonio Cestero—as Secretaries of the Interior, Foreign Affairs, Justice, and Finance, respectively, and General Gregorio Luperón as Minister for War, the President undertook his arduous task.

But the country, lamentably enough, proved unfitted for the experiment which Espaillat proposed. The sole constructive measure which Espaillat had time to offer, the creation of local banks of issue under Government supervision, to stabilize the national credit, was misunderstood, misconstrued, and died abortive. The President had hardly been in office two months before the intrigues of General Baez, manipulating from his headquarters in Curaçao, and the propaganda of General González, who had established himself in Mayaguez, proved effective in creating the outbreak of revolutionary movements along the Haitian frontier. These early attempts at rebellion were crushed by General Eugenio Valerio and General Ulises Heureaux, but by midsummer the revolution had spread, and the Cibao eventually fell into the control of armed adherents of General González while the southern Provinces were dominated by the forces of the Baecistas. The energetic measures adopted by Espaillat's Minister for War, which had instilled new life and more especially new discipline into the Governmental armies, for a time controlled the situation. The President himself evidenced a sturdy determination to maintain the Constitution and his Government.

In letters written to his loyal friends one can read the gradually increasing sense of discouragement which beset Espaillat, and the feeling of bitter loneliness which came over him as one after the other of those who had at first supported him in his work of reform deserted his Administration. One of these letters, written to General Cabral late in the month of July, is worthy of quotation:

"You already know, doubtless, that what was in the beginning the insignificant foray of a small gang has today assumed the proportions of a formal insurrection which the legitimate authorities of the Cibao are struggling with all their power to suppress.

"That means that I, who made the immense sacrifice of accepting the Presidency because of the compelling argument that my acceptance of the office was absolutely essential if public order was to be preserved, have now to consent that the force of arms, civil war, be the means of maintaining me in power; power of which I never was enamored and which I am exercising with profound distaste.

"And if in offering my name, until now respected as that of a man of worth, lacking unworthy ambition, as that of an honored patriot—if in offering this name, which is the sole legacy which I desired to bequeath to my children, as a sacrifice upon the altar of the duty of a public man, I could have the assurance that I was doing it as a tribute to that portion of the Dominican people who still have some esteem for honor and the dictates of 'men of order,' I would make the sacrifice in all resignation; but when there is not a day that passes since I assumed the fatal presidency which does not bring with it a bitter disillusion from those from whom I least expected it; when I see that instead of comprehension of my situation and instead of loyal and vigorous assistance

I encounter only unjustifiable demands, unfounded discontent, indifference and aversion on the part of the men whom I truly esteem and upon whose loyal coöperation I most counted; when I find, in place of the assistance necessary to save the country and to obtain its welfare, that to these very men public misfortunes are a matter of indifference, and when I find that upon invoking their aid to put out the conflagration which is commencing they turn their backs upon me as if the conflagration were only going to destroy me, and as if my Administration were alone interested in restraining it, then, my dear General, a feeling of absolute hopelessness gains possession of my soul. What, after all, can I think or hope of such insanity, such madness?

"Two months ago the presence of these men in the north, once Gabino (Crespo) was defeated by General Heureaux, made triumph sure, and would have calmed all passions, implanting confidence in our friends and respect among our enemies. Today, it is necessary to ruin the Republic, calling upon the south to rise against these egotistical and factious rebels. What an aftermath of deplorable consequences can one foresee!

"I do not know what excuse they can offer to public opinion, to God, to their own conscience, those very men who not three months ago raised me to the Presidency; and I without giving them the least motive, without changing in the slightest degree either my program of administration or my principles, both of which were fully known beforehand; today it seems as if they took pleasure in discrediting me and in bringing about my downfall, as if they had solely wished to elevate me in order to obtain the satisfaction of casting me down.

"I have the right to count upon the men of worth, General, my friend, and the men of worth have not the right to turn their back upon my necessity. Let me know if you think that I am right and then act in accordance with your own convictions."

In the early Autumn the President made public a final appeal to the leaders of all parties to overlook their personal ambitions and to forget their party strife in order that the Government might have the support of all.

"Dominicans, of all parties," he besought them, "help me in reëstablishing order, and seek by supporting the law the road to the salvation of the country and the honor of our national fame. To this end you may resort to all legal methods, when, after peace is restored, elections are possible, and through the press or in public assembly you may determine upon the candidate whom you may desire to succeed me in the Presidency in accordance with the Constitution. But, otherwise, no usurper shall impose himself by violence, unless those who rejoice in soaking our sacred land with blood first pay for their dastardly enterprise as they deserve.

"Fellow Citizens! I call you all, not excepting the leaders of the Revolution nor my opponents, to my side to safeguard law and order, liberty and civilization. I appeal to your patriotism, which you have so often demonstrated under a thousand adverse circumstances, and I promise to be the first to contribute to the return of peace and of general well-being."

The situation, however, had gone far beyond the possibility of controlling it through an appeal to reason. On October 5th, a group of malcontents in the capital seized the seat of Government and proclaimed themselves a national Dictatorship, announcing their intention to maintain their posts until General González could return. Espaillat was thus forced to resign. On December 20th,

Espaillat issued a farewell message to his people, and returned to his home in the Cibao where he died soon after, profoundly disillusioned, a broken-hearted man.

5.

González's return to power lasted barely forty days.

"González and his gang were no more than the spider which ensnared Espaillat; Baez was the hawk. González and his followers were the rats which ran to devour the skeleton of the Republic; but behind them came Baez who was the cat." [1]

Immediately after his return to the capital, General González had sent his Minister for War, General Villanueva, to the Cibao, where the latter entered into a conspiracy with General Cáceres and other Baecista leaders, who declared themselves supporters of Baez rather than of González. Puerto Plata was captured by these chieftains; the revolutionary troops marched upon the capital, and González again fled from the country. Then, for the last time, Buenaventura Baez, the "Great Citizen" returned to power.

Installed as Dictator on December 27, 1876, Baez once more formed a Government in which there figured the familiar names of the same men who had so long been associated with him. In March of the following year he was declared elected President of the Republic by a National Convention, selected *ad hoc*, on the dubious constitutional ground that

"The heroic Dominican people, in the exercise of their inherent sovereignty, had unanimously proclaimed the

[1] Luperón, "Notas Autobiográficas," Vol. II, p. 354.

Great Citizen, Buenaventura Baez, President of the Republic."

Baez's inaugural address was, as ever, replete with assurances. Among other specious promises, the people were guaranteed exemption from imprisonment, exile or other punishment for political offenses; a free press; the right of free speech; assembly in public meetings; religious toleration; the inviolability of private correspondence. That the Dictator did not place entire reliance upon the "unanimous proclamation of the heroic Dominican people" was made apparent by a confidential message sent the American Secretary of State by his Agent in the Dominican capital:

"In private conversation General Baez says the only salvation for the country is annexation and is still hopeful of its accomplishment." [1]

As was to be anticipated, a general revolution broke out almost immediately. The first signs of revolt were manifested at Juana Méndez on the Haitian frontier, where General Benito Monción and Don Maximo Grullón commenced a guerrilla warfare. The revolution gained added impetus from the support given the Dominican "emigrados" by the President of Haiti, General Boisrond Canal, who had been persuaded of the mutual advantages which lay therein by General González who had taken refuge in Port-au-Prince. Appeals for assistance were at once directed by Baez to the American Government, upon the ground that the Haitian authorities were supporting the revolution because of their belief that the Great Citizen desired to sell his country to the United States, and that, since in that contingency Haiti would eventually

[1] Mr. Paul Jones to Secretary Fish, January 16, 1877.

likewise be absorbed, the Haitian Republic would not be safe so long as Baez remained in power.

As the result of repeated representations, made both through Baez's Agent in Washington, Don Joaquín Montolio, and through the American Commercial Agent in Santo Domingo, the Department of State at length instructed the American Minister in Port-au-Prince to make plain to the Haitian Government that, while there was no purpose on the part of the United States to revive the plan for the annexation of the Dominican Republic, it was hoped that the Haitian Government would restrain marauders from entering Dominican territory. Small importance was attached to these representations, and the assistance lent by the Haitian authorities to the increasing number of Dominican revolutionaries became more open and effective as the weeks passed.

Baez's next move was an attempt to convince Secretary Evarts, who in the Hayes Administration, had succeeded Hamilton Fish as Secretary of State, that the Government of the United States was indebted to the Dominican Government to the amount of some $300,000 for the occupation of the Bay and Peninsula of Samaná under the rejected treaty of 1869, the amount claimed being the sum of the payments due the 1st of January of each of the years 1870, 1871, and 1872, deducting the advance originally paid by General Babcock. The claim continued to be pressed not only throughout Baez's tenure of office but during the term of his successor as well, and was only dropped upon receipt of the final conclusive statement of Secretary Evarts that

"It is obvious that the convention pursuant to which a claim is made for money due from the United States to the Dominican Republic was never completed as its conditions required, and consequently no such claim has any valid or legal vindication." [1]

As soon as the revolt commenced, Baez at once had recourse to the acts of cruelty and repression which had distinguished his previous periods of authority. In May, the President caused the arrest of fifty of the leading inhabitants of the capital, and upon their discharge by the courts on the ground that no commission of crime could be proved against them, the President announced his intention of substituting more pliant individuals for the judges who had flouted his wishes. All guarantees granted by the Constitution were then formally suspended, and both nationals and foreigners were indiscriminately arrested and imprisoned without any cause being assigned or charges preferred. In November, over one hundred persons—among them the Peruvian Consul, an old man dying of consumption, as well as three citizens of the United States—were sent from Puerto Plata to be thrust into the already overcrowded prison in the capital. The army was increased by daily drafts upon the rural population. The popular reaction was depicted in a further despatch from the American Commercial Agent to the Secretary of State:

"All classes unite in attributing economic conditions to the bad management of Baez. If it were not for the fear which he inspires owing to his malignant character and the savage vengeance he inflicts upon his enemies he would not be suffered to remain in the country forty-eight hours . . I have never known such intense bitterness and hatred as is expressed against Baez." [2]

[1] Secretary Evarts to the Dominican Minister for Foreign Affairs, April 2, 1878.

[2] Mr. Paul Jones to Secretary Evarts, July 20, 1877.

Although temporarily the revolution died down for want of unity among its leaders, with the first month of the year 1878, it broke out again with renewed fury. Padre Meriño, at the time Vicar of the Province of Seybo, was instrumental in fomenting the rise of the inhabitants of that Province against the Dictator, and a great number of Seyban troops headed by General Cesareo Guillermo marched against the capital. Soon after, the Province of Azua, so long responsive to the behests of the Baez family, joined the movement. The Cibao was already under arms. During the first week of February the contending parties were attacking the Government armies on all sides of the capital, and on February 18th, the Governmental detachment in Pajarito, across the Ozama River from the city of Santo Domingo, was almost annihilated by the troops under Guillermo. Baez now reached the conclusion that he had not the wherewithal to hold out any longer. Delaying for a few days the final negotiation of his capitulation with the leaders of the insurgents, the Dictator collected all the customs revenues which he could force the local merchants to pay in advance, amounting to some $70,000, and then, on March 2nd, abdicated his authority and set sail once more for Puerto Rico. During this last period in the Presidency the Great Citizen was enabled,

"by withholding the salaries both from civil officials and the soldiers in the field, to accumulate a sum of more than $300,000, which was sent abroad for deposit." [1]

6.

On March 3rd, the revolutionists commanded by General Guillermo marched into the capital, where a Pro-

[1] Mr. Paul Jones to the Secretary of State, March 19, 1878.

visional Government headed by their chieftain was at once established. For a while an anomalous situation existed, since at the same time that the Provisional Government of General Guillermo was functioning in the capital and controlling the more important seaports of the Republic, a second Provisional Government of which General González had been proclaimed the chief was functioning in Santiago, and controlling the Cibao.

Had the desire of the people for peace not been so great—for the struggles of the preceding year had reduced the country to a condition of misery commensurate only with that which existed subsequent to the revolt against Spain—a new outbreak of civil war might have at once ensued. But the destitution of the populace and the counsels of such leaders as General Luperón contributed to a peaceful solution of the dispute, and it was determined to resort to the polls in determining the choice for the Presidency. A reconciliation was likewise effected between General González and General Luperón, resulting in a joint manifesto addressed by them to the people, urging the support of all classes and of all parties for the candidacy of the Chief of the Santiago Government. Consequently, in the general elections held in May of the same year General González was once more elected President.

Immediately after his inauguration, which occurred in the first days of the month of July, 1878, General González attempted to secure the continued support of General Luperón by offering him any post in the Government which he might desire. Upon Luperón's refusal to accept office, the President, apparently fearing an implied threat against his supremacy, refused to carry out the promises which he had made previous to his election to the redoubtable chief of the "Blue" party, among them the promise to appoint General Heureaux as Governor of Puerto Plata. Indignant at this disregard of his wishes, General Luperón at once resorted once more to revolution, and on August 3rd captured the fort in Puerto Plata and took possession of the city. A Provisional Government was once more constituted in Puerto Plata under the control of Luperón's adherents, among them Alfredo Deetjen and Generals Heureaux and Federico Lithgow. When he learned of the outbreak in Puerto Plata, President González despatched a small body of soldiers to that city on the American steamer *Tybee*. As soon as the insurgents were apprised of the presence of Governmental troops on board the vessel, which had anchored some three miles outside the harbour, they demanded the delivery of the soldiers on board, and the Government war vessel held by Luperón, re-enforced by eighty men fully armed, was sent to capture the *Tybee*, but the latter, steaming swiftly for Cape Haitian, arrived in safety before it was overhauled by the insurgent vessel.

Steps were then promptly taken by the Provisional Government to march upon the capital, but not swiftly enough to prevent the prior arrival there of General Guillermo, who himself had lost no time in proclaiming a revolution against González after his defeat in the elections.

By August 24th, Guillermo's forces had invested the capital both from the east bank of the Ozama River and from the western side of the city. On the following day, an engagement resulted, but as the President had only some 200 men to defend the city and no prospects of obtaining additional forces, he was forced on September 2nd to abdicate, and sailed for Curaçao. On September

3rd, General Guillermo entered the city, to quote the American Commercial Agent,

"at the head of some 600 of the most villainous looking ruffians it was ever my misfortune to behold." [1]

For the time being, the Chief Justice of the Supreme Court was permitted to hold office as Provisional President, General Guillermo assuring his own control of the situation by seizing the Portfolio of War in the Provisional Cabinet; and finally, as the result of further elections held on January 26th, 27th, and 28th, General Guillermo forced his own election as Constitutional President, and was inaugurated on February 27th, 1879.

General Luperón, who had not unwisely declared his determined refusal to accept election to the Presidency in view of the fact that General Guillermo had already secured possession of the capital, left the country and embarked for Europe. The only other rival momentarily feared by General Guillermo, General Manuel A. Cáceres, was removed from the scene through assassination. Seated one evening in the house of his friend, Don Juan de la Cruz Alfonseca, he was shot from the street through the open door.

For a while the country sank into the uneasy rest of exhaustion. The new President evidenced neither interest in the welfare of his country, nor desire for reform in the national Administration, nor did he manifest even that aptitude for dictatorial government shown by his more powerful predecessors in office. A mulatto from the Province of Seybo, he had served during many years the dictates of Baez, and had been, with his father, a leader in the extermination of all those who had remained faithful

[1] Mr. Paul Jones to Secretary of State, April 2, 1878.

to General Santana during the years of the latter's struggle against his chief rival. He had distinguished himself as a "ferocious and pitiless persecutor of all who were not adherents of Baez and had made himself feared as a man without scruples and without pity." [1] Utterly lacking in education, he possessed no ambitions beyond the lust for power and the desire to obtain as much profit as he might during the days that he remained in office. During the months of his Administration the country lay prostrate beneath the repeated atrocities of his subordinates and found itself, if possible, in a worse plight than that which had existed during the last months of the Dictatorship of Baez.

The movement for Guillermo's overthrow was instigated by Luperón, who returned from Europe in the autumn. Proclaiming a new revolution in Puerto Plata on October 6, 1879, Luperón constituted a Provisional Government and called to his support his chief adherents, appointing as members of the Provisional Cabinet Generals Heureaux and Lithgow, Alfredo Deetjen and the brothers Maximiliano and Eliseo Grullón. Protesting against the reëstablishment of a dictatorship, the Provisional Government openly accused Guillermo of responsibility for the murder of General Cáceres, of having converted the public treasury into the private property of his followers and of himself, and proclaimed that the revolution was led by

"the soldier of democracy, Gregorio Luperón, who never unsheathed his sword but to safeguard the independence of the Nation and to protect the liberties, the securities, and the rights of his fellow-citizens."

[1] Luperón, "Notas Autobiográficas," Vol. III, p. 23.

The contest against the Dictator commenced immediately thereafter. President Guillermo, who was at least not deficient in personal valour, went out in person at the head of his troops to meet the rebels. Establishing his headquarters on the southern side of the pass known as San Pedro, which commanded the highroad from the capital to Cotuy, he was there surprised by the revolutionary troops commanded by Heureaux and routed, being compelled to fall back in utter disorder upon Santo Domingo. One-third of the Dictator's troops reached the capital; the remainder deserted. After fortifying the capital, General Guillermo marched swiftly to the Seybo, which he supposed remained still loyal to him. There he succeeded in recruiting some 800 men, but being again taken by surprise was once more defeated, and, deserting his own soldiers, returned to Santo Domingo on November 10th with only ten men.[1] The capital was immediately surrounded by the revolutionary forces and all communications and means of supply were thus cut off. After the city had been reduced to the point of starvation, President Guillermo realized that his time had come, and, failing to obtain the assistance from the Spanish Captain-General of Puerto Rico for which he had secretly negotiated, he took refuge on December 6th upon a Spanish man-of-war which lay conveniently outside the harbour of Santo Domingo and fled to Puerto Rico.

The Government of the Republic was now vested in the hands of General Luperón, who insisted upon retaining the seat of his authority at Puerto Plata, delegating General Heureaux as his representative in the capital.

[1] Mr. Paul Jones to the Secretary of State, December 8, 1879.

7.

The first steps taken by the Provisional Government were indicative of Luperón's honest desire to pacify the country and to accomplish what he might, during the limited time the Provisional Government should remain in office, to bring order out of the chaos which the state of anarchy of the preceding years had produced. The Provisional President himself at once announced his determined refusal to accept the Constitutional Presidency of the Republic. A Constitutional Convention was summoned to meet in the capital to amend the Constitution, and the electorate was officially informed that general elections would be held as soon as the Constitution had once more been revised. In the meantime, General Luperón and his Ministers set themselves to the task of reforming the administrative machinery of the Government, in particular that of the Department of Finance.

A law of conscription was passed and the national army was completely reorganized; measures were adopted to improve local administration in the various provinces, both military and civil; and the national arsenals, depleted as the result of the successive revolutions, were replenished with modern arms and ammunition. The salaries of the employees of the Government, which had remained unpaid during the three previous Administrations, were promptly paid by the Provisional Government, although their total, amounting to some $200,000, was a severe strain upon the limited resources of the national treasury. Adjustments of the pending foreign claims were reached and concessions granted by the previous Administrations were canceled wherever it was shown that the terms of such concessions had not been strictly complied with. The Provisional President, who had inveighed against the treaty negotiated by General González in 1874 with the Haitian Government, made evident his continued disapproval of the agreement entered into by refusing to accept from President Salamon all installments offered on the amounts owed to the Dominican Republic by Haiti under the provisions of the treaty.

Finally, General Luperón rendered official tribute to an occurrence which had signalized the last Administration of Baez and which the latter had neither the inclination nor the opportunity to commemorate.

On September 10, 1877, during the course of repairs made near the High Altar of the Cathedral of Santo Domingo, the leaden coffin containing the bones of Christopher Columbus was discovered under the pavement of the Cathedral. It had been previously assumed that the coffin had been removed from Santo Domingo to Havana in 1796 by the Spanish authorities, but since the records and archives of the Cathedral had been destroyed some years before, it was evident that the ecclesiastical authorities at that time exercising authority over the Cathedral, entrusted to the Spanish officials, through error, the coffin containing the remains of Columbus's son, Don Diego Colón. As soon as the discovery of the true coffin was made the remains were exhumed and examined in the presence of the ecclesiastical authorities, the officials of the Government, and the Consuls of the foreign Powers, "amidst the booming of cannon and the music of the military band."[1] Subsequently, they were again enclosed in a wooden box covering the original leaden coffin, sealed with the official seals of the Consuls and other authorities, and entrusted to the custody of Padre Francisco X.

[1] Mr. Paul Jones to Secretary of State, September 29, 1877.

Billini in the Church of the Regina Angelorum. From that day, no further importance had been attributed to the discovery, and General Luperón, by a decree issued in Puerto Plata April 1, 1880, allotted $10,000 from the public treasury of the Dominican Government as the first portion of a fund destined towards the erection of a monument in Santo Domingo to the memory of the discoverer of the American continent, and by official communications addressed to the Governments of all the American Republics and to those of Spain and Italy requested further assistance towards the erection of the monument. While the Governments so addressed, with the exception of that of Spain, which still maintained that the remains transferred in the 18th century to Havana were the true remains of the Great Admiral, expressed their gratification at the discovery, no further action was taken for a long period. At length, the remains were once more removed to the Cathedral and there deposited under a monument, erected solely with funds raised in the Dominican Republic, which stands within the main entrance of the edifice.

During the months in which General Luperón was laying, with notable success, the foundations for stable government in the Republic, he was at the same time endeavouring to obtain a candidate, satisfactory to himself and responsive to the requirements of the nation, to succeed him as Constitutional President of the Republic. His first selection was Don Pedro Francisco Bonó of San Francisco de Macorís. Señor Bonó was a citizen of proved patriotism, of the highest personal integrity, generally esteemed by reason of the prominent part which he had taken in the Restoration. A planter and merchant, there had been no sacrifice too great for him to make towards the liberation of his country from the rule of Spain, and although he had never consented to take an active part in governmental affairs, he had ever assisted so far as he might as a private citizen in promoting the establishment of democratic government. He proved utterly unwilling, however, to accept the honours which the Provisional President desired to have conferred upon him, protesting his lack of personal ambition and his fear that he did not possess the necessary strength to undertake the arduous task which the assumption of the Presidency implied. Luperón then turned, for second choice, to Padre Meriño.

Fernando Arturo de Meriño had for many years been a distinguished figure in the life of the Republic. An outstanding patriot even before the cession of the Republic by Santana to Spain, he had gained widespread influence by his fearless opposition to the barter of his country's sovereignty, as the result of which he had been forced to flee the country. An orator of extraordinary eloquence, of imposing presence, a man of the greatest force of personal character, dominating, intolerant, he had become identified with that small group in the Republic who had persisted in their opposition to all infringements of the nation's liberties, and he had opposed with all the force at his command the tyranny of the series of Dictators who had despoiled the land to their own profit. A politician more than a priest, Padre Meriño had for many years enjoyed the intimate friendship of Luperón, and had not unnaturally become identified with the political aspirations of the leaders of the "Blue" party. Although at times divergence of opinion threatened to disrupt the close friendship which existed between these two arrogant men, Luperón's true estimate of the man whom he now selected as the one to replace him in office was later written down in his memoirs:

"It is men like Meriño who represent the moral force of this world. Inspired by noble sentiments and supported by their own courage, they are the center of all progressive social renascence." [1]

There is no better indication of the sincere desire of Luperón for his country's well-being, and no better proof of his ability to sink his own interests in his efforts for the Republic's salvation, than in this decision to refuse office himself when he could so easily have retained it, and in his selection of two such outstanding patriots as Pedro Francisco Bonó and Padre Meriño as fit elements to further the true welfare of the nation.

On May 29, 1880, General Luperón addressed a public manifesto to the Dominican people urging upon them the election as their President of Padre Meriño. Granted this immense support, Padre Meriño was elected without opposition, and was inaugurated President of the Republic on September 1, 1880. In view of the favour bestowed upon Padre Meriño by the Provisional President, two candidates who had at first presented themselves—General Heureaux and General Francisco Gregorio Billini—withdrew their candidacy prior to the election, and were rewarded by their appointment by the new President as Ministers of the Interior and of War, respectively, in the new Cabinet. The other Ministers whom the President selected were General Casimiro N. de Moya, Don Eliseo Grullón, and Don Rodolfo Roberto Boscowitz as Ministers of Foreign Affairs, Fomento and Hacienda. Clothed in his clerical robes, Padre Meriño took the oath of office

[1] Luperón, "Notas Autobiográficas," Vol. I.

and read his inaugural address, but if any malcontents believed that the clerical garments in which their new President was garbed covered any weakness, any pity for the evil-doer, or any reluctance to punish the insurgent, they were grievously mistaken. No more vigorous rule, no more decisive sway, had ever previously been exercised by any Dominican President.

8.

During the first year of the new Government there were two attempts at revolution. The first, headed by General Braulio Alvarez, who led an uprising near the capital, was mercilessly crushed by General Heureaux. The second, which threatened to become more serious— a landing of insurgent forces near Jovero in the east under the leadership of General Cesareo Guillermo, who had embarked his troops from Puerto Rico with the connivance and assistance of the Spanish authorities—was likewise speedily put down, and the ringleaders of the rebellion, with the exception of Guillermo, who succeeded in making his escape, were executed without pity. Prisoners, the wounded, even boys of fifteen, captured under arms, suffered the extreme penalty. During the remainder of President Meriño's term of office he had no valid cause to fear rebellion.

The peaceful months under the Provisional Government of General Luperón and the firm control exercised by President Meriño brought, as a natural result, an immediate return of material prosperity to the Republic. Imports rapidly showed a great increase, and it was during this period that the extensive planting of the sugar estates on the southern shores of the Republic, which now form a material portion of the country's natural wealth, was commenced. Immigrants from Cuba and from Puerto Rico entered the country in considerable numbers, and the activities of these settlers added renewed impetus to the development of the agricultural resources of the country.

Perturbed by the first attempt at revolution which had been perpetrated, and induced thereto by the rumour of the imminent insurrection of Guillermo, and likewise incensed by the antagonism of the Senate, which was insistent that his Administration render a public accounting of its disposition of the public monies, President Meriño, on May 30, 1881, issued a decree announcing his assumption of power temporarily as Dictator of the nation. On the same day, a proclamation was issued abolishing the right of asylum in foreign Consulates, as the result of which many suspected malcontents were arrested and incarcerated in the prisons of the capital. The energetic measures taken by the President were probably responsible for the failure of a conspiracy against him engineered by followers of the ex-Presidents, Baez and González, although the time lost by the conspirators in wrangling over the question of whether Baez or González should be entrusted with the Government, were the revolution to prove successful, was presumably of no small assistance to the chief executive.

The vigorous measures adopted by the President were openly supported by General Lithgow and other leaders of the "Blues," who organized a series of public meetings throughout the Republic in commendation of the steps taken. General Luperón himself, absent in Europe as diplomatic emissary of the Government, and engrossed, as he recounts in his memoirs with somewhat naïve satisfaction, in conferences with Lord Granville and Mr. Gladstone, with the Duque de Fernan Núñez, and with

FERNANDO ARTURO MERIÑO
President of the Dominican Republic 1880-1882
and later Archbishop of Santo Domingo

FROM BAEZ TO HEUREAUX

prominent statesmen in France, in an attempt to solve
the outstanding difficulties between his Government and
those of Great Britain, Spain and France, had no words
of censure to direct against the energy displayed by the
man whom he had been instrumental in placing in office.

At length the time came for the Government to pre-
pare for the national elections in which Padre Meriño's
successor in the Presidency was to be selected. On May
31, 1882, the President promulgated a decree convoking
the elections for the following July 1st, 2nd and 3rd. In
accordance with the custom then existing, the voting took
place in the various ayuntamientos, the votes cast each
day being counted by the members of the ayuntamiento
at five o'clock in the afternoon. In those localities where
no ayuntamiento existed, the Alcalde and two fellow-
citizens appointed by him computed the returns, and all
returns made were sent directly to the Congress, a copy
being sent to the Minister of the Interior, and a third
copy being retained in each ayuntamiento or alcaldía.
Inasmuch as the candidacies of General Ulises Heureaux
as President and of General Casimiro N. de Moya as Vice
President were supported both by President Meriño and
by General Luperón and his adherents, the Governmental
ticket was naturally elected by a great majority.

On September 1, 1882, the new President and Vice
President were inaugurated, and immediately thereafter
a Cabinet composed of personal partisans of the new
President, General Wenceslao Figuereo, General Segundo
Imbert, General Generoso Marchena, Don Alejandro Woss
y Gil and Don Juan Tomás Mejia, was appointed. Thus,
for the first time in the history of the Republic save one,
a President was regularly elected and installed in accordance with the Constitution.

CHAPTER VII

THE DICTATORSHIP OF ULISES HEUREAUX

1.

THE date, September 1, 1882, marks the commencement of an epoch of seventeen years during which the interests, the development and even the fate of the Dominican people as a sovereign and independent nation were obscured and merged in the destinies of one man, the negro Ulises Heureaux. The absorbing interest of the period lies not alone in the vicissitudes of the Republic which came to pass in consequence of the Dictatorship. It lies as well in the human drama evolved from the protracted struggle of one man to maintain himself in power by every means known to his ingenuity; in Heureaux's gradual consolidation of his authority; in his attempt to quench through terror the last sparks of the longing for liberty which lingered in the souls of those whom he oppressed, until his swift, violent death brought with it the end of the most pitiless tyranny known to the Republics of the American continent.

The intrinsic viciousness of Heureaux's rule, it must be clearly realized at the outset, lay not so much in the oppressive character of his Government, in his efforts to betray the sovereignty of his people for his own profit, nor in his gross corruption; not in his cold vindictiveness, nor in the blood-lust which ravaged the man; the history of democracy, and the democracy of the Western Hemisphere not excepted, bears spread upon its pages lives of those as evil as Heureaux. The significant threat to the fundamental health of the Dominican nation, the danger which increased with each month of Heureaux's domination, lay in his appeal, so frequently successful, through fear, through the hope of personal advancement, or through vulgar bribery, to the basest instincts of the natural leaders of public thought. The latent patriotism of the nation's manhood became corrupted; and what was infinitely more tragic, and of far graver import to the country's destiny, in the hearts of the future generation the ideals of valour, integrity, liberty and freedom, for which the founders of the Republic had sacrificed themselves, became adulterated and perverted.

The narration of the history of Heureaux's dictatorship constitutes the depiction of a period lacking all that which is most inspiring in western civilization, save for those brief and futile struggles of a few patriots to raise their land from its long-continued subjection. The sensation of the times can only be compared to the ominous portent of one of those black, hot, tropical nights in the Dictator's own country when the atmosphere is charged with the oppression of the approaching cyclone. The certainty exists that eventually the lightning will flash and the storm will break and the sun will rise again; but even after the dawn the horror lingers. So in the hearts of Heureaux's countrymen, after his assassination the horror of his times still persisted.

2.

The origin and antecedents of Ulises Heureaux are to some extent shrouded in obscurity. That he had no Dominican blood in his veins has always been well established, and that fact was responsible for the modification, during the Presidency of his predecessor, Padre Meriño, of the Constitution, which had previously provided that only those who were Dominicans both by birth and parentage could aspire to the Presidency. It is, however, likewise possible that he was born in the Island of St. Thomas, and not in Puerto Plata as he himself claimed. The date of his birth is also uncertain. It is generally accepted, however, that he was born on October 21, 1845, in the city of Puerto Plata, the illegitimate son of a Haitian, d'Assas Heureaux, by a negress of St. Thomas named Josefa Lebel. In his earliest years, in accordance with the common Dominican custom, a nickname was bestowed upon him by his mother—that of "Lilis"—and it was by that nickname of his early childhood that Heureaux was destined to be known so long as he lived.

Such education as Heureaux obtained in his childhood he gained at a school maintained by an Englishman, a Methodist missionary, pastor in the city of Puerto Plata. Apprenticed for a brief period in the store of a French merchant, the future Dictator soon freed himself from a restraint to which he felt himself in no wise suited, to undertake a career which promised more adventure. Fortunately for him, he early attracted the attention of General Gregorio Luperón, to whose fortunes he attached himself until the time arrived when he concluded that the patronage of that patriot and popular hero was no longer necessary to enable him to fulfill his own ambitions. At the age of eighteen he took part in the war of the Restoration with conspicuous valour, a quality which distinguished him among his fellows throughout his whole career. General Luperón, notwithstanding the utter ingratitude which Heureaux displayed in after life to the man who had made possible his own rise to power, later penned this tribute to him:

"Heureaux, with loyalty and decision, accompanied his chieftain in all of his campaigns, through all his exiles, through all difficulties and dangers, and never showed in any conflict the least discouragement. Devoted to his work, he displayed such ability that eventually he was the chief of the General Staff of his General and the officer in whom the latter placed most confidence when the most difficult tasks had to be carried out." [1]

Utterly fearless, he displayed throughout the revolutionary campaigns waged by General Luperón during the score of years subsequent to the Restoration such energy and enterprise, such marked intelligence in military affairs, such popularity among the Dominican troops, that his appointment by President Meriño as Minister, granted his relations with General Luperón, was a foregone conclusion.

The activity which Heureaux displayed as the Minister of Meriño might readily, however, have given pause to those who were about to elevate him to the Presidency, even though they lacked prophetic vision. It was Heureaux who executed the notorious decree which the President was induced to promulgate, dubbed by popular sarcasm the decree of San Fernando, which provided that all those seized under arms would suffer the penalty of death. It was by virtue of this decree, when the two rebellions of Meriño's first Presidential year broke out, that Heureaux perpetrated, without the President's knowledge, the first of the long series of legalized executions which were later to make his name execrated. Among the rebels captured under arms when the unsuccessful revolt of General Cesareo Guillermo in the Seybo was crushed, were his antagonist of long standing, General Juan Isidro Ortea, and his own brother-in-law, Luís Pecuña, against whom

[1] General Luperón, "Notas Autobiográficas," Vol. III.

Heureaux bore an especial grudge for some reason not then disclosed. It is related that Pecuña, confident that his life would be spared because of his close relationship to the leader of the Government forces, was called after his capture before Heureaux. His confidence rendered more secure by the apparent kindliness of his brother-in-law in ordering that he be brought food, and a change of clothes to replace the garments worn by the exposures of a long and arduous march, Pecuña was appalled when he was coolly informed by Heureaux that the orders had been given solely in order to make it possible for him to bear himself with more composure and thus not disgrace his family when he was brought before the firing squad. His protestations unavailing, he was then summarily despatched, immediately after the execution of Ortea.

Notwithstanding these and many other instances of the savage cruelty peculiar to the man, possibly because of the faith which they placed in his sponsors, Luperón and Meriño, Heureaux came to the Presidency with the enthusiastic acclaim of his fellow-citizens. Rendered quiescent by the tranquillity and the increasing prosperity which the preceding governments of Luperón and Meriño had bestowed upon them, they little knew what the assumption of the Presidency by Ulises Heureaux held in store.

At the time Heureaux became President he had long since emerged from the chrysalis of his barefoot days in Puerto Plata, and from the transition state of his arduous wanderings with Luperón. The time was far past when his need was such that he had had his own arm shattered, and had murdered one of his companions, in a struggle to retain possession of a blanket with which to cover himself. He had by now become the resplendent figure of his later period. In the prime of life—for he was then some thirty-seven years of age—he was already affecting extreme elegance in his dress and personal appurtenances. Inordinately vain of his personal appearance, he was ever mindful of the completely negroid aspect of his face, which he attempted to mitigate so far as Nature made it possible by resorting to the most elaborate uniforms, to the most immaculate clothes. Tall, with splendid carriage, his body was beautifully proportioned, being that admirable welding, often found in the African race, of a suave, almost feline, surface under which there rippled the muscles and sinews of an immensely powerful resilient frame. His physique was untiring and untirable, and his nerves ever under the most perfect control, due in part, no doubt, to his life-long abstinence from both alcohol and tobacco. His sole weaknesses, if so they can be termed, were those of the savage—his domination by his sexual passions, which never were satiated, and his lust for blood. Courageous in the highest degree, confident of his own powers, astute with native shrewdness, possessed of the innate suspicion of the savage, polished with the veneer of civilization which he had acquired, rapacious, merciless, pitiless, filled with unquenchable dæmonic energy, such was the figure which was now for so long to dominate the scene.

3.

The first Presidential term of Heureaux may be termed almost uneventful. The Dictator, convinced of the truth of the old adage, "Il faut reculer pour mieux sauter," played his part with consummate guile. There was liberty of speech and liberty of the press. Deferent to the advice of the prominent leaders of his party, he was conciliatory to all. The two years of this first term passed like a pleasant dream. The Administration, in a financial sense, was far more fortunate than its predecessors, since the revenues of the nation continued to increase, and the President, as the result doubtless of his immediate efforts to conciliate the Government of Haiti by entering into flattering but futile negotiations for the conclusion of a new treaty with the neighbouring Republic, was the recipient of a secret donation from the Haitian President, General Salamon, of the sum of $50,000 with which to pave the way for his own return to power. Claims of Dominicans against their own Government were rapidly paid off, and if upon the termination of his Administration it was found that notwithstanding that the annual expenditures of the Government had amounted only to some $800,000, and the yearly income had exceeded $3,000,000, there still remained a total deficit of some $300,000, surely the fault could not be attributed to the President nor to his Secretary of Hacienda, General Generoso Marchena, proclaimed loudly by Heureaux to be the greatest economist of the whole Republic. But few probably possessed the pessimism, or perhaps the good sense, of Luperón when he wrote regarding Heureaux's Minister:

"There exists in the Dominican Republic the mistaken theory that any man who can figure must be an economist, and it is for that reason that almost always, through some fatality, Governments appoint a Minister of Hacienda who has failed in his own business and who fails consequently to a greater degree in the business of the State." [1]

Only one brief outbreak marred the peaceful course of events. On November 16, 1883, a revolution was pro-

[1] General Luperón, "Notas Autobiográficas," Vol. III.

claimed in the town of Moca by General Cartagena. Marching immediately at the head of his troops to the scene of the rebellion, the President by vigorous measures promptly suppressed it and thereafter continued his march through the Cibao to Puerto Plata, where a magnificent reception rewarded his triumph.

In the spring of 1884, the time arrived when Heureaux found it necessary under the Constitution to make plans for the selection of his successor. Although his own prestige and his authority had been greatly enhanced during his term of office, and his personal popularity was great, he did not yet feel himself sufficiently secure to risk the grave dangers which would undoubtedly have arisen had he attempted so early to undertake a revision of the Constitution in order to permit his own retention of office. Had such an attempt been made at the time, Heureaux was sure that the immense influence of General Luperón and of the other outstanding figures in the "Blue" party would most certainly have been exerted against him. There existed still unity and cohesion among these leaders. The fruition of his own ambitions, he realized, must depend upon the breaking up of the leadership of the party which had placed him in power. What more satisfactory and facile method could there be than his utilization of the thirst for power among these leaders in order to destroy the force in the country which that party represented?

His first open step towards that end, after months of secret intrigue, was taken on March 24, 1884, when he summoned to his private house the members of his Cabinet; the Governors of the Provinces; the ex-President, Padre Meriño; General Francisco Gregorio Billini, one of the outstanding aspirants for the Presidency; the more prominent military and civil officials of his Administration; and the editors of the Dominican newspapers of most importance. With consummate shrewdness, Heureaux proposed—and did not omit to cause the publication of his proposal—that in the coming elections for the Presidency his party support but one candidate in order that a diversity of candidates, bound to create personal enmities fatal to the country, might be avoided, and further volunteered the assurance, that were his proposal unfortunately not to be accepted, his Government would in any event maintain the strictest neutrality. The conference resulted in no decision, as Heureaux had well foreseen, as the prospective candidates—with the exception of Padre Meriño, who resolutely refused under any conditions to return to the Presidency—having each secretly been advised by the President of the favour with which he looked upon their aspirations, were unwilling to abandon their ambitions. The scheme so far had worked admirably.

It now became necessary to undermine the influence of General Luperón who, although he had announced his own unwillingness to assume office, had already declared his intention to support Don Pedro Francisco Bonó as his first choice for the Presidency. Upon the repeated refusal of the latter to accept office under any conditions, the field narrowed down to the following prominent leaders: the Vice President, Don Casimiro N. de Moya; General Billini and General Segundo Imbert. The first, the representative of a family which had long held the Province of La Vega as a satrapy, was a leader of marked ability supported not only by his feudal province but likewise by many of the more prominent leaders of the Cibao; the second had been advanced by Padre Meriño as a man of recognized integrity, whose administration of governmental affairs would prove a valid guarantee to all; the third, General Imbert, a valiant military leader of the Restoration, was vociferously acclaimed by General Benito Monción, the cacique of Monte Cristi, and finally secured the support of General Luperón upon the refusal of his earlier candidate, Don Francisco Bonó, to accept the distinction which Luperón desired to bestow upon him.

The increasing rivalries between the candidates, and the exacerbation of the tempers of their supporters as the campaign progressed, created exactly the situation for which Heureaux had plotted. Traveling to Puerto Plata upon the ostensible pretext of obtaining the advice of Luperón, Heureaux called a meeting of all the prominent leaders of the party to assemble on May 14th. As the result of the deliberations of this assembly the famous "Capitulations" of Puerto Plata were agreed upon both by the President and General Luperón, and by the three candidates for the Presidency. The agreements so signed could not have proved more satisfactory to Heureaux. They provided that the three candidates might continue without restriction their respective campaigns; the candidates announced, personally or through their representatives, that they would jointly support the candidate elected and would employ their utmost efforts to secure the support of their respective followers for the President-elect; the successful victor in the elections was obligated to appoint to his Administration individuals who had supported the opposing candidates, and the President agreed to guarantee the impartiality of the Government authorities during the elections, and, jointly with General Luperón, to see that the "Capitulations" should be carried out.

As soon as Heureaux ascertained that Luperón was

definitely committed to the candidacy of General Imbert, he announced, with apparent reluctance, his own support of the candidacy of Meriño's favourite, General Billini. Subsequently, General de Moya withdrew his candidacy for the Presidency and consented to run for Vice President upon the ticket with General Imbert. General Alejandro Woss y Gil was thereupon selected by the sponsors of General Billini as the Vice Presidential candidate upon the latter's ticket.

The issue was now squarely launched. Luperón's prestige as leader of his party was at stake. Notwithstanding this first move in opposing the desires of his former chief, Heureaux felt that the time had not yet come when he could afford an open break. Hence the following letter to Luperón written during the course of the elections:

"My dear General:

"By Tuesday's mail I wrote to you under the impulse of the impression that your letter of June 25th caused me.

"Today I write you again to communicate to you my sincere desire for peace. If Imbert triumphs in the elections I will support Imbert, who will be served by me; if Billini triumphs and you consider that the victory of this General might become a pretext for disorder, advise me immediately and he will resign the same day that he is proclaimed elected by the Congress. Give me beforehand your orders regarding the candidacy which should be presented and the manner in which you wish me to have it done. I await your instructions . .

"Here everything is quiet. The election returns are beginning to come in but we do not yet know even approximately the result of the elections in the Cibao.

"Your affectionate son,

"U. HEUREAUX." [1]

[1] President Heureaux to General Gregorio Luperón, July 3, 1884.

GENERAL ULISES HEUREAUX

It is unnecessary to add that the chieftain at Puerto Plata was not greatly mollified by this communication, since he had already received the information that Heureaux, through his agents, had stuffed the ballot boxes in many of the districts where the election was close. Even so, in the capital, where every measure was resorted to in order to defeat the Imbert ticket, Billini received a sparse majority of 400 votes. In the final returns the Billini ticket was announced as obtaining 35,000 votes, while the Imbert ticket was declared defeated with a total of only 33,000 votes. The fact that, because of the delay in communications, the supposed triumph of General Imbert was being celebrated in Puerto Plata, Santiago and Monte Cristi, where he had outdistanced his rival at the polls, at the same moment that Billini's victory was proclaimed in the capital, did little to quiet the passions aroused during the electoral period.

4.

Upon the inauguration of General Billini as President on September 1, 1884, the unity of leadership in the "Blue " party which had persisted without serious impairment during a period of twenty years had been shattered. It now remained for Heureaux to obtain the confidence of the leaders of the various factions into which his party had been split, and then to cause the disappearance from the scene of General Billini, who, he soon found, was not as tractable as he had supposed. Upon becoming convinced that General Billini would not prove subservient to his desires, and assisted in his enterprise by the absence from the Republic of General Luperón, Heureaux seized upon the decree of amnesty promulgated by the President soon after he assumed office to stir up dissatisfaction with the existing régime. Under guise that the amnesty which had permitted the return to the Republic of General Cesareo Guillermo was a measure aimed against General Luperón and his political friends, a vicious campaign was waged under cover against the President. The success of this propaganda was almost immediately reflected in the attitude of Congress, which promptly refused to coöperate with the Executive, and rendered sterile a considerable part of the commendable initiative which General Billini displayed, particularly in his efforts to improve the condition of the agricultural classes and in attracting emigration to the Republic from Spain. Within six months the President was forced to the realization that he had to make his choice between suppressing the insurrection which had by now become inevitable, and resigning his high office. Primarily a man of peace he selected the latter alternative, and on May 16, 1885, presented his formal resignation to the Congress which immediately accepted it. He was immediately succeeded in office, in accordance with the Constitution, by the Vice-President, General Woss y Gil, who appointed a new Cabinet composed of the partisans of Heureaux and of the adherents of General Luperón.

One more obstacle had thus been removed from Heureaux's path. The continued presence in the country of General Cesareo Guillermo next claimed his attention. Upon his instigation a detachment was sent by the Government on the night of June 28th, to seize the ex-President in the hotel where he then was lodging in the capital. Guillermo, who was seated in the patio of the hotel when the soldiers entered, instead of surrendering when ordered to do so, dashed the lamp under which he had been sitting to the ground, and made his escape, shooting at the officials who had been sent to arrest him. An innocent bystander, an American named Platt, was shot and instantly killed, a casualty for which the Government was later forced to pay an indemnity to his heirs of some $33,000. Making his way to Azua, Guillermo lay in hiding for some months, and in the first days of the following October, challenged the Government by proclaiming a revolution which obtained the support of many Azuans who had small cause to support the Administration.

Thereupon Heureaux displayed his accustomed energy. Taking command from the President as Commander-in-Chief of the Government troops, he at once chartered the American steamship *Santo Domingo,* of the Clyde Line, and arrived at the head of 400 men at the port of Azua on the night of October 11th. At the same time, General Marchena was sent to Baní, and General Espaillat to San Cristóbal, at the head of considerable reënforcements. Upon finding that the road from the port to the town of Azua, which lies some half mile distant from the coast, was blocked by revolutionary forces, Heureaux made a strategic move and landed the troops under his command on the following morning at Boca Villa. The fighting commenced immediately upon the beach where the Government forces landed, the revolutionists soon being surrounded by Heureaux's troops. The former were rapidly routed; Heureaux was enabled to take possession of the town of Azua itself without firing a shot, and proceeded thereafter to arrest those who he surmised were the ringleaders of the movement. At first Guillermo was believed to have escaped into Haitian territory, but on November 8th, it was learned by officials of the Government who had remained in Azua that he was in hiding not far from Orégano where he had attempted to procure

food and water at a countryman's hut. Surrounded by
twenty men of the Government forces and ordered to
surrender, the fugitive committed suicide. When Guillermo died he was stark naked, his clothing torn from
his body by the cactus jungle through which he had
been forced to flee; his feet were bandaged with the
sleeves of his shirt, and his body was lacerated terribly
by thorns. Disinterred from the rude grave into which
it had at first been thrown, his decomposed corpse was
later brought to the town of Azua in order that Heureaux
might assure himself of its identity and rest certain that
he had no more to fear from this opponent. Again an
obstacle had been removed.

Confident now that he himself might once more safely
return to power, he awaited the Presidential elections
which were scheduled to take place in the first days of
July, 1886. To Luperón, who had once more returned to
Puerto Plata, there could be only one solution were he to
regain the authority which had so rudely been shaken in
the previous elections—the "Blue" party must present but
one ticket to the public. Won over, apparently, by the
specious professions of loyalty on the part of Heureaux,
to which Heureaux's extermination of their common
enemy, Guillermo, had inclined him, Luperón resolved to
support the candidacy of Heureaux and to urge the candidates of the previous election, who had once more come
to the fore, to eliminate themselves in Heureaux's favour.
This General Imbert proceeded to do, and was consequently rewarded with the place of Vice President on
Heureaux's ticket; but General de Moya, to whom the
Vice Presidency had first been offered, stubbornly refused
to accede to the repeated urgings of his leader. His opposition to Heureaux had now become intense, and gaining

the support of General Billini, he persisted in his own candidacy for the Presidency, with General Billini as his Vice Presidential candidate. The Cibao was in a ferment, and excitement throughout the Republic was intense.

Notwithstanding, the elections passed off quietly, resulting, as his opponents should have anticipated from past experience, in the election of General Heureaux by a majority of more than 20,000 votes. In the capital the faction of de Moya was so far in the minority that on the first day of the elections, after polling only 500 votes, the leaders of the party protested, and abandoned the contest. Fearing a resort to violence, President Woss y Gil immediately after the elections traveled to La Vega to attempt to induce General de Moya to give in to the inevitable, and to return to the capital with him to offer his support to the President-elect. Failing in his mission, the President left La Vega on the 20th of the month, and immediately thereafter the revolution was proclaimed by the adherents of the defeated candidate. The revolutionists at first met with success, but after repeated struggles they were driven back from Santiago, which they had at first seized, and took refuge in La Vega, awaiting the results of the campaign commenced by General Monción, who, after he had announced his support of the revolution in Monte Cristi, had established himself securely in Guayubín. At the end of August, General Heureaux, once more appointed Commander-in-Chief of the Government forces, succeeded in capturing La Vega, whence General de Moya and General Villanueva, his principal associate, succeeded in escaping to the Haitian frontier.

Since the Congress, because of the revolution, had been unable to assemble in special session to go through the official form of counting the votes cast and proclaiming the validity of the elections, September 1st, the date upon which the new President should have been installed, passed, and no proclamation of the new Administration could constitutionally be made. The Government of General Woss y Gil consequently, in disregard of the Constitution, announced its own continuance in power until an opportunity might be afforded the Congress to proclaim officially the election of Heureaux. By the middle of November, the last signs of revolution in the frontier Provinces had been obliterated with the defeat of General Monción. On November 22nd, General Heureaux made his way back to the capital by way of Samaná, and refusing to receive a public ovation which was tendered him, repaired to the Cathedral to prostrate himself in gratitude for his victory, and subsequently retired quietly to his home to receive there the homage of a group of his supporters.

On November 25th, the Congress met to proclaim the President and Vice President elect legitimately elected, and on January 6, 1887, General Heureaux once more was inaugurated, this time to hold office for the remainder of his life.

The appointments to Heureaux's new Cabinet were indicative of the new policy upon which he had determined. Henceforward racial lines and party lines were to mean nothing to him. His supporters were to be chosen from all ranks. Thus, Don Manuel Maria Gautier, a man of pure Spanish descent, for decades identified with the interests of General Baez and willing, notwithstanding his conspicuous ability, to serve the dictates of any tyrant, was appointed Minister for Foreign Affairs, and General Miguel A. Pichardo, one of Heureaux's most determined adversaries in the recent revolution, agreed to accept the post of Minister for War. The other portfolios were granted to men representing all factions and all classes. The Dictator, when questioned as to the reasons for his unexpected selections, delivered himself of this sententious platitude:

"Patriotism and love of country demand that in civil war there be no victor and no vanquished; all are brethren of one good family who should be willing at all times to grasp each other's hands across the bloody chasm of war in order to bring lasting peace and tranquillity to the Nation." [1]

This estimable sentiment provided but a scant screen for the campaign which Heureaux now consistently carried on throughout the period of his tenure of office. Overtures were made to all the important leaders in the "Blue" party; to the chieftains of the remnants of the "Red" party which still existed after the death of Buenaventura Baez, which had occurred some five years before; and to those constituting the small group which had remained faithful to the fortunes of General González. Were the lure of public office not to prove sufficient, bribery was resorted to. So successfully had this latter policy been carried out during the de Moya revolution that the saying became general: "Although Lilis could not have put down de Moya's revolution with lead, he was signally successful in quelling it with gold." Were neither appointment to office nor corruption to prove successful, decrees of exile were promulgated, or did the opportunity present itself, assassination was resorted to. It was not only with the outstanding figures in the country that Heureaux occupied

[1] Mr. H. H. C. Astwood, American Consul, to the Secretary of State, January 12, 1887.

himself, however; as soon as the Dictator learned that any member of the younger generation showed exceptional talent or gave promise of becoming a man of prominence, an agent of the President invariably approached him to attempt to secure his support for the Dictator. Those few who refused to become sycophants and who resisted, soon were taught the bitter lesson of long imprisonment or continued persecution. The policy of the Dictator proved on the whole effective; one by one the men of prominence and ability either accepted the inducements offered or were swiftly removed from the local scene.

5.

There remained to Heureaux two essential requirements still to be satisfied. The first of these—the assurance of his own continuation in office—was relatively simple. Through his agents, and by appealing to the weaknesses of popular opinion, Heureaux commenced the creation of an artificial demand for a revision of the Constitution in order that the Presidential term might be extended from one of two years' tenure to a term of four years. Submissive apparently to this demand on the part of the public, and in reality to the orders given by the President, a Constitutional Convention, in November, 1889, promulgated a new Constitution which fixed the commencement of the next Presidential term as from February 27, 1889, and lengthened the term in accordance with the Dictator's desires. In the same Constitution, the system of direct election which had previously existed was replaced by that of the election of the President by an electoral college, bound in the future to facilitate the indefinite reëlection of Heureaux to the Presidency.

The second requisite was the removal of all elements of

danger to his Administration from those foreign Powers chiefly concerned with the Dominican Republic. After a few years in office, domestic politics had lost their flavour when all danger of open opposition had been safely removed. But the great game of international relations never lost its fascination for Heureaux. It was, moreover, a game in which he showed conspicuous ability. There is, in fact, no more interesting chapter in the modern history of the Americas than the chapter which contains the account of the manner in which the Dictator of a small country, with but small resources and of but potential importance, played off, one against the other, the United States of America and the great European Powers.

In his first Administration Heureaux early gained the enthusiastic support of the American Consul in the Dominican capital, a negro named Astwood appointed by President Hayes. Although Astwood was subsequently dismissed by President Cleveland on the double ground of his having purloined funds entrusted to the Consulate and of his having initiated the "indecent proposal" by which he and his partner would have toured the United States with the bones of Columbus as a side-show in circuses and expositions, Heureaux was no less successful in obtaining the friendship of Astwood's more reputable successors. At first his overtures to the American Government were somewhat hesitant. They consisted of assurances that although General Luperón favoured the lease of Samaná Bay to a French syndicate to be utilized in the event that the Panama scheme of Ferdinand de Lesseps were to prove a success, he himself was determined to thwart the scheme, and would lease the territory once more to the defunct Samaná Bay Company of San Domingo should the American Government so desire, and of vague requests that he be assisted in obtaining a loan in the United States.[1] He soon went further. In October, 1883, the Dominican Government officially requested the American Department of State to consent to a revision of the Commercial Treaty of 1867 between the two countries by negotiating a reciprocity convention which would permit free entry into the United States of the principal articles of export from the Dominican Republic, in return for the free entry of four or five classes of American products into the Dominican Republic. These negotiations were undertaken in the early summer of 1884 through the Agent of the Dominican Government in Washington, Don Manuel de Jesús Galván. On June 16th, the latter officially communicated to Secretary Frelinghuysen the draft of the reciprocity convention proposed by the Dominican Government. In his reply, the Secretary of State assured the Dominican envoy of his willingness to enter into the negotiations proposed, which evidenced in his opinion

"The promptings of good-will as well as a convincing sense on the part of the Government of the Dominican Republic of its true relationship with this country."[2]

The Secretary referred to the fact that the draft proposed followed substantially the lines of the convention concluded between the United States and Mexico, and although he accepted in principle the establishment of reciprocal commercial privileges he expressed himself as yet unprepared to determine upon the detailed list.

The close supervision exercised by Heureaux over the progress of negotiations was evidenced by a letter addressed

[1] Mr. H. H. C. Astwood, American Consul, to the Secretary of State, February 26, 1883, and March 8, 1883.

[2] Secretary Frelinghuysen to Señor Manuel de Jesús Galván, July 9, 1884.

by him to the President of the United States two days
before the expiration of his first term of office:

"Only a few days remain before the term is concluded
during which I have held power as Constitutional President of this Republic, and before leaving office I have
deemed it to be a high duty on my part to send Your
Excellency the expression of my gratitude and appreciation for the favorable welcome which the Minister
Plenipotentiary of this Republic, Citizen Manuel de Jesús
Galván, has received, as well as for the kindness with
which his negotiations for a limited reciprocity treaty
between the United States and the Dominican Republic
have met." [1]

Assuring President Arthur that the negotiations initiated
by his Government were supported by the great majority
of the Dominican people, as a means of increasing their
commerce and of drawing closer their relations with the
United States, Heureaux urged him to receive his letter as
an additional proof of his earnest desire that the negotiations be brought to a successful conclusion during President
Arthur's Administration. The negotiations continued in
Washington in accordance with the hope expressed by
Heureaux, and were eventually brought to fruition in the
conclusion of a reciprocity convention between the two
countries during the last weeks of President Arthur's Administration. The treaty was not destined to become effective, however, since it was withdrawn from the Senate by
President Cleveland soon after he assumed office.

It was not only in direct negotiations with the American Government, however, that Heureaux manifested his
desire to secure the good-will of the United States. Ameri-

[1] President Ulises Heureaux to President Chester Arthur, August 29, 1884.

can enterprise of all descriptions was sought. Concessions to American citizens were granted for the building of railroads, for the establishment of a national bank, and for the construction of public utilities. Unfortunately both for the Dominican Government and for the credit of the United States, the concessionnaires were, in the words of the American Consulate, mainly

"adventurers who are dissipated, dishonest, and immoral, who come to have a good time generally, spending freely in the gambling dens and drinking saloons the hard earned cash of some capitalist, and who return to the United States bankrupt with some exaggerated statement detrimental to the interest of both countries to cover up their own debauchery." [1]

But notwithstanding the discouragement which Heureaux must have encountered when the concessions so liberally granted so rarely materialized into banks, railroads, or public utilities, he continued to be, so far as the American Consul at the time was concerned,

"a great friend of Americans and American enterprise and holds out every inducement to American capitalists and is desirous of infusing the progressive spirit of our institutions into those of this Republic." [2]

Appeals both to the American capitalist and to the American colonist were frequently resorted to through the American press. The response to such propaganda was generally, however, of the character of which the following communication, addressed to the American Consul, is a typical example:

[1] Mr. Astwood, American Consul, to the Secretary of State, June 10, 1886.
[2] Mr. Astwood, American Consul, to the Secretary of State, June 10, 1886.

"Honored Sir:

"I see from the New York *Sun* an invitation from His Excellency General Heureaux, President of the Dominican Republic, to the colored people of the United States to settle in San Domingo. I have written by this mail to His Excellency for some information respecting the invitation. I wish to say here, if the Dominican Government will employ an agent for the purpose of engaging intending immigrants, the immigration scheme from this section would be made a grand success. There are fully 5,000 well-to-do farmers in this section who would willingly emigrate to San Domingo if they knew the true condition of the country. I have suggested to the President that an agent should be employed . . I am selling a life-sized picture of Toussant L'Ouverture, which sells at sight here. Do you think it would sell well in San Domingo? I also have the noted silver plater. Do you think I could do much in the Island with it . .

"(Sgd) . . .

San Marcos, Texas.

"P. S.—The Separate Coach Bill has passed and I am anxious to get out of Texas." [1]

6.

The liberal manner in which Heureaux had early accustomed himself to expend the resources of the national treasury soon brought his second Administration to dire straits, although the crisis had been keenly felt during the intervening Administrations of General Billini and General Woss y Gil. The national revenues were barely sufficient to meet current expenses, and consequently revolutionary claims, readily admitted, were disregarded, and salaries long overdue remained unpaid. The Government's sole

[1] Mr. Durham, American Consul, to the Secretary of State, June 23, 1891.

recourse lay in obtaining loans from local merchants, or
domestic "credit companies," in return for which it was
obligated to pay interest of frequently 10% monthly. At
the time that his overtures to the American Government
for assistance were first made, Heureaux was even then
endeavouring, without success, to obtain a loan in Europe
in order to pay off the growing mountain of the nation's
floating indebtedness. The imposition of extra duties; the
increasing of import duties by 10%; the levying of duties
on materials for the use of sugar plantations already operating, while still exempting machinery and materials
required for the construction of new sugar centrals; all
were resorted to, without creating any material improvement in the situation.

During the Administration of General Woss y Gil,
Heureaux had persuaded the President to formulate a
more concrete request for the assistance of the United
States Government than had previously been made. It was
determined, therefore, to resort once more to the time-
worn inducement of the lease of Samaná. Calling the
American Consul to a conference with President Woss y
Gil and with his Secretary of Hacienda, Don Roberto
Boscowitz, General Heureaux outlined the proposition
which the Administration would be willing to make.[1]
The Consul was requested to advise his Government officially that the Dominican Government would be willing
to lease, under conditions of absolute temporary sovereignty, for a term of years to the United States, the Bay
of Samaná with all its keys, in return for a loan not to
exceed $4,000,000, at a rate of interest to be subsequently
determined by the two Governments. But the same project which had elicited so enthusiastic a welcome from

[1] Mr. Astwood, American Consul, to the Secretary of State, January 21, 1886.

previous Administrations in the United States, met with no response from President Cleveland. Negotiations, likewise, between Heureaux, when he had once more returned to the Presidency in 1887, and representatives of certain financial interests in New York, finally came to nothing, although the Dominican Government agreed to issue $3,000,000 of bonds, and to grant American capitalists the power to undertake the direct collection of 30% of all of the national revenues to cover interest and amortization charges, in return for the advance of $1,350,000 gold.

At length General Generoso Marchena was sent to Europe as the President's Agent to secure the financial assistance without which, Heureaux appreciated, his Administration could not endure. The prime impediment in Marchena's efforts to obtain aid lay in the opposition offered by the holders of the outstanding bonds of the old Hartmont loan. Although the Dominican Government had never received more than the initial installment of this loan—the sum of approximately $150,000, promptly squandered by Baez in 1869—and the Dominican Senate had canceled the loan contract in 1870, bonds totaling £750,000 had been issued and sold in London by the Hartmont syndicate. In 1872 the loan had gone into default. It was now maintained by the bondholders, supported by the British Government, and by the British interests in the Dominican Republic, notably those represented by Sir Alexander Baird, constructor of the Samaná-Santiago Railway, that no further lien might legitimately be placed upon the nation's revenues, until the claims of these bondholders had been satisfied.

After repeated efforts, Marchena finally met with response from Westendorp and Company, of Amsterdam, and secured a contract. By the terms of this contract the

Dominican Government was to authorize the creation of £770,000 thirty-year 6% gold bonds. Of this amount, £142,860 was to be employed in the conversion of the outstanding bonds of the Hartmont loan at the rate of one to five, £151,660 was to be expended in the payment of the interior floating indebtedness, while the remainder was to be bought by Westendorp and Company at 78% of the bonds' nominal value.

The sole method by which the Dominican Government was enabled to obtain this contract was by indicating its willingness to secure the loan by making its interest and amortization charges a first lien upon the customs revenues. It was moreover compelled to go much farther, by agreeing to authorize the issuing firm to collect directly through its agents all the national customs duties, to retain such amounts as might be necessary to meet the loan charges, and thereafter to turn the remainder over to the Government. These agents appointed by Westendorp and Company, organized into a board known as the "Caja de Recaudación," or "régie," were to commence their duties upon the 1st of November, 1888.

The constitution of the "régie," implied that although Dominican officials, headed by the "interventor," or "collector," were still to continue in each custom-house, from now on the authority was in reality to be vested in the hands of foreign deputies, since it was to them that all customs payments must be remitted for transmission to the Director of the "régie" in Santo Domingo.

By this alien board of officials, therefore, it was provided by the terms of the loan contract, the annual charges upon the loan, amounting to some 30% of the total revenues of the Republic, were to be collected and transferred to the issuing company; by it a monthly dole of $75,000 was to be paid to the Government from the customs duties; and its own expenses and compensation were assured by the monthly retention of $3,000, as well as by an added commission should the yearly customs revenues exceed a certain figure.

In his message to the Congress urging the immediate ratification of the contract signed by General Marchena, Heureaux recommended that, once the proceeds of the loan were available, the unpaid salaries and all other obligations of his Administration be paid at par; and that the internal debt and the unpaid salaries of prior Administrations be paid off at fifteen cents on the dollar. With this inducement the contract was ratified on October 26, 1888.

The Westendorp loan at this time saved the situation for Heureaux. The increasing clamour of the claimants against the Government, the rise of general dissatisfaction due to the non-payment of Governmental employees, he had been unable to still because of the increasing pressure brought to bear by the British Government to prevent the Dictator from continued default upon the Hartmont loan. For a time a breathing space was afforded him. It is not remarkable that he continued to acclaim General Marchena as the greatest financial talent the country had known, and to welcome him upon his return to the Republic with every sign of distinction. For the Dominican Republic, however, the ratification of the Westendorp contract implied a radical departure, and by the admission of extraneous intervention in the collection of its customs revenues there was inaugurated a system which has prevailed until the present day and which will probably continue for some years to come. Had this infringement of the nation's sovereignty been adopted as a sacrifice required imperatively in the public interest, or as the sole method by which the latent resources of the nation might be developed, the end might have justified the means; but this sacrifice, forced upon the Dominican people, was made solely in order to fortify Heureaux's own position, and to secure the stability of the Dictatorship.

7.

For a brief period in the autumn of the year 1888, the Dictator was forced temporarily to devote himself once more to domestic politics. The danger which threatened his own prestige so long as General Luperón remained alive came constantly to the fore. Urged thereto by those of his closest friends whom Heureaux's Government had antagonized, Luperón at length consented to proclaim his own candidacy for the Presidency for the term beginning in the following year. A large group rallied about the old leader of the "Blues" and for a time Heureaux's authority was shaken. Acting, however, with his usual wit, the Dictator maneuvered the situation in such a manner that he made it appear that his own candidacy was forced upon him, against his will, by those of his new satellites who had in the past opposed Luperón, and who now feared the latter's return to power. He even induced Luperón to join with him in signing a manifesto addressed to the public, announcing that the two leaders had reached the friendly decision to present their opposing tickets in the coming elections, and that they had obligated themselves mutually to countenance no fraud or coercion during the electoral period. If Luperón was in fact taken in by the assurances so readily given by Heureaux, he was rapidly disillusioned. Luperón's followers in various towns, among them Matanzas and Samaná, were soon thrown into prison by the orders of the President, and the situation harboured such elements of danger that Luperón, who had lost somewhat the intrepidity of his earlier years, finally determined to withdraw his candidacy, which he did by means of a proclamation which contained the most bitter charges of disloyalty and corruption against Heureaux.

Although the resort to revolution was resolutely decried by Luperón, it was apparently impossible for him to control his partisans. Revolutionary movements broke out in Puerto Plata and later in other parts of the Cibao. The rebellion in Puerto Plata was almost immediately crushed, and the leader, General Almonte, imprisoned by order of the Dictator, was summarily assassinated in the prison into which he had been cast. The second effort at revolution, which broke out in Santiago on the 17th of February, 1889, and in La Vega under the leadership of General Samuel de Moya on the following day, was likewise suppressed, this time by the Dictator in person. Placing some seventy of the more conspicuous leaders of the rebellion in irons, he cast them into the hold of the Government cruiser *Presidente* and brought them with him to the capital where upon his return they were incarcerated in the fortress. Once more, and for a considerable number of years, all serious opposition to the continuance of the tyranny had been crushed.

The new Administration was inaugurated on March 1, 1889, again in the absence of the President-elect, who was engaged in stamping out the last remaining signs of rebellion in the Cibao district, with the Vice President, Don Manuel Maria Gautier, assuming the Presidency temporarily. Gautier appointed, in accordance with the orders of his chief, a Cabinet composed of the most representative men of all affiliations who could be selected in the Republic. General Ignacio Maria González, proclaimed, almost twenty years before, the hope of those who desired reform and honest administration, consented to take office under the Dictator as Minister for Foreign Affairs; Generals Alejandro Woss y Gil and Federico Lithgow, prominent representatives of the "Blues" and for years apparently devoted to the ambitions of their leader, General Luperón, received appointments as Ministers of Fomento and of War; Don Genaro Pérez, an outstanding figure in the Republic, known for his personal integrity and his undoubted ability, consented to serve as Minister of Justice; while General Juan Francisco Sánchez, son of the famous "Trinitario," was appointed to the Department of Hacienda, and General Wenceslao Figuereo, an elderly mulatto ever subservient to Heureaux's interests, was appointed Minister of the Interior.

8.

His financial needs amply satisfied for the time being by the Westendorp loan; all signs of domestic rebellion utterly crushed; the principal leaders of all parties ensconced within his Cabinet, General Heureaux could now once more devote his preferential attention to the foreign relations of his Government.

The situation in Haiti gave him well grounded cause for alarm. At the time two parties were struggling for the ascendency in the neighbouring Republic. In Cape Haitian the partisans of General Hippolite were struggling to displace General Légitime, installed in Port-au-Prince. The latter, resenting the material assistance advanced Hippolite's party by Heureaux, had permitted the Haitian capital to become the rallying place of the Dominican partisans of General Casimiro N. de Moya, who had taken refuge there. Despatching a commission headed by General

González, his new Minister for Foreign Affairs, Heureaux succeeded in reaching an agreement with Légitime, as the result of which de Moya and his Dominican fellow-exiles were expelled from Haitian territory, and a convention was negotiated similar to the agreement entered into by General Salamon with the Dominican Government in 1880, providing that each Government would maintain strict neutrality so far as the internal politics of the other were concerned, and would take effective measures to prevent the fomenting within its territory of revolutions against the Government of the neighbouring Republic.

Upon the subsequent overturn of Légitime and the assumption of the Presidency by Hippolite the same tactics were pursued, and by means of a personal conference between Heureaux and the Haitian President, which occurred upon the Haitian frontier near Cape Haitian, a working agreement was again reached between the chiefs of the two Governments. Notwithstanding his repeated and open protests, so often made for public consumption, against the intrigues and treachery of the Haitian authorities, there was no time throughout his long term of office when Heureaux ever had valid ground for fearing the hostility of his Haitian neighbours. In fact, Haiti was to him a mine to be exploited. Were the Government of the adjacent Republic in straits, he would wrest from its officials large sums as payment for his neutrality or his secret support; were the Government of Haiti, on the contrary, to be stable temporarily, and his own position threatened by revolution organized on Haitian soil, he would assure that Government's benevolent neutrality to himself by means of bribery. And the alarm of an imminent war with Haiti proved invariably a ready means of distracting the attention of the Dominican people from the iniquities of his own Administration.

For some years, Heureaux, resentful of the fact that the Government of the United States had established a diplomatic mission in Port-au-Prince, whereas it had refrained from doing so in the Dominican Republic, had been pressing the Department of State through his agents in Washington to maintain a diplomatic mission in Santo Domingo. The desires of the Dominican President were finally acceded to by the appointment of the Minister in Port-au-Prince as American Chargé d'Affaires in Santo Domingo. The first American Chargé d'Affaires, Frederick Douglass, appointed in 1889, arrived in Santo Domingo on February 23, 1890. Owing to the fact that General Heureaux was on the eve of his departure to confer with President Hippolite, the Chargé was received by the Vice President, Don Manuel Maria Gautier. Mr. Douglass, who had visited Santo Domingo some nineteen years before as secretary to the Commission of Inquiry sent there by President Grant, was impressed with the growth of the capital city and

"with its well built and well-kept market, its street railways, its well-regulated police and its prevailing quiet and order." [1]

In a despatch to the Secretary of State, he related that notwithstanding the fact that he had been officially received by the Vice President, since President Heureaux was about to leave for the Haitian frontier, no sooner had he returned to his hotel from the Palace than he received a note from the President inviting him to come to his

[1] Mr. Frederick Douglass, American Chargé d'Affaires, to Secretary Blaine, February 26, 1890.

private house in the afternoon. Upon arriving at the President's residence, he found Heureaux at the door of his house engaged in sending off the luggage he was to take with him on his trip to Haiti.

"It was pleasant to see a man in his position attending to the carting of his own luggage instead of leaving it to others, as he might have done without touching it with one of his fingers . . He is a tall slender bright-eyed man of dark complexion and well defined negroid features. He gave me his age as forty-two,[1] but he looks even younger than that. He is of wiry make-up and has apparently a large capacity for work. He has a military bearing . . Beside his native language he speaks French and English, the latter remarkably well. He is a man of energy and intelligence and his history proves him to be well versed in statesmanship."[2]

During the conversation, which lasted an hour, the President appeared especially desirous of disarming criticism for having omitted to represent the Dominican Republic in the Pan-American Congress which had taken place in Washington under the auspices of Secretary Blaine, and gave as his main reason for not having done so the alleged neglect of the United States in failing to ratify the reciprocity treaty negotiated in 1884. Stating that that treaty overshadowed in importance the deliberations of the Pan-American Congress, Heureaux declared that no department of the United States Government had ever communicated to him the reasons for the withdrawal of the treaty, and in view of this neglect he said that he

[1] Ulises Heureaux was forty-five years of age at this time.
[2] Mr. Frederick Douglass, American Chargé d'Affaires, to Secretary Blaine, February 26, 1890.

felt the proper attitude for his Government was one of aloofness.

Touching upon the earlier proposals he had made concerning Samaná, and

"Speaking of the principle of progress and natural development, of the ever increasing power of the large States and their disposition to encroach upon the smaller States, he told the story of the rich cacique who, refusing to disclose and surrender his riches to the Spaniards, was finally induced to do so by his wife, who was wiser than he, and thus consent to give up what would be taken from him anyway by force. 'If,' said Heureaux, 'you take ten years to decide whether you will make a request of me, you must give me a little time in which to decide whether I can grant it.' When a hint was thrown out as to the possible needs of coaling stations in different parts of the world, a thing likely to be created by the growth of commerce and the extensive use of steam navigation, President Heureaux's eyes flashed with animation as he spoke of the proceedings of the English in Egypt and gave other instances to show that strong governments are likely to take by force what they need if it be denied and withheld." [1]

As the result, no doubt, of the feeling displayed by the Dominican President regarding the treatment accorded the reciprocity treaty previously concluded with the United States, and owing, doubtless, as well to the sudden interest displayed by the Harrison Administration in the Samaná proposals, negotiations were once more taken up between the two Governments. Don Manuel de Jesús Galván was again sent by Heureaux to Washington with

[1] Mr. Frederick Douglass, American Chargé d'Affaires, to Secretary Blaine, February 26, 1890.

the approval of the Congress, to negotiate a commercial convention on the basis of reciprocity between the two countries. This time negotiations proved more successful, and on June 4, 1891, the new treaty was concluded and later ratified, by virtue of which the United States accorded the privilege of free entry to certain Dominican products, notably sugar, molasses, coffee and hides, the Dominican Government in return therefor granting free entry to certain American exports enumerated in twenty-six classifications.

Due to the failure to secure from the Haitian Government the cession of the Môle St. Nicolas, coincident with the conclusion of the new Dominican Reciprocity Treaty the Cabinet of President Harrison determined to press vigorously for the lease of Samaná Bay. A proposed contract was thereupon entrusted to the Dominican Chargé d'Affaires, Señor Galván, in order that the latter might secretly present it to General Heureaux, as secrecy, in the opinion of the Dominican Dictator, was essential. But in July of the same summer, due to the mysterious visit of an American worship to Samaná, rumours of the negotiations leaked out. So much popular agitation was raised against the project, and Heureaux was consequently so incensed, that he caused the *Gaceta Oficial* to publish an official statement denying that overtures had been made by either the American or Dominican Governments for the sale or lease of Samaná Bay. His complaints to the American Consul were vigorous:

"The great difficulty is your American press. Whenever a Dominican editor writes anything objectionable or puts my picture in his paper as a caricature I put him in prison. That settles it. In the United States, the writers

abuse their privileges and your ruling men do nothing.
That article in the *Gaceta Oficial* will quiet the people. Then Mr. Blaine can send instructions. We can go to
work some months in the future secretly. If we succeed it
will be done before anybody can make any noise. If we
obtain no good result, there will be no bad feeling. The
great difficulty about the Môle St. Nicolas was that your
papers gave it more importance than it deserved and thus
put weapons into the hands of Hippolite's enemies. He
became frightened and the people of the United States
became his enemies. I want no such result." [1]

Although Heureaux insisted upon discontinuing negotiations for the time being, he reiterated his willingness to
consider any proposition which might be made to him
privately the following year,[2] and even communicated to
the American Consul his own proposals modifying the
American project which had originally been communicated to him, as follows:

"1. No sum to be paid by the Government of the
United States for the lease of Dominican territory;

"2. The two Republics to enter into an offensive and
defensive alliance; the United States to enjoy
the privilege of establishing stations in Dominican ports and of fortifying them;

"3. Should the Dominican Republic make war upon
Haiti, the Government of the United States
should then determine whether the reasons for
the Dominican aggression were justifiable and
should it deem them so, to supply two vessels
of war and a loan of $1,000,000.

[1] Mr. Durham, American Consul, to General John W. Foster, July 22, 1891.
[2] Mr. Durham, American Consul, to General John W. Foster, August 25, 1891.

"4. The Dominican Government would seize the Môle St. Nicolas as security for the funds due it by the Haitian Government under the treaty of 1874, the United States to agree to hold the said harbor in the name of the Dominican Government." [1]

While the negotiations for the lease of Samaná continued secretly throughout the winter of 1892, public attention was distracted from them by reason of the fact that the German, British and French Governments had filed official protests against the reciprocity agreement concluded with the United States, which they claimed infringed upon their rights under the most-favoured-nation clauses of their respective treaties with the Dominican Republic. In a letter addressed by Heureaux to General John W. Foster on October 6, 1891, the Dominican President expressed his gratitude for the opinion rendered by General Foster that any unfriendly attitude displayed by the European Powers towards the Dominican Government because of the reciprocity agreement would be regarded as an attitude unfriendly to the United States; but rendered uneasy by the violence of the French Consul (notwithstanding the assurances proffered by the French Premier, M. Ribot, that no ulterior consequences might be expected from the Consul's protests), he continued to request the official communication of Secretary Blaine's opinion as to the course the Dominican Government should pursue, and pressed for the statement of the position which the American Government would definitely take in the event that the protests of the European Powers materialized into action.

[1] Mr. Durham, American Consul, to Secretary Blaine, January 16, 1892.

In February, the British, French and German Governments were joined by the Governments of Italy and the Netherlands, and in April, 1892, the situation took an alarming trend, so far as Heureaux's own position was concerned. The German Government, which had previously limited its protestations to formal admonitions, now threatened tariff reprisals against the Dominican Government. Such action on the part of Germany would have gravely prejudiced the sale of the Dominican tobacco crop, which at the time ranged annually from 175,000 cwt. to 70,000 cwt., most of which was sold to Germany, and for which no other market had ever been established. The German menace held political significance, and this the German officials with their habitual knowledge of political affairs in Latin-America well understood. Since the whole of the Cibao depended upon the marketing of its tobacco and its cacao, for which latter crop Germany likewise provided the market, and since unrest had already been occasioned in the Cibao provinces by the rumours of the negotiations with the United States regarding Samaná, German tariff reprisals were bound to create such general agitation that a revolution would undoubtedly ensue. In this emergency, Secretary Blaine's suggestion that the Dominican Government defend itself by counter reprisals was worse than futile, since Heureaux found himself face to face with conditions which might provoke an uprising at any time.[1] The only solution lay in the hope that the United States would consent to make some arrangement for the acceptance of Dominican tobacco, and of this there seemed no likelihood.

For a time, General Heureaux contemplated giving the year's notice required by the commercial treaties between

[1] Mr. Durham, American Consul, to Secretary Blaine, April 16, 1892.

the Dominican Republic and the European Powers looking towards their abrogation, but he hesitated, hoping still
to obtain assistance of one kind or another from the
American Government with which he could stave off the
European Powers. Time and again the French, German,
and Italian Consuls reiterated their protests to the Dominican Government. Invariably they were put off by the
Dictator, who asked them what authority they had to
take up the matter; what instructions they had received
from their Government; or urbanely replied that their
protests had been received and would be considered, that
an answer would later be sent, and so on.[1] Finally, an
ultimatum was delivered, and the Dominican Government
was forced to promise to reply by July 1, 1892, as to
whether or not it would accede to the claims advanced.

Once more Heureaux turned to the United States:

"President Heureaux begs me to say to you that he is
in a very difficult position and that he begs you to use
your good offices to procure the settlement of this reciprocity trouble. He reproached me this morning privately. He says that but for our assurances he would
not have made the reciprocity arrangement. He had a
very close shave about three weeks ago and had it not been
for the promptness of his people in that district, the
tobacco people in the Cibao would have been in open
rebellion. Many prisoners were brought here." [2]

On June 7th, Mr. Durham was summoned to attend a
Cabinet meeting considering the German protest. While
great satisfaction was expressed at Secretary Blaine's promise of "moral support and friendly intervention," President

[1] Mr. Durham to Secretary Blaine, May 3, 1892.
[2] Mr. Durham to General John W. Foster, May 23, 1892.

Heureaux interposed in the conversation in his "character-istic practical way":

"When we accepted the assurances of Washington and made the treaty, the European Nations protested; and all we get from the United States is a reply four months later in which we are made friendly promises and in the mean-time Germany threatens an ultimatum which will cause the ruin of the whole Cibao . . Germany's course defi-nitely indicates her purpose in combating the growth of American influence in the Republic. She has raised her mission in Santo Domingo to a legation and intends to make her influence felt both in Santo Domingo and in Port-au-Prince." [1]

Finally, the Dominican President received from the United States Government the assurances which he had been seeking. He was officially advised on July 2nd, that should he take a firm stand against the European Powers in the reciprocity matter he would be sustained by the United States Government. Consequently, when the Con-suls of Italy and Germany, on the same day, addressed a joint note to General González, the Dominican Minister for Foreign Affairs, reminding him that they had been promised a reply to their protests on the reciprocity ques-tion on July 1st, and threatening to notify their Govern-ments accordingly, were no reply immediately forth-coming, they were advised in a communication addressed to them on July 12th that the Dominican Government re-fused to accede to the contention of the European Powers, and that it was unable to grant the European nations the advantages already granted the United States, unless it received equivalent benefits from them. They were assured,

[1] Mr. Durham to Secretary Blaine, June 14, 1892.

however, that the Dominican Government would attempt to arrange an agreement with the United States for a modification of the reciprocity treaty, so that those benefits resulting from that agreement, which the Dominican Government could not extend to other nations, would cease in the case of the United States. And there the matter dropped.

Throughout these months when the support of the American Government was so essential to him, the negotiations regarding Samaná had progressed most amicably, though to the eyes of the American Consul,

"The more President Heureaux reflects upon the proposition, the more is he inclined to magnify its importance to the United States and to increase his terms." [1]

There were two major reasons, however, which prompted Heureaux's desire to postpone any definite conclusion, and without offending the susceptibilities of President Harrison and Secretary Blaine, whose friendship was at the time so necessary, he prolonged negotiations and made no definite commitment. The basic causes for this policy lay in the fact that a Presidential election must be encountered within a few months, and the fact that as the financial necessities of the Government once more required the making of a new loan, additional to two already negotiated with Westendorp and Company, the lease of Samaná Bay might prove an invaluable trading point in such negotiations. Consequently, negotiations were frequently checked by such statements from Heureaux as:

"Señor Galván had no authority to propose a draft of a contract for the lease of Samaná;

[1] Mr. Durham to Secretary Blaine, January 16, 1892.

or

"If your Government wants a station it must permit me to study the question;" [1]

While General Heureaux made many inquiries about the possibility that the United States would advance large sums to meet the Dominican Government's expenses in "smoothing the way" for the lease of Samaná, or concerning the possibility that the United States might be willing to guarantee the service of the foreign debt, the American Consul warned the Secretary of State that although General Heureaux wanted money for his Government he could not forget that an American company had once contracted to pay $150,000 a year for the privilege of leasing Samaná. Finally, the Dictator made the following proposition:

" 'Personally and as President' Heureaux engages himself to call a special session of Congress in July or August, 1892, and to cause legislative ratification of the Samaná contracts proposed at Washington for the establishment of a coaling station for the United States, providing he can receive on account of the first instalment of $250,000, the sum of $200,000 immediately after the Dominican Congress shall have effected the ratification. He desires me to explain that he fears a revolutionary movement as soon as Congress acts on the Samaná matter and that he will require money immediately thereafter to provide for preserving peace." [2]

Advised by the Consul of the constitutional difficulty which prevented the American Executive from advancing

[1] Mr. Durham to Secretary Blaine, March 27, 1892.
[2] Mr. Durham to Secretary Blaine, in a private letter dated April 25, 1892.

money not authorized by act of Congress, the Dictator replied with undeniable logic:

"You know my situation. I cannot ask insurgents to wait until I receive money from the United States with which to fight them." [1]

That Westendorp and Company were by no means averse to the conclusion of the rumoured negotiations for the lease of the Samaná Bay territory to the United States was soon made known:

"On my arrival in Santo Domingo in March, 1891, Mr. Dentex Bondt, the superintendent of the Company, visited me at Santo Domingo and asked me whether the United States still wanted Samaná Bay. He stated that he suspected the reason for my visit to Santo Domingo and that he would help me if I would help him. He confessed that his Company's affairs were almost hopeless and that they wanted to get out. He outlined a plan and I told him to see Heureaux, who agreed to encourage him while he looked over the ground. The proposition of Mr. Dentex Bondt was that the United States guarantee the payment of the interest on all the debt of the Dominican Republic, in return for which it would have a lien on the customs revenues of the Republic and obtain a lease for the period it desired, of Samaná Bay." [2]

On condition that his letter be regarded as strictly private and be shown to no other individual, not even to General Foster, General Heureaux, on April 25, 1892, addressed a letter to Secretary Blaine offering definite conditions for the lease or cession of Samaná to the United States. Upon favourable consideration by the Harrison

[1] Mr. Durham to Secretary Blaine, in a private letter dated April 25, 1892.
[2] Mr. Durham to General John W. Foster, July 1, 1892.

Administration of this communication, Mr. Durham received final instructions in the matter on August 6th. In these instructions he was reminded that he had already been apprised of the informal negotiations conducted during the preceding year for the lease by the United States of a coaling and naval station in the Bay of Samaná and that the terms of this lease had actually been agreed upon by General Foster and the Dominican Envoy, Don Manuel de Jesús Galván, in Washington; that Heureaux had later expressed his willingness through confidential communications to carry out immediately the terms of the lease on condition that the initial cash payment provided for in one of the articles be made immediately upon the ratification of the lease by the Dominican Congress; that the United States Congress had therefore been applied to for an appropriation equivalent in amount to that necessary to meet this condition, that Congress had made the appropriation, and that the money had been placed at the disposal of President Harrison. Mr. Durham was therefore instructed to proceed at once to Santo Domingo, and should he find the Dominican Government prepared to carry out the proposals advanced by General Heureaux he was to sign the convention for the lease under the terms agreed upon, with the understanding that the Dominican Congress should be called immediately to ratify it. An engrossed copy of the convention was even entrusted to Mr. Durham. The convention proposed read as follows:

"Article I. The Dominican Republic grants to the United States exclusive possession and occupation for the purposes of a coaling and naval station in the form of a lease of the Island of Carenero in the Bay of Samaná . .

The Dominican Republic further grants to the United States of America the right to construct upon the land and in the waters adjacent to the above described Island whatever wharves or other improvements the latter may deem necessary; the right of free use and occupancy of any of the waters and shores of the Bay of Samaná and the right to erect whatever defenses it may deem necessary for the protection, occupancy and use of the aforesaid station and waters.

"The United States shall have the right to possess and occupy the above described territory during a term of ninety-nine years from the date of the proclamation in Washington of the present convention with the privilege on the part of the United States of a renewal of the lease for a like term of years, upon an annual rent to be agreed upon by the two Governments or by an arbitrator in accordance with the methods stated in Article V, and at the expiration of said term the territory and premises above described, with all the permanent improvements thereon, exclusive of supplies, materials, and armaments, shall be delivered to the Dominican Republic without compensation therefor.

"It is understood that the Dominican Republic does not cede its right to the control and free navigation of the waters of said Bay, except as herein expressly stated.

"Article II. The United States shall pay, as a consideration for the rent and occupation of said territory, within thirty days after the proclamation of the present convention, to the Dominican Republic, the sum of $250,000, and annually for the first five years after said date the sum of $50,000, and annually thereafter until the expiration of the term of lease and occupancy the sum of $25,000 . . .

"Article III. It is agreed on the part of the Dominican Republic that, so long as the lease and privileges herein

stipulated shall remain in force, it will not lease or otherwise dispose of or create any lien upon or grant any spécial
privileges or rights of use in or to any of the waters of the
Bay of Samaná or any of the territory in the maritime
district of Samaná to any other Power, State, or Government.

"And it is further agreed by and between the High
Contracting Parties that in case the Dominican Republic
may become involved in a civil or foreign war, the waters
of the Bay of Samaná shall be held to be neutral territory;
and the Governments of the Dominican Republic and of
the United States shall have the right jointly or severally
to enforce such neutrality.

"Article IV. The Dominican Republic agrees that during the existence of this lease it will . . arrest and surrender . . all deserters from the Service of the United
States found within the territory of said Republic. . .

"Article V. The two Contracting Parties agree that the
doubts which may arise on the interpretation or execution
of this convention shall be submitted when the means to
adjust them directly by friendly accord may have failed,
to the arbitration of a single arbitrator to be selected by
mutual agreement.

"Article VI. This convention shall be ratified by the
two Governments in accordance with their respective
Constitutions but it is understood that it shall not be
binding on either Government until the necessary appropriation of money for the first payment herein provided
for has been made by the Congress of the United States.

"The ratifications shall be exchanged at Washington as
soon as possible after this appropriation."

Immediately after the receipt of these instructions, Mr.
Durham started for Santo Domingo, where he arrived
August 20th to find the President absent "conciliating"

public opinion in the Cibao. Upon Heureaux's return, the Chargé d'Affaires advised General Foster that

"not to offend González and the Vice-President, I have been going through the motions of conferring with them, but nothing will be done until Heureaux's return." [1]

The inopportune publication by the New York *Herald* at this time of reports to the effect that the Westendorp loan was to be transferred to the Government of the United States through the agency of a private corporation created a storm of excitement in the Republic. The center of the protests lay in Santiago, and the President deemed it advisable to return there immediately from the capital in order to assure the public that his Government would not permit the rumoured transfer. Rendered more indignant than ever against the American press, General Heureaux refused to permit Mr. Durham to join him in Santiago, as he had intended, in order to avoid gossip. Returning finally to the capital on September 15th, Heureaux insisted upon postponing negotiations on the pretext of ill-health. While the Dictator stated to Mr. Durham that were he well he would not hesitate a moment to conclude negotiations, but that since he was sick he had to move with caution, Mr. Durham advised his Government that he had gained the impression that the real reasons for postponing the decision lay in the President's desire to secure money from the syndicate in New York, which had already been negotiating for the transfer to it of the Westendorp loan.[2]

Four days later, the American Agent was convinced that negotiations had failed. Several days later his hopes

[1] Mr. Durham to General John W. Foster, August 25, 1892.
[2] Mr. Durham to General John W. Foster, October 6, 1892.

were again partly raised by a letter which he received
from the President:

"Esteemed Friend:

"As I offered you the day before yesterday, I have today
taken up very carefully the matter to which I referred
in my note, and although I have not obtained the result
which I hoped to reach, at least something has been
accomplished.

"It is imperative to give heed in these moments in which
the lack of agreement may easily cause one's best efforts
to fail, so I am of the opinion that it will be better to let
things go along little by little. If you are in agreement
with me and wish to follow my premonitions, wait.

"I have in addition to this matter another to place under
your protection. My city properties located in this City
have a total value of about $200,000 in gold. Knowing,
as I do, things in my country, and having to foresee the
dangers which may affect my own person and perhaps my
interests as well, I should be glad to place the latter under
the protection of the American Nation, leaving to your
judgment the manner and the form in which that desire
may be realized.

"It is unnecessary for me to tell you that you merit all
my confidence in this matter . . .

"I have complied with your requests and I remain
always,

"Your affectionate friend,

"U. HEUREAUX"

By the end of October, Mr. Durham had once more
reached the conclusion that it was impossible for him to
make any advance in the Samaná negotiations. The matter had been fully discussed in the meetings of Heureaux's
Cabinet and it had been determined that in view of the

recent revolutionary movements, of the ill feeling in the tobacco districts created by Germany's threatened tariff retaliation, and because of the general ferment caused by the approaching Presidential elections, it was inexpedient to conclude the proposed agreement. This, in fact, was the conclusion of the President himself, and although the Minister for Foreign Affairs, General González, asked Mr. Durham to write an official note requesting the formal decision of the Dominican Government, Mr. Durham determined to withdraw all papers informally, and therefore no entry remained upon the official records of the Dominican Government. The decision so arrived at was reaffirmed three months later when the Department of State was once more advised that by reason of Haitian agitation, opposition in Europe, conspiracy in Santo Domingo, and general popular apprehension, General Heureaux was unable to complete the Samaná negotiations at that time.[1]

9.

The Dictator did not lack other irons in the fire.

Within two years after the first Westendorp loan had been obtained, Heureaux had been forced once more to turn to the same company for further assistance. His appeal resulted in the contraction of the so-called "railroad loan," calling for the emission of bonds amounting in all to £900,000, redeemable in fifty-six years and bearing an interest rate of 6%. The contract specified that the loan was to be secured by a first mortgage upon the railroad to be built from Puerto Plata to Santiago with a portion of the loan proceeds, and by a second lien upon the customs. The "régie" was again entrusted with the

---

[1] Mr. Durham to General John W. Foster, January 28, 1893.

collection of the funds to meet the service of the
loan, which amounted to an additional charge of £57,000
annually upon the scant revenues of the Government.

With the approach of the year 1893, the ready funds
obtained by Heureaux from this second operation had
already been dissipated. His secret expenses constantly rising, as the pay-roll upon which were carried his paid supporters, his agents and his spies, lengthened, he applied
again for advances to the local merchants. When this
market became glutted with his paper, he resorted to an
ingenious arrangement by which, in return for cash advances, local importers were exempt from the payment
of customs dues. It was scarcely surprising, therefore, that
in 1892 the customs revenues remaining after the budgetary requirements had been met proved far less than
the sum necessary to meet the service of the foreign
bonds. The Government promptly defaulted.

Although to remedy this situation a compromise was
later reached whereby the Government agreed to permit
the "régie" to retain 35% of all port revenues to meet
the charges upon the defaulted bonds, when Heureaux
once more applied for additional advances to Westendorp and Company, he was met by a blunt refusal. That
source of supply had run dry.

Consequently, while the advantages offered by the
projected Samaná Convention with the United States
were eminently satisfactory in so far as they implied the
open support of his Administration by the American Government, financially they seemed far from alluring. During the very period that the State Department was
anticipating the successful outcome of the negotiations,
Heureaux was undertaking conversations for further

financial assistance, in which he believed the lease of Samaná might prove a strong card, not only with the agent of Westendorp and Company, as reported by Mr. Durham, but likewise with a financial syndicate supported by John Wanamaker, Postmaster General in the Harrison Cabinet, and with a group in New York headed by Messrs. Smith M. Weed and Charles W. Wells.

It was from the syndicate headed by these two, later organized under the laws of New Jersey as the San Domingo Improvement Company of New York, that Heureaux was at last enabled to obtain further financing. Acquiring the rights and assuming the obligations of Westendorp and Company in May, 1892, the new Company agreed to undertake two new loans, both guaranteed by the customs revenues; one for £2,035,000 for the purpose of refunding the prior obligations of the Dominican Government; the second for $1,250,000, to meet various items of indebtedness incurred by Heureaux, aggregating but one-third of the amount so authorized, or $438,000. The "régie" was continued, under the direction now of the Improvement Company, although it was provided, as a means of enhancing the Republic's credit, that in the event of default the "régie" was to be controlled by an International Commission composed of bondholders, appointed, one from each nation, by the Governments of the United States, Great Britain, France, Holland and Belgium.

The facility of the operations so provided for, authorized by the Dominican Congress on March 23, 1893, led Heureaux to repeat them within a few months by contracting for a new loan almost identical in purpose and amount to the second loan negotiated with the Improvement Company. To the Dictator it was a matter of supreme indifference that under the new agreements the Government received but $90,000 silver a month from the customs revenues, and still less that the "régie" was saddled upon the Republic for a term of sixty-six years.